A THEORY OF
REASONS FOR ACTION

A THEORY OF
REASONS FOR
ACTION

BY

DAVID A. J. RICHARDS

OXFORD
AT THE CLARENDON PRESS
1971

Oxford University Press, Ely House, London W. 1

GLASGOW NEW YORK TORONTO MELBOURNE WELLINGTON
CAPE TOWN SALISBURY IBADAN NAIROBI DAR ES SALAAM LUSAKA ADDIS ABABA
BOMBAY CALCUTTA MADRAS KARACHI LAHORE DACCA
KUALA LUMPUR SINGAPORE HONG KONG TOKYO

PRINTED IN GREAT BRITAIN
AT THE UNIVERSITY PRESS, OXFORD
BY VIVIAN RIDLER
PRINTER TO THE UNIVERSITY

To
Mim, Dad, and Di

'Is it mischief, is it not benefit to understand what it is we mean?'

JEREMY BENTHAM, unpublished manuscript, cited on p. 17 of Everett's introduction to *Limits of Jurisprudence Defined*

'O Wort, du Wort, das mir fehlt!'

ARNOLD SCHOENBERG, Act II, scene 5, *Moses und Aron*

ACKNOWLEDGEMENTS

THIS book is a revised version of my doctoral dissertation which was accepted by Oxford University in February 1970. As such, it has given rise to many debts of gratitude which it is a pleasure to acknowledge.

In roughly chronological order, I owe much to my undergraduate experience at Harvard College during which I had the good fortune to study under Professor John Rawls. Not only did I learn much from Professor Rawls's supervision of the senior thesis which contained the seeds of chapter 9 of this book, but generally Professor Rawls (through his tutorials, seminars, lectures, and published and unpublished writings) taught me much that is now embodied and developed in this book both regarding general orientation and specific arguments and viewpoints on the theory of rationality, morality, and the nature of moral feeling. Thus, this work is very much the product of a student and disciple; as such, I hope that, with little claim to originality or finality, this book will further reveal and develop the profundity and fruitfulness of Professor Rawls's ideas. For Professor Rawls's own seminal and admirable development of these ideas, see his recently published *A Theory of Justice*, Harvard University Press, 1971. I am also indebted to Professor Rawls for reading through an earlier version of the dissertation and giving me his advice on rewriting.

At Oxford, during my first year, I profited greatly from discussions with my thesis supervisor during that year, Professor H. L. A. Hart, whose patient criticisms produced nearly any clarity which chapter 2 of this book may have. And during the second year, when the bulk of the dissertation was written, I incurred a special debt of gratitude to my thesis supervisor, Mr. G. J. Warnock, who patiently digested and wisely criticized so much material, and without whose advice, support, and liberal regime I am sure the dissertation and this book would never have been written. I am also thankful for Mr. Warnock's continuing kind support and concern during the period of revision and rewriting after I left Oxford. I should also like to express my very deep appreciation to the readers of my dissertation, Professor R. M. Hare and Dr. A. J. P. Kenny, whose extremely detailed criticisms were invaluable to me in reworking the dissertation; the prod of their criticisms made a tiresome task stimulating and engrossing. I must, in this connection, especially express very real gratitude for Professor Hare's unflagging generosity in continuing to give me the benefit of his deep and serious thought on the subject of morality.

Also, I should like to acknowledge with thanks the intellectual stimulation I have received from conversations with many friends, among whom I should mention Robert Lawry, John Moore, Stephen Morris, Saki Numata, Richard Parker, and, especially, Raymond Frey, presently of Liverpool University.

In addition, I must note my appreciation to Harvard University for a Frank Knox Memorial Fellowship, which made my first year in Oxford possible.

Finally, it is a pleasure to express my deep gratitude to my parents, Mr. and Mrs. Armand J. Richards, who assisted me in financing my second year in Oxford, and whose support has sustained me throughout all my work on this book; and to my sister, Diane, who was of invaluable assistance in criticizing both substantive arguments and style and syntax.

D. A. J. R.

Orange, New Jersey
September 1970

CONTENTS

CONTENTS

INTRODUCTION

THIS work is an attempt to offer, in an exploratory and constructive spirit, a systematic account of the concept, reasons for action. The main thesis of this study is that there exists an adequate and true theory of the meaning of sentences using 'reasons for action' and related terminology—a theory which analyses or elucidates their meaning in terms of certain propositions (which may be truly or falsely asserted), which provides an account of the use of these sentences in performing various acts by speech (e.g. advising), and which clarifies the moving appeal to action which the utterance of these sentences often, or typically, has. Coherent with this general thesis, the work has the theoretical objective of presenting a plausible (not necessarily a true) formulation of such a theory, so that at least some good constructive reasons will have been given for believing the thesis to be true, and some good reason given for others to work further in developing a more accurate expression of the truth which is here perhaps only dimly perceived and incoherently expressed.

Consonant with the book's general thesis and theoretical objective, an attempt is made to formulate a structure of principles which will account for reasons for action associated with the concept of rationality (Part I) and with the concept of morality (Part II). In both parts of the book, the same constructive pattern of argument is systematically applied. First, principles are formulated and explained. Secondly, an attempt is made to show how these principles clarify propositions which certain 'ought', 'under an obligation', 'there is good reason', etc., sentences express. Thirdly, an explanation is sketched regarding how the propositional account elucidates the use of these sentences in accomplishing the various characteristic speech acts that they do accomplish. And fourthly, an attempt is made to explain and clarify the moving appeal to action which the utterance of these sentences typically possesses.

Throughout, the orientation of this work is tentative and exploratory. No claims to finality or conclusiveness are made. Rather, a general approach to doing normative philosophy is suggested, one which re-examines and questions the fruitfulness of sharp divisions between analytic and substantive inquiries. The reader is invited to consider whether and how this approach may be usefully developed further.

PART I

THE CASE OF RATIONALITY

1

PROBLEMS AND METHODS

(1) You ought to learn the calculus; it's an invaluable tool.

(2) You ought to learn how to swim; it may, someday, save your life.

(3) I don't think you ought to make him your partner; he's so un-reliable that it will just make your job harder.

(4) You ought to learn how to ride a horse; it's such fun.

(5) You ought to visit the Hermitage, if you're going to Leningrad; it has a splendid art collection, which you will enjoy.

IF one were asked to characterize the most important logical properties that the above expressions share, several things would, I think, be mentioned as obvious. (1) The first halves of 1–5 seem to be typically used to indicate that there is a reason for action, which the second halves of 1–5 more specifically indicate. (2) The reasons so indicated and specified are reasons of that general sort which relate to the agent's own self (as opposed to the desires, needs, etc., of others). (3) The indication of these reasons often has force in an advisor–advisee relationship. However, when one seeks for a deeper philosophical understanding of the concepts expressed by such sentences, especially the concept of a reason for action, matters seem far less obvious, far more obscure and difficult. What is it for something to *be* a reason for action? What, exactly, is the relationship between such reasons and advising, between reasons and rules, between reasons and human desires, etc.?

One of the fundamental problems, to which the philosophical examination of expressions 1–5 leads, is the issue of the exact status of such assertions of reasons as between our beliefs and our will. Thus, in so far as 1–5 seem to be used to *indicate* the existence of reasons for action, it seems plausible to say that they express propositions that can be truly or falsely asserted; for example, the person to whom (1) is addressed may rebut it by indicating the irrelevance of the calculus to his intellectual interests, and the speaker may maintain its truth by indicating new work in the other's field whose authors have found the calculus relevant and illuminating, etc. On the other hand, after considering the use of such expressions to advise, many would deny that 1–5 primarily express propositions. This general view in reference to moral language has, of course, been the main analytic claim of Stevenson's emotivist theory and Hare's more recent (and more plausible) prescriptivism.[1] But, the view has been taken explicitly in reference to self-regarding, non-moral or technical, 'oughts' by B. J. Diggs; while Diggs allows, following Hare, certain cases which are purely propositional,[2] he goes beyond even Hare in suggesting that some 'ought'-expressions have no propositional content at all: 'strictly speaking, "ought" sentences are not statements.'[3] On Diggs's view, the use of 'ought' in 1–5 should be analysed in the same sort of way as the imperative mood, where used in an order from father to son, 'shut the door', or a command of a sergeant to a private, 'attention!'. The distinctive feature of the use of these linguistic expressions, in the appropriate context of a known and acknowledged personal relationship involving some elements of authoritative or other superiority between the commander and the commanded, is that the speaker typically intends that the commanded person will do what he tells him to, *by means* of the commanded's recognition of that intention, as communicated or signalled (in the language) by the non-propositional imperative mood.[4] Similarly, Diggs would argue, 'ought' in 1–5 does not express any proposition, but is, in the language, a special kind of word which is used to express some aspect of the speaker's will which, in the appropriate circumstances, is used to guide the actions of others without mediating propositions. Diggs suggests that the aspect of will generally expressed by 'ought' is an intention to 'propose or express a decision on action to be taken';[5] other non-propositional theorists might alternatively hold that the word is used to grade or commend or prescribe. However, all would agree that expressions 1–5 are analytically related to the speaker's will; so that, reasons *are*, in essence, a certain type of expression of will.

While both (*a*) indicating reasons for action and (*b*) advising seem to be equally important aspects of 1–5, it seems to me mistaken to suppose that (*b*) compels the abandonment of the propositional character of (*a*), which one, I think, pre-analytically feels it as having. Of course, it is often necessary in constructive philosophy to re-examine and, perhaps, ultimately to revise or reject (as confused) certain pre-analytic judgements; but there seem, in this case, to be good reasons for supposing that 1–5 do, in fact, express propositions. First, as I mentioned briefly above, forms of argument, typical of the form of reasons for believing the truth or accepting the falsity of propositions, can and do occur in reference to these expressions. Thus, I suggested that the relevance of the calculus to one's interests might be disputed in the case of (1); and similarly, in (2), facts about the complete certainty of never coming near any expanse of water; in (3), facts about the person's family connections with great and wealthy capital investors that more than compensate for his unreliability; (4), facts about the countervailing dangers; (5), facts about the interlocutor's distaste for all forms of art, etc. Further, as Geach has pointed out in arguments against nonpropositional theories generally (not only of moral concepts but of logical and epistemological ones), many putatively non-propositional expressions have the logical manipulability typical of all propositional expressions.[6] Thus, in reference to our particular problem, note that an 'ought'-expression can appear in an 'if'-clause, where it does not have any of the properties non-propositional theories ascribed to it. Thus, one could, on the basis of (1), form the new expression 'if you ought to learn the calculus, then you must go to summer school at this college', where the 'ought' in the 'if'-clause is *not* being used to grade or commend or prescribe or express a decision of some sort. Further, the non-propositional theorist cannot respond by claiming that 'ought' in an 'if'-clause has a varying use from that in other contexts, for it may be pointed out that 'you ought to learn the calculus' and 'if you ought . . ., then . . .' *can* be joined as premisses for a modus ponens. Here, the two occurrences of 'you ought . . .' must have the same sense if the modus ponens is not to be disallowed by an equivocation. And if a theorist holds that 'you ought' does not express a proposition at all, it is up to him to show how this expression can quite sensibly stand as a premiss in this way. Similarly, one may also, following Searle on 'good',[7] point to the use of 'ought' in 'ought I to learn the calculus?', 'I wonder if I ought to learn the calculus', and 'I don't know whether I ought to . . .' where, again, non-propositional accounts seem clearly inaccurate. Such theories seem to have gone wrong through their sole attention to the question: what act is performed when it is *said* that someone ought to do *x*, or when something is *called* good, etc., whereas, in the contexts mentioned here, it is hypothesized that someone ought to do *x*, or wondered about, and so on.[8] When such contexts are considered, non-propositional theories seem much less plausible, for one naturally supposes that 'ought' means the same whether I ask if I ought, hypothesize that I ought, or assert that I ought; and what *seems* common here is some proposition.

Given these considerations, there seem good reasons for believing that sentences of the kind 1–5 do, indeed, express propositions, and thus are true or false. Of course, good reasons are not conclusive reasons. And it would be a mistake to suppose that the arguments just offered irrefutably establish a propositional theory of reasons for action, since non-propositional theories have been conclusively refuted. On the contrary, neither the one has been conclusively shown, nor the other conclusively refuted. Thus, on the latter question, the arguments offered above could, I think, be answered by non-propositional theories. For example, in reference to the claim that various facts can be adduced of a similar sort to those presented as reasons for believing certain propositions, it is a well-known feature of non-propositional accounts, e.g. those of Urmson and Hare on the concept of good,[9] to draw a distinction between the meaning of a certain moral concept and the conventionalized criteria in terms of which it is applied to certain things; and it is, thus, open to a non-propositional theory to account for the seemingly objective or descriptive features of a certain expression in terms of the conventionalized criteria that govern its use, and to separate this issue from the question of normative *meaning*. Further, if one cites the logical manipulability of 'ought'-expressions, and demands from the nonpropositional theorist some account for this, it is always open to him to develop a special normative logic for the use of these expressions; or, he may, like Hare, grant that normative expressions have a propositional content, which is not, however, their *primary* meaning content, *qua* normative expressions.[10] Moreover, a non-propositional theorist, like Diggs, may strongly riposte that no propositional theory can adequately account for the crucially important advisory *force* of expressions of the type 1–5. This counter-argument would only be the reflection in the area of non-moral or technical 'oughts' of the quite common argument of non-propositional moral theorists concerning the incapacity of propositional theories to account for the relation of moral concepts to action and practical life. Thus, it was one of the central claims of Stevenson's emotivism that propositional theories failed to account for the 'magnetism' of ethical terms, their hold on our motivations and consequent persuasive influence on our actions.[11] And surely, if a moral theory cannot account for the 'moving appeal', in Perry's phrase,[12] of ethical utterances, it would be inadequate. Similarly, Hare's prescriptivism crucially argues that propositional theories cannot adequately account for the role of moral terms in performing various speech acts, e.g. commending.[13] And clearly, if this were true, propositional theories would be philosophically unacceptable.

What is required in order to give the arguments sketched above greater, and perhaps conclusive, force is a positive and constructive analytic account of the propositions expressed by sentences 1–5, an account which will also provide a philosophical elucidation of the important use of such expressions to advise, and some clarification of the relation of these propositions to human motivation, such that they have some influence on human conduct. If this can be accomplished, we shall have done what non-propositional theorists have claimed to be impossible, provided a propositional account of 'ought'-expressions which also accounts for the role of such expressions in practical life. Indeed, one may establish here three criteria for the adequacy of the positive theory I shall propose in subsequent chapters: (1) the expressions comprising the proposed theoretical analysis must indicate propositions which, upon reflection of the whole theory, a thoughtful person would accept as identical with the propositions indicated by the original expressions; at a minimum, if the above is too strong a requirement, the analysis must retain the truth values and logical relations of the defined expression (e.g. if the expression 'x is in your interest' has a logical relation to 'you ought to obtain x', then the defining expression for 'you ought' must preserve this relation; see here, chapter 4); (2) the theory must provide an illuminating account of how certain things are done in using the defined expression, e.g. advising; (3) the theory must relate the account of (1) to some plausible view or theory of human motivation which will explain the influence that the utterance of the defined expression has on human conduct. These criteria for theoretical adequacy not only apply to the account of reasons associated with the concept of rationality, which will be developed in Part I of this book, but have, I think, quite general validity, and will be applied to moral concepts also, as I hope to illustrate in Part II. The same point has, in fact, recently been made by Warnock in reference to moral reasons when he suggested the applicability of Austin's threefold distinction of locutionary, illocutionary, and perlocutionary acts to the analysis of moral discourse.[14] Thus, the three criteria just elaborated can quite easily be mapped onto Austin's distinctions. Assuming the expression in question is propositional, the analysis of (1) clarifies the proposition expressed, what, strictly, is typically meant by the locutionary act of uttering the expression in question—a concept of meaning which Austin equates with Frege's notion of sense and reference.[15] The analysis of (2) elucidates the relation of the proposition expressed to the illocutionary speech act performed (e.g. commending, praising, advising, etc.). And the account of the relation of the proposition expressed to human motivations (3) clarifies what is done by using the expression in question, e.g. the possibility of the success of the perlocutionary acts of persuading.

These criteria of theoretical adequacy, and the basic method of analysis behind them, represent, I think, only a more sophisticated statement of long-standing methods and orientations of ethical theorists such as Plato, Aristotle, Hume, Kant, W. D. Ross, Richard Brandt, and John Rawls.[16] That is, one assumes, as these theorists do, that people generally make a certain class of judgements about normative questions, and that certain of these judgements are marked by being likely to be made seriously in conditions of impartiality by reasonable and moral men who are in full control of normal mental and judgemental capacities.[17] Such considered judgements are the empirical data of normative philosophy. The task of the philosopher is to provide a theoretical account of normative concepts which, given people's nature and predilections, naturally and readily explains the normative judgements which people do make; the only distinctive feature of my view is judging the adequacy of an account by its capacity to mirror these judgements in the three ways specified above. Generally, if after considerable reflection on the account and its capacity to mirror our considered judgements, it falls short, then one is justifiably *entitled* to reject it. I use the permissive locution of entitlement because it is always possible to revise one's considered judgements to match a plausible account, to 'clip the ragged edge of common use', in Sidgwick's phrase, instead of rejecting the account.[18] What one will do will depend on the systematic plausibility of the account, as well as on background assumptions of various sorts; for example, empiricists in semantics have rejected forms of rational intuitionism despite their supposed adequacy, in other respects, as philosophical accounts;[19] and other empiricists have rejected objectivist theories, despite their admitted fit with ordinary language, because they supposed them to be incompatible with a consistent empiricism.[20]

One final point. Conspicuous by its absence, so far, has been any mention of the so-called naturalistic fallacy, which has been supposed to establish conclusively the unsoundness of all propositional theories.[21] Of course, as the fallacy was originally formulated by G. E. Moore, it was not directed against all propositional theories, since Moore was himself defending a propositional account. However, as various theorists have, for good reason, rejected intuitionism, because based on an unsound semantics, the naturalistic fallacy has been viewed as the conclusive refutation of all forms of propositional theory that were not otherwise semantically unacceptable. It seems to me important to try to respond to this conception, in order to rebut the presumption of the indefensibility of propositional accounts. First, Moore's formulation of the fallacy has been described by Frankena as a case of the 'definist fallacy', i.e. the process of confusing two different properties.[22] If this is all the naturalistic fallacy amounts to, then it cannot be used against non-intuitionist propositional accounts *prior* to systematic investigation of whether a supposed propositional account does or does not express the same property as the expression to be defined. Yet, Moore's use of the fallacy, in refuting many naturalistic theories, precisely begs the question in so far as it does seem to claim *a priori* authority against all non-intuitionist propositional accounts. Secondly, apart from Moore's attempts to show that various proposed propositional accounts (utilitarianism, etc.) do not in fact correspond to our considered moral judgements, there is one argument which does claim more *a priori* authority, i.e. the famed open-question argument.[23] This argument runs as follows. Suppose you have two terms, '*P*' and '*Q*', and it has been suggested that they mean the same. Now, a test of whether they really are identical in meaning would be this: It is the case that no one can doubt that the concept of being P is equivalent to the concept of being P; but if the concept of being P is equivalent to the concept of being Q, then, by substitutivity of identity, it should be the case that no one can doubt that the concept of being P is equivalent to the concept of being Q. But, in fact, one can always doubt this; it is always an open question. Thus, synonymy can never hold. There is, I think, a glaring and obvious fallacy in this form of argument: its failure to recognize that in contexts of believing, doubting, etc., substitutivity of identity does not hold. This is simply one instance of the well-known fact of the referential opacity of belief contexts.[24] In so far as the open-question argument depends on such contexts, it must be construed as a fallacious argument with *no a priori* force against propositional accounts. In so far as the open-question argument is construed as an appeal to the implausibility of the truth of the sentence '"Whatever is P is Q, and vice versa" is analytic', it seems inconclusive.[25] In fact, it will, I think, rarely be the case that any really complex meaning analysis will not be initially doubted, and the claim of analyticity found implausible (how, one feels like asking, can the simple words 'know' or 'true' or 'right' mean anything so complex?); and yet one may, after reflection, be prepared to grant that the defined and defining expressions are synonymous, even if, using Brandt's phrase, 'covertly' so.[26] Thirdly, quite apart from Moore's understanding of the naturalistic fallacy, it has also been widely construed as pointing up the logical gap between a merely propositional account of moral terms and their actual uses: for example, Hare attacks naturalistic analyses of good because, he thinks, they make commending, in certain contexts, impossible.[27] This conception of the naturalistic fallacy has, in fact, already been discussed above. The answer to this view is simply to show that no such logical gap exists, that what it claims to be impossible can, in fact, be done. Let us proceed to this.

2

SOCIAL RULES AND PRINCIPLES

THE general approach to the analysis of the concept of reasons for action, in the following chapters, will appeal at bottom to the notion of certain principles of action associated with the concepts of rationality and morality. While the main interest of the account, no doubt, will be the analysis given the concepts of rationality and morality, another distinguishing feature of it is the role that principles of action play in the analysis. Indeed, the use to which the theory puts the notion of principles of action is all that will fundamentally distinguish the theory from certain other views, e.g. from Gauthier's similar account of rationality and morality; that is, where Gauthier specifically eschews the view that some form of rule is fundamental to the concept of reasons for action ('this position . . . I have endeavoured to combat throughout this study'),[1] the present account brings a form of rule—principles—into the very centre of the analysis. This being so, the present chapter will attempt to clarify the concept of principles of action. The generality and abstractness of this discussion will, I hope, be compensated for by the detail of example which is to follow in subsequent chapters.

Before undertaking this discussion, however, it is, I think, important to be clear about two different uses of the concept of principles of action: (1) the notion of my or your principles as something that one person has and another does not, and which is naturally expressed by such locutions as 'that is against my principles' and (2) the notion of *the* principles, for example, of punishment. In the latter case, the one which concerns me here, one is thinking not of the standards which a particular man has accepted, but of the basic standards or rules which provide the final justification, in the considered judgements of reasonable and moral men, of the institution of punishment, for example, distributive principles of fairness for determining when people shall be liable for punishment, deterrence grounds for how much, etc.[2] The appeal to the *judgements* of reasonable and moral men is, simply, an appeal to what the concepts of morality and reasonableness specify as justifying principles for the institution of punishment; whatever principles are proposed as specifying the requirements of morality in this case will be tested against such judgements. It can, I think, easily be seen that this latter inquiry is logically different from that which (1) involves (i.e. finding out what principles a person accepts); for not just anything a person explicitly accepts as his standard morally justifying punishment, in fact justifies it. And, just because a person explicitly rejects, as his moral principle, a certain principle justifying punishment, that does not mean that it is not the one (or among the ones) which morally justifies it. It is a notorious truth, in moral philosophy, that even men of sound and enlightened moral convictions may rather completely misunderstand and mis-state the logical nature, and substantive basis, of their moral beliefs, a frequent claim made, perhaps justly, against the classical utilitarians, Bentham and Mill; so that, the principles they claim to underlie their moral beliefs do not in fact do so, and the principles they reject as justifying their beliefs may, in fact, justify them.[3] And then, of course, there are the examples of men of warped moral character whose acceptances and rejections have no weight in deciding what count as moral principles. This latter point should not be lightly taken; for it is not a merely formal question, of no substantive importance, when Hare ignores this point and adopts a view of the nature of moral principles which compels him too easily to accept what one's deepest moral convictions eschew—the logical possibility of the actual (versus the supposed) morality of the principles of intolerance used by a sincere, universalizing Nazi.[4] In clearly distinguishing (1) and (2), it is my hope to avoid the temptation to conflate the different questions involved in their respective analyses—a conflation which may have led both to the widespread view that moral principles bear some *logical* relation to having been accepted by an act of free choice,[5] and to Hare's kind of attempt to view even quite corrupt moral attitudes as centrally relevant to the question of what are, in fact, moral principles. Thus, for example, since people sometimes believe or suppose quite insane things to be moral principles (which are not moral principles at all), a moral theory (like Hare's), which conceives its *central* task to be giving an account of how even quite insane things can be a person's accepted and believed moral principles,[6] is quite likely to confuse this inquiry with the question of what are moral principles. Once, however, (1) and (2) are clearly distinguished, such views seem less attractive; indeed, as regards the relation of principles to having been chosen, it seems more correct to say that principles, in sense (2), at least certain moral principles, define what we have the *right* or *liberty* to choose, rather than principles being defined, in part, by our freely choosing them.[7]

A useful way to clarify the notion of principles of action is to compare them, along several dimensions, with social rules (of which, I take customary rules of etiquette, rules of games, and rules of law to be examples), since by comparing principles of action to their conceptual relatives (both social rules and principles being species of the genus, general standards of conduct), we may come to understand the former's distinctive features among standards of conduct. This method is adopted here, both for the above reason, and because the explanation of certain technical terminology here adopted will be thus made easier, since that terminology was adapted from the case of social rules. For present purposes, examples of principles of action are the principles of rational choice, justice, efficiency (Pareto optimality), fairness, consideration, and non-maleficence.[8]

I. *Existence Conditions*
(a) *Social Rules*

Social rules are, crucially, rules of groups. The existence conditions for particular social rules, thus, seem to be that those rules are, in some sense, part of the critical attitude of some group of people, which results in the group's general observance of the rule. The critical attitude is shown not only by the observance of the rule, but by the attitude taken toward obeying the rule (viewing this as justified by the rule) and toward not obeying it (viewing demands that others follow the rule, and criticisms of not following it, as justified by the rule; feeling oneself inhibited from disobeying it, and feeling guilty when one does voluntarily break it, being disposed to apologize and make reparations).[9] The sense in which the existence of a social rule depends on the critical attitudes of some group of people varies with the kind of social rule in question. Thus, customary rules of manners, like 'men are to take off their hats to ladies', must be widely accepted and used to regulate conduct in a social group before one is prepared to say that this social rule exists. Similarly, the rules of games, e.g. baseball, must be accepted at least in various sub-groups of social groups (i.e. players of the game), as regulating various moves, plays, and related matters, before one is prepared to say or think that such a rule exists. Similarly, particular rules of law must, at least, be part of a system of rules which satisfies certain fundamental rules of legal authority (e.g. 'what the King in Parliament enacts is law'), which must be accepted as standards of conduct at least by the officials (legislators, judges, executives, lawyers generally) before one is prepared to admit that such a legal rule exists.[10] In none of these cases does the existence of a social rule imply that every individual in the society accepts the rule. Quite the contrary. In the case of customary rules of etiquette or rules of games, a person may wholly reject such rules; yet rules still exist and apply to him; and others who accept the rule view themselves as having reasons to criticize him, if he transgresses the rules. And in the case of the modern legal system, it is often the case that people do not accept a legal rule as a standard of conduct, which none the less applies to them, and for disobedience which others hold them justifiably punishable.[11] But still, in all these cases, there is a point at which, when a rule is not accepted by a group or sub-group, the rule's existence will be denied, and truly denied.[12] And thus, it will not be possible to make true or false statements about that rule's requirements, since, *ex hypothesi*, it applies to no one.

(b) Principles

We have seen that the existence of a certain social rule is dependent on the existence of a certain sort of critical attitude, which underlies a certain pattern of behaviour. One cannot make true or false statements concerning the requirements of such a rule, unless it is actually part of the behaviour and critical attitudes of people. None of this is the case with principles of action. A certain principle (e.g. a principle of justice) could be accepted by no one at a certain period in history, and yet it may be true to say that what they are doing is wrong. Thus, imagine a society of human beings (constituted as men normally are), which is a slave economy, where there is no social or moral pressure to treat *all* persons fairly, and the slaves accept their positions as being ordained in what they view as the divinely established organism of the state. Yet it is, I think, one's judgement that members of that society, given certain assumptions, had the right to be treated in accordance with principles of justice and equality, and that slaveholders, with the exception of special cases,[13] had a duty to abolish slavery in line with the requirements of justice. There is a sense in which a particular moral principle can exist and be applicable, such that persons are under moral obligations to obey it, without *that* principle being accepted by the society as part of their critical attitudes. We may suppose people in that society to have moral concepts not unlike ours, but with a sociological arrangement or historical background which has made certain exploitative human relations seem natural and unquestionable. No doubt, something like this is involved in one's reactions to Aristotle's arguments justifying slavery as an institution;[14] moral obligations forbidding that institution then existed, though not correctly recognized because of mistaken factual beliefs about different kinds of human nature, etc. Similarly, one thinks of the case of a moral reformer who enters into such a society, and condemns its institutions in terms of principles of justice; if talk or thought of principles depended on existing social attitudes, then the reformer would be talking nonsense; yet there is a perfectly intelligible and clear sense in which the moral reformer could truly make his claims, apart from any such existing rules.[15]

If the existence conditions for principles cannot, thus, be found in actual critical attitudes, they may, I think, alternatively be found in people's capacities for having the concepts with which principles stand in an important relationship (the rationality principles with the concept of rationality, and the other principles mentioned above, and others, with the concept of morality). A way of understanding what these capacities are is by attempting to clarify what it is for people to *have* the concepts of rationality and morality. Adapting Geach's account to my purposes,[16] to say of a person that he has the concept of rationality is to say that he has certain special capacities of judgement, thought, belief, and knowledge, capacities which are centrally shown to others by the mastery, in the appropriate contexts, of the linguistic usages which surround the notion in the language. What having the concept of rationality or morality does not, *per se*, imply is any desire to act rationally or morally; that is a different question (for example, consider the amoralist, who may well understand what counts as a moral man or action, but who experiences no inclination to let this understanding influence his conduct). Nor does having these concepts, *per se*, imply the existence of the relevant capacities of control and action, which are necessary for the principles to apply to someone (it is, therefore, possible for people to have the concept of principles which do not apply to anyone). Drawing on the above account of a person's having a concept, one may say that the principles of rationality or morality exist in the relevant sense, if people have the various general capacities of thinking about, describing, and classifying human action and human character which having the concepts of rationality or morality requires. Note that this account of the existence conditions of principles of action does not require that people specifically have the concepts of rationality or morality, so that it is possible that no one has these concepts and yet, if the general capacities of thought and other requisite capacities of control and action exist, these principles will exist and apply, in the sense that people's conduct can *be* rational or irrational, moral or immoral (depending on whether the content of the principles of rationality or morality is relevant, given human nature and the circumstances of life). This is, of course, an ontological question, which must be distinguished from the question of the conditions for thinking or saying that conduct is rational or irrational, moral or immoral (where having the concepts of rationality or morality would form an important part of one's account of such conditions). Further, note that, even where people have these concepts, there is an enormous difference between people's having the same concept of morality and their thinking that morality requires the same things in certain circumstances, a distinction on which my slavery example above was built. Much rather superficial cultural relativism is, I think, due to the failure to see the force of this distinction.

What I shall try to clarify in the following chapters is the sense in which the concepts of rationality, morality, and principles are logically related. The case of rationality is the easiest and will be dealt with first. The case of morality is, of course, the more difficult. Here one wishes to ask what it is that makes a principle a moral one; what it is that makes Mrs. Foot's principle of not walking on the lines of the pavement ineligible as an ultimate moral principle (though a neurotic, 'very probably mad', in

Harrison's phrase, could hold it as a moral principle), while
Kant's principle of equal liberty is a moral principle?[17]

11. *Normative Propositions and Rule Expressions*

(*a*) *Social Rules*

One of the most important, if little noted, aspects of our
language and thought in terms of social rules is the difference
between the language used to express the content of these rules
(rule expressions) and the language in terms of which we talk and
think *about* the rules (normative propositions), a distinction first
made by Kelsen and von Wright.[18] What Kelsen and von Wright
noticed, and picked out for analysis, was the important distinction
between expressions of the type (*a*) 'citizens at twenty-one arc to
serve in the military', 'citizens shall serve . . .', 'citizens will
serve . . .', etc. (which might appear in a legal code book, containing a written record of the country's laws) and expressions of
the type (*b*) 'you are legally under an obligation to serve in the
military at twenty-one', 'legally, you ought to serve' (as these
might be used by a lawyer in explaining to his client his legal
position under the law). Sentences of type (*a*) seem directly to
express the rule itself, and do not seem to be capable of truth or
falsity; thus the name, rule expression. Sentences of type (*b*), on
the other hand, seem to express a proposition about legal rules,
namely, that the rules apply in the client's case, which could be
true or false. The distinction cannot, however, be drawn between
all employments of sentences of type (*a*) and (*b*). For example,
sentences using the 'are to' and other forms of type (*a*), can,
depending on the context of communication, be either rule
expressions or propositional expressions whose truth depends on
the existence of rules—a phenomenon which Cavell noted as the
'complementarity of rule and statement'.[19] Thus, standing alone,
the sentence 'children are to be seen and not heard' may be used
to express a certain customary social rule; but if 'in this society'
were placed before the sentence (as part, say, of an anthropolo-
gist's report), the sentence would be propositional. And, of course,
the 'are to' and other forms not only have a non-propositional
employment in rule expressions, but also in legislative enactment
and in giving commands (e.g. a father's command to his daughter,
'you are to be in by midnight'). Thus, it is important to note that

I am here concerned only with that use of 'are to' and related forms, where they are used in formulating the content of rules. Note also that, besides the forms mentioned in (a), there are a diversity of other linguistic expressions which are used in rule expressions, including the simple indicative, e.g. 'When no "Odds" are given, the first move is decided by lot' (from Milton Bradley's 'Rules of Chess').[20]

While it is not possible to discuss here at any length the exact logical status of 'are to' and other forms, as used in formulating social rules, it is of interest that philosophers have usually viewed them as a form of prescription (thus, Kelsen remarkably explains their not being true or false by saying that it is 'parce qu'elles constituent des prescriptions';[21] and von Wright, speaking of 'prescriptions, and perhaps other types of norms',[22] assumes that prescriptive command is the central case of a rule). It seems clear that the use of the concept of command here is one of philosophical art, like Hare's notion of prescriptivity. In viewing both rules and commands as species of the artificial genus prescription, one attempts to clarify their common features: their setting authoritative guides to others' conduct, which is often expressed non-propositionally. As long as distinctions are not blurred (e.g. the typically fugitive and unique nature of the thing commanded, as opposed to the generality of rules), there seems nothing objectionable here. The only further, rather tentative, point that may be worth making is that, in the language, the 'are to' form seems often to play for social rules a similar function to that of the imperative mood in the case of commands. Thus, the imperative mood is an appropriate way of commanding because it is a form in the language, typically intended to be used, and understood to be used, to communicate a person's own intention about another's actions, where there is some context which typically makes these intentions effective. Similarly, the 'are to' form, as in 'you are to take off your hat', may be used to demand or order on the basis of a rule, perhaps because 'are to' is a linguistic form typically (though not always) intended to be used, and understood to be used, to express the content of a seriously felt critical attitude, involving some general standard of conduct, in a context where expressing one's critical attitude will be typically (though not always) effective. *If* this were so, perhaps more abstract uses of 'are to', in formulating the content of actual or possible rules, would be susceptible to an analysis depending on the above use. Thus, given that a certain pattern of action and attitude exists in a certain group of people, we may abstract from the particular group of people, and talk solely about the content of their critical attitudes, i.e. the rule expressed by 'men are to take off their hats to ladies'. We might discuss such an actual rule quite apart from any particular knowledge of the people whose rule it is. But, the understanding of the use of the above sort of sentence, in expressing the rule, will depend on our understanding that perfectly self-conscious and fully informed people would hypothetically be prepared to use such 'are to' sentences to express the content of their critical attitudes, and that actual people do use the 'are to' form to express their critical attitudes, in appropriate contexts of demand, order, and the like. Alternatively, we may discuss a certain rule, e.g. 'women are to take off their hats to men', in abstraction from that rule's ever having been accepted anywhere, discussing the content of a possible rule. Here, our understanding of the above expression would derive from our understanding that 'are to' would be a form of expression used by a group of people to express their critical attitudes, if such a group of people with such a critical attitude existed. The same pattern of analysis can, I think, easily and plausibly be extended to other forms when used as rule expressions, e.g. 'shall' (very commonly used in formulating statutes), 'will', the simple indicative, and the like.

As indicated above, the 'are to' and other forms used in rule expressions can also be used to express normative propositions.[23] However, another form of normative proposition, and one of special importance for my purposes, is that expressed by the language of 'ought'. Of course, 'ought'-expressions occur variously throughout the language, but I am at this point concerned with their use in reference to social rules. In order to abstract from non-social rule uses, here I shall always frame the normative propositions by a tag referring it to the social rule which is its specific context, e.g. 'legally speaking' or 'in terms of customary etiquette', etc. Further, I am here concerned with a general and undifferentiated use of 'ought' which does not distinguish between 'ought' and 'are under an obligation', the latter being often the more natural way to express normative propositions for legal rules. Sentences using 'ought', in this sense, express propositions either about the general requirements of a rule in all cases to which it applies, e.g. 'legally, all citizens at twenty-one ought to serve in the military'; or about the requirements of the rule in a particular case to which it applies, e.g. 'legally, John Doe ought to serve in the military'. I propose to distinguish these two sorts of 'ought' sentences by calling what they express, respectively, primary and derivative normative propositions. The relation of these normative propositions to rule expressions may be stated as follows: the existence of social rules, and thus of certain critical attitudes, expressed, e.g. by 'citizens at twenty-one are to serve . . .', provides the truth grounds for the assertion of such normative propositions.

(b) *Principles*

While, of course, the 'ought' terminology does occur in the case of principles (as will be elaborated in subsequent chapters), principles of action do not have, in the language, any rule expressions of the 'are to' type found in the case of social rules. The explanation for this is not, I think, far to seek. Social rules are rules which vary from social group to social group, and of which a person is often unaware; so that, people often have to read rule books to learn the rules of games which they do not know, and have to consult their lawyers or code books to find out about laws of which they are unaware; thus, there is a need for forms of words in which the rule may be formulated, i.e. rule expressions. By contrast, principles, and the concepts of rationality and morality with which they are associated, are normally part of the ordinary conceptual equipment of a man; and there is no need for him to be made aware of what he was previously wholly unaware.

However, though this is the case, there is a special theoretical enterprise, that of normative philosophy, which is concerned with formulating the content of principles and relating them to the concepts with which they are associated. In the case of social rules, formulating their content in rule expressions is a relatively easy task. One may, for example, appeal to rule books, or to collections of statutory law, or to the tendency of court decisions, in order to decide a debate about what the content of a particular rule is. But when it comes to principles of rationality and morality we have no such easy appeal, no such simple and straightforward procedures to formulate them. Here, one has the phenomenon of the reasonable man, the person of sound moral convictions and practical wisdom, who is thrown into confusion and puzzlement when he begins reflecting about the principles which underlie his judgements, a story as old as Plato's increasingly puzzled Euthyphro,[24] and as recent as Ryle's contrast of 'knowing how' and 'knowing that',[25] and the psychologist Piaget's finding that 'verbal judgment lags behind practical judgment'.[26] Here, we must construct various formulations of principles and their priority relations to one another, and see which formulations most accurately mirror judgements—a task of constant revision, elaboration, and puzzlement. Moreover, what is especially needed here are not the ordinary moral capacities of judgement and action, though these importantly provide the data of the inquiry, but specialized philosophical capacities for ingenuity, controlled hypothetical thinking, systematic examination, and detailed argument.

Though it is the case that the 'are to' form does not typically appear in ordinary language in contexts of principles, for purposes of philosophical investigation (which are uniquely concerned, among theoretical enterprises, with the formulation of principles of action) we may extend this form of words as technical terms to the case of principles, as the linguistic form which I will use to formulate the content of principles. The technical use of 'are to' may be understood in two ways: (*a*) in the formulation of both the principles of rationality and morality, it may be understood as the form of words which a *hypothetical* person, with the critical attitudes of rationality and morality and the complete philosophical capacity to express the content of his critical attitudes in detail, would use in expressing these attitudes; and (*b*) in the formulation of the principles of morality, it may be understood as a kind of quasi-enactment formula which *hypothetical* contractors (of which the reader will hear perhaps too much in Part II) would use in deciding on the content of moral principles. As long as one is aware of the precise sense that I intend this technical use of 'are to' to have, there should be no difficulties here. Further, this use has the advantage of emphasizing the fact that principles themselves, like all rules, are not true or false.

III. *Normative Propositions and Reasons for Action*
(*a*) *Social Rules*

A way of elucidating the origin of my terminology of primary and derivative normative propositions is to set out the following sort of inference:

(1) Legally, citizens at twenty-one ought to serve in the military

(2) John Doe is a citizen at twenty-one

(3) Legally, John Doe ought to serve in the military and thus, (3*a*)
Legally, you (John Doe) ought to serve . . . and thus, (3*b*) Legally,
I (John Doe) ought to serve . . .

where the sense in which propositions of type (3) are derivative,
and those of type (1) are primary, seems clear. Another use of this
inference might be as an example of legal reasoning. It is important
to see what, exactly, such a claim involves.

In the discussion of the existence conditions for social rules,
I emphasized the important place that the notion of a certain kind
of existent critical attitude plays in the notion of an existent social
rule. This attitude might be characterized as involving two crucial
features: (1) a certain type of belief, and (2) a corresponding
effective desire (not a mere velleity) to act according to the rule.
The belief aspect of such a critical attitude could be indicated by
such a logical pattern of normative propositions as is expressed
in the above inference, and by the further belief that this order of
propositions represents a reason for action applied to the particular case. That is, John Doe, who, let us assume, accepts the
rule, would, other things being equal, view the primary normative
proposition as the reason for his acting in accord with the rule.
It is absolutely important to distinguish here, (1) the truth or
falsity of these normative propositions as statements about the
requirements of existent social rules, and (2) the truth or falsity
of the assertion that the primary normative proposition is, in fact,
a reason, or a good reason, for action. So far, all that has been said
is that there is a logical relation between (*a*) the existence of a social
rule, (*b*) the existence of certain critical attitudes in members of
a social group, (*c*) the truth of certain normative propositions which
describe the requirements of the existent social rules, and (*d*) the
belief, on the part of those who accept the social rule, that such
normative propositions are reasons, and good reasons, for action.
On this view, social rules could exist because people *view* certain
religious beliefs about divine sanctioning of the organic social
order, or sociological concepts of the minimum requirements for
social cohesion, as justifying the rules, when such beliefs and concepts may not, in fact, comprise good reasons or reasons for action
at all.[27]

This is not an unimportant point, I think. For example, in reference to legal rules and legal systems, there has been in political and legal philosophy, at least since Cicero and the Roman lawyers, a tradition of thought called natural law theory which has maintained that the concept of a legal rule, or, more plausibly, the concept of a legal system, logically implies that the law or the system is, in some strong sense, morally justified.[28] And this view has, in turn, been opposed by a school of thought, known as legal positivism, which has maintained that the concept of law and the legal system do not imply, at least in any strong sense, its satisfying substantive moral criteria.[29] Here, we have an important intellectual dispute which has absorbed the energies of legal and political philosophers throughout two millenia. Yet, it seems to me that the simple logical view just delineated can significantly clarify the dispute, and indeed indicate a solution to it, one favourable to legal positivism, understood in the narrow sense just defined. Thus, a plausible definition of a legal rule is this: a rule is a legal rule if it is part of a system of public coercive rules, meant to be used as a guide to behaviour and a basis for legitimate expectations, defining the basic constitutional agencies with a monopoly of coercive power and final effective authority over a well-defined territory, and marked by the fundamental nature of the things effectively regulated (property, use of coercion, etc.) and the basic nature of the interests secured (life, property, etc.).[30] However, the existence of a legal system implies only that a certain sub-group of people (legislators, judges, executives) accepts, as legitimate standards, the fundamental legal rules of authority of the system. But they may accept such standards for what are, *in fact*, the worst of reasons or for no good reason at all, and yet the legal system will exist, given that they *believe* it justified, and the other features of legality are present. Thus, one may grant to a natural law theorist like Lon Fuller that, implicit in the concept of a legal system as a system of public rules, intended to be used as guides to conduct and the basis of legitimate expectations, there is an 'internal morality of law'.[31] That is, such rules must be administered impartially and regularly (a notion expressed by the common-sense rules: no one is to be the judge of his own case; equal cases are to be treated equally);[32] as prospective guides to conduct (there being no retrospective legislation, and there being general observance of the rule: *nulla poena sine lege*); without making such impossible demands on people that the rules cannot be used as guides to conduct (a notion expressed by the maxim: ought implies can). Such properties, and others, comprise 'the morality that makes law possible',[33] in the sense of logical possibility, in so far as, if any of them were systematically lacking, the system of rules would not count as a legal one, since it would not satisfy its underlying purpose of being a guide to conduct. However, such a system of rules is compatible with the most vicious injustices; for laws establishing institutional systems of racial separation (e.g. apartheid) and ethnic genocide (e.g. Nazi Germany) *may* be publicly, impartially, and regularly administered, maintaining legal morality while systematically pursuing substantively immoral aims with, *pace* Fuller, great clarity of purpose.[34] Such a system will exist, though it is substantively evil, and though the legal system is accepted for what are, in fact, insufficient or even evil reasons. Believing the rules to justify actions is sufficient.

(b) Principles

As indicated previously, a social rule can exist and apply to a person who wholly rejects the rule; such rejection may derive not merely from considerations of self-interest, but from a non-acceptor's view that the rule is not morally justified. On the basis of social rules *per se*, we have no way to resolve the conflict of beliefs between the acceptor and the non-acceptor. The non-acceptor may agree that certain normative propositions, e.g. those expressed by 'legally, citizens of twenty-one ought to serve in the military' and 'legally, you ought to serve . . .', are true; but, using a more general sense of 'ought', which has yet to be discussed, say: 'I ought not to serve in the military.' This fact is a consequence of the above-mentioned logical relation of social rules and reasons for action, i.e. that the existence of social rules only implies certain supposed reasons for action, not that there *are* such reasons. In order to tend in the direction of resolving the non-acceptor's and acceptor's disagreement, we must move to a wholly different level of rules, where the relation of reasons and existing rules is not that of supposition or belief, but one of fact.

One class of considerations, in terms of which social rules are justified, seems to have a special priority and importance, namely those considerations which are defined by principles. Thus it may not often be a satisfactory answer to 'ought I to obey this law?' to respond with the reason, 'yes; the law requires you to obey', unless some further standard is being tacitly assumed. But, it is, often, a good and sufficient answer to that question to point out the relevance of the principle of fairness in bearing the burdens after having accepted the benefits of a co-operative, mutually beneficial system. Or, to take a more complex case, a citizen, asking from the moral point of view, 'ought there to be legal institutions of punishment?' would not seek an answer by appealing to the requirements of legal rules, though there is the purely legal use of 'ought' where this would be apt.[35] But, often, it would be a good and sufficient answer to point out that legal systems, as systems of coercive rules, underpin and support the application of various principles to social life, e.g. principles of justice and efficiency, non-maleficence, etc.; and in so far as they secure the application of such principles and stabilize institutions which satisfy them, and are themselves just (e.g. not punishing the innocent), then they are justified.

One of the marks of a principle, then, is that, *ceteris paribus* (other principles being satisfied), the principle provides the final justification in the string of standards, the final court of appeal of a reasonable and moral man's critical judgement. Such ultimateness is a crucial mark of the concept of principles *simpliciter*, whether they are principles of justification or explanation. Consider, for example, the principles of economics, or psychology, or mathematics, where the sorts of things that count as principles are either the ultimate explanatory laws which are believed to explain a certain range of phenomena (e.g. the rationality postulates of economic theory, and laws of supply and demand; or the stimulus-response linkages which much psychological theory has emphasized), or the ultimate justifying axioms and rules, from which a particular formal theory is derived, as in mathematical theory or formal logic. Principles of action are only one special class of this genus, namely, that species concerned with justification in matters of human action.

In addition to their distinctive finality in justification, another feature of principles of action, as with principles generally, is their generality: they lack proper names and definite descriptions. At first glance this may seem to be a relatively weak mark of principles, since social rules are also general in this sense, e.g. legal rules which, by their own terms, apply to particular persons are regarded as deviations from the central case (thus, consider the jurist Austin's remark that Roman *privilegia* are 'anomalous').[36] Indeed, one of the minimal lines of distinction between commands and rules seems to be the latter's generality, at least in the sense of applying to possibly recurrent acts, if not in the above sense of generality; and thus it would seem generality in either sense cannot be a useful distinguishing mark of principles. However, the generality of principles, in the sense of their lacking proper names and definite descriptions, may provide some clarification as a distinguishing criterion of principles versus social rules, if one recalls the claim of both Kelsen and Hart that the concept of a legal system requires, as part of its adequate logical analysis, some notion of an ultimate rule of validity, or basic norm, which contains a definite description of some person or persons as being the final authority on what counts as valid law in the system (e.g. the King in Parliament).[37]

And finally, a last mark of principles of action, which distinguishes them from social rules, is their universality: they apply, or can apply, to the actions of all persons, by virtue of their having the capacity to understand and act on them. Unlike many social rules, principles are not formulated in terms of some artificial sub-class of persons (as defined by social class, local community, nation, etc.), but in terms of all persons, including special situations into which all persons may enter (e.g. giving and receiving kindness, benefits from a co-operative scheme, etc.). Of course, this characterization of universality is extremely tendentious. For present purposes, however, it serves the useful function of giving an intuitive formulation of a concept which later chapters will try to analyse more precisely.

So far, quite abstract claims have been made about some kind of analytic relation between true normative propositions on the basis of principles and there being reasons for action. However, I have not yet considered in any detail the 'ought'-expressions associated with principles, or even the principles themselves. The whole account is, as it were, in the air; we must now try to give it a firmer, more plausible basis.

3

THE PRINCIPLES OF RATIONAL CHOICE

WHAT I propose to do in this and the following two chapters is the following: (1) in this chapter, to set out the principles of rational choice and discuss in some detail the distinctive features of my formulation of them; (2) in chapter 4, to relate these principles to an account of normative propositions made on the basis of them, and an account of reasons for action, in both the justificatory and explanatory uses of this notion; and to show how the propositional account makes prudential advising possible; (3) in chapter 5, to relate this propositional account to an analysis of the natural attitude of rationality, thus clarifying the influence that the utterance of sentences expressing such propositions often has on human action. In following this pattern of argument, I am strictly adhering to the criteria of theoretical adequacy outlined in chapter 1.

1. *The Principles of Rational Choice: their Rule Expressions*

I propose to offer here the rule expressions (in the technical sense outlined in chapter 2) of four principles of rational choice, which, I think, represent a plausible specification of an important part of the content of the ultimate standards of deliberation involved in the concept of rationality, at least as this notion is associated with reasons for action (it is also associated with reasons for belief). The formulation of these principles is derived not only from a consideration of the traditional literature, but, perhaps as fruitfully, from recent accounts of the problem of rational choice by various economists, game theorists, and philosophers.[1] After presenting the rule expressions, I shall try to clarify the precise sense in which these principles are to be understood and the distinctive features of this account. Throughout, it should be clear that this particular formulation of these principles is merely *an* attempt to specify the content of these standards. Systematic work at alternative formulations is needed in this field.

The four principles, with some explanatory remarks occasionally appended, are:

1. *Effective means*: given a desired end, one is to choose that action which most effectively, and, at least cost, attains that end, *ceteris paribus*.

2. *Dominance*: given several plans of action, one is to choose that plan which secures all the desired ends of other plans, and more, *ceteris paribus*.

3. *Lottery*: given a plan of action which achieves x, the object of a desire, with probability p ($0 \leqslant p \leqslant 1$), and y, the object of *another* desire, with probability p' (where $p' < 1-p$), and another plan which achieves x with probability p_1 and y with probability p_1' (where $p_1' < 1-p_1$), then that plan is to be chosen in which the probability of securing x is greater than or equal to the probability in the other plan, *and* the probability of securing y is similarly greater than or equal to that of the other plan, except where $p = p_1$ and $p' = p_1'$, when the plans are to be indifferently chosen. Where plans of action secure the same ends (e.g. x and y, as above), and $p = 1-p$, and $p_1' = 1-p_1$ (i.e. the probabilities being exclusive), then that plan is to be chosen which gives a higher probability to the more preferred alternative. And if there are the same probabilities in two plans of action, which secure entirely different ends, that plan is to be chosen which secures ends, at least one of which is preferred (the others being indifferently preferred) to one of those secured by the other plan, all *ceteris paribus*.

This last standard is called the lottery principle, since the simplest case of it is when the plans of action between which one must choose are lottery tickets which yield objects of desires with different probabilities. For example, a rational person typically prefers a lottery ticket which gives higher probabilities to winning the prizes; and, where probabilities are exclusive, a rational man typically prefers the lottery ticket which gives a higher probability to winning a yacht, as opposed to a typewriter; and, given two lottery tickets with equal probabilities of a person's winning different things, a lottery ticket with yachts and cars as prizes is usually preferred to one with tables and chairs as prizes. By its terms, the lottery principle does not apply to cases where the probabilities or ends desired are not as specified in the above rule expressions. For example, it provides no solution to many cases where there are non-exclusive probabilities in two alternative plans involving the same ends, one of the plans giving a higher probability to x, and the other to y; nor does the principle apply where the x and y involve the same end, e.g. different amounts of money as the lottery prize. Such a case would fall under the principle of effective means (1)—which would presumably require the choice of that plan with the highest expected money outcome. The importance of the lottery principle can be seen in cases of military planning of defence systems for various contingencies. As Hitch and McKean have pointed out,[2] even though one system of defence seems to be dominant because it secures against more contingencies than other systems, if it is quite ineffective against the most probable situation, it would be rejected, and rejected, I would add, on the basis of the lottery principle.

4. *Postponement*: one is to postpone making a choice among plans of action which secure certain desired ends, when it is not clear at the time of choice what these ends will be, or how they will be best secured, *ceteris paribus*.

An example of the application of this principle is the case where a parent must choose between alternative plans of education for his child: the parent, not having adequate information at the time of choice about the child's later capacities, interests, and desires generally (whether the child will later rationally prefer being a musician, or mathematician, etc.), is to postpone the choice of a specialized education, instead giving the child the most general background possible, compatible with a wide range of later interests, as they develop. Similarly, as Koopmans has pointed out, in the economic consumer case, enterprises, governments, and private consumers, when choosing between plans for the provision of future goods and services, are to postpone now making a choice of plans for specific goods, since one must allow for consumers' both learning more about their own preferences as time goes on, and changing them; and on the production end, planning is to be flexible, through postponing now making choices which preclude taking advantage of later information about how production processes work out and about better techniques, discovered through research and development.[3] Similarly, in the military planning case, the problem of research and development opens up an enormous area where the principle of postponement applies; in the United States, for example, the military services have only after hard experience learned the irrationality of giving too detailed requirements for advanced systems, and not allowing flexibility in

their planning.[4] Once again, where there is uncertainty, postponement seems relevant.

11. *The Principles and the Problem of Preference Orderings*

Discussions of rational choice assume that the desired ends
satisfy several conditions. Thus, it is universally supposed that a
person has an ordering of the various things he in fact wants, i.e.
he prefers x to y to z. And, it is usually assumed, in economics
and game theory, that the desires underlying such preferences
satisfy certain properties, i.e. (a) completeness, (b) consistency,
(c) non-satiation, (d) continuity, and (e) convexity.[5] That is, (a)
a person could order *all* the things he wants in terms of preference
and indifference relations; (b) the preference relations which
express these desires are such that if I prefer x to y to z, I prefer
x to z. (c) Normally, more of anything is always wanted, and thus
preferred to less. (d) Given $\alpha =$ amount, wants are such that, if
$(a+1)$ α of x, (b) α of y is preferred to (a) α of x, (b) α of y, then
there is some α (n) of y (greater than b), such that $(a+1)$ α of x,
(b) α of y is indifferent to (a) α of x, (n) α of y; if this requirement
is satisfied for every amount of x and y, it follows that the utility
indifference function, which plots all the amounts of x and y
which are indifferently preferred, is continuous in the mathematical
sense (intuitively, there are no gaps or jumps in the function).
(e) Finally, the more a desire is satisfied, the more of that object of
desire one will be willing to give up to receive the object of a less
satisfied want; such a fact about desires will yield a convex
indifference utility function.

The empirical status of several of these properties has been
rather searchingly questioned, especially the transitivity of indifference relations and the associated question of continuity.
Thus, the economist Armstrong has endeavoured to construct a
theory of cardinal utilities (giving numbers, capable of summation
by addition, to desires) based upon the alleged intransitivity of
indifference relations, which has the consequence that indifference
functions are discontinuous. And Rothenberg has pointed out the
independent objection to continuity that certain desired things
may not be substitutable for other desired things, e.g. a certain
minimum level of water for some fine damask. Wants may be in
some 'lexicographic' order, such that one does not satisfy certain
wants unless certain others have already been satisfied.[6]

Whatever may be the accuracy and force of these and related criticisms (and Rothenberg, for example, rather questions them),[7] in the case of a normative theory of rational choice, i.e. an account of what it means to talk and think in terms of rationality, the properties of completeness and consistency seem especially crucial, particularly the latter. An agent who is inconsistent in his preferences, such that he prefers x to y and y to z, but z to x, seems a primary example of irrationality for he will never be able to settle on a preferred course, constantly moving in a self-defeating and frustrating circle of deliberations. Transitivity, at least of preferences and preferences over indifferences (so that if z is preferred to y, which is indifferent to x, which is preferred to w, then z is preferred to w), seems crucial to the concept of rationality; intransitivity of indifference, in Armstrong's sense, does not seem equally objectionable. And the notion of completeness of preference order seems to express that aspect of paradigmatic rationality (at least as expressed in principles 1–3), which assumes clarity about things wanted and their preference relations. Thus, the principles of rational choice 1–3 apply to a complete, consistent preference order. Principle 4 applies precisely to those cases where the uncertainty of the future makes it unclear what one will want later or what means will best secure wants.

In speaking of preference orderings, it must be clear that there is often a difference between a person's actual preference ordering (which may be quite complete and consistent), and his capacity actually to say, accurately, what his preferences are, a distinction long recognized by those students of rational choice who have thought about ways of giving the question some experimental substance.[8] Luce and Raiffa, for example, suggest that building a model of a person's preference ordering poses a statistical problem of a person's having 'actually (or latently or genotypically)' a certain preference ordering which appears in his verbal responses, confounded by random errors.[9] For my purposes, it is important to see that rationality does not imply previously setting out or thinking about one's preferences in detail; it only implies that a complete and consistent preference order in fact exists.

III. *Desires, Self-regarding and Other-regarding*

These principles are clearly relevant only to deliberation about people's actually desired ends, whether general objects of

self-regarding desires (e.g. hunger with the end of eating food)
or other-regarding desires (e.g. benevolence and helping another),
for their very rule expressions, as formulated above, indicate that
they apply given certain desires. Thus, when people claim that
the concept of reasons for action only applies when persons have
certain desires, they may be supposing that all reasons for action
are defined by the principles of rationality. Thus, in philosophy,
Miss Anscombe seems to take such a view when she sees the
crucial mark of practical reasoning in all its forms as being a
calculation of 'the way of getting or doing the thing wanted'[10]—
a view followed by Foot, Melden, D'Arcy, and Findlay.[11] Similarly, economists and game theorists often suppose that all reasons
for action are associated with the process of pursuing our desired
ends, whether our own narrow interests, or other-regarding ends,
like 'altruism and spite' (Luce and Raiffa), 'general standards of
equity' (Arrow), a 'consistent value system' (Schelling), or 'self-
denying charity' (Downs).[12] While I shall, in Part II, indicate why
such a general theory of reasons for action is mistaken, in the
present context it seems incumbent on me to provide some clarification of the concept of desire, since at least the class of reasons
associated with rationality assumes this concept. First, I shall
discuss the general notion of desire, and my own distinction of
self- and other-regarding desires. After that, the conceptual limits
of these notions will be further delineated by relating them to the
notions of (a) wants, (b) interests, (c) needs, and (d) well-being or
welfare.

Desires are distinguishable by their general objects or ends,
e.g. hunger as the desire for eating food, thirst as the desire for
drinking liquids, sexuality as the desire for sexual stimulation,
curiosity as the desire to find out or discover something through
study, reading, investigation, etc., competence desires as the desire
to have or develop or exercise various capacities and talents, and so
on. Having a desire, *per se*, does not imply having certain thoughts
or beliefs about the objects of desires, for animals and babies
have desires, yet we often would not want to attribute to them
thoughts or beliefs. And, indeed, relatively mature persons may
have certain desires, without having any clear idea, or any idea at
all, of what the objects of those desires are (e.g. the adolescent boy
who first experiences the twinges of sexual desire, without realizing
what the desire is; or the grown woman, who may experience a

general uneasiness without realizing it is the desire for children).[13] Yet, desires, importantly, have objects, objects which, when achieved, attained, or realized, *satisfy* the desire, which does not imply having a certain sensation or distinctive quality of feeling.[14] However, having desires as part of various human attitudes, like pride, the sense of justice, shame, fear, etc., does imply having certain thoughts or beliefs about the object of those desires. Thus, condemning someone out of a sense of justice implies not only the desire to act on the principles of justice, but the belief that these principles have been violated; and, leaving one's home out of fear, implies not only the desire to avoid something, but the belief (or thought) that something injurious or dangerous is approaching.

However, in the human case, there seems to be a deeper and more general relationship between belief and desire; that is, in the explanation of human *actions*, there is a relation of epistemic interdependence between the knowledge of the agent's thoughts and beliefs, desires, and capacities.[15] One cannot know that one of these is a part of the explanation of a certain human action without knowing the other two. A classic case of the interdependence between belief and desire is Geach's example of Dr. Johnson doing penance in Uttoxeter market place by standing bareheaded until it rains; we can infer that he expects rain only if we know that he desires to get wet in order to do penance.[16] The converse dependence, that of knowledge of desires on knowledge of belief, has been questioned by Kenny on the basis that what a man believes and says sincerely that he wants, may not be what, in fact, he wants.[17] This objection is not to the point, for the relevant sense of knowledge or belief is not knowledge of the agent's beliefs about his own desires, but knowledge of the agent's beliefs and thoughts about the factual situation before him (c.g. that the object over there is something to eat or that it will rain), about his moral or social relation to that situation (e.g. in Johnson's case, his belief that morality required penance for his filial disobedience in the past), and the like. Even in the clearest case of Kenny's kind of example, so-called psychoanalytic unconscious desires, the knowledge of certain thoughts or beliefs, e.g. that one's father murdered one's mother, and that thus you are entitled to murder him, and all people like your father, is a necessary part of understanding the desire to kill people who resemble your father, a desire which a psychoanalyst may claim to have uncovered. The importance of knowledge of capacities in explaining human actions can also be seen in the Dr. Johnson example, for if we knew that he lacked all capacity for religious attitudes so that doing penance was something he could not, really, do, then we could not characterize his standing in Uttoxeter as doing penance, though he may have the appropriate desires and beliefs; he may *try* to do penance, but, like Hamlet's desperate uncle, he may conclude:

> My words fly up, my thoughts remain below:
> Words without thoughts never to heaven go.[18]

This use of the concept of desire, in the explanation of human action, suggests certain associated marks of the general notion of effective desire (as expressed, I think, by the verb forms of 'want')—a point Anscombe first made in recent philosophy, followed by Gauthier, Kenny, and others.[19] Thus, if wanting is to be distinguished from a mere velleity at the thought or sight of an object or from hoping, one must note that the concept of wanting x implies the notion of a readiness to try to get the object of desire (assuming x is not, under the same or a different description, the object, or part of the object, of being foregone by another stronger desire), and the knowledge or belief that the object of desire, which one does not now have, is there to be had or is achievable by action in the future.[20] Further, the employment of the notion of wanting x, e.g. in 'I want a pin', is not normally fully understood, until some characterization of why the pin is desirable is given. Anscombe made this point by saying that the intelligibility of 'I want x' typically requires some characterization, until one comes to some final desirability-characterization, where one sees 'what he wants under the aspect of some good'.[21] Anscombe's conception is, I think, somewhat inaccurate, for it is not unintelligible when a person says, without explanation, 'I want a pin', but rather such a usage is not fully understood, until this desire is shown to relate to more basic desires. There is, I think, an underlying assumption or presupposition in ordinary language and thought about a certain constant pattern of human desires which are regarded as ultimate in the explanation of human actions; thus, one can understand what a person means in saying 'I want a pin', but if such expressions of desire are not understood to relate to more basic desires, they will, without special explanation about a certain irregularity in human desire, not be fully understood;[22] one is left with the explanatory puzzlement of why anyone would want *that*. Among self-regarding desires which are viewed in ordinary thought (yet uncorrupted by reductionist psychological theories) as ultimate, are, perhaps, the desire for health, hunger, thirst, sexual appetite, the desire for love and personal intimacy, competence desires, curiosity, desire for play, etc. And among other-regarding desires viewed as similarly ultimate are love, sympathy, pity, benevolence, the sense of justice, the sense of moral right, as well as hate, jealousy, envy, and malevolence. Anscombe's view that the notion of the good is relevant here is quite compatible with my account, if the notion of the good is analytically related to satisfying basic human desires (see chapter 14).

In introducing the concept of a self-regarding desire, I intend to characterize a feature of the objects of a certain class of one's own desires, namely, that the *object* of these desires has reference to, and is thought or believed to have reference to, the satisfaction of oneself. Thus, the end of hunger, eating food, satisfies the self; the end of sexuality satisfies oneself (without necessary reference to the satisfaction of another, one of the differentiae of sex and love); the end of the desire for love, getting loved, has reference to the satisfaction of oneself (not implying the desire for the satisfaction of others' desires); and similarly with thirst, curiosity, competence desires, and the like. Other-regarding desires, on the other hand, have *objects* which have, and are thought to have, reference to the satisfaction or dissatisfaction of other selves. Thus, love has as one of its objects satisfying the desires of the person loved; the sense of justice has the object of realizing principles which have a clear reference to the justified satisfactions and dissatisfactions of others, as well as one's self; hate has the object of causing harm or dissatisfaction to others; envy has the object of belittling and thus lessening the satisfaction of another in his achievements and capacities; and the like. The distinction between self- and other-regarding desires is not, then, a moral or evaluative distinction, for many other-regarding desires are contemptible in a way that many self-regarding desires are not. It is a distinction in the objects that distinguish desires from one another. Of course, such a distinction is logically completely separate from the logical truism, mentioned above, that when the object of a desire is achieved, the agent's desire is satisfied, whether that desire is the hunger for food or the hunger for justice. The failure to distinguish this logical truism from the concept of the objects of desire is the rock on which many theories of psychological hedonism are dashed.[23]

Given this general view of the concept of desire, it is illuminating to contrast it with certain related notions.

(a) Wants

The ordinary language notion expressed by the noun 'want', like the related notion expressed by 'doing x for pleasure',[24] seems especially appropriate when thinking about spontaneous self-regarding desires; for wants seem typically to be desires whose satisfaction involves oneself, in a context where a person is at liberty positively to pursue his self-regarding ends as he sees fit, neither being coerced by another, nor being in circumstances where all the alternatives of choice frustrate, in some degree, self-regarding desires, nor being under any prudential or moral requirement to act or not to act in a certain way. As a consequence of this, the concept expressed by the noun 'want' is not identical with the concept expressed by the verb 'want', for there seem to be many things which I may want, which do not correspond to wants of mine.[25] Thus, the objects of wanting to be fair, or wanting to improve one's health are not always, or typically, thought of as one's wants, but rather as things which one must or ought to do.[26]

The confusion of wants and the general notion of practical desire has led, I think, to some extremely strange views of moral motivations, as if one could act from a moral belief, *per se*, with no desire present *at all*. This is a consequence of viewing all desires as wants, then noting that the desire to be moral is not a want, and thus inferring that it is also not a desire, but something else. In contemporary philosophy, Hampshire has drawn the distinction between acting from wants and acting from moral considerations as being between the explanation of action in terms of desire and its explanation in terms of moral belief; and this is evidenced by naturalness of explaining other-regarding actions as things one must or ought to do, and others as things which are one's wants.[27] In traditional philosophy, this sort of view is, I think, in part behind Kant's extreme distaste for all theories of moral motivation in terms of desire.[28] However, such views can seem plausible only if one has assimilated wants and desire; and it is this, precisely, which must not be done.

(b) Interests

The notion of one's interests seems logically related to self-regarding desires, but as a concept of the generalized means to the achievement of many self-regarding ends, a point recently made in Barry's useful discussion.[29] Among the things that are in one's interests are health, money, security from destruction of one's person or property, the possession of unrestricted authoritative or coercive power over others, and the like, all of which enable one to pursue and achieve the objects of many self-regarding desires.

That the concept of interests is, in this way, relative to the achievement of self- and not other-regarding ends, can be seen by considering the fact that there is no logical impropriety in the claim that a course of action is in one's interests, but is so at the expense of frustrating one's friendships, loves, general desire to do what is right, and, indeed, all one's other-regarding ends. Indeed, note that it is quite natural to say of a secular saint (thus, abstracting from considerations of an after-life, where benevolence in this world will ultimately be in one's interests)—who pursues an other-regarding end of general benevolence valued more highly than all his other ends together, and thus incurs poverty, ill-health, insecurity, powerlessness, and even death—that he has frustrated his interests. And this would be so, although all might agree that, given the saint's value system, this was his most rational course of conduct. Further, note that this account of the concept of interests is quite compatible with cases of interests seemingly arising from other-regarding desires, e.g. a person's interest in his children's future happiness after he is dead. For, in such cases, the desire for others' welfare may be explained not in terms of love, or the like, but in terms of self-regarding desires like the desire to be loved and honoured after death, or the desire for self-preservation (one's children and their children, etc., being conceived as a kind of eternal self).

(c) Needs

The concept of needs does not imply the notion of desire, for one may speak of the needs of plants or primitive animal life, where the concept of desire is inapplicable. Rather, the notion of a need is relative to some view of what is required for the survival and/or minimal functioning of some other things.[30] In the case of organisms, not all things which are part of the functioning of an organism are thought to be needed, but only those which are typically related to sustaining life, whether the life of the organism or that of other organisms. Thus, in reference to human beings, we speak and think of oxygen, food, water, the exercise of bodily functions of elimination, sexual intercourse, etc., as human needs, because they are viewed as things without which we could not survive, either because they are directly necessary to sustain life (oxygen), or because they are part of the minimal organic functioning by which the life of the organism is sustained (elimination), or the life of the species is sustained (sex). By analogy to this view of bodily needs, what is meant in talking of psychological or spiritual needs like the need for love is that such love is required if a person is to attain some minimum level of satisfactory psychological functioning; and no doubt, part of the appropriateness of the concept of needs in the description of such a phenomenon is that one has an underlying idea that, if persons lack such love, the capacity to sustain life may be undermined, with accompanying notions of spiritual death (as, for example, in Strindberg, later Ibsen, and Bergman) and, perhaps, even actual suicide.

While the notion of a need is related to one's view of the requirements for survival and minimum organic functioning, it is, of course, the case that things needed are often the objects of our desires; for example, many human needs are the objects of those recurrent and regularly periodic desires that psychologists have dubbed 'drives'. Further, while a thing judged to be needed is not necessarily judged to be a want, the concept of wants does seem to imply some of the urgency of the self's needs; it seems, in short, a logical fact about things judged to be a person's wants that, over some range of them, they are judged to ensure the person's minimally adequate functioning, i.e. they are judged to fulfil his needs.[31]

(d) Well-being or Welfare

Like needs, things which are judged to lead to one's well-being or welfare do not seem necessarily to be things which are judged to be desired.[32] Indeed, doing things 'for' another's welfare is a typical way of rejecting the other person's own desires in the light of one's own conception of what is objectively required for well-being, a common phenomenon in parent–child relationships. What theoretical adequacy not only apply to the account of reasons associated with the concept of rationality, which will be developed in Part I of this book, but have, I think, quite general validity, and will be applied to moral concepts also, as I hope to illustrate in Part II. The same point has, in fact, recently been made by Warnock in reference to moral reasons when he suggested the applicability of Austin's threefold distinction of locutionary, illocutionary, and perlocutionary acts to the analysis of moral discourse.[14] Thus, the three criteria just elaborated can quite easily be mapped onto Austin's distinctions. Assuming the expression in question is propositional, the analysis of (1) clarifies the proposition expressed, what, strictly, is typically meant by the locutionary act of uttering the expression in question—a concept of meaning which Austin equates with Frege's notion of sense and reference.[15] The analysis of (2) elucidates the relation of the proposition expressed to the illocutionary speech act performed (e.g. commending, praising, advising, etc.). And the account of the relation of the proposition expressed to human motivations (3) clarifies what is done by using the expression in question, e.g. the possibility of the success of the perlocutionary acts of persuading.

These criteria of theoretical adequacy, and the basic method of analysis behind them, represent, I think, only a more sophisticated statement of long-standing methods and orientations of ethical theorists such as Plato, Aristotle, Hume, Kant, W. D. Ross, Richard Brandt, and John Rawls.[16] That is, one assumes, as these theorists do, that people generally make a certain class of judgements about normative questions, and that certain of these judgements are marked by being likely to be made seriously in conditions of impartiality by reasonable and moral men who are in full control of normal mental and judgemental capacities.[17] Such considered judgements are the empirical data of normative philosophy. The task of the philosopher is to provide a theoretical account of normative concepts which, given people's nature and predilections, naturally and readily explains the normative judgements which people do make; the only distinctive feature of my view is judging the adequacy of an account by its capacity to mirror these judgements in the three ways specified above. Generally, if after considerable reflection on the account and its capacity to mirror our considered judgements, it falls short, then one is justifiably *entitled* to reject it. I use the permissive locution the quite common argument of non-propositional moral theorists concerning the incapacity of propositional theories to account for the relation of moral concepts to action and practical life. Thus, it was one of the central claims of Stevenson's emotivism that propositional theories failed to account for the 'magnetism' of ethical terms, their hold on our motivations and consequent persuasive influence on our actions.[11] And surely, if a moral theory cannot account for the 'moving appeal', in Perry's phrase,[12] of ethical utterances, it would be inadequate. Similarly, Hare's prescriptivism crucially argues that propositional theories cannot adequately account for the role of moral terms in performing various speech acts, e.g. commending.[13] And clearly, if this were true, propositional theories would be philosophically unacceptable.

What is required in order to give the arguments sketched above greater, and perhaps conclusive, force is a positive and constructive analytic account of the propositions expressed by sentences 1–5, an account which will also provide a philosophical elucidation of the important use of such expressions to advise, and some clarification of the relation of these propositions to human motivation, such that they have some influence on human conduct. If this can be accomplished, we shall have done what non-propositional theorists have claimed to be impossible, provided a propositional account of 'ought'-expressions which also accounts for the role of such expressions in practical life. Indeed, one may establish here three criteria for the adequacy of the positive theory I shall propose in subsequent chapters: (1) the expressions comprising the proposed theoretical analysis must indicate propositions which, upon reflection of the whole theory, a thoughtful person would accept as identical with the propositions indicated by the original expressions; at a minimum, if the above is too strong a requirement, the analysis must retain the truth values and logical relations of the defined expression (e.g. if the expression 'x is in your interest' has a logical relation to 'you ought to obtain x', then the defining expression for 'you ought' must preserve this relation; see here, chapter 4); (2) the theory must provide an illuminating account of how certain things are done in using the defined expression, e.g. advising; (3) the theory must relate the account of (1) to some plausible view or theory of human motivation which will explain the influence that the utterance of the defined expression has on human conduct. These criteria for the notions of well-being and welfare do analytically seem to imply is some view of what is required for the health, viewed generally, or sound functioning of another, where this may be assessed along several dimensions, e.g. 'material' or 'spiritual' welfare.[33] Thus, these concepts imply more than just what is minimally required for survival, suggesting instead some conception of maximal or flourishing function, the full realization of the species' potential capacity—a characteristically Greek way of thinking.[34] Thus, among things that are regarded as ingredients of well-being or welfare are adequate housing facilities, medical care, adequate diet, sanitation, education, etc., since these things are required for the maintenance and full development of human capacities.

Given this account of welfare as a concept without logical reference to desires, it should, none the less, be clear that, as in the case of needs, things for one's welfare are often the objects of our desires, indeed, are in one's interests, since they realize the conditions of mental and physical health, which are a means to many self-regarding ends.

IV. *Intention and the Concept of Plans of Action*

Another important feature of the principles of rational choice formulated above is the use of the concept of plans of action between which the principles are intended to be standards of adjudication. I am using this concept to cover much of the same ground that the concept of intention covers in ordinary language and thought.[35] What I intend to do, in ordinary language, as opposed to specialized uses, as in the law,[36] covers the aim of my action (the end I am trying to achieve, e.g. enjoying myself at the theatre, having a good meal, etc.) and the means I knowingly envisage or am using to secure that end. Of course, as Anscombe and D'Arcy have taught us, actions and intentional actions may be described and redescribed in many different ways.[37] However, the use of intention with which I am concerned is not any intermediate means-end relation, but rather the means leading to the final end, or ends of action in reference to which 'why?' does not arise or does not arise in the usual way.[38] My notion of a plan of action is related to this form of intention in that it expresses a possible intention in acting, covering various possible means of securing one's ends.

v. *The Importance of the Dominance Principle*

There are two reasons for the special importance of the formulation of the dominance principle in my account of rational choice.

(*a*) At least one extremely influential account of practical reasoning (Hume's)[39] views the essential role of reasoning as discovering the most efficient means to the desired end, where the agent either knowingly or unknowingly desires that end. In the latter case, reasoning not only performs an efficiency calculation, but also performs inferences which make known to the agent certain latent desires to act which he does not realize are relevant in a particular situation (e.g. making inferences from seeing the shadow of a man with a gun, which indicates the relevance of the desire for survival). This view largely conceives the role of reason in terms of my first principle, that of effective means, wholly missing one of the central aspects of human reasoning, i.e. those cases where the agent tries to adopt plans of action which secure as many ends as possible, and where, thus, the pursuit of various ends is co-ordinated in plans covering various time periods. Such a time-plan may cover one day's activities, trying to act in such a way as to secure as many ends as possible (e.g. adopting a plan whereby en route to the library I may stop at my bank, visit a friend, buy some food for dinner, buy theatre tickets, etc.); or it may cover quite extended *life* plans, such as seem relevant at the time of choice of college, career, marriage and marriage partner, having children, and the like. This feature of human reasoning is, perhaps, what Butler was attempting to clarify through his concept of 'self-love';[40] and it is certainly the aspect of human reasoning which, in several articles, Mabbott has urged us to take account of.[41] Mabbott has emphasized the many cases where time-plans may alter desires, not taking them as always given, as Hume supposed. Thus, postponing desires may allow them to weaken or disappear ('Count ten when you are angry'); the occurence of a desire can be avoided by anticipating it, e.g. eating before you are actually hungry; a person can check a desire's operation by insuring that it will be difficult to satisfy it, e.g. not carrying cigarettes if he wants to stop smoking; also, one may subordinate the extent to which one or more desires are satisfied, so that a number of weaker preferences are satisfied also; and a person may refuse, entirely, to act on one desire because it is incompatible with the satisfaction of many other desires. It is possible, I think, to supplement Mabbott's list with the cases where reason not only weakens or eliminates desires, but where it can, in a sense, create them. Consider, for example, the case where a person is able to choose a certain system of education which he knows will develop in him a set of sensitivities and desires which he did not previously have.[42] Unlike Hume's cases, where the desires to be satisfied are always assumed to pre-exist, here an agent makes a choice to enter into certain circumstances where he knows, as some form of psychological law of attitudinal transformation, that new desires will be created. Throughout all these cases (whether of creating new desires, reducing the satisfaction of given desires, or trying to eliminate such desires entirely by habitual non-satisfaction), the central importance of the dominance principle is, I think, clear; for it is this principle which seems crucially involved in our understanding of the rationality of these actions. In its dynamic formulation, it requires that plan to be chosen which secures more new desires and capacities for enjoyment and civilized response; and its static form, which applies when an existing system of desires is given, requires less or a negligible satisfaction of those desires whose pursuit interferes with the satisfaction of many other desires, and requires the attempt to eliminate, perhaps by habitual non-satisfaction, a certain form of desire satisfaction, which may seriously interfere with the satisfaction of other desires. Thus, the rationality of eliminating the desire to smoke derives from the causal relation of smoking to cancer and death, for, by the principle of dominance, one ought to act on a plan of action which substitutes a different form of satisfying the desire, which is presently satisfied by smoking, so as both to satisfy that desire, and many others as well (e.g. chewing gum as an alternative way of satisfying the desire to keep pleasurably occupied).

Generally, the principle of dominance only applies where people value their ends in some equal way, and thus it has its chief relevance in regulating the pursuit of self-regarding ends, where persons often do not have any special preference for one end over another, but rather seek to advance the satisfaction of all, or most, rather than any one. Thus, the dominance principle does not apply in the case of other-regarding ends like being moral, or being benevolent, where it is the case that, in terms of the dominance principle, a person might better secure his self-regarding ends, if he lessens the satisfaction of such humanistic ends, which inhibit his pursuit of his interests; for, such ends are typically valued so much more highly than self-interest, that it is irrational not to pursue such other-regarding ends, even if this frustrates one's self-regarding ends. Indeed, the principles of rational choice are primarily intended to apply to self-regarding ends, though, of course, they apply in the pursuit of other-regarding ends: e.g. the concept of rational love (as love which effectively does good for the beloved), and the just mentioned notion of rationally pursuing one's desire to be moral. This primary applicability to self-regarding ends is a consequence of the fact that the pursuit of certain other-regarding ends (e.g. being moral) is regulated by principles of morality, so that even if a person does not value the pursuit of morality at all, he is not to pursue his interests in violation of morality. Because this is so and because it will considerably simplify the analytic task, I shall, in the rest of this chapter and the rest of Part I, only consider the rationality principles applied to self-regarding ends; the appropriate place for considering their application to other-regarding ends will be after I have provided some account of the principles which define certain of those ends (see chapter 12).

(b) The second aspect of the distinctive importance of this formulation of the dominance principle is that it does not imply internal comparisons of strengths of preferences. One plan dominates another plan if it secures all the ends the other plan does, and more. This principle provides no standard of comparison between plans which secure different self-regarding ends, situations where comparisons of preference intensity may seem relevant. Rather, if the principle is to apply, overlapping ends must be assumed. Indeed, it is a general feature of the four principles, as applied to self-regarding ends, that they never involve a comparative *weighing* of preference intensities; the effective means principle (1) applies to securing an individual end; the lottery principle (3) assumes that either the same things are being compared in two (or more) plans, or that both things in one plan are preferred to both things in the other plan; and the postponement principle (4) is essentially a form of dominance principle, since it is trying to assure that more ends in the future are realized, not frustrated. Thus, if one views the notion of dominance, as it is viewed in economics and game theory, as the concept that x is to be preferred to y only if

x secures as much as y secures, and more, then principles 2, 3, and 4 are all forms of dominance principle.[43]

VI. *The Incompleteness of the Decision Procedure for Rational Choice: a Contrast with the Traditional View*

Given the way in which I understand the use of these principles, they will not always yield a unique or any decision between plans of action: the decision problem for rational choice is not complete. Thus, for example, if the only real alternative plans of action involved non-overlapping classes of self-regarding ends, in a case where only principle 2 was relevant, then the principles provide no way of resolving the decision problem. To cover such cases, and thus make the set of rationality principles more complete, the following principle may be formulated:

5. If principles 1–4 do not apply, and *ceteris paribus*, one is to choose that plan which, after a dispassionate, well-informed weighing of probabilities and preference intensities, will better secure one's desired ends.

However, even though this is a real possibility, it should be made clear that it is often not necessary to resort to principle 5. As Richard Brandt has suggested, it is often possible to break down seemingly incomparable plans of action into various sub-plans which are comparable. Thus, consider Brandt's professor who must decide whether to take a sabbatical at Los Angeles or Oxford. This question, which might seem to involve incomparable ends, can be reduced to questions like: Will I have stimulating students? Will I have stimulating colleagues? Will there be enough theatre to satisfy my theatre interests? etc. Using such a parsing device, it may be possible to conclude that there is sufficient overlap of ends to permit application of the principles. Thus, Brandt suggests that, first, the alternative plans be parsed into the kinds of things that will be secured, and then you are to see if there is overlap. Then, if it is not the case that the same kind of things will be achieved, one sees if things which satisfy the same sort of desire will occur, e.g. knowledge, entertainment, etc. Finally, if the same kind of desire-satisfying things does not occur, you line up the things secured on either plan, and make a judgement of 'the comparative worth of things of different kinds', e.g. reading Plato with drinking milk shakes; and if one plan yields all things of greater or equal worth, and more things, then that plan dominates.[44]

Further, it is important to note that such parsing may be required not only to compare seemingly incomparable plans of action, involving different ends, but also to provide discriminating comparisons between seemingly quite comparable plans, involving the same ends. For example, the process of choosing rational plans to satisfy the desire for aesthetic pleasure often involves quite extensive parsing of alternative plans of action in terms of the disparate criteria on which aesthetic satisfaction turns, a process of decision quite as complex as that of Brandt's professor. Thus, in the case of the dramatic theatre, such criteria as aesthetic credibility, stylistic unity, quality of language, development of plot, etc., are all often consulted and weighed in rationally deciding which play to attend. And, in the case of music, the sophisticated and rational music-lover often must consult such quite disparate (and sometimes irreconcilable) criteria as beauty of melody, complexity of harmony, colour of orchestration, lucidity or complexity of structure, rhythm, and the like. Such inquiries may, in turn, assume considerable analysis and comparison of different traditions of taste. The complexity of this rational process makes the existence of the discriminating, informed critic a matter of considerable social utility, since his special training will aid others in identifying and weighing the criteria of aesthetic value in terms of which plans of aesthetic satisfaction may be parsed, and then compared.[45]

The general capacity for parsing of the above kinds is one of the fundamental features of human rationality, though this has rarely been recognized in traditional accounts of rational choice. Part of the problem is that this point is only clearly seen when considering specific problems of rational choice. On a general level, notions of maximizing satisfaction may seem sufficient; but when specific analysis of cases occurs, such abstract conceptions are less than useful, and may be positively misleading. In this context, consider the results of contemporary operations research and systems analysis, in applying rationality criteria to specific economic and military problems; thus, Hitch and McKean report that general conceptions of maximizing satisfaction or military worth are useless as operational criteria, and espouse a search for more 'proximate' criteria.[46] The form that the latter finally take is invariably some form of the dominance principle, emphasizing the theoretical need for the parsing of alternative plans. As they put it:

In many cases, the analyst's ingenuity may be more rewardingly exercised in trying to find ways of satisfying multiple objectives than in devising common measures for them.[47]

The emphasis, throughout, is on the need for *ingenuity* in developing plans which will accommodate diverse ends. I would only add that such ingenuity and resourcefulness is a general feature of human rationality.

However, even given this possibility of so parsing plans that the dominance principle applies, it must, again, be admitted that there will be cases where principles 1–4 do not supply a solution. By contrast, traditional philosophical views often supposed that the problem of rational choice required some common thing one could use in order to calculate about otherwise incomparable ends, in order to render a complete decision procedure for all cases. Consider, for example, Aristotle's statement that in deliberation about so many different things 'there must be a single standard to measure by, for that is pursued which is greater';[48] St. Thomas's view that there must be some ultimate end, which orders all others, for 'if sport were an end in itself, the proper thing to do would be to play all the time';[49] Kant's idea that a feeling of pleasure must be the basis of calculation, 'otherwise how could one make a comparison with respect to magnitude between two determining grounds, the ideas of which depend upon different faculties, in order to prefer the one which, affects the faculty of desire to the greater extent';[50] and Sidgwick's conception that 'Happiness' is required in order to compare the human ends pursued.[51] Further, this view was, I think, a primary philosophical motivation behind hedonism and the conception of reasoning solely in terms of effective means. Thus, given this general idea of some common thing by which various ends could be compared, it was not uncommon to identify it with some notion of pleasure. Needless to say, there was a deceptive ambiguity behind this conception. When the view was thought of as philosophical doctrine, it was conceived in terms of the general conception of coherent desire satisfaction, or happiness; but when the view was considered in terms of calculation, some identifiable qualities of sensation, or, in Sidgwick's phrase, 'agreeable . . . feelings' were imagined.[52] Further, thinking of reasoning in terms of some common thing, it was, I think, quite natural to suppose that the essential role of reason was to discover the most efficient means to get that thing.

In any event, my conception quite explicitly rejects such a view. It does not seek any common thing which will render all choices decidable, but accepts, as a fact, that the rationality principles 1–4 will provide only a partial ordering of alternative plans.

VII. A 'Satisficing', Not a Maximizing Conception

Principles 1–4, as stated, seem to be maximizing conceptions, requiring the choice of that plan which *most* effectively or *most* dominantly secures certain ends. I wish, however, quite explicitly to eschew such a viewpoint. In the process of deliberation, it is normally impossible, given the costs of prolonged decision making, to consider *all* the possible alternative plans, and to choose the maximal one in the light of *all* the relevant facts. What seems to be required here is not a maximizing conception, but what Herbert Simon has called 'satisficing'.[53] That is:

An alternative is *satisfactory* if: (1) there exists a set of criteria that describes minimally satisfactory alternatives, and (2) the alternative in question meets or exceeds all the criteria.[54]

How high or low one will pitch the criteria of satisfaction will depend on what the prospects of satisfaction in fact are, and whether a marginal increase in better securing the desires in question is worth the marginal increase in costs of deliberation, costs which might be better expended on some other decision problem; thus, the criteria will be set rather high when a person chooses a fundamental life plan like marriage with someone, since the interests involved are so fundamental and the costs of deliberation seem, by comparison, slight; and, the criteria will be set rather low when a busy executive has to choose to buy a pair of scissors, for here the price of extended deliberation would be too costly, given the small benefits which result and great costs in terms of forgoing the exercise of deliberation on more difficult and important decision problems. The satisfaction of arbitrarily chosen scissors seems here enough, though special circumstances could change this judgement (a pair of scissors with a special mark contains the secret to a great fortune), as they could in the case previously described (e.g. there is a realistic threat of death unless you marry a certain person immediately). The importance of such a satisficing conception is seen not only in such examples from ordinary life, but also in the case of applying rationality criteria to complex economic and military problems; as Hitch and McKean report, 'Frequently, we can demonstrate that system A is better than system B even when we cannot show that system A is optimal.'[55] However, while satisficing seems an important part of rational choice in general, note that, if decision costs could be reduced in some technological or other way (computer data processing may indicate a way), then satisficing levels would begin to move towards the maximizing level.

Thus, given this discussion, the rationality principles are to be understood as requiring that plan which is, for example, satisfactorily effective in securing a certain end (principle 1), or which satisfactorily dominates other plans (principle 2), etc.

VIII. *The Importance of the* Ceteris Paribus *Conditions*

The use of these principles, individually, is always subject to the *ceteris paribus* conditions which I have appended to each of them. These conditions cover two things: (*a*) the priority relations between the principles themselves, and (*b*) their priority relations to the principles of morality.

(*a*) Within the class of principles of rational choice, the *ceteris paris* conditions involve two different kinds of priority relations: (i) the relation between the principles as applied to other-regarding ends, valued absolutely higher than self-regarding ends, and the principles as applied to self-regarding ends, and (ii) the priority relation between the principles as applied to self-regarding ends alone. Since I have limited myself to the explanation of the principles as applied to self-regarding ends, only the latter relation will here be discussed.

The *ceteris paribus* conditions of (ii) imply that the effective means principle is not to be used unless the dominance principle has first been satisfied. Thus, if a man wants alcoholic drink, and a certain plan satisfactorily secures it, this will not necessarily be the plan to be chosen, even on self-regarding grounds alone. For if drinking alcohol will impair the man's health, then the dominance principle will exclude this plan (since it frustrates many self-regarding desires), instead requiring a plan of action which secures the desire satisfied by drinking alcohol, but in a non-deleterious way, and also secures one's other self-regarding ends as well. And, even the dominance principle does not seem properly applied until the lottery principle has been: in a case where probabilities of a plan's success are relevant, then the plan which best allows for the most likely probability is to be chosen, even if another plan is dominant (secures the same and more ends), but does not secure the most likely contingency nearly so well. Thus, the *ceteris paribus* conditions here imply that there is a lexicographical priority order in the application of the principles; that is, just as in the dictionary ordering, a lexicographer will only go on to place words with 'abce' after he has placed all words with 'abcd' (observing a strict order based on alphabetic succession), so, one here has an order of principles where a successive principle is only applied to a situation which has passed muster by the requirements of the previous principle. I shall assume that the priority order here is expressed by the following rule expressions:

Given self-regarding ends, one is to apply principle 3 (lottery); if plans equally satisfy this principle, or this principle is irrelevant, then principle 2 (dominance) is to be applied; if plans equally satisfy the above or the above are irrelevant, then one is to apply principle 1 (effective means); if plans equally satisfy the above, or the above are irrelevant, principle 4 (postponement) is to be applied; if the above are irrelevant, then principle 5 (dispassionate weighing) is to be applied, *ceteris paribus*.

This is, of course, only a suggestion, which requires much refinement before it can accurately express the outlines of rational deliberation in this area.

(*b*) That I still need blank cheque *ceteris paribus* conditions, in formulating the principles' priority relations, should be clear, quite apart from the priority mentioned in (*a* (ii)), above. As Diggs pointed out, just because a plan, e.g. killing the major, most effectively secures a certain end, even where other self-regarding considerations are not relevant and where the agent has no other-regarding desire that would involve not killing in such circumstances, it does not follow that one 'ought' to do the act.[56] In short, principles of morality seem to be in some kind of priority relation to the principles of rational choice. The consequence of this view is that one cannot fully specify the principles of rational choice until he has presented an account of the principles of morality, since moral principles form part of the content of the *ceteris paribus* conditions of the principles of rational choice. This task remains as a *theoretical* requirement for the adequacy of my account of rational choice.

4

NORMATIVE PROPOSITIONS, REASONS FOR ACTION, AND ADVISING

IN this chapter I shall relate the above two chapters to a propositional account of certain 'ought'-expressions, and present an account of self-regarding reasons for action in both the justificatory and explanatory uses of that notion; and shall then show how this view makes an account of prudential advising possible. The limitation of this account to self-regarding reasons for action is a consequence of the fact, mentioned in the previous chapter, that I propose in Part I only to consider the applicability of the principles of rationality to self-regarding ends.

I. *Normative Propositions*

'Ought'-sentences are often used to express propositions about the requirements of the principles of rational choice. Of course, in the discussion of normative propositions made on the basis of social rules (chapter 2), 'ought' was isolated as serving a similar purpose. But, there I noted that, in order to isolate the relevant sense, it was necessary to preface the propositions by 'legally', etc., and that, in many cases, 'ought' would be an unnatural form of word to use. However, in the present context, none of these qualifications seems to be necessary. Thus, consider the sentences listed at the beginning of chapter 1:

(1) You ought to learn the calculus; it's an invaluable tool.

(2) You ought to learn how to swim; it may, someday, save your life.

(3) I don't think you ought to make him your partner; he's so unreliable that it will just make your job harder.

(4) You ought to learn how to ride a horse; it's such fun.

(5) You ought to visit the Hermitage, if you're going to Leningrad; it has a splendid art collection, which you will enjoy.

The use of 'ought' in such sentences seems understandable without any proviso about 'rationally speaking' or about an unnatural, technical use of 'ought'. Indeed, it seems as though the uses of 'ought' I discussed in the social rule case must be specially distinguished precisely because, without qualification, we will tend to understand 'ought' in this, or some related (the moral 'ought'), use.

At this point it is necessary to make a central theoretical distinction, one already introduced in the discussion of social rules, i.e. that between primary normative propositions which describe the general requirements of certain rules in all cases to which they apply and derivative normative propositions which concern the requirements of certain rules in a particular case to which they apply. Thus, one can set out the following sort of logical relation between primary and derivative normative propositions in this context:

1. One ought to choose a satisfactorily effective plan of action to secure a certain self-regarding end, *ceteris paribus*.

2. Learning how to ride a horse is a satisfactorily effective plan of securing the self-regarding end of having fun for person x, and no other principles are relevant.

3. X ought to learn how to ride a horse.

3–*a*. If you are x, you ought to learn . . .

3–*b*. If I am x, I ought to learn . . .

Derivative propositions, such as those expressed in 3, are the typical form of normative proposition expressed in the context of the principles of rational choice. Given that the other principles of rational choice and morality are satisfied or not relevant, and given the truth of 2, then the use of such 'ought'-sentences expresses true propositions about the requirements of the rationality principles in a particular case. Of course, this presupposes that the moral and rationality principles exist and apply—a subject already sufficiently discussed in chapter 2.

Three important properties of these normative propositions must be noted.

(*a*) The truth-value of *these* 'ought'-expressions differs from person to person, a consequence of the application of the principles of rational choice to self-regarding ends, the specific nature of which varies from person to person. Thus, while one person may have the desire for fun, he may so lack various physical capacities of co-ordination, or have such a psychological history, as not to have the desire to realize this end through riding horses. Relative to this person, 'you ought to learn how to ride a horse' (3*a*, above) is false, since the mediating premiss (2, above) is false. In an important sense, then, *these* normative propositions, unlike many others, are *relative*; their truth value depends on contingent circumstances about the specific nature of the self-regarding desires of a particular person. Thus, here, the demand for uniformity of action, so appropriate in the context of moral principles, is stupid and irrational, dogmatic and illiberal.

(*b*) Given my formulation of the principles of rational choice, the logical relation of such normative propositions to the concept of interests is understandable. In brief, the concept of interests implies the generalized means to many self-regarding ends; and the dominance principle, on the basis of which, *ceteris paribus*, 'ought'-expressions can be truly asserted, precisely requires the adoption of plans which secure more as opposed to less ends, and thus often requires the pursuit of things in one's interests. Thus, the logical relation of '*x* is in your interests' to 'you ought to obtain *x*', in many contexts of speech and thought, is explained.

(*c*) It is important to see that 'ought'-expressions of the type that here interest me, when used *simpliciter*, are true only *ceteris paribus*, where this is a convenient tag for the complex of priority relations mentioned at the end of the previous chapter. What one ought to do, in this sense, importantly assumes that the principles of morality are not relevant, as they would be where special moral relationships exist (e.g. where a man's imprudence will have untoward effects on his wife and children), or where there is extreme irrationality likely to lead to the frustration of the agent's basic interests. As a consequence of this, when a man refuses to do what he ought to do (no moral principles being relevant), we do not regard ourselves as justified in interfering. Indeed, while one may question, as I did in chapter 2, the validity of a view of moral principles as things freely chosen, it may be a tolerably accurate view of the relation to choice of the principles of rational choice, applied to self-regarding ends; the agent may choose to act or not to act on rationality principles, as he wishes; the burdens and benefits of rational choice being his alone, he is at liberty, free. However, such a view of the relation of principles and choice, even in the present context, is not completely accurate, since, on my account, it is not the case that persons can, logically, choose the sorts of things that *count* as rationality principles, though they are at liberty to act or not to act on these principles, *ceteris paribus*. Even the systematic irrationalist, who rejects the rational life as incompatible with the supreme value of spontaneity, does not, by the same token, adopt a different concept of rationality, for he may be quite clear about, and insistent upon, his being an irrational man.

11. *Self-regarding Reasons for Action*

In chapter 2 I suggested that the relation of existing principles of action to actual reasons for action was an analytic one, unlike the existing social rule case where the logical relation seemed to be to supposed or believed reasons for action. This view must now be given more precision in the light of my formulation of the principles of rational choice, and my conception of the normative propositions of which these principles are the truth grounds.

(a) The Justificatory Concept of Self-regarding Reasons for Action

I outlined above a logical inference of primary and derivative normative propositions. Another such inference might go as follows:

(1) One ought to choose the satisfactorily dominant plan of action, *ceteris paribus*.

(2) The plan of adopting a certain career (*m*) will be satisfactorily dominant over alternative career plans for person *x*, and no other rational or moral principles are relevant here.

(3) *x* (you, I, if = *x*) ought to choose career *m*.

Such a form of inference represents the skeletal outline of a process of reasoning. The act of choosing career *m* is justified by (1), which is to say that (1) expresses the reason for adopting career *m*. Unlike similar examples in the case of social rules, it is not logically possible to accept the truth of propositions (1) and (3) and reject the proposition that there is a conclusive reason for choosing career *m*.

Three types of reasons for action must be distinguished here: (1) there is *conclusive* reason for choosing something, (2) there is a *good* or *generally sufficient* reason for choosing something, and (3) there is *some* or *a* reason for choosing something, (1) The notion of there being a conclusive self-regarding reason for choosing *x* is equivalent to the notion that the choice of *x* is a requirement of the principles of rational choice applied to self-regarding ends, *ceteris paribus*. Thus, the proposition expressed, in a self-regarding context, by 'you have a conclusive reason for choosing *x*' is equivalent to that expressed by 'you ought to choose *x*', where no other rational or moral principles are relevant. In this sense, if it is true that there is a conclusive self-regarding reason for an agent to choose *x*, it is also true that the act of choosing *x* is the rational course of conduct in the circumstances, for a conclusive reason for action is to the knowledge of the rationality or morality of an act what a conclusive reason for belief is to knowledge of matters of empirical fact. (2) The notion of there being a good or generally sufficient self-regarding reason for choosing *x* is equivalent to the notion that the choice of act *x*, in many typical contexts of choice of which one has good reason to believe the present choice situation is one, is required by the principles of rational choice applied to self-regarding ends, *ceteris paribus*. A proposition about there being good reasons for doing *x* may be used as evidence for the truth of 'you ought to do *x*', but it is not equivalent to what is meant by the latter expression, for one may have good reasons for doing *x*, which may turn out not to be conclusive reasons. (3) Both the above notions of reasons for action must, in turn, be distinguished from the notion that there is some or a reason for choosing *x*, for I may well truly assert that there is some reason for choosing *x*, which is no good reason, and also truly say: ' "you ought to choose *x*" is false.' The explanation for this is clear: there may be some reason for choosing *x*, and other good and perhaps conclusive reasons for not choosing *x*. Here, the analytic relation of reasons to principles seems to be this: the concept of there being some or a reason for action is identical with the concept that some principle of rational choice requires that action, without implying that *ceteris paribus* conditions are satisfied. For example, some reason for choosing a career might be that it most effectively secures one of my self-regarding ends, say, the desire to use my hands, in abstraction from considerations of dominance which have priority here, if they are relevant. Or, in the light of the principle of effective means, there is some reason for a drunkard's drinking alcohol, if he wants such a drink, but such a reason may be insufficient because, in terms of the prior dominance principle, there is good or conclusive reason for not drinking (e.g. ruining one's health).

Note that the distinction between good and conclusive reasons for action importantly clarifies the distinct issues involved in the questions of the rationality or irrationality of acts and agents. That is, the rationality of an act x is to be understood in terms of there being conclusive reasons to do x. However, the concept of a rational agent is not to be construed in terms of the agent's systematically and consistently acting on conclusive reasons for action, for this would involve such great costs in terms of careful deliberation and such hesitations in acting that it would not, perhaps, result in as rational a course of conduct, on balance, as if the agent more generally acted on good reasons for action. As a consequence, the rationality of an agent is understood in terms of his generally acting on good self-regarding reasons for action, though this may result, in particular cases, in his doing an act which is, in fact, irrational (because of some unavoidable mistake in belief or deliberation).

Thus, the principles of rational choice, in my view, establish self-regarding reasons for action, in the sense that, given the existence and applicability of these principles, certain normative propositions are true and do justify certain actions, *ceteris paribus*. The contrast of this view to Gauthier's could not be more dramatic, for where Gauthier emphasizes the logical primitiveness of reasons and the role of principles as summary generalizations of them,[1] I place principles as the basic concept in terms of which reasons are to be understood. Of course, I cannot claim to have provided a defensible alternative to Gauthier, until the account is generalized to moral reasons.

Here, of course, I have been concerned with what may be called the *justificatory* concept of a self-regarding reason, for, in this sense, reasons for action are offered as a justification for a course of conduct, in propositions which may be truly asserted quite apart from the agent's readiness to accept them. A person, for example, may have the concept of rational choice (understanding what it means to say that he has self-regarding reasons to act, and granting that this is true), and yet he may reject this concept as a way of living, preferring the life of planless spontaneity.

(b) The Explanatory Concept of Self-regarding Reasons

However, there is another important use of the concept of reasons, which is logically dependent on the justificatory notion.

This is, as Baier pointed out, the use of the notion of reasons in the explanation of someone's actions,[2] what I shall call the *explanatory* concept of a self-regarding reason. Of course, there is a quite trivial sense in which a notion of reasons is related to the concept of explanation, i.e. the sense in which any true explanation of *x* gives the or part of the reason for *x*. This relation holds on all levels of explanation, whether of physical events or human behaviour, for an appropriate answer to 'why?', in the context where an explanation is desired, is 'the reason for it is the law of gravitation' or 'the reason for this has to do with quantum mechanical law of energy leaps' or 'the reason for his action is the deep ambivalence of his feelings toward his mother', and so on. Further, on the level of the explanation of human behaviour, the or part of the reason for someone's behaviour, in this sense, may take as many different forms as there are true explanations, e.g. certain electrical discharges in the brain in response to certain internal or external stimuli, certain chemical levels in the blood-stream, etc. However, when the explanation for certain behaviour is truly given in terms of the agent's reasons for action, then that explanation must take a *special* form, which will distinguish it from other types of explanation. One of the necessary, though not sufficient, marks of *this* type of explanation is that the agent must be, in a sense to be explained, aware of it.[3] This condition is unnecessary in the case of other types or levels of explanation, with the exception of Anscombe's mental causes,[4] e.g. the appearance of a face at the window which explains one's jumping with fright, and of which one must be aware in order for it to be true that the face's appearance caused one's frightened behaviour. Indeed, some philosophers, e.g. Benn, Peters, and Findlay,[5] have seen the distinction between explanations in terms of reasons for action and other types of explanation as being so profound that they have claimed, or pleaded,[6] that to talk truly of the agent's reasons for having acted in a certain way is to eschew the notion of causal explanation altogether. Such views seem to me to be exaggerated distortions of the simple fact that explanations in terms of the agent's reasons for action take a special form and must, therefore, be distinguished from the general notion of explanation which 'the reason for' expresses. But, of course, they *are*, still, causal explanations, and this fact should not be obscured or denied.

Perhaps a good way to clarify the explanatory use of self-regarding reasons is by first sketching a general account of explanation, and then showing the special form that this takes in the case of self-regarding reasons. Employing Hempel's useful notions, what seems essential to the general notion of explanation is the application of a generalization about the causal relation of two events or circumstances to a particular instance of that generalization.[7] In the case of an explanation by good reasons for action, this view would imply that an explanatory answer to the question 'why did A do x?' must take a form of which the following would be a schematic representation:

(i) A was in situation B.

(ii) A was a rational agent in that situation.

(iii) In a situation of type B, any rational agent will do x.

(iv)   Therefore, A did x.

From this abstract scheme, one can see that the notion of explanatory reasons is conceptually parasitic on the notion of justificatory reasons, for to speak of being a rational agent in (ii) implies a complex set of attitudes which involves the understanding of the principles of rational choice and the desire and capacity to use them in situations of type B. Further, in the causal generalization or law of (iii), the rationality principles are also implied, for they indicate what a rational agent, given the situation, would do.

The point may perhaps be put a little less abstractly. In the discussion of the concept of desire in chapter 3, I claimed that, in ordinary language and thought, the explanation of human *actions* crucially involved three epistemically interdependent features, i.e. thoughts or beliefs, desires, and capacities. There the beliefs, desires, and capacities were of a fairly specific and lower-order character, e.g. the expectation of rain, or the desire to do penance. However, in the case of the explanation of action in terms of good self-regarding reasons, these features are transferred to a more general level, involving the beliefs associated with having the concept of rationality, the desire to act on the principles of rational choice, and the capacity to do so. Given that the agent was rational at the time (all these higher-order features being effectively present), then truly to explain his actions in terms of good self-regarding reasons is truly to apply a causal generalization about what rational agents do in the sort of circumstances he is in.

Thus, the crucial difference between explanations in terms of reasons for action and explanations in terms of mental causes, however alike in other respects, is that the latter do not imply anything about the agent's rationality and the relation of his rationality to the explanation of his actions, whereas this is crucially implied in the former. It is, for example, quite inappropriate, in the case of a startled jump caused by the appearance of a face at the window, to inquire how the jump was supposed to advance the agent's ends, and what those ends were, for no such explanation, in terms of the agent's rational pursuit of his ends, is here either appropriate or true. Further, explanations in terms of mental causes apply in the case of infants and animals, where the principles of rational choice have no explanatory relevance at all (e.g. an animal's running in fear at hearing a certain sound).

So far I have spoken quite pointedly of the explanation of acting for good reasons; but, given this account, the concept of explanations of acting for reasons, generally, seems clear. For example, when a person does an act for an insufficient reason (e.g. drinking alcohol, where this frustrates many other ends), then to explain his action is truly to apply a causal generalization about a certain type of irrational agent to his case (perhaps he lacks the full desire to be rational, though he has the concept and capacity). A similar account seems possible for other cases where there are true explanations in terms of an agent's reasons.

It is, I think, important to note that, for a person to have acted for reasons (of any kind), it is not required that the reasons in question actually were entertained prior to action, or that any reasoning process occurred at all.[8] Thus, for example, in ordinary language and thought, it is sufficient for a person x to have acted for self-regarding reasons if he, in fact, regulated his conduct by the principles of rational choice applied to his self-regarding ends, which is usually shown, as Alexander has pointed out, by eliciting from x, *after* his acting, that he had certain reasons in acting.[9] The fact that one must be able to elicit such reasons clarifies the sense in which the agent must be aware of them (unlike other kinds of explanatory reasons). However, the process of eliciting reasons may not be a clear-cut and easy process, for the agent may require some time for thought about his reasons; indeed, he may initially err sincerely in expressing his reasons, and thus need the suggestion by others of more accurate ways to express his reasons, before he clearly expresses them himself. What seems clear is that, for an agent to have acted for a certain reason, he must, in ordinary non-Freudian thought, at least at some point be able honestly and accurately to say that *that* reason was his reason for acting, or, perhaps more exactly, at least be able to formulate the thought or conviction that *that* was his reason, if he is not able fully to express it.

It is, I think, necessary to be careful in stating what this view precisely involves, for it is easy to misunderstand it and suppose it to be mysterious.[10] Here, it seems to me important to distinguish between, on the one hand, thoughts (which pass through the mind or are entertained) and, on the other hand, beliefs (which can exist without actually being part of one's thoughts at some particular time).[11] Given this distinction, note that what acting for certain reasons implies is that these reasons are part of one's beliefs, not necessarily part of one's actual thoughts in conscious deliberation (it, of course, also implies the desire to regulate one's conduct in accord with these beliefs). But it is, as I had occasion to remark in chapter 2, a notorious fact in moral philosophy that people may have certain beliefs which they have great, even insuperable, difficulty in expressing clearly, of which the above difficulty in expressing one's reasons for action is only a special case. Thus, when I say that the principles of rational choice are logically implied in people's acting for self-regarding reasons, and that people must be aware of such reasons, I am not claiming that these facts imply that people consciously deliberate from primary to derivative normative propositions. A view of my account as a psychological process, as Anscombe said of her account of intention, 'would in general be quite absurd. The interest of the account is that it described an order which is there whenever actions are done with intentions.'[12] What such normative propositions describe is a reasoning process which could be elicited as the logical structure of belief which the agent regards as justifying his act when he acts.

Generally, given the pervasive problem of costs of decision making, raised in chapter 3, it seems absurd to suppose that acting for reasons always requires active prior deliberation. Many situations are recurrent, and our ends relatively constant, so that redeliberating each time is wasteful of valuable energies. Deliberation should be reserved for the novel and changing, where habitual decisions are inappropriate. Of course, it is quite possible to make a semantic decision here that the habitual is to be sharply opposed to reasoning, which is crucially related to the novel, a view which Ryle's *Concept of Mind* suggests and which Nowell-Smith seems to adopt explicitly.[13] But such views seem obviously to distort the notion of acting for reasons which is quite intelligibly applied in cases of unreflective, habitual actions, e.g. my making my breakfast in the morning is as habitual an action as can be imagined, yet I do it for a good reason.[14] That questions of rationality draw our main attention in cases of new problems should not lead us to forget the contexts of habitual and undeliberated action in which they are importantly implicit.

III. *Advising and Normative Propositions*

In chapter I I noted that sentences like 'you ought to learn the calculus' seem to have two important logical aspects in that they both express propositions and have a certain advisory force. I opposed the view that the advisory function of such sentences required them to be viewed as non-propositional, and have endeavoured to provide an account of what sort of proposition I take to be expressed by such sentences. If this view is correct, I must now show that such a propositional account is quite compatible with the advisory force of these sentences.

First, of course, it is necessary to know what is the act of advising in the self-regarding case, so as to distinguish it from the many other kinds of use of words by one person, 'in consequence of' or 'because of' which other people act (e.g. persuasion, inducement as reward or bribe, threat, command, etc.). All these speech acts, when successful, have several common properties.[15] (i) In all of them the other person knows of and understands the significance of what the speaker has said. (ii) The first person's words or acts are part of the reasons for acting of the second person. (iii) The second person only forms the intention to do the act, after the first person's intervention. However, what is expressed by these speech acts is different in each case. In the case of a sincere threat or bribe, the speaker expresses his intention of doing some harm to the other's interests if he does not do what the speaker wishes him to, or of advancing his interests if the other does do what the speaker wishes him to. Normally, the second person understands that these intentions are expressed and, if influenced by them, believes that the speaker's intentions are likely to be executed.

In a sincere command, the speaker expresses his intention that the other person do something, where there is a context of authoritative or coercive superiority which typically gives the speaker's intention effect. For the command to be effective the other must understand the speaker's intentions are being expressed, and also believe that there is the appropriate superiority. In the case of persuading someone to do something, the speaker expresses any views which are intended to influence the other to do something; for the persuasion to be effective, the second person must understand what is being said, though it is not, of course, necessary that the second recognize the speaker's intention that he shall do something (unlike, for example, commands, where it seems part of the concept that this information is typically communicated). The minimal content of sincere prudential advising, I think, is the intention to communicate to another one's beliefs about what course of action is most self-regardingly rational in a particular case. One is not necessarily communicating anything about one's intention to harm or advance the other's interests, nor one's intention that the other do something on the basis of an authoritative relationship, nor just *any* ideas or arguments which are intended to influence another to do something. Even in the case where advice is successful not because of a careful consideration of the relevant reasons for acting, but because of trust in a particular person's judgement or experience, the act is still basically done in the belief that this is the rational course of conduct, as evidenced by the advisor's known judgement and experience and consequent competence in evaluating self-regarding reasons for action.

Two kinds of advising seem distinguishable: advising someone about or upon some course of conduct and advising someone to do some action.[16] Advising about or upon some course of conduct is marked by the intention of communicating one's views about reasons for or against some action, without necessarily desiring or intending that the agent adopt a certain course of conduct. This form of advising is quite different from the other types of speech act mentioned above, since it does not involve, as they all do, the intention that the person spoken to do something. Advising someone to do something seems to go beyond such a discussion of pros and cons, and implies the speaker's recommendation of a certain course of conduct, and, perhaps, his intention that the other should do what he is advised to do (though he may not privately want this). However, this kind of advising is distinguishable from the above speech acts in that the beliefs communicated are of a certain special kind, pertaining to relevant self-regarding reasons for action.

Clearly, advising is of great importance in a society such as ours where the natural attitude of rationality is widespread. People want to know what rationality requires in particular cases, and thus there is a social need for forms of communication which a person can use in order to communicate to another his views of what the principles of rational choice require in the other's particular case. In such ways, one person's experience and judgement about matters of fact and principle can be made available to others.

Given these facts about the importance of advice, one might expect the existence of some form of language which was reserved (and understood to be reserved) for signalling the performance of this important act. Of course, such expectations are fulfilled, for there is a form of words which is understood, in the language, to perform, *ceteris paribus*, this act, i.e. 'I advise you to do *x*'. However, such a performative utterance[17] is not our only linguistic resource in advising, just as 'I warn you' is not our only means of warning. Rather, there are other linguistic expressions which are used to perform such acts, i.e. sentences which express propositions which are so related to the aim of such acts that, in the appropriate circumstances, they can be used to do the act. The act of warning is, perhaps, a relatively clear example of this. The typical intention or aim of such acts is to make others aware of some impending danger or inconvenience to them, so that they may be made ready to take whatever action they deem appropriate (usually, avoiding it); and this act may be performed, *ceteris paribus*, by 'I warn you that . . .'. However, it seems quite clear that various sentences which express propositions, which are related to the aim of warning in the relevant situation, can be used to warn, e.g. 'There is a bull in the field behind you', 'The rope he wants you to use on your mountain climbing trip is too weak', 'The man you're travelling with is quite capable of murdering you', and even 'The cat is on the mat' (where, for example, the cat is a tiger, and one is pointing out to one's friend that it is standing on the mat before his tent).

Given the aim of self-regarding advice which I have just delineated, i.e. communicating to a person one's views about which course of conduct in a specific situation is justifiable on self-regarding grounds, then it should be obvious that there is, in the language, a form of expression which is ideally suited to accomplishing this aim, i.e. 'ought'-expressions. I have argued that certain 'ought'-sentences express true or false propositions, i.e. that a certain act is justified by the principles of rational choice. But this kind of proposition is exactly the form of information which it is the aim of advising to communicate. Thus, these propositions can and are used to advise, in the appropriate contexts.

I set myself, in chapter 1, against the view that a propositional account of 'ought'-expressions is incompatible with their advisory force. I have argued here that, so far from being incompatible, the adequate analysis of the way in which such sentences are used to advise depends on the propositions they express, which provide the grounds for making the speech act. The second criterion of theoretical adequacy, presented in chapter 1, is then satisfied. But the task will not be complete, in accounting for self-regarding reasons, until some account of the moving appeal to action of such utterances is offered.

5

THE NATURAL ATTITUDE OF
RATIONALITY

IN a sense, to ask for an explanation of the moving appeal to
action of certain propositional 'ought'-expressions is a quite
trivial question with a quite trivial answer. That is, for a
propositional theory of such utterances, it seems clear that the
answer must be: as a brute fact of human psychology, there is a
widespread desire to be rational, and thus the information conveyed by 'ought'-expressions has an intelligible relation to human
desires and thus to human actions, which those desires, in part,
motivate. This seems to be a quite general solution to the problem,
of which the most familiar examples come from propositional
theories of moral utterances, e.g. Prichard's claim that we must just
accept, as a fundamental fact, 'the existence of a desire to do what
is right', and admit that having moral concepts does not imply
having such a desire.[1] Strictly speaking, however, it is not true
that propositional theories *must* accept this distinction, for it is a
possible form of propositional theory to hold that the proposition
expressed by 'doing *x* is right' is equivalent to that expressed by
'doing *x* is what I desire now'. Such a view, as far as I know, has
never been held by a serious philosopher; but Westermarck and
W. D. Falk have held dispositional forms of it, where the proposition expressed by '*x* is right' is equivalent to that expressed by 'I
have a tendency to feel required or compelled to do *x*, when fully
informed, disinterested, etc.'[2] Such first-person 'moral-sense
theories', to use C. D. Broad's tag,[3] illustrate that it is not part of
the inexorable logic of propositional accounts to appeal to brute
facts as the explanation for the moving appeal to action of the
analysed expressions. It will depend on the view taken of the
propositions expressed. But, of course, my propositional account
of certain 'ought'-expressions does not involve the claim that these
expressions are analytically linked to occurrent desires—nor even
to dispositions to desire impartially, as Westermarck and Falk

might suggest. In my view, what is *meant* by my saying '*x* is what you ought to do' is not that I am impartially disposed to desire *x*, but that the principles of rational choice require *x*; this holds quite independently of my desire that the person addressed do what the principles require, and of his inclination to do what they justify. In Frankena's useful terminology, mine is an externalist account of self-regarding 'ought'-expressions; the propositions expressed by such expressions as 'you ought to do *x*' do not logically imply any desire that *x* be done.[4]

Thus, given the form of propositional account advanced above, I am committed to some form of the brute facts thesis. However, such accounts differ, importantly, in terms of the informativeness of their explanations of the relation of concepts and desires. Thus, intuitionist accounts in ethics, like those of Prichard and W. D. Ross, suffer from the fact that having identified rightness with some intuitable property, they are compelled to explain moral motivations in terms of an inexplicable desire for that intuitable property.[5] Naturalistic forms of propositional account seem, by contrast, more informative, since such theories at least provide some clarification of the objects of our moral desires. For example, whatever the other difficulties in Benthamite utilitarianism, the moral theory does clarify why benevolence is the primary moral motivation, as Bentham evidently thought it was;[6] for, since morality is understood as maximally satisfying the desires of all, which may require a considerable sacrifice of one's individual interests in a particular case, then the notion of benevolence, implying a rather unusual willingness to advance others' interests even at the expense of one's own, seems apt.[7]

The propositional account that I advanced above is naturalistic, in the sense that it explains the concept of rationality in terms of certain principles which have a logical relation to the natural facts of self-regarding desires. It is, therefore, open to me to provide some explanation of how the concept of rationality in fact relates to the natural attitude which is called rational, a matter discussed under the rubric of explanatory reasons for action in the previous chapter. What I shall do here is to elaborate that account, showing how the principles of rational choice enter into the concepts of the self and the virtue of prudence; and how such a view provides some understanding of the concept of regret. Using the criteria of theoretical adequacy outlined in chapter 1, I am trying to clarify, first, the logical relation of the concept of rationality to various other notions (part of criterion 1), and second, the desire to be rational, by providing some further understanding of the natural attitude of which it is a part (satisfying criterion 3).

1. *The Self and the Principles of Rational Choice*

A way of getting at the relation between the self and the principles of rational choice is to ask: among human beings, what is the logical relation of a self or person to his body? The view of this relation which I shall offer represents an interpretation of the concept of 'self-love' found in Bishop Butler's second sermon, a notion which seems to me roughly identical with the concept of the ego used in theories of ego psychology, e.g. that of Erik Erikson.[8]

First, the concrete unity that, in ordinary life, is called a human being is not itself the self; rather, the self is something that, in Erikson's interesting terminology, is capable of 'a feeling of being at home in one's body'.[9] At first sight, this may seem paradoxical and even absurd; for, in ordinary life, the criteria of personal identity importantly include criteria of bodily identity.[10] But consider the following sort of case which can be *sensibly* imagined, one where we might be prepared to say that there is a person in a body, but the person does not have a body that he views as *his*: a body's movements and reactions show that the *body* is in pain or subject to the desire for drink (thirst), but there is *no* ordered, purposeful sequence of *thoughts, volitions,* or *bodily movements* with the end of relieving the pain or thirst; and this occurs in the case of *all* the desires of the body. It is possible to imagine a person being in this body, and dispassionately noting the existence of the thirst, pain, etc., but one would not be prepared to claim that it is, in the full sense, that person's body; for if the person did view the pain or thirst, etc., as being his, he would at least *try* to relieve them through planned behaviour. Consider, here, Hampshire's remarks about a similar sort of case:

The idea of a thinking observer who could form from his experience no notion of making a movement, or, more generally, of doing something, is one that can scarcely be entertained, if one tries to follow its implications through to the end. For instance, he would have no reason to make any kind of identification of himself with his body, as 'his' body would only be for him one physical object among others.[11]

While I doubt whether there is any psychotic disorder which involves such profound psychic disorientation and self-alienation, at least *something* like this seems to occur in people one talks with who are extremely fatigued or intoxicated, or under the influence of certain hallucinogenic drugs—certain behaviour or whole sequences thereof are quite clearly *not theirs*; and people are in the strange and disturbing position of being a dispassionate contemplator of their desires, with a loss of the capacity for agency in respect to their satisfaction. What this sort of case seems to reveal is that at least part of what is meant, in the typical case, by a person regulating *his* body is that there exists the capacity and effective desire to formulate and execute plans which effectively satisfy the body's occurrent desires.

Consider, now, a different, perhaps more realistic, case: a person has a body, in the sense that when the body is thirsty, the capacity to formulate and execute plans goes into action to relieve the thirst, but here the person systematically drinks all the water without regard to the future; generally, the person is incapable of acting now on the basis of a recognition of future probable desires (e.g. conserving some water for later thirst) and is, further, incapable of adjusting the satisfaction of an occurrent desire to the satisfaction of others. In this case, the person lacks Butler's 'judgement, direction, superintendency',[12] the capacity and desire to formulate and execute time-plans of action, which adjust desires according to the requirements of the dominance principle, and which allow for distantly future desires in terms of the postponement principle. As a systematic occurrence, this phenomenon occurs in humans only among young children and perhaps certain sorts of neurotics and psychotics (all cases where we regard the ego or self as undeveloped or damaged). But it seems systematically to characterize animals; for, while animals have the capacity to satisfy occurrent wants (even if the notion of plans of action is inapt here), they typically lack the characteristically human capacity to adjust and postpone desire satisfaction over time, as a matter of rational plan and not of instinct.[13] Thus, another aspect of the relation of a person to his body is that there exists the capacity and effective desire to formulate and execute plans of action which satisfy the principles of rational choice (especially dominance), regulating the body so as to satisfy desires equally over time. A way of further confirming this view is to note, as Ryle has pointed out, that the most important contexts where the use of 'I' does not seem replaceable by 'My body' are those where exercises of self-control are called for, as against various occurrent appetites which claim sole attention;[14] for this evidences the central role of these capacities of higher order planning in the concept of the self or person. Where, on the other hand, the speaker does not intend any contrast between the planning capacities and the body's occurrent desires, they will often be viewed as identical, for the purpose at hand; thus, the 'I am' in 'I am in pain' is replaceable, without meaning distortion, by 'My body is'.

Consider, finally, another person, like Erikson's schizophrenic Jean, who, though having a body regarded as his own, still could not remember himself as the person who planned to satisfy desires in the past or think of himself as the same person who would satisfy desires in the future.[15] This sort of case, exemplifying a severe breakdown in ego functioning and the resulting loss of the sense of personal continuity, brings out a further feature of the logical relation of a self to its body: typically, this includes the self-conception of the higher-order planning capacity and desire having been in that body in the past up to the present and continuing in that body into the future. Such a self-conception enables the capacity for human intelligence to be exercised, since a person can learn from *his* past experiences.[16] The ingenuity and plasticity of human responses to changing circumstances, developing new rational plans of action on the basis of one's own and others' collective experience (a systematic and refined form of which is empirical science), seems one of the distinctive marks of human activity, in contrast to the frozen, instinctive 'stupidity' of animals, e.g. Tinbergen's herring gulls.[17] However, it is not, in fact, true, as these remarks might suggest, that humans and animals differ crucially in intelligence, for animal intelligence seems to be an established fact. The difference comes in the distinctive form that such intelligence takes in the human case, the use of universal and dated propositions in reasoning about matters of fact, as Bennett noted in his illuminating investigation of human rationality, a study mainly of reasons for belief.[18] From the point of view of my study of reasons for action, one need only supplement Bennett's views by noting that what makes reasoning about matters of fact relevant to human rationality, in my sense, is that it leads to knowledge of, or reasoned belief in, matters of fact which are relevant

F

to developing more effective, dominant, etc., plans of action, especially in novel circumstances where many factual matters require inquiry.

By virtue of such 'pathographic' considerations as I have just gone through,[19] one begins to see, by negative example, what is positively required for there to be a self which is functioning well in *its* body: i.e. there exists (1) an effective higher-order desire and capacity to formulate and execute rational plans of action and (2) the self-conception that this capacity has existed in this body continuously up to the present and will continue existing into the future. What seems clear is that the principles of rational choice importantly enter into any adequate account of the typical case of the human self.

11. *The Natural Attitude of Rationality, the Virtue of Prudence, and Regret*

A person who is fully rational satisfies three separable criteria: (*a*) having certain thoughts and beliefs, (*b*) having certain desires and capacities (which define the virtue of prudence), and (*c*) being disposed to certain sorts of feelings if he deviates from rationality (feelings of regret).

(*a*) The thoughts and beliefs that an existing attitude of rationality implies are the thoughts and beliefs that having the concept of rationality implies. That is, the rational man believes that the principles of rational choice define what are self-regarding reasons for action, a belief shown by the sorts of expression (e.g. 'you ought to do *x*', 'you have good reason to do *x*'), which the man claims or admits to express true propositions about some or good or conclusive reasons for action in a self-regarding context. But, of course, so far, on my view, the rational man is no different from other men, who reject the attitude of rationality but who have the concept. They, too, may admit that such propositions are true, and yet they may not act on them.

(*b*) What is further required is the capacity and desire to be rational. To say that beings have this capacity is to say that they have the psychological equipment to do what the principles of rational choice require. They are creatures of a kind who are able to perceive and understand their present and future circumstances and desires, to satisfy their wants, and to suppress, subordinate, or adjust the satisfaction of present occurrent wants to future

perceived wants. They have the capacities of imagination, ingenuity, inventiveness, a firm grasp of facts and possibilities, the
power of relevant and controlled hypothetical thought (involving
Bennett's dated and universal propositions and the capacity to
use them, for example, in inductive reasoning about matters of
fact). Further, there must be the desire to use these capacities in
formulating and executing rational plans of action.

To say of a man that he has such capacities and desires, which
explain a large class of his actions, is to say that he has the virtue
of prudence.[20] Virtues are, I believe, systematically related to the
various principles of action which specify them, for virtues identify
the capacities and desires which a person who acts on and from a
certain principle must have (a view to be elaborated somewhat in
chapter 14, where I shall try to show how many traditional virtues
can be organized under various principles). Prudence is that virtue
which is associated with the principles of rational choice, since it
identifies the capacities and desires which explain a man's acting
on the principles of rational choice. Thus, the characteristic marks
of the prudent man, e.g. pursuing his long-term interests, carefully
weighing up costs and benefits to himself of various plans of action,
shrewdness and ingenuity, planning, etc., are precisely those
features of capacity and motivation which a man acting on the
principles of rational choice should have. Thus, it is no accident,
and there is no mystery in the fact, that prudence is a virtue; given
the logical relation of virtues and principles, its being a virtue is
explicable.[21] Indeed, if, as Mrs. Foot has claimed, the virtues must
be things which a man wants, as being to his advantage, then
prudence, above all, would be a virtue.[22]

(c) If a rational man (having the concepts, desires, and capacities
just described) in a particular case fails to do what the principles
of rational choice require (because of his own lack of self-control
or judgement), and his interests are consequently harmed, he will
be disposed to feel *regret* for his failure. There is, of course, a
usage of the notion of regret which is far more general than this:
for example, W. M. Sibley has suggested that 'the presence of
regret is a sign that he did not act in the direction of his basic
preferences',[23] where basic preferences include the desire to be
moral; and Hampshire construes regret quite broadly as relative
to failure to live up to 'standards of humanity'.[24] Similarly, Kenny
seems to be interpreting regret rather generally when he relates

it to 'something thought to be evil'.[25] While I would not claim that such accounts are incorrect, I am concerned here with a more specific use of regret, which can be intelligibly distinguished from shame, guilt, remorse, embarrassment, and the like (see chapter 13).

Regret, in this restricted sense, is crucially marked by two features: (i) the characteristic way in which having the feeling is explained and (ii) the ways in which it is possible to dispel it. (i) The agent typically explains his feelings of regret by expressing his *belief* (or, at least, the thought) that his self-regarding desires have been frustrated because of his adopting an irrational course of conduct. But such beliefs are not sufficient for one to feel regret, for a man could have the concept of rationality (and thus believe that he violated the principles of rational choice) and the capacity to be rational, and yet, if he did not desire to be rational, he would not be disposed to feel regret for his irrationality. As with the amoralist and the feeling of guilt, we might say that he ought to feel regret for what he did, and yet we would understand why he did not feel it: 'He is completely irrational.' Having the full natural attitude of rationality (beliefs, desires, and capacities) seems a necessary condition of the propensity to regret; and the suscepti- bility to regret seems a necessary condition of having the natural attitude of rationality, given the normal circumstances of the fallibility of human judgement and the fragility of human self- control. On this view, if a man never made a mistake in under- standing and rationally pursuing his self-regarding ends, he would be (as Aristotle describes his perfectly good man) 'a person who knows no regrets'.[26] Further, if men associate the rational pursuit of their self-regarding ends with larger social groups, of which they are a part, they will be susceptible to feeling regret with respect to the decisions of that social group, in so far as they view these decisions as irrationally frustrating the group's aims, and, as a consequence, their associated ends. For example, a Frenchman may regret his government's gold policy, because of its long-term irrationality, relative to France's, and his own, interests; or a resident of London may regret the government's decision not to finance a new opera house; and the like. (ii) In addition, there seems to be a characteristic way in which we dispel our feelings of regret: we resolve or set ourselves to act differently in similar situations in the future. Given that regret typically implies a belief about frustrating one's own interests through irrationality (not harming the interests of others), it seems quite natural that the principal way to resolve one's sense of failure is to try to act differently in the future. In this, regret seems similar to shame, and different from remorse and guilt (see chapter 13).

III. *Summary Remarks on Part I*

In chapter 1 three criteria for the adequacy of a propositional account were offered: it must provide an elucidation of the proposition expressed, account for the use of such propositions in speech acts like advising, and explain the moving appeal to action of such expressions. In chapters 2, 3, and 4, I endeavoured to clarify the kind of propositions expressed by the class of 'ought'-expressions in which I was interested; in the latter part of chapter 4, I showed how such propositions could have advisory force. And, in this chapter, I tried to clarify the moving appeal of such expressions. Admitting that my view simply accepted as a brute fact that people desire to be rational, none the less I tried to characterize further such a natural attitude, especially showing how the principles of rational choice importantly enter into the analysis of such an attitude. In terms of my three criteria, then, the account seems adequate.

However, at every point of my account, the primacy of the principles of morality to the principles of rationality was emphasized; the characterization of these principles is, clearly, a theoretical requirement on the adequacy of my account of rationality, for the principles of morality importantly determine when the principles of rational choice apply. The claim of theoretical adequacy is, then, simply not valid, until I characterize the principles of morality in some detail. This so far empty promise I must now try to fulfil.

PART II

THE MORAL CASE

6

THE CONCEPT OF MORALITY

THE task before me now is to extend the mode of analysis of Part I to another class of 'ought'-expressions, as well as to certain 'under a duty'- and 'obligation'-expressions, and to a related class of expressions concerning moral reasons for action. In this chapter I shall consider the concept of morality, presenting my own constructive account of this notion, which is derived from Kant. In chapter 7, after delineating a summary and schematic account of the principles of morality which I take my account to establish, I shall present and explain a division of those principles into institutional and individual ones, and the non-overlapping division of them into principles of obligation or duty and principles of supererogation. In the following four chapters, the specific nature of the principles and their exact relation to the concept of morality will be discussed in much greater detail. In chapter 12 I shall consider the relations of these principles to various normative propositions, especially propositions concerning moral reasons for action; and shall try to show how this account makes possible the explanation of various speech acts. In chapter 13 the moving appeal problem will be considered, relating the propositional account to the analysis of moral and related feelings (especially shame and guilt) and to plausible genetic theories of moral development; in both cases I shall try to render plausible an alternative view to the Freudian one. Finally, in chapter 14, I shall consider how this account enables us to understand the notion of human virtues, and the classic question—why should I be moral?

1. *Rationality versus Reasonableness*

Perhaps the first thing to do, in undertaking an account of so difficult a notion as the concept of morality, is to get somewhat clear about the general conceptual area that one is trying to clarify. I should like to use this strategy in sharply distinguishing moral questions from other problems with which philosophers often confuse them, i.e. the confusion between questions of rational choice and questions of reasonableness, issues which Sibley has rightly insisted that philosophers should clearly distinguish.[1] Roughly, in terms of their application to acts, the distinction may be put thus: questions of rationality involve the agent's aims and the best way to realize them, whereas questions of reasonableness involve the assessment of the pursuit of one's own aims in the light of the morally justified claims of others. As applied to persons, the description of a man as rational does not carry with it any information about his moral character or sensitivity, and is relevant to his doing what is reasonable and right only in so far as the agent has an overriding desire to do what is right, or, failing that, in so far as there is a coincidence between the requirements of prudence and morality, which will not, obviously, always occur.

This view of rationality was, of course, behind my account of self-regarding reasons in Part I. The view outlined there differs from Sibley's in two respects. First, it emphasized the relation of rationality to satisfying self-regarding ends, to the realization of the agent's advantage and interests, whereas Sibley holds that rationality is relative to the achievement of any end, presumably including the desire to do what is right, if that is the agent's over-riding end. However, the limitation of the concept of rationality to self-regarding ends was, as indicated there, only a matter of convenience; and thus my general view of the concept of rationality agrees with Sibley's in maintaining that what strictly differentiates rationality and reasonableness is not the restriction of the former to self-regarding ends, but rather the fact that the notion of the rational brings with it no information about the pursuit of any particular class of ends, as opposed to any other, whereas the notion of the reasonable conveys information about a certain class of moral ends. But second, Sibley does not clearly distinguish the application of 'rational' and 'reasonable' to acts and persons, and thus seems to claim that what is correct about the application of these terms to persons (namely, that a person is rational or reasonable if he has the desire to be rational or reasonable) to be also correct about their application to acts (namely, that an act is only rational or reasonable if the person has the desire to be rational or reasonable).[2] Once, however, the application of these terms to acts and persons is distinguished, the temptation to Sibley's confusion is removed. For example, a course of action may be the one that is rationally justified, yet the agent may have no desire to be rational, either occurrent or dispositional; whereas a rational person is one with such a desire as well as with associated concepts and capacities, and whose actions are explained in terms of good reasons for action (see chapter 5). None the less, Sibley's general point concerning a distinction between the notions of rationality and reasonableness seems clearly correct, and it is an important one to note if we are to keep ourselves on our analytical target— i.e. moral reasons for action.

The damage to philosophical adequacy, in failing to make this distinction, can be clearly seen in those theories, like Anscombe's, Melden's, and Foot's, which seem to relate analytically the concept of reasons for action to the agent's wants, and which, with Sibley, do not clearly distinguish the justificatory and explanatory uses of the notion of reasons for action. Such theories reflect much that is involved in human rationality; they capture, for example, the important fact that there being a certain class of reasons for action depends on the formulation and execution of plans to satisfy fully the agent's desires. But these theories mistakenly assimilate this case to that of moral reasons for action, where there may be such reasons quite apart from the agent's particular desires, wants, or needs. A theory which would be correct for a certain class of reasons for action is incorrectly generalized to the class of all reasons for action, and this in part derives from the confusion of rationality and reasonableness.

Such damage may, I think, be equally seen in theories which do not analyse all reasons for action in terms of the agent's wants, and which clearly distinguish the two uses of the notion of reasons for action, i.e. the theories of Kurt Baier and G. R. Grice. Baier, for example, was one of the first persons in recent philosophy to insist on the different uses of the notion of reasons for action in the justification and explanation of human actions. However, after presenting his account of moral reasons for action, Baier states that the notion of their being *reasons* requires him to prove further that an agent's using such reasons will cause him in his own case 'to maximize satisfactions and minimize frustration', which leads him to what seems an ultimately circular attempt to justify moral in terms of prudential reasons, as though this were logically required by the concept of a reason for action.[4] What seems behind this sort of argument is the confusion of rationality and reasonableness, so that, in offering an account of the latter concept, Baier finds it *necessary* to incorporate also features of the former notion. Similarly, G. R. Grice clearly distinguishes the different uses of reasons for action and provides a suggestive account of moral reasons in terms of his 'contract ground'; but Grice's account is theoretically weakened by his conflation of the notion of there being a moral reason to do *x* with *x*'s being the rational course of action, for this leads him to state some obviously false propositions. For example, his claim that his 'Master Criminal', who escapes the sanctions on his moral misconduct by exercise of his ingenuity and who has no desire to be moral, is acting irrationally, seems both an unnatural way of speaking and false, as does his general claim that the immoral is equivalent to the irrational.[5] Grice's problem here—and it is more explicit in his case than for any of the above theorists—is his failure to distinguish rationality and reasonableness; and much that is obscure and strained in his account could be clarified by this simple distinction.

Though the above will have suggested it, I do not mean, at this point, to propound the view that there is an exact equivalence between the reasonable and the moral in all contexts.[6] Thus, it may be a counter-example to such a view that a saint or hero who insists on moral beneficence, when his interests will be severely harmed, is often called unreasonable, where this means something like: he refuses to modify his preferences in the light of prudential reasons that most men of good moral character, but lacking such saintliness or heroism, would regard as overriding. Without discussing the exact relation of the moral and reasonable at this point, it is, however, important to see that the notion of reasonableness can introduce at least a subclass of moral considerations which are clearly not conceptually, and often not extensionally, equivalent to the claims of rationality.

Finally, throughout all the following discussion of the concept of morality and moral principles, I shall regard the concept of morality as being the same as that expressed by 'right', at least in those contexts of use where 'right' may be replaced, without distortion of meaning or change of truth value, by 'morally right'. This qualification is required, because 'right' (like 'rational' and 'reasonable'), as well as 'wrong', are quite sensibly used in non-moral contexts, associated with reasons for belief and the concept of truth, e.g. 'that is the right (or wrong) answer', 'you are wrong in thinking that', and so on.

With these remarks in mind, the territory of morality will, I hope, not be confused at least with what it clearly is not.

11. *Morality as an Ideal Contract*

The presentation of my own constructive account of the concept of morality might profitably proceed by means of a detailed consideration of several views of morality which have great plausibility, but which are in various ways inadequate, a strategy which might wisely use Frankena's recent typology as a starting-point.[7] However, such a comparison would perhaps clarify my own private process of reasoning in arriving at my constructive account, rather than clarify that account itself; and lengthen an already lengthy account with matters not strictly necessary to understanding my views. I shall, therefore, simply present my account, and use other views of morality only by way of cursory comparison to elucidate its distinctive features. While this method may sacrifice something in terms of the initial plausibility of the theory, I hope *this* defect will be amply remedied by the plausibility of the principles to which I will relate the account in subsequent chapters.

What I should like to suggest is that the concept of morality may be analysed in terms of a certain sort of ideal agreement or contract which rational men in a certain defined situation would unanimously make. The idea I have in mind here is not unlike that which several economists and political scientists have recently suggested as relevant to the normative assessment of certain economic and political questions. For example, Harsanyi, seeking a more acceptable form of the utilitarian principle as a criterion for economic distribution, has suggested that a way of understanding the nature of impersonal value judgements of right distribution is by likening them to the choice of principles governing the distributive effects of certain institutions which each rational man would agree to when he was 'in complete ignorance of what his own relative position (and the position of those near to his heart) would be within the system chosen'. He suggests that, in such a choice situation under the constraint of uncertainty, rational egoistic men would adopt a Laplacean strategy, resulting in their agreement to a principle which maximizes average, not total, utility.[8] Similarly, Buchanan and Tullock try to clarify the normative issues involved in the choice of a constitutional voting procedure like majority rule, or two-thirds rule, in terms of the unanimous choice of self-interested rational maximizers from an original position where each person is 'uncertain as to what his own precise role will be in any one of the whole chain of later collective choices that will actually have to be made'. By making the assumption of such choice of institutions under uncertainty, where the choosers can only assume that their position will be randomly distributed in terms of the effects of the particular institution, Buchanan and Tullock claim to have delineated a view where 'the purely selfish individual and the purely altruistic individual may be indistinguishable in their behavior'.[9] The views of Harsanyi and Buchanan and Tullock are incomplete in so far as they do not systematically extend their analyses to the concept of morality generally; Buchanan and Tullock, for example, are clearly working within the constraints of certain moral assumptions.[10] What I should like to suggest is the extension of this sort of view to morality generally and the particular form of account which seems to me most suggestive and useful.

The view that I propose, one also suggested by John Rawls,[11] is this: the concept of morality and moral principles is equivalent to the concept of those ultimate standards of conduct which, if publicly known and generally acted on, perfectly rational egoistic men (consisting of all persons), from a position of equal liberty, and in the absence of any knowledge of their own *particular* desires, nature, and circumstances, but with knowledge of all other circumstances of human life and desire, would agree to as the standards to be used in regulating their actual relations to one another, whether in their common institutions or apart from them.

Let me try to clarify each part of the analysis.

(i) 'those ultimate standards of conduct which, if publicly known and generally acted on': the contractors understand that they are deciding on the ultimate standards of justification, which are to be prior to all other standards, when they apply; thus, they will see themselves as setting the boundaries within which it is justifiable for them to pursue other standards, e.g. the rationality principles. *By hypothesis*, possible ultimate standards are to be considered on the assumption of their being publicly known and generally acted on as ultimate standards. Thus, the contractors are to construe their task as agreeing to standards which people are generally capable of using to regulate their conduct, as a stable public order. Standards are publicly known, in this sense, if each person knows they are the ultimate standards, knows that the others know, and knows that the others know that he knows, etc. The publicity requirement excludes the acceptability of those possible standards whose stable existence depends on their remaining secret, e.g. 'one is to make a promise, always knowing one will not keep it'.[12]

(ii) 'perfectly rational egoistic men': the assumption of egoistic rationality depends *solely* on the concept of rationality outlined in Part I, and is in no way circular. That is, I assume that the members of the original position have the concept of the principles of rational choice, and the capacities and desires necessary to their completely successful use in judgement and deliberation. Thus, the solution of the decision problem before the contractors depends solely on what each individual's perfect rationality requires him to choose as ultimate standards in such a choice situation, a problem which will be clarified in chapters 8–11.

(iii) 'consisting of all persons': the class of members of the original position includes, in a hypothetical sense, *all* persons, who have lived, live now, or will live; the notion of a person is defined by a creature's having the capacity of rational choice, and the capacity to act on the principles that will be chosen from the original position, whether these capacities are fully developed or not. On this account, not only actual age is irrelevant to the moral point of view (in the sense that moral status does not begin or end with any age group, not in the sense that age may not be a relevant moral consideration in certain circumstances, e.g. duties of care owed to children or of deference owed to the aged); but also, one's membership of a historical age is irrelevant. Thus, unlike G. R. Grice's use of a similar contract conception (which limits the contractors only to living adults), this account provides, in its basic structure, for the moral relations of older generations to children and infants, as well as different historical generations to one another, moral facts which Grice claims can be established and justified by 'no remotely respectable argument'.[13] Further, the fact that people are construed as members of the original position even if their capacities are undeveloped includes also the mentally deficient and insane, whose undeveloped capacities of rationality are sufficient for them to be considered, in a hypothetical sense, members of the original position.

(iv) 'from a position of equal liberty': members of the original position are all equally free from restraint and coercion to the greatest extent possible. The idea is that the moral point of view abstracts, by definition, from the unequal liberties which may prevail in ordinary life, and is, thus, a point of view from which such unequal liberties may be criticized. This feature of my analysis of the concept of morality distinguishes my view from the otherwise similar sorts of analysis found in Baier, Gauthier, and G. R. Grice.[14] Each of these philosophers has suggested that moral principles in some way make *everyone* better off, thus proposing some application of Pareto optimality to the analysis of the concept of morality;[15] and G. R. Grice used the notion of a contract to give expression to this view (since his contractors will only be able to agree to what makes everyone better off)—at least in his analysis of 'basic obligations'.[16] The problem with these views, as stated, is that they leave unclear from what point of view moral principles make everyone better off. For example, certain quite immoral principles make everyone better off from a position of initial exploitation (e.g. chattel slavery), and yet this seems hardly decisive of their morality. Grice, of course, sees this problem, and, to defend against it, requires that his contract idea only apply when no person or group of persons is favoured by an 'entrenched legal, or quasi-legal institution'.[17] This qualification, while a significant advance beyond Baier and Gauthier, still leaves one unsatisfied, since it encourages a suspicion of circularity; that is, a main class of moral acts is analysed into some notion of acts that it is in everyone's interest to contract to do, and then the proviso is added on—'unless the relation of the contractors is itself immoral'.[18] My view, on the other hand, avoids such an *ad hoc* and circular appearance by incorporating the notion of an initial equality into the very concept of morality.

(v) 'and in the absence of any knowledge of their own *particular* desires, nature, and circumstances': each of the persons in the original position will not, for example, know his own sex, age, native talents, particular degree of his capacity for self-control, race, religion, social or economic class and position, the age in which he lives, or the particular form of his desires (e.g. whether he likes asparagus or spinach; or is homosexual or heterosexual in his sexual aims). On this analysis, such particular differences between persons are irrelevant to their equality from the moral point of view, thus further supplementing the sense of equality of (iv). Another and perhaps more exact way of putting this requirement is to say that the members of the original position are under a sort of moral amnesia as to who they are, and thus as to what they are like specifically.

The underlying idea here is that the choice of *moral* principles by definition implies that the choice is made without favouritism to one's class or race, clan or caste, talent or nationality. Such favouritism is here made impossible by the ignorance of the contractors. Or, put differently, the idea may be expressed thus: from the point of view of morality, it is utterly and at bottom fortuitous that a person is born in one social class rather than another, or in one racial or ethnic group rather than another, or in one body (with associated endowments of physical beauty, intelligence, perception, talent, etc.) rather than another, and the like. Since these differences between persons are fortuitous, they cannot be of fundamental weight in deciding what count as moral principles. The ignorance requirement gives expression to this idea by depriving the contractors, who are deciding on moral principles, of the knowledge of their fortuitous position in the natural and cultural lottery.

This ignorance requirement is, I think, the main distinction between my theory of morality and the otherwise quite similar view of R. M. Hare. That is, I think my requirement that moral principles be something that all persons could consent to comes very close to Hare's notion of universalizability.[19] The difference comes in Hare's willingness to allow into the notion of the choice of moral principles all sorts of factors that are excluded from that choice, in my view. Thus, Hare supposes that each person, given all his attitudes, no matter how distorted, and all his beliefs, no matter how prejudiced and unwarranted, chooses what *are* moral principles, as long as he chooses sincerely using the moral 'ought'. Hare grants that bona fide moral judgements cannot be based on beliefs known to be false; but he argues that, once a person has acknowledged and given weight to the facts in so far as they can be reasonably ascertained, he is logically at liberty to give moral significance to whatever residuum of prejudice remains immovable under rational scrutiny. Thus, Hare claims that even the principles of genocidal intolerance of a sincere Nazi can be moral principles if the Nazi sincerely universalizes those principles on the basis of his prejudice against Jews, a prejudice which remains intact even after fully acknowledging the genetic and historical facts.[20] By contrast, the ideal contract view, by its requirement of ignorance, tends to make *such* a choice of moral principles less likely, since the contractors do not know the special facts about themselves which might lead to such distortions. Indeed, since the contractors are by definition perfectly rational, they will precisely be able to do what Hare's universalizers cannot do, namely, to exclude from moral significance those prejudices which do not correlate with any rational basis (in the same way that a rational man will master and subdue a fear which rational scrutiny has shown not to be based on any real harm foreseeable in the future).

A further important difference between Hare's theory and the ideal contract view is that the ideal contract conception views the choice of moral principles not, *pace* Hare, as an individual matter, but as a matter of unanimous choice of *all* persons, *qua* perfectly rational men, from an abstract choice situation. Thus, even assuming that the rational contractors were to give weight to the desires of a certain class of persons for the elimination of another class of persons, the circumstances would have to be quite extreme before the contractors would give such weight to these desires as to agree to principles of genocide. Even assuming that the intensity of these desires for elimination completely outweighed the intensity of the survival desires of the class of persons to be eliminated, the rational contractors would not agree to a principle allowing such elimination as long as one contracting person found it rational not to agree to such a principle. By definition, the ideal contract theory defines morality not in terms of the choices of one person or of many or even of most, but of all. To the extent all would not agree, the principle is not a moral one.

However, one must not let the differences between Hare's theory and the ideal contract account blind one to the important similarities; indeed, so similar are Hare's notion of universalizability and the ideal contract view's idea of universal consent that it is plausible to suppose that the theories reflect different aspects of the same phenomenon. Perhaps, the truth of the matter is this: Hare's view is basically concerned with the question of characterizing the individual's process of moral deliberation, within the constraints of his limited knowledge and sympathy, in deciding what it is morally right for him to do in a particular situation; but the ideal contract theory is basically concerned with the question of what are the general principles of morality, in abstraction from the constraints of an individual's moral deliberation about a particular problem. Thus, the theories' differences relate to their divergent emphases on micro-moral and macro-moral questions: Hare's view is oriented to the particular situation where people lack the knowledge and catholic perspective of the ideal contractors, and thus universalize in order to work their way out of the constraints of subjectivity and to discover the knowledge of what is objectively morally right; the ideal contract view, on the other hand, addresses itself to generally recurrent fact situations and to the question of what principles all persons, assumed fully to have all properties necessary to moral objectivity, would agree to as the general standards to govern conduct in such recurrent situations. These questions are obviously interdependent, and so are the theories oriented to these different questions. Indeed, it seems to me not unlikely that, to the extent Hare's universalizers attain perfect rationality and knowledge of all facts and are required to give equal weight to the interests of all affected by the principles they prescribe, Hare's procedure would, epistemologically, yield belief in or knowledge of a structure of principles very like the structure of principles the rational contractors would agree to. However, unlike the usual relation of micro- and macro-theories, here the macro-theory (the ideal contract view) seems to be the more fundamental account; for Hare's universalizers are but individual men who universalize in order to approximate to the condition of the rational contractors, whose choices ultimately define what is morally right.

(vi) 'but with knowledge of all other circumstances of human life and desire': while the contractors do not know who they are, nor their distinctive characteristics of body or mind, they know that they are persons (in 'sense (iii)), and are aware of all other facts pertaining to the well-being and desire satisfaction of persons. Thus, they know about the general capacity and incapacity (e.g. akrasia) of persons to regulate their lives by the principles agreed upon—facts which importantly will influence the sorts of standards agreed upon; e.g. their knowledge of akrasia will lead them to agree to certain standards as regards deterrence for the weak-willed (note, by hypothesis, the ultimate standards are only *generally* acted on). Further, the contractors know what typically harms and advances human interests, including whatever true scientific theory is relevant to such questions (including economics, sociology, medicine, etc.). This includes knowledge of the relation of human interests to various forms of institution which advance or prejudice such interests. The contractors, as part of their ignorance, do not know what institutions they are in; their view of the relation of institutions to interests will, thus, be determined only by whatever true facts are presented to them.[21] The contractors only bring the general institution of language with them to the original position, a condition of their rationality; but their ignorance deprives them of knowledge of what specific language they have; rather, it is assumed that the contractors have some universal means of communication.

(vii) 'would agree as to the standards to be used in regulating their actual relations to one another, whether in their common institutions or apart from them': on this view, moral principles are, by definition, ultimate standards to adjudicate the conflicting claims of people when they come into relation to one another, whether such claims arise within their common institutions or in some non-institutional state of nature. Given the rationality of the contractors (ii) and their knowledge of certain facts (vi), the requirement of their unanimous agreement means that the set of ultimate standards agreed upon will be that set which, if publicly known and generally acted on, best advances human desires, from the point of view of the original position. I assume that the members of the original position lack any morality prior to their choice (an assumption not made by such traditional contract theorists as Locke and Rousseau)[22] and are deciding what is to be morality here.

The notion of unanimous *agreement* is meant to express the basically distributive character of the concept of morality, where each person's interests are given equal weight, and no persons' interests are required to be sacrificed to those of another (unless the sacrificing person consents). In this, the ideal contract theory may be usefully contrasted with ideal observer accounts, which view the concept of morality as depending on the approbation of *one* person, under certain ideal conditions of perfect sympathy, impartiality, full knowledge, etc.[23] Such a view has sometimes been used, e.g. by Hume,[24] to suggest that the choice of moral principles depends on whatever principles such a perfectly sympathetic observer finds most pleasurable, after sympathetically identifying with the pleasures and pains of all affected.[25] Thus, Hume (like Hare, who uses a strikingly similar sort of argument)[26] naturally ends up with a form of the utilitarian principle, since such a principle, requiring the maximum amount of pleasure over pain, results in the maximum amount of pleasure with which the ideal observer identifies. Such a view commits the profound conceptual error of assimilating moral principles to individual rational choice. It supposes that what is legitimate in the case of rational choice, namely, to satisfy certain desires less in order to satisfy certain other desires more, or to refuse to satisfy certain desires because of wishing to satisfy other desires later, is legitimate in the case of the moral choice of satisfying the desires of different persons.[27] This is shown by the fact that such a view naturally leads to the utilitarian principle, a main objection to which, since Price, has been its failure to note

the difference between communicating happiness to a *single being* in such a manner, as that it shall be only the excess of his enjoyments above his sufferings; and communicating happiness to a *system of beings* in such a manner, that a *great* number of them shall be totally miserable but a *greater* number happy.[28]

By contrast, my own theory, by making the choice of moral principles depend on the agreement of *all* persons, not just one, provides in its basic structure for the fact that, as Findlay put it, 'the separateness of persons . . . is . . . the basic fact for morals'.[29] The consequence of this crucial provision of the ideal contract theory, as will be elaborated later on, is that certain principles are rejected as moral principles which involve the above criticized consequence of ideal observer theories, viz. sacrificing the satisfaction of certain persons' basic wants in order to advance other persons' desires more, or refusing to satisfy certain persons' desires at all in order better to advance the desires of other persons later on, or, at least, principles requiring such sacrifices are accepted only in the most exceptional and circumscribed kinds of circumstance.

In addition, it is interesting to note the different way in which the ideal contract view interprets the concept of moral objectivity as opposed to the ideal observer view. Whereas the latter account supposes that persons approach moral objectivity to the degree that their knowledge of facts becomes more complete, as well as their sympathies more extended, etc., the ideal contract view supposes that persons' moral judgements approach moral objectivity to the degree to which they *lack* knowledge about their particular desires and circumstances, and view others in the light of a constrained and highly abstract choice situation. On this view, various particular facts about oneself are irrelevant, by definition, to the moral point of view, a conception which, I think, gives expression to the intuitive view that morality involves treating persons as persons, apart from the irrelevancies of class or colour, clan or caste, talent or nationality.[30]

However, once again, one should not let the important differences between theories blind one to important similarities.[31] Thus, both the ideal observer theory and the ideal contract view agree crucially that both the ideal observer and the rational contractors have (1) at least fully to be informed about all universal truths (viz. truths expressible without reference to individuals) and (2) to ignore totally particular facts about individuals, when they frame their universal moral principles (viz. moral principles expressible without reference to individuals). The ideal observer theory accomplishes these ends by making the ideal observer aware of all facts (including laws of nature) and requiring that the observer be disinterested and impartial, which presumably implies that the observer will *ignore* particular facts about people the advertence to which would be incompatible with the observer's giving impartial weight to the interests of all persons. The ideal contract view, on the other hand, ensures that the contractors are fully informed in the relevant sense by giving them knowledge of almost all facts and secures impartiality by depriving the contractors entirely of knowledge of their particular nature and circumstances. Note that the ideal observer theory's requirement that the observer ignore certain knowledge which he is assumed to have is the functional equivalent of the ideal contract theory's requirement that the contractors lack certain knowledge entirely. Both views in similar ways are trying to give expression to the concept of moral impartiality and objectivity.

I regard the ideal contract account of the concept of morality as an attempt to formulate non-metaphysically Kant's view of the concept of morality, which seems to me, in its basic idea, the correct view. Some of the ways in which I regard this account as related to Kant's are the following: the notion of an equal position of equal liberty is meant to give expression to Kant's concept of noumenal selves as equal members of the kingdom of ends;[32] the notion of the contractors' lacking particular knowledge expresses Kant's conception of autonomy;[33] the idea that the contractors come from all ages expresses Kant's notion that noumenal selves do not operate under the category of time;[34] the idea of a contract is suggested in Kant's general theory of morality[35] and is quite explicit in his political theory.[36] The introduction and use of the rationality assumption, while suggested in Kant, is not precisely what Kant had in mind, since he seems to have thought that the noumenal selves come to a determinate choice of principles on the basis of their desire to express in the phenomenal world their equality as ends in themselves, and thus as persons of intrinsic worth.[37] While Kant's exact view may be useful and productive (cf. Vlastos's recent use of such assumptions),[38] I have myself not been able to do much with it; and I have therefore preferred the use of assumptions of egoistic rationality under a constrained choice situation as better expressing Kant's underlying idea. The use of such assumptions of egoistic rationality makes available to us the vast literature on the subject in economics and game theory; and it certainly does not seem to me in principle implausible that this literature may have relevance in the philosophical analysis of morality, as it has had already, in Part I, in the analysis of rationality.

One difference between Kant's view and mine is the way in which Kant viewed the relation of phenomenal and noumenal selves, for Kant supposed that, *as noumena*, we actually will our following the moral law. Thus, he was an internalist in ethics, since he supposed that, to be under a moral duty, one has, in a sense, actually to will the duty.[39] My view, on the contrary, is an externalist account, since it analyses the concept of morality into a purely hypothetical contract and does not introduce actual consent in any sense. The hypothetical contract is a form of contract in the sense that the hypothetical contractors are agreeing that certain principles will apply to their conduct, if they have the requisite capacity to act on moral principles: in this sense, the contractors are binding themselves. But the applicability of the principles is quite distinguishable from a person's wishes, wants, and volitions, as I maintained in Part I, and shall further elaborate later on.

In terms of the recent arguments over whether the concept of

morality is strictly formal or also incorporates substantive elements,[40] the ideal contract view at first sight seems highly formal,
in the same way that the ideal observer and Hare's accounts are
highly formal: viz. all these theories do not write any moral content
into the accounts which they give of the meaning of 'morally right'.
Nothing is said in the statement of any of these theories about
which specific principles the contractors, observers, or universalizers would accept or prescribe. However, while this is so, the
ideal contract view (like the other theories) puts quite severe constraints, I think, on the kinds of standards that count as moral principles. For example, the account excludes immediately standards
that contain proper names and definite descriptions; nor does
it seem that particular principles involving special bargains, such as
Grice expects of his contractors,[41] would be accepted. Since the
contractors lack all particular information about themselves, there
will be no point in even proposing standards of such kinds. Mrs.
Foot's standard of not walking on the lines of pavements would
not be such an ultimate standard, since—in such an abstract
choice situation—it would stand little chance of being accepted by
perfectly rational men. In general (i.e. in the case of the ideal
contractor, ideal observer, and Hare's theories), the formal theory
is not enough to determine the specific content of the principles.[42]
In order to do this, one has to attribute to the rational contractors
(or, to the ideal observer or the universalizer) both factual knowledge and a strategy of choice on the basis of which they can choose
principles. But this brings us to the relation of the ideal contractor
account of morality to substantive principles, a matter on which
I shall dwell for the next few chapters.

Finally, a natural objection to the ideal contract view, as so far
baldly proposed, is that it is too artificially theoretical, even superficial, to begin to express the reality of moral experience for which
it claims to be an explicating account. Where, one may ask, in
actual moral deliberation and moral experience do we find anything
like these hypothetical rational contractors who seem to be creating
morality *de novo*? However, there is, I think, nothing artificial
or superficial about the concepts of human equality and the
fortuitousness of human differences in nature and situation, the
central notions which the account endeavours to articulate.
No one, for example, who has thought seriously about moral
experience can fail to have been moved by the thought that there is

nothing *at all* on which any person can base a claim for deserving the nature with which, or the situation in which, he was born. The thought or conviction of such fortuitousness is one among our deepest and most real moral intuitions. No little evidence of the depth of this idea, at least in Western culture, is that it seems to comprise at least the moral (though not the purely religious) substratum of the pervasive religious idea of man's utter unworthiness, his incapacity legitimately to make any claim of deserving the gifts with which he has been bestowed. Thus, there is nothing artificial or superficial about the ideas which the ideal contract view is trying to articulate: these ideas are as real as our oldest and most haunting collective myths. The point of the theoretical elaborateness of the ideal contract view is not artificially to sophisticate these profound and durable ideas, but rather to provide or suggest some way in which these ideas may be so expressed that one may fruitfully indicate how these notions establish the specific and determinate structure of our moral experience. The notion of contractors deciding what count as moral principles must be understood from this point of view: as a way of giving workable expression to certain deep and permanent features of moral thought, not as a way of suggesting that each person facilely creates morality on his own. Like men, theories should be judged by their fruits. Thus, whatever artificiality the ideal contract theory seems to involve (it seems to be not inconsiderable), the account must ultimately be judged in terms of the creative usefulness of such theoretical intricacy in providing tools with which we may take hold and better understand not only the nature of some of the most abstract and difficult concepts which we employ, but also how such concepts are specifically applied to the variegated circumstances of human life. Let us proceed to this.

7

MORAL PRINCIPLES:
A CLASSIFICATION

IN this chapter I propose briefly to sketch a survey of the class of principles that I take to be moral, and to explain two different and non-overlapping subdivisions of them, which seem to me of special importance. This will involve a consideration of the concepts of obligation and duty, as well as of rights and liberties, and their relation to the concept of morality.

1. *Institutional versus Individual Principles*

In proposing, in the previous chapter, that moral principles exist to regulate human relations both within and apart from institutions, I mean to suggest that the rational contractors of the original position will find it in their interest to agree to two sorts of principles: (1) principles that apply (*a*) to institutions and (*b*) to persons in so far as they voluntarily accept the benefits of such institutions, and (2) principles that apply to persons independently of their relations under common institutions, such that they would logically apply in a state of nature (defined as the absence of common institutions). It will, I think, be useful if the reader has some general idea of some of the principles I have in mind, so that he will know what is the systematic outline of the account. The exact formulations and explanations of these principles, and the presentation of other related principles, will be the task of the next four chapters.

(1*a*) In speaking of institutions (to which principles apply), I mean, quite generally, to include any rule-defined activity in which more than one person co-operates, and which produces benefits and imposes burdens related to the stability of the institution. Thus, among institutions, I include political constitutions and legal systems, economic systems of production and exchange (markets), social and economic classes, family institutions, as well as promising and the general use of language to communicate. Two principles will be accepted that apply to such institutions, those of (i) justice and (ii) efficiency.

(i) Principles of justice: these standards require the existence of certain equal liberties in the basic structure of the institution, and allow inequalities in benefits and burdens only to the extent that they relate to making the worst off in the system better off (as compared both with complete equality and other sorts of unequal distributions).

(ii) Principle of efficiency: given that an institution is just by the principles of justice, this principle requires the institution to be efficient, where an institution is efficient if and only if it is not possible by any change of the institution to make the average person in one typical sort of situation better off, and no other average person in another sort of situation worse off.

(1b) A principle of fairness will then be accepted, which determines when institutional rules are to be obeyed, viz. given a just institution, those persons who voluntarily accept the distributive benefits of such an institution, and who depend on other participants in the institution doing their part in bearing the burdens associated with the stability of the institution, are to bear such burdens, when their turn comes.

(2) Principles applying to individuals, in abstraction from their relations under common institutions, define what is due other persons, as persons, apart from their being members of different, or the same, nations, tribes, or clans. These principles are of two kinds: those of (a) duty and those of (b) supererogation, a distinction to be discussed shortly.

(2a) Six main principles of duty will be accepted from the original position: (i) a principle of natural justice requiring each person, who can, at little cost, advance the existence of just institutions, to do so; (ii) a principle of mutual aid requiring that, when a person is in a position where he can do a great good to another person, at little cost to himself, he is to do that good; (iii) a principle of non-maleficence proscribing killing or inflicting pain on those who do not rationally wish their deaths or such pain; (iv) a principle of consideration requiring people to make allowances in their own plans for the feelings and concerns of others by not arbitrarily annoying them; (v) a paternalistic principle requiring, among other things, interference with, and guidance of, the actions of highly irrational or as yet non-rational persons (the insane and children), which can be reasonably expected to frustrate interests severely; and (vi) a principle of moral development which requires each person to expose himself and others to the causal conditions facilitating the development of the attitude of being moral if the person may do so at not substantial cost.

(2b) Four main principles of supererogation would be accepted in the original position: (i) a principle of civility requiring people not arbitrarily to show ill will or bad feeling to others, instead observing a minimal level of affability; (ii) a principle of mutual respect requiring persons to show equal respect for all human persons, as equal members of the kingdom of ends; (iii) a principle of mutual love requiring that people should not show personal affection and love to others on the basis of arbitrary physical characteristics alone, but rather on the basis of traits of personality and character related to acting on moral principles; and (iv) a principle of beneficence according to which people are actively to advance the interests of other persons.

In presenting this general division of principles into those that are institutionally related, and those which are not, I should like to emphasize that this is a wholly unoriginal division of moral principles, one which many traditional theorists, differing on many other issues, have made, suggesting the distinction represents a *natural* division in our moral concepts. Among utilitarians, consider, for example, Hume's distinction between the artificial and natural virtues, where the notion of the artificial virtues marks off moral considerations which arise in the context of institutions like property and promising, while the natural virtues arise between persons apart from such institutions.[1] Similarly, Sidgwick's general distinction of moral duties into those that arise in the context of a system of existent expectations which would be violated by a transgression of duty, and those duties which do not assume such expectations, represents a similar division.[2] In Kant, the division appears in his distinction between the perfect juridical duties which arise in the context of legal institutions (to which the external principle of right applies) and the imperfect duties of virtue which do not similarly arise.[3] And, closely analogous to Kant's view, note Price's similar distinction between determinate particular duties, like veracity and justice, and indeterminate general duties like beneficence, where there is a general duty to do good to others, but not to do any particular act of goodness.[4]

11. *Obligation and Duty and Morality*

The tradition of post-Greek moral philosophy has typically tended to view all moral principles as essentially principles of duty and obligation, though often theorists made some attempt to account for the fact that these notions did not seem to apply without qualification to all moral principles. Kant, for example, viewed duty as the central normative term, using it to explain both juridical *duties* and the imperfect *duties* of virtue, though clearly he is trying, in the latter part of his moral philosophy, to account for the lesser stringency of certain of our duties.[5] Similarly, Price considers the possibility that 'duty' may not be the appropriate term for certain moral principles, especially beneficence, but ultimately rejects this idea, alternatively seeing the special feature of such principles in terms of their establishing a general duty to do one or several of a class of certain acts, not a particular duty to do any one.[6] Sidgwick also tries to account for the inappropriateness of the term 'duty' in indicating certain moral requirements, and offers his extremely interesting supply and demand theory of praise and blame to explain this; yet, he clearly admits that his utilitarian theory does not allow him to depart basically from the view that duty is the appropriate notion in describing moral requirements.[7] Similarly, in recent moral philosophy, W. D. Ross has, with unimportant qualifications, viewed the right and obligatory as equivalent;[8] and Findlay, even after making an interesting distinction between minatory and hortatory principles, still insists on using the concepts of obligation and duty throughout.[9] Such views, I think, derive in part from the seductive assumption that, in moral contexts, the use of 'ought' is everywhere interchangeable, without distortion of meaning, with 'under a duty' or 'obligation'; indeed, some theorists have gone so far as to maintain that even the use of 'ought' in prudential contexts can be similarly replaced, for example, Sidgwick and Price,[10] though not Kant.[11] As against these theories, I wish to maintain, in the basic structure of my account of moral principles, that there is a distinction between moral principles of obligation and duty and those of supererogation, a view which will make possible such utterances, in certain moral contexts, as 'you ought to be willing to die that another may live' where there is no plausibility in claiming that the sense of the sentences could also be expressed by 'you are under an obligation . . . '.

First, I shall develop a general view of the concepts of obligation and duty as well as of related notions like rights and liberties through a consideration of some alternative views that seem to me inadequate. Then, I shall suggest a way of distinguishing obligation and duty, while granting that there is the same underlying notion of requiredness involved in both. Finally, this account will be related to the case of moral principles.

(a) The Concept of Obligation and Duty

Four interesting views of the concept of obligation and duty have been taken: (i) the intuitionist, (ii) the priority relation, (iii) the predictive-coercive, and (iv) the justificatorily coercive theories. After considering the weaknesses of the first three theories in succession, I shall adopt the fourth theory as my constructive account, and illustrate its plausibility by reference to the legal case, which includes showing how the view clarifies the notions of rights and liberties.

(i) The intuitionist view of obligation has often attracted thinkers, because they have despaired of any other solution. Thus, Sidgwick reviews the various suggested attempts to define moral duty (internal feeling or such a feeling socialized, social pressure, God's sanctioned commands), finds them inadequate, and therefore, since he assumes our judgements of duty are characterizing acts as having some property, concludes that there is a simple indefinable notion which 'cannot be resolved into any more simple notions'.[12] This is *the* characteristic mode of argument among intuitionists against various naturalistic definitions of ethical concepts, though they do not, of course, always agree on which ethical notions are the simple ones.[13] If this is so, it seems that one can adequately answer the intuitionist analysis by doing what they claim has not or cannot be done, viz. provide an analysis of duty or obligation without appealing to their *sui generis* concepts and associated non-empirical intuitions.[14]

(ii) The priority relation theory of duty and obligation, suggested by Gauthier, maintains that questions of obligation only arise where there are countervailing considerations, and the essence of reasons of obligation is that they 'take precedence over whatever other reasons may be relevant to what I may do, necessarily out-weighing them'.[15] Such a theory fails to account for the cases where principles or reasons are in a priority relation to other principles or reasons (e.g. the principle of moral beneficence to the principles of rational choice; the rationality principle of dominance to that of effective means), and yet it makes little or no sense to speak of the prior principles as obligatory. For example, it may be that one ought to do some quite extraordinary good for others, even where this completely contravenes the requirements of prudence; yet there seems little plausibility in calling this an obligation.

(iii) A natural place to look for the distinguishing characteristics of obligation is in the notions of coercion and force which seem so separably related to it; and what easier way to relate them than the view that the concept of obligation is equivalent to the concept of the likelihood of coercion, if one omits doing what is required? While this sort of view has been widely held as an account of both legal and moral obligation, here I wish to consider it only in terms of its adequacy as an account of legal obligation, since its inade-quacy there will suffice for its rejection as a general account of obligation.[16] A common objection to this theory has been that it can give no informative explanation of the sense in which 'why am I being punished for doing x?' can be intelligibly answered by 'because there is a legal obligation not to x', since the account makes the latter statement redundant.[17] This objection is simply not valid, for it is open to a predictive-coercive analysis to claim that legal obligation statements are to be analysed not in terms of the probability of a particular act's being punished, but of the probability, in general, of certain sorts of acts' being punished under the system. Thus, a general statement of probabilities can be intelligibly used to explain a particular act of punishment as falling under that general statement. But, another objection does seem to me still to have force despite the above sort of reinter-pretation of this view, viz. the objection that probabilities of sanc-tions are importantly irrelevant to the meaning of legal obligation.[18] That is, even if it were the case that, generally, acts of sort x did not have a probability of being punished, still those acts could be one's legal obligations, were this the law and given that the legal system has not generally broken down. The case of unenforceable or unenforced laws are, no doubt, deviant ones in a generally effective legal system, but there is nothing in the description of such cases as unenforceable which leads us to think them less legally obligatory. An account which misses this conceptual fact has failed to render the meaning of legal obligation.

(iv) The justificatorily coercive account of obligation, suggested by J. S. Mill, was first explicitly formulated by H. L. A. Hart. Hart develops his theory of obligation in terms of the requirements of customary social rules (in the sense of chapter 2) which are more firmly accepted than others, such that:

the general demand for conformity is insistent and the social pressure brought to bear upon those who deviate or threaten to deviate is great.[19]

From this, he develops this general view: to say that a rule is obligatory is to say that coercion is thought to be justified, in the last resort, to get people to do what the rule requires. This coercion takes two forms: first, prior to the threatened disobedience, the demand that they should not disobey, and the willingness forcibly to stop them from disobeying, if possible; and second, if they have disobeyed, severe criticism and punishment in some form. The two forms of coercion are interrelated: what typically backs up the demand prior to disobedience is the credibility of the punishment if one disobeys, since it is rarely possible actually to stop the action. In the case of the legal system, one of the logical marks of which is the final authority over the use of coercion (whether as compulsory compensation, incarceration, fine, or the like), the nature of many, though not all, the rules is exactly such as to satisfy Hart's analysis of obligation; and these are typically the cases where the concept of obligation is appropriate. That is, the structure of a modern legal system consists of what Bentham called the 'principal' and Austin the 'primary' laws, directing us, e.g. not to murder, which laws are supported by the sanctions stipulated by the 'subsidiary' or 'secondary' law, sanctions to be applied if the primary law is broken.[20] But this is to say that certain rules are of such a kind that coercion is viewed as justified, in the last resort, to get people to follow them, where the persons who hold this view are, at least, the judges, legislators, etc., who man the legal system.

The account of the relation of coercion and obligation, in the legal case, is not open to common objections brought against the predictive and crude Hobbesian view of this relation. As opposed to

Hobbes, it does not build into the concept of obligation that, to be under an obligation, one must actually fear the sanctions, nor does it make the related mistake of Alf Ross and suppose that a member of the legal system must view the rules as justified before he is under legal obligations.[21] This latter point is sometimes obscured by Hart's statements that persons in a legal system, who do not accept it as justified, will not use 'obligation' utterances, for this has led Baier to claim that Hart's account does not decide whether or not non-acceptors are under legal obligations.[22] After Hart's own criticisms of Alf Ross on just this point,[23] his view seems to me quite clear about this: in terms of what is strictly meant by legal obligation, all persons in the system, non-acceptors and acceptors alike, *are* under legal obligations, though, since the use of 'obligation' in speech typically evinces acceptance, non-acceptors will not tend to use this form of words, though there is nothing logically odd in their so using it. Finally, this analysis is not open to the above objection against the predictive view, since it does not require that, for a legal obligation to exist, the sanctions associated with a delict must be either likely in this particular case or generally likely in cases of this kind. Rather, it proposes that what makes certain legal rules those which impose obligations is that the application of sanctions is viewed as justified, if the rules are broken; and this will typically, though not always, be determined by an examination of the content of the primary and secondary rules of the existing system.[24]

Finally, I should like to elaborate a view of the concepts of legal liberties and rights which this sort of account makes possible, an account coinciding with Hart's.[25]

Legal rights were divided by Hohfeld into four types: (i) claim rights, (ii) liberties, (iii) powers, and (iv) immunities. Hohfeld's typology is a useful starting-point in getting some idea of the diversity of legal rights, though I shall not follow him completely.[26] (i) The central example of a claim right is the case of a contract where A agrees by contract to sell to B goods for which B has paid, such that, on a certain date, B has a right to the delivery of the goods, and A has a duty to deliver. Another, somewhat different, example of a claim right is a tort case where A, an owner of land, has a right against a trespasser B that he shall not trespass, and B has a duty not to trespass. The difference between these cases is that the obligation not to trespass is not incurred by contract, nor

are the persons bound not to trespass limited to the trespasser
(rather, corresponding duties fall on nearly all in the legal system).
The similarity in these cases is that there are correlative duties on
other persons in both cases; and one can talk of a person having
the right to enforce the duty, if he wishes, or extinguish it, if he
wishes, where such rights are supported by some rule of law. (ii) By
contrast to claim rights, liberties do not imply correlative duties,
but rather the absence altogether of a duty to do or not to do the
thing one has a liberty to do. Thus, using Hart's example of two
men who both see a ten dollar bill, both men have various legal
duties not to kill or injure one another in the process of trying to
pick up the bill first; but with respect to the act of picking up the
bill, both have an equal liberty in being first, since neither has a
duty to or not to pick up the bill.[27] (iii) In the case of legal powers
(e.g. the right to sell my watch, or bequeath my books), legal rules
of a certain type are implied in the notion, though they are not the
rules involved in claim rights. Rather, to have a legal power assumes
the existence of certain kinds of power-conferring rules which
provide procedural facilities (often of a ritualistic kind) by the
use of which legal relationships may be altered.[28] Thus, such rules
make possible the fact that uttering 'I do', in the appropriate
matrimonial context, alters the personal and property legal
relations of the parties in question; and similarly, such rules make
possible, with the appropriate witnesses and documentation, the
act of bequeathing property, or of selling, etc. (iv) The notion of
rights is often used in the case of immunities from legal change,
e.g. one's right to his own house, where a person is not liable to
have ownership rights divested.

Legal rights, in these examples, seem all to assume the concept
of liberty in some form. Thus, apart from liberties themselves,
claim rights involve highly specific liberties plus certain
powers in relation to others' duties. A person who has contracted
for the delivery of certain goods is not under a duty to force or
not to force the other to give him the goods in question, and has
the power of enforcing the duty of the person he has contracted
with, or not enforcing it, as he wishes. Similarly, powers assume
the notion of liberty, in that the person can exercise his power of
changing legal relationships at his option. Thus, clubbing someone
over the head changes legal relationships, but, since it lacks the
requisite legal liberty, is not a legal right. At the heart of the

concept of a legal right is a liberty to do or not to do certain sorts
of actions; and this is divisible into not obstructing actions
(liberties) and giving opportunities for choice (claim rights,
powers). The notion of rights as immunities can be understood in
terms of these sorts of rights, which it guarantees or protects (e.g.
the right to one's house as a right against deprivation of one, or
several, of the above rights, a cluster of which comprises ownership).

However, this theory of legal rights is clearly designed only to
cover rights in the civil law, where the concept of legal rights is
most typically applied by lawyers, for it clearly does not cover
rights in the criminal law; thus, the rights to property and personal
safety (of which political theorists and common men often speak)
do not allow persons any choice whether they should be enforced
and no power to extinguish the associated duties. Of course, there
is some analogy here with the above sorts of rights, since the right
to personal safety, for example, facilitates choice at liberty, in so
far as the law secures persons' choices from threat, coercion, and
damage. However, the clearest common element in all these cases
of having rights seems to be this: having a right implies at least the
justifiability of coercion, under the law, in enforcing what one
has a right to, whether the individual has the additional liberty of
choosing whether they shall be enforced (contracts in the civil
law) or whether he does not (right to personal safety in the criminal
law). Shortly, I shall try to show that this is the strongest logical
relation between moral and legal rights.

(b) Obligation versus Duty

In the above discussion of obligation and duty, I assumed that
they involved an undifferentiated concept of requiredness. However, it is, I think, possible to show that, in ordinary language,
there is a special naturalness in the use of 'obligation' in certain
contexts and 'duty' in others.[29] My constructive use of this
distinction later on will not, perhaps, follow ordinary language
scrupulously; but it is, I think, important to be clear about the
precise way in which my technical terminology may be related to
ordinary use, since it takes its departure from there.

In this context, Brandt's consideration of ordinary use, in his
article 'The Concepts of Obligation and Duty', seems to me
especially accurate and useful. Brandt suggests that there are

paradigm uses of 'obligation' and 'duty' in ordinary language, which are related to their different historical origins; and that these paradigm uses are widely departed from in ordinary language to the point of practical interchangeability in many, if not most, contexts. The paradigm features of obligation are:

(a) A roughly specifiable service is 'required' of one person. (b) Two parties are involved: the one who is required to perform a service, and the one for whom, or at the bidding of whom, the service is to be performed. (c) A prior transaction, the promise or benefaction, is the source of the relationship.

And those of duty are:

(a) An individual occupies an office or station in an organization or some kind of system. (b) A certain job is deemed of some value for the welfare of the organization. (c) This job is associated, somehow or other, with the office occupied by the individual. (d) Performance is expected and 'required' of him.[30]

Given such ordinary usage, legal theorists interestingly developed a distinction between legal obligation and duty on the basis of it.[31] Obligation was said to imply a special relation between determinate persons, whereas duties exist apart from such special relations. Obligation, thus, was associated with the civil law and rights *in personam*, e.g. a right of contract with the obligation on the other to deliver; whereas duty was associated with the criminal law, whose requirements involved the general normative relations between persons apart from their special relations (e.g. not stealing or murdering). Here, the notion of duty, as related to an institutional station, was stretched, by analogy, to a notion of a man's station, as man.

(c) Moral Obligation and Duty

It is not, I think, difficult to see how obligation and duty are related to the concept of morality, given the discussion of morality in chapter 6 and the account of obligation and duty developed above. I have argued that the concept of moral principles is equivalent to the concept of ultimate standards of conduct which would be accepted by rational men from a certain defined choice situation, given their knowledge of pertinent facts of human life. As I suggested in chapter 6, among the general facts which the rational contractors know are those pertaining to the capacity (broadly construed) of people to regulate their conduct by the standards to be agreed to; thus, the contractors know that *some* people wholly reject such principles as their standards of conduct because they are not in their individual interest, and that *some* other people's effective desire to use them will either be over-ridden by countervailing appetites or desires of self-interest (temptation and akrasia), or quite distorted by their particular situation, limitations of knowledge or sympathy, etc. (e.g. the criminal who falsely regards his conduct as morally right since he is redistributing wealth from the rich to the poor). It is because the rational contractors know such facts that the concepts of obligation and duty are introduced into the choice of ultimate standards. That is, because the contractors know *some* people will not tend to act on moral principles, they will find it rational that coercion be justifiable, in the last resort, in getting the recalcitrant to act on them, i.e. certain principles will be ones of obligation and duty.[32] Not all the principles decided upon, however, will be of this kind, since the rational contractors, while they wish to encourage certain sorts of behaviour (e.g. civility, mutual respect, and beneficence) by agreeing upon principles that make such behaviour right and moral, and contrary behaviour wrong, will not find coercion the apt means to enforce them; these are the principles of supererogation.

It is important, I think, to be clear about exactly what the concepts of obligation and duty involve here. To say that the rational contractors view coercion as justified in enforcing certain principles is not to say that coercion is appropriate in the same way, or even in all cases, where these principles are transgressed. For example, the justification for coercion (including the kinds permitted) obviously differs in the case of forcibly stopping a person previous to his act and in the case of punishing the person after his act. In the latter case such coercion must reasonably be expected to secure *general* obedience to the principles in question, a consideration not present in the former case.[33] And if, as I shall argue, the rational contractors will generally regulate the use of coercion by principles of justice, as embodied in a legal system, then it may well turn out that, though a moral principle has been violated, it will not be, in fact, possible justly to impose coercion, and thus coercion may not be, on balance, justified in that case (though it is in the generality of cases). All this will be elaborated in subsequent chapters.

On this view, the notions of obligation and duty could disappear from the concept of morality without substantially altering the sense of it. This would occur, were it the case that persons have holy wills, in Kant's and Sidgwick's sense, for both these philosophers believed that the concepts of obligation and duty were appropriate only assuming the possibility of counter-desires, a view also implied in Marx's withering away of the state under communism.[34] My account gives expression to their idea by claiming that the rational contractors introduce obligation and duty into morality only because they know about the frailty of the human will in its application of principles that often conflict with self-interest. But these notions would presumably wither away from our concept of morality, were human nature substantially to change: people retaining 'ought' but discarding 'duty' and 'obligation'. What is crucial to the concept of morality are the ultimate standards of judgement which the contractors agree upon; obligation and duty are secondary and derivative.

Within this general view of principles of obligation and duty, it is possible to subdivide these principles further into those of obligation and those of duty—an account which is suggested by the distinction between these notions in legal theory. Thus, I propose to use the term 'principle of obligation' to refer to the principle of fairness, since this standard applies in those cases where persons have voluntarily entered into special relationships with others under common institutions and is enforceable, in the last resort, by the use of coercion. And I propose to use 'principles of duty' to refer to the non-institutional principles, which the contractors view coercion as justified in enforcing, e.g. the principles of non-maleficence and mutual aid. The use of 'duty' here is, perhaps, less natural than that of 'obligation' for the above principle; and some, e.g. Hart and Gauthier, have questioned the appropriateness of the notions of duty or obligation in reference to non-maleficence *at all*, and others, e.g. Baier, in reference to mutual aid.[35] But the use of 'duty' here, introduced as a quasi-technical term, rightly suggests that men, as men and apart from their special institutional relationships, are in moral relationships to one another, a view of the concept of duty surprisingly suggested by Gauthier, who fails to see its relevance to there being a duty of non-maleficence.[36] Indeed, it may well be that D'Arcy is correct in supposing that 'duty' is a wholly natural form of words in a context of non-maleficence or mutual aid, and that recent philosophers have over-reacted to the improper extension of the concept by traditional philosophers (mentioned above) by unduly contracting it.[37] If this is so, as I suspect, my account of the concept of duty will not be a completely technical one; but, in order to forestall unfruitful debate over this question, I will rest content with the more modest claim that this is a quasi-technical extension of the concept, which is useful in understanding the nature of our moral concepts. Finally, I propose to refer to principles applying to institutions (justice and efficiency) as 'principles of duty', using the natural sense of 'duty' in which it is associated with roles like legislator, judge, citizen, and the like.

This view of moral obligation and duty can, I believe, be also plausibly used in the analysis of the concepts of moral liberties and rights, on the analogy of my discussion of the notions of legal rights and liberties above. Thus, the notion of being morally at liberty to x can be analysed as the notion of not being under a moral obligation or duty to x or not to x. The concept of moral rights is importantly dependent on the notions of moral obligations and duties, because a person's having a moral right implies that it is justified to use coercion in getting other persons to respect this right;[38] and the morally justifiable use of coercion is exactly what principles of moral obligation and duty define, either by their presence or their absence. This applies both to rights associated with the principle of obligation (e.g. the right of a co-operating participant in a legal system that others obey the law, just as he does) and with principles of duty like non-maleficence (e.g. the right to personal safety), as well as the rights guaranteed by the principles of justice; in all these cases, coercion is justifiable, at some point, in getting people to obey these principles, and those who benefit from such obedience may thus coercively demand that people obey. Even in the case where one is morally at liberty to do x, and where one, thus, has a right to do or not to do x, part of what having such a right implies is that coercive interferences with it are not justified; and coercion is justified to stop such interference, if necessary. The concept of moral rights thus seems to me the same whether they are rights against a special class of persons engaged in a particular co-operative practice or against all persons, *qua* men; and the minimal content of the notion of a right (that is, the justifiability of coercion in securing it) seems present here, as it was in the case of legal rights.

On this general view of moral obligations, duties, rights, and liberties, note that the moral categories into which acts fall will be at least five:[39] (i) right acts which are in accord with moral duties and obligations, and thus which one has no moral right not to do; (ii) wrong acts which omit to do what moral duties and obligations require, and thus which one has no moral right to do; (iii) right acts which are morally at liberty, and which are morally indifferent, e.g. acts pursuing prudential rationality within the constraints of right; (iv) right acts which are in accord with the principles of supererogation, and which it is good to do, but which we are morally at liberty to do, and thus have a right to do or not to do; and (v) wrong acts which omit to do what principles of supererogation require, and which it is bad and offensive to do, but which we are morally at liberty to do, and thus have a right to do or not to do.

8

INSTITUTIONAL PRINCIPLES:
JUSTICE AND EFFICIENCY

I N this chapter I propose to consider the principles which the
rational contractors of the original position will accept as the
standards applying to the common institutions which they may
share, viz. principles of justice and efficiency. It should be clear,
from the outset, that I do not claim to present here a complete
account of justice or efficiency as applied to institutions, let alone
a complete account of justice or efficiency as applied to individual
acts, persons, and even events. At best, the account below will
present a quite schematic view of the principles which certain
completely just institutions satisfy; but since no such institutions
in fact exist, it will remain a serious problem to characterize the
proper relation between actual institutions and the ideal, the
problem of reform and, if necessary, revolution. My remarks on
this subject will, I fear, be sketchy and not altogether satisfactory.
However, my reason for undertaking a discussion of the relation
of substantive principles to the concept of morality is not to get
the matter correct in all its details, but to suggest that the account
can present the *rough* outlines of the sorts of principles that are
moral, and their relations to one another. It would be preposterous
to claim, or hope to claim, that such an investigation will yield
precise answers in all cases, especially in untypical shipwreck
examples where our moral concepts often have no clear implications. Generally, this whole area of inquiry cries out for discussion
and argument; and my remarks in this and the next few chapters
are to be taken only as tentative suggestions, which will hopefully
be criticized and refined by others.

1. *Principles of Justice*

The discussion of the principles of justice will profitably proceed
in the following stages. First, the general problem of justice will
be outlined, drawing upon Hume's still unrivalled discussion of the

subject. Then, I shall discuss what strategy of rational choice the contractors would use in agreeing to such principles, and thus explain why they would not agree to the utilitarian, perfectionist, or Pareto optimality principles as principles of justice, or even the modified utilitarian principle of Harsanyi. After this, I shall outline the principles which the rational contractors would agree to, with special reference to basic legal, social, and economic institutions. Having so far considered the application of such principles as among all living persons within a given institution at some given time (both children and adults), I shall consider the moral relations between succeeding generations (some yet unborn) which will share the same institutions, and between different systems of institutions (especially, nations). Finally, a view of the proper relation of actual institutions to institutions which are ideal by the principles of justice will be presented.

(a) The Circumstances of Justice

When the rational contractors of the original position consider which principles will be the ultimate standards of justice, they will have put before them a certain set of circumstances which are likely to arise in their actual lives, a set of circumstances associated with problems of justice, and by reference to which they will decide upon certain ultimate standards to adjudicate claims. The finest discussion of these circumstances is still Hume's, on whose account I shall draw quite explicitly.[1]

In the process of a rather extended argument, most of which is in the *Treatise*, but parts of which are also found in the *Enquiry Concerning the Principles of Morals*, Hume presents four circumstances which are characteristically associated with problems of justice. First, individual men are not self-sufficient, having a limited ability to satisfy their wants and having extensive wants which cry for satisfaction.[2] Secondly, men typically have only 'confin'd generosity': they generally desire their own good and the good of only a small circle of family relations and friends, so that they are not indifferent to others getting things which could come to them and their loved ones.[3] Thirdly, the typical circumstances of the material goods that satisfy men's desires (e.g. food, clothing, shelter, etc.) are neither ones of complete abundance, so that distributive problems do not arise, nor ones of absolute necessity, so that co-operation and distribution are nugatory.[4] Rather, the typical range of such circumstances is between these extremes, with that scarcity of goods which makes co-operation and the division of labour both feasible and desirable. And fourthly, there is a rough measure of equality in men's capacities and aptitudes, so that society together is possible without 'absolute command on the one side, and servile obedience on the other'.[5] For Hume, even prior to the organization of government and legal systems, men join together into mutually beneficial, co-operative enterprises in the way that 'Two men, who pull the oars of a boat, do it by an agreement or convention, tho' they have never given promises to each other.'[6] In such circumstances, there being a need for some form of rules which regulate the distribution of benefits and burdens involved in such co-operation, certain rules of justice (for Hume, actual institutions like property and promising), called 'fundamental laws of nature', necessarily arise, ensuring the survival of the society.[7] Hume's view could, I think, easily be translated into a problem of rational choice, where a person is trying to design a system of rules which must satisfy certain constraints on their generality and lack of complexity, so that people could understand and easily and inflexibly apply the rules, which, when accepted, would lead to the stability of systems of co-operation which arise under the circumstances of justice. Indeed, Hume seems to understand the proper role of the legislator (as a sort of governmental ideal observer) to be the solution to such problems of rational choice, especially in creating rules to stabilize the pre-existent rules of justice.[8] And in so far as the correct solution to such a decision problem will best satisfy the desires of all, people will tend to support that government, so that, when there is an ideal government, there is a stable, self-supporting feedback mechanism, like that which Downs suggested in his analysis of government functioning some two centuries after Hume.[9]

The chief difficulty with Hume's particular formulation of the rules of justice comes, I think, with his understanding of the way in which the moral acceptance of such rules is 'requisite, both to the support of society, and the well-being of every individual'.[10] Hume's insistence that rules of *justice* work out to the well-being of *every* individual seems to be an important and correct point; and goes a great way toward answering the common criticism of utilitarian theories, namely, that they fail to make any allowance for the moral constraints of equality upon the application of the utilitarian principle—the sort of objection that has led rule-utilitarians like Brandt to claim that not just utility is to be maximized, but the intrinsic value of equality.[11] However, Hume's interpretation of the sense in which *everyone* is made better off by justice quite destroys the value of his general requirement, for he supposes that without such rules of justice, 'everyone must fall into that savage and solitary condition, which is infinitely worse than the worst situation that can possibly be suppos'd in society'; that is, the sense in which everyone is made better off by the acceptance of the rules of justice is interpreted relative to the benchmark of the state of nature.[12] By this sort of criterion the society with the most grave social and economic injustices (caste system, slavery, contrasts of enormous wealth and near starvation, etc.) will be just, since people in such societies will presumably be much better off than they would be in the brutish and solitary state of nature. But Hume's general account of the circumstances of justice seems to me correct; and it is by reference to his account that the problem of justice will be introduced to the rational contractors.

(b) *The Maximining Criterion and the Utilitarian, Perfectionist, and Pareto Principles*

In defining the concept of moral principles, I claimed they were the ultimate standards, which, if publicly known and generally acted on, would be unanimously accepted by rational men, from an original position of equal liberty, in the absence of any knowledge of their own *particular* desires, nature, and circumstances, but with knowledge of all other circumstances of human life, as regulating their relations both within their common institutions and apart from them. On this view, the contractors' decision is a problem of rational choice under uncertainty. That is, each contractor is assumed to be a fully rational egoist who is trying to choose those principles which will make him best off, where he does not know who, in fact, he is, or what he is specifically like; thus, he is making a rational choice among principles, where he cannot assign any probabilities to his holding one position in society or another, to his being highly gifted and brilliant or a dullard and boor, to his being Negro or Caucasian, and the like. Further, because each rational contractor has no knowledge of his particular desires, he cannot make his decision to accept a certain principle in the light of his plan to maximize the satisfaction of his particular desires (e.g. preferring steak to kidney pie), but must choose in terms of getting the most of those general goods which typically promote the satisfaction of many desires (e.g. liberty, opportunity, property, money, personal safety and security, health, and the like).

The question of rational choice under uncertainty has been, and continues to be, a vexed and unresolved problem in decision and game theory, since at least four different choice strategies have been plausibly suggested as being variously appropriate.[13] However, in the choice situation under uncertainty of the original position, two of these strategies are specially relevant and plausible, the maximin and the Laplacean. According to the maximin strategy, when a rational person is choosing a certain course of action, where he does not know the probabilities with which the various results (or pay-offs) of the action will occur, he is to choose that course of action which has the best worst result. Thus, if I am trying to decide whether to go out with or without my rain-coat, where I do not know the probabilities with which it is likely to rain or be sunny (assuming there is no intermediate bleakness), I have the following possible pay offs before me: rain+raincoat (great relief), sunny+raincoat (slight annoyance), rain+no rain-coat (great annoyance), sunny+no raincoat (slight relief); on the maximin principle of choice, I am to choose to take my raincoat, since that choice has a better worse result than the choice of not taking my raincoat (slight as opposed to great annoyance). On the Laplacean (or Bernouillian) strategy, or the principle of insufficient reason, when one is uncertain about the probabilities of various circumstances, one is to assign an equal probability to each possible result and a numerical value representing their respective utility outcomes, and then choose on the basis of that choice which yields the highest sum, or highest expected utility. Thus, in the above example, one is to assign an equal probability of one-half to its being sunny and raining, then assign some numerical values (measuring utility) to the various possible outcomes (say, rain+raincoat $= u_1$, sunny+raincoat $= u_2$, rain+no raincoat $= u_3$, sunny+no raincoat $= u_4$), and then choose on the basis of that choice which yields the greater sum (here, whether $\frac{1}{2}(u_1+u_2)$ is greater than, less than, or equal to $\frac{1}{2}(u_3+u_4)$). While the application of this strategy may result in the same choice as that given by the maximin strategy in the above case, it will not do so in all cases;[14]

and it is thus both extensionally and intensionally non-equivalent to the other.

Interestingly, the theorists who have also suggested the use of this sort of contractual choice in the analysis of normative notions have importantly differed over which rational strategy would be adopted. Thus, Harsanyi clearly supposes that the Laplacean principle would be used, and this leads him to the view that the rational contractors would choose, as the principle of economic distribution, a modified form of the utilitarian principle which maximizes average, as opposed to total, utility.[15] It is, I think, easily seen how this sort of result would follow from the above contractual conception, were the Laplacean strategy adopted; each contractor in the original position would assign an equal probability to his ending up in each of the standard positions in the society, and then each would agree to that distributive principle which, if publicly known and generally acted on, maximizes the sum of the utilities associated with all such positions, weighted by the equal probabilities, since this principle maximizes expected utility from the point of view of the original position. Thus, if a society consists of four standard positions—landowners, soldiers, farmers, and rulers—each of which has a different utility value (u_1, u_s, u_f, u_r), then, on this strategy, the contractors would choose the principle that maximizes $\frac{1}{4}u_1 + \frac{1}{4}u_s + \frac{1}{4}u_f + \frac{1}{4}u_r$, which is mathematically equivalent to a principle which maximizes $\frac{1}{4}(u_1 + u_s + u_f + u_r)$, i.e. a principle which maximizes the average of utility—Harsanyi's modified utilitarian principle. Similarly, Buchanan and Tullock's use of the contractual notions suggests the Laplacean strategy, since they assume that the contractors are randomly distributed among the various positions (e.g. the majority and the minority) which are possible under the voting rules they consider.[16] On the other hand, John Rawls, by suggesting that the calculations of the rational contractors would so occur as if they were 'those a person would keep in mind if he were designing a practice in which his enemy was to assign him his place', seems to be supposing that the maximin strategy would be used; and this supposition is made clear elsewhere.[17]

Rawls, it seems to me, is correct in thinking that the rational contractors of the original position will use the maximin principle; this can, I think, be seen by showing that the usual circumstances where this strategy is not appropriate do not obtain with the choice

from the original position. That is, the usual objection to the use
of the maximin strategy under uncertainty is that it has too conservative a bias, and leads to irrational and counterintuitive results
in certain cases.[18] For example, consider the case where one has
a choice between two acts, a and b, where two circumstances, S_1
and S_2, of whose exclusive probabilities of occurrence one has no
knowledge, condition the result of these acts, leading to the following pay-off matrix:

$$\begin{array}{c} & S_1 \quad S_2 \\ a & \begin{bmatrix} 0 & 100 \\ 1 & 1 \end{bmatrix} \\ b \end{array}$$

assuming that the numbers within the matrix measure utility in
some way. According to the maximin criterion, a man choosing
between a and b, in such circumstances, must choose b, since this
leads to the highest lowest result of the two acts open to the man.
And this, it is claimed, is irrational, where the difference between
the lowest results (0 and 1) is minute, and the difference between
the higher results is substantial (100 and 1). The point could be
made more strikingly by changing the '1' under S_1 to '0·00001'
and changing the '100' to '10⁶'. However, this objection will not
do against the use of the maximin criterion in the original position;
for, it is not the case, as a matter of sociological and moral fact,
that the lowest positions, which different substantive moral
principles justify, differ inconsequentially in their utilities, and
that the utilities of the highest positions, by contrast, differ substantially. Consider, for example, the difference between Aristotle's
use of his perfectionist principle in justifying chattel slavery, and
Kant's use of his equal liberty principle to condemn this institution
ab initio, a comparison which indicates that the lowest positions
allowed by substantive ultimate standards differ quite dramatically.
The contractors of the original position will be aware of this, which
will indicate to them that the special circumstances where maximining is not appropriate do not obtain in the choice from the
original position.

   More positively, it seems correct to point out that the contractors of the original position *will* be conservative in their bias
towards the rational choice problem before them. What is at stake
here is not merely an isolated gamble, where a person may indulge
his taste for risk-taking, at no great sacrifice to his life on the whole;

but the choice of the basic and ultimate standards to which he will be able to appeal in justifying changes in distribution throughout his whole life, where there is no possibility of recouping possible gambling losses later on. Further, since these principles will apply not only to each contractor, but to those he may love and support, the possibility of exercising a gamble, which may be disastrous not only to himself but to those he loves, will further inhibit the propensity to risk-taking. Thus, the spirit of gambling is excluded from the original position by definition of the rationality of the contractors: the strategic importance and deep seriousness of their choice to their whole life plan and prospects are such that the adoption of the maximin strategy best advances the contractors' ends. Or, at least, such a spirit of gambling is excluded when the contractors decide on the basic moral principles which affect the fundamental life prospects of persons. Once such principles are agreed upon, the contractors may rationally use another choice strategy giving some expression to the desire for gambling, in deciding on principles which apply when the requirements of the prior basic principles have been satisfied. I shall later suggest that this will be so when the contractors decide on the principle of efficiency and the principle of beneficence.

The use of the maximin criterion by the rational contractors can be clarified, I think, by considering what the attitude of the contractors will be to certain principles which have been proposed as *the* moral principles governing at least distributive questions, and often all moral questions—the classical utilitarian principle, the perfectionist principle of Aristotle and Nietzsche, and the Pareto optimality principle. By the classical utilitarian principle, I mean the view that an act is right if and only if it tends to produce the maximal balance of desire satisfaction among sentient beings, the sort of principle that seems clearly present in Sidgwick, and that is at least strongly suggested in Hume and Bentham.[19] It is not, I think, difficult to see why the rational contractors would not accept this principle as the ultimate standard governing the distributive aspects of their common institutions. It would, if publicly known and generally acted on, not provide the highest lowest result of the various principles that might plausibly be considered in the original position; and the maximin criterion would require its rejection. That is, even if factual assumptions are made (as they were made by utilitarians)[20] about similar utility functions and

diminishing marginal utility, the utilitarian principle will require
severe disadvantages to persons and groups (including not only
unequal distribution of goods and services, but unequal political
rights and liberties, basic opportunities, etc.) if this maximizes
desire satisfaction summed over the whole of society.[21] Further, the
contractors will know that the empirical assumptions, which give
the utilitarian principle *some* plausibility, are themselves dubious.
It is certainly *not* clear that people do not have different capacities
of desire satisfaction and correspondingly different rates of
diminishing marginal utility, whatever the difficulties in comparing
them; and the members of the original position will not accept a
principle whose only tenuous acceptability depends on further
tenuous assumptions. While the rational contractors would not
agree to the utilitarian principle, it is interesting, I think, to
consider what kind of change in assumptions about the defined
choice situation might be required if the acceptance of the utilitarian principle were likely to result. Thus, if we assumed that
all the contractors were rational saints, each of whom effectively
desired what the others rationally desired (the others also rationally
desiring this), then it might be rational, I think, for them to
accept the utilitarian principle, since this principle would give
expression to the desires of mutual love and benevolence that
such saintliness would involve (i.e. if any person's interests
were ploughed under by the classical utilitarian principle, he,
as a rational saint, would rationally desire this, since thus a
higher sum of utility satisfaction is attained).[22] If this were so,
it would be an interesting fact, because it would help to clarify the
relationship between utilitarianism and benevolence, which is such
a typical feature of utilitarian theories of morality, though utilitarian theories, at least before Sidgwick, tended to explain this
relationship by an ideal observer theory of morality like Hume's.
It is as though such theories could be supposed unconsciously to
have assumed a contractual view of morality, but used different
assumptions about the contractors to arrive at their ultimate
standard.[23] On the contractual view under egoistic assumptions,
however, the principle of utilitarianism will not be wholly excluded
from the concept of morality, for I shall eventually try to show that
the contractors would accept a form of it as a principle of supererogation. What they would *not* do is to accept such a principle as
imposing *duties* on distribution which persons have no *right* to omit.

For similar reasons, the rational contractors would not, I believe, accept Harsanyi's modified form of the utilitarian principle, which maximizes, as indicated above, the average of utility of all the standard positions in the society. While this principle might not allow some of the low levels of individual desire satisfaction which the classical principle might require, it does not specify that the lowest rung of society (in terms of institutional rights, money, status, etc.) should not be indefinitely lowered (e.g. to the point where chattel slavery is allowed) if this maximizes average utility *across* the society; the contractors will reject this principle in favour of another that requires such constraints and thus leads to a higher lowest. But, again, it is interesting to see what sort of change in assumption would lead to the rational contractors' accepting this principle. Here, we have Harsanyi's explicit construction where he assumes that the process of deciding under uncertainty would imply rational gamblers with a willingness to undertake the fair chance of winning or losing, depending on where they ended up in the social system.[24] And thus, they would use the Laplacean strategy, which, as indicated above, would lead to the modified utilitarian principle.

The perfectionist principle, suggested in Aristotle and Nietzsche,[25] maintains that acts are right if and only if they produce the greatest possible exercise and display of developed capacities of talent, creativity, and general excellence. The exact forms of developed capacity to which this principle is meant to apply are not always clear, especially in Nietzsche; the description of 'developed capacity', *per se*, excludes almost nothing, e.g. the developed capacity to walk; but clearly, both theorists placed a special emphasis on intellectual creativity; and in Aristotle, the emphasis on theoretical excellence is such that it is a matter of dispute, in Aristotelian exegesis, whether the practical virtues are only excellent by virtue of their relation to facilitating the exercise of the theoretical. Further, there is the general difficulty with this view of providing comparative measures for the exercise of such capacities, by comparison with which the problems of interpersonal comparisons of desire satisfaction, in utilitarian theory, seem slight indeed. However, without elaborating the difficulties of definition and measurement that such a principle involves, it seems quite clear that it, of all the principles so far considered, would most clearly not be accepted by the contractors of the original position. Since the developed capacities which define the scope of the principle exist in only a certain class of persons (and, for Nietzsche, perhaps uniquely himself), all persons lacking these capacities will literally be the tools and instruments (Aristotle's very words)[26] which may justifiably be used in facilitating the greatest possible exercise of talent and creativity. In Aristotle and Nietzsche, there are quite explicit justifications for slavery, caste systems, aristocracies, etc.,[27] since these are compatible with their perfectionist principles. In the case of the utilitarian principles considered above, at least each person has some intrinsic relevance to the standard in so far as they have desires, so that the utilitarian calculus gives *some* weight to each person's interests; but, with the perfectionist principle, the interests of whole classes of persons are by definition excluded from the scope of the principle; and the interests of the talented, or potentially talented, alone have relevance. The contractors of the original position, who rejected the utilitarian principles because they permitted too low a level of satisfaction for persons when this maximized total or average utility on the whole, will thus *a fortiori* reject the perfectionist principle, which more strongly requires low, perhaps negligible, levels of satisfaction for the untalented if this leads to exercise of capacity by the talented. Thus, the whole idea of a society whose institutions are solely regulated by perfectionist principles, the sort of meritocracy, so frighteningly described by Michael Young in his fascinating book,[28] would be unacceptable to the members of the original position. Indeed, unlike the above cases, it is difficult to redescribe the original position in such a way as to result in the acceptance of the perfectionist principle by the rational contractors. Thus, if we restrict the choice situation to all talented persons, who know, generally but not particularly, about their own and others' talents; or if we assume that the members of the original position all acknowledge and accept a prior duty (to God?) to maximize the exercise of superior talent, or admire the exercise of such talent as the only intrinsic value—then perhaps the perfectionist principle would be accepted. That the choice situation which defines the concept of morality should have to be so distorted in order to accommodate the perfectionist principle illustrates, I believe, how much strain there is in viewing it as a moral principle, unlike the utilitarian principle which has a much greater plausibility.

The Pareto optimality principle maintains that a distribution of goods is optimal if and only if there is no redistribution of the goods which will make some better off (in terms of their rational preferences) and none worse off (in terms of their rational preferences). The principle is, of course, a form of the utilitarian principle, which was introduced by Pareto in order to avoid the fine-grained interpersonal comparisons of desire satisfaction that the application of the classical utilitarian principle involves.[29] Thus, for the application of the Pareto principle, only intrapersonal comparisons of utility are required (is one man better off or worse off or the same as before), as opposed to the classical and modified utilitarian theories which both require some way of weighing some men's being better off as against other men's being worse off, in order to compute that act which will maximize total or average utility. The Pareto standard has not only been used by economists as at least a partial criterion of optimality in distribution, but has also been suggested by Buchanan and Tullock as the main normative criterion that should regulate political choice, and by Runciman and Sen as at least a sufficient condition of social justice.[30] And, in chapter 6, I indicated that such a principle seemed involved in the moral theories of Baier, Gauthier, and Grice. However, from the point of view of the original position, it is, I think, clear that the rational contractors would not accept the Pareto principle as the basic principle of justice, since, by this criterion, a slave-owning society could be Pareto-optimal, because it could be the case that there was no change from it which could make some (the slaves) better off without making others (the slave owners) worse off. The contractors will not accept a principle which does not exclude such low social and economic positions as unjustifiable *ab initio*, since, as maximiners, they want a higher lowest. Further, the Pareto optimality criterion will not be accepted by the rational contractors because it provides no determinate principles of justice; there are, on this criterion, an infinite number of possible distributions which are optimal, a point which can be seen by drawing the usual Edgeworth box diagram for distributions of goods x and y between persons a and b (see opposite page).

The diagram plots the distribution of x and y exclusively between a and b; and the concave curves of a and convex curves of b (but concave if the diagram is read from his point of view) represent their indifference maps between amounts of x and y. Each of the

points where their indifference curves are tangent represents a
Pareto optimal point, and the dotted line plots the infinite number
of such possible points. From the point of view of the rational
contractors, such a normative conception is too indeterminate a
conception of justice, and this fact will supplement their reasons

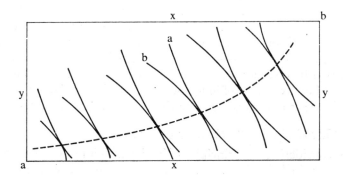

for rejecting this principle. However, as in the case of the classical
utilitarian principle, it does seem to me that the principle will
occupy some part of morality, since it would be accepted as the
principle of efficiency.

Finally, I should like to make clear that in questioning the
relation of various of the above principles to morality, I do not
mean (except for the perfectionists) to question the moral characters
or beliefs of the philosophers who held such views. The classical
utilitarians, for example, were often among the most enlightened
and liberal men of their time; however, I do wish to question
whether utilitarianism is, in fact, the best theoretical justification
for the sorts of beliefs that utilitarians espoused, and which I, in
large part, share. Even with utilitarianism in its most plausible
rule-utilitarian form (i.e. an act is right if and only if it conforms to
that ideal set of rules which, when publicly known and generally
acted on, maximizes the desire satisfaction of all sentient beings),[31]
the general difficulty remains that this principle allows quite low
desire satisfaction for some, if it maximizes desire satisfaction on
the whole. And if this result is hedged against by supplementing
the value term (utility) maximized with 'equality' as an intrinsic
value (Brandt's move), or with 'considerations of impartiality and
respect for persons' (Benn and Peters's way of supplementing

counter-intuitive results of the utilitarian principle), then the whole distinctive force of utilitarianism is, I think, undermined.[32] And we are involved in a theoretical dead-end, not unlike that found with ideal utilitarianism, which multiplies intrinsic goods to be maximized as fast as theoretical gaps are located. As I remarked in chapter 7, theoretical desperation implies the use of intuition. And this remark holds whether intuition is construed in the narrow epistemic sense which rational intuitionism involves, or in the more general sense, relevant to the views of Brandt and Benn and Peters, as well as Brian Barry's notion of 'evaluation',[33] where intuition involves a notion of independent value terms which are weighed up by a sense of judgement. But, before we fall into such a cul-de-sac, we must investigate the theoretical alternatives.

(c) The Principles of Justice for a Given Institution

In considering the principles of justice which would be accepted in the original position, a strict deductive argument would require considering all possible principles of justice, and picking the one which justifies the highest lowest position, which the maximining rational contractors would accept. This theoretical ideal cannot be realized here, where only a tentative approach to the formulation of moral principles is being undertaken; and I shall therefore only suggest principles which seem to me plausible, and at least more satisfactory than the alternatives discussed above. I do not claim theoretical conclusiveness, only relative plausibility.

When the rational contractors deliberate about which standards to accept to regulate their institutions, they will know certain general facts about those institutions and their situations of life, which I called the circumstances of justice. They will, for example, have knowledge of true sociological and economic theories pertaining to the functioning of social and economic classes, markets, and the like. This will include acknowledging things like liberty, opportunity, property, money and status as general goods, which men typically want if they want anything at all; and they will understand that the distribution of such goods has incentive effects on the exercise of special talents and capacities. By institutions, here, the contractors will understand certain social rules of the logical type that I discussed in chapter 2, and of which legal, social, and economic systems are examples. That is, institutions are said to exist if and only if a certain group of people generally act in a certain way, and have the critical attitude toward such actions which views criticism of actual or threatened deviants as justified by certain standards, and conformance as justified by these standards. The special feature of institutional social rules is, of course, that they often define, and enter into the logical possibility of, the actions and activities which they regulate.[34] Thus, a run or strike in the game of baseball logically depends on the rules of that game which define certain acts in the way that makes these descriptions possible; contrast this with the act of walking down the street, which describes a natural act without reference to any similar sort of special social institution. In the legal case, compare the description of an act as marrying or making a will and the description of an act as intentionally killing someone.[35] Generally, institutions are constituted by social rules which regulate and define a certain sphere of activity, establishing the appropriate moves and claims within the institutions; this includes such diverse phenomena as rules of games, promising, markets and currencies, class or caste systems, educational and family systems, and, of course, legal systems (including the sub-institutions of parliaments, executives, judiciary, citizenry, and so on) which typically support and stabilize other institutions through the monopoly and finality of their use of coercive power.

The principles of justice that would be accepted by the rational contractors will, I believe, be two; the first of these is completely Kantian, and the second is partly Kantian and partly that of Rawls (whose theory of justice, in general, is far more elaborate and detailed than the mere sketch attempted here).[36] I claim no originality. The principles would be formulated as follows:

1. Basic institutions are to be set up and arranged so that every person in the institution is guaranteed and secured the greatest equal liberty and opportunity compatible with a like liberty and opportunity for all.

2. Inequalities in the distribution of general goods like money, property, and status by institutions are only to be allowed if those inequalities are necessary as an incentive in order to elicit the exercise of superior capacities, and if the exercise of those capacities advances the interests of typical persons in all standard classes in the institution (as compared with equality) and makes the life expectation of desire satisfaction of the typical person in the least advantaged class as high as possible.

The first principle of justice applies to three different sorts of basic institutions: (i) the legal system, (ii) the educational, cultural, and family system, and (iii) the economic system of jobs. (i) As applied to the legal system, it requires that it guarantee by law the equal right of all persons to the liberties of thought (speech, press, religion, association), civic liberties (impartial administration of civil and criminal law in defending property and person), political liberties (the right to vote and participate in political institutions), and the freedom of physical movement, where the exercise of these liberties does not itself infringe the requirements of the greatest equal liberty and opportunity. The notion of liberty here is to be understood by reference to not being coerced to do or not to do, where this is guaranteed by law, e.g. in the basic constitution. (ii) As applied to the educational, cultural, and family system, the first principle requires that, as regards children and young adults, the educational, cultural, and family system ensure that persons have an equal opportunity to develop their capacities and sensitivities, especially their rational conception of their own good in terms of a coherent life-plan, and the capacity to bring it to realization—matters in which early training and nurture, as well as later education are indispensable. (iii) As regards the economic system of jobs, the first principle requires that all adult persons have an equal liberty and opportunity to be chosen for any job, as long as their capacities are such as to qualify them equally for the job. And, if the second principle applies, so that different social and economic classes exist, then every person is to have an equal liberty and opportunity of movement in the class system in line with his capacities.

It is not, I think, difficult to see what the rationale of the contractors is for accepting this first principle of justice. In the choice situation of the original position, each contractor is trying to find those principles which regulate institutions in such a way that the lowest position in the institution is the highest possible (compared with the alternative principles that could be chosen). In considering such a question, the contractors are thinking from a highly abstract point of view, deliberating about the general effects of various institutional forms on the rational expectations of desire satisfaction over the whole life-plan of the persons occupying the institution, assuming such persons typically have the concept and capacities of rational choice. Given this highly abstract orientation, the contractors will agree upon the first principle because it requires the existence of institutions which enable the most disadvantaged class to have a higher rational expectation of desire satisfaction over their life-plan from these institutions than any alternative principle, which requires inequalities in basic institutional liberties and opportunities. In effect, the use of the maximin strategy in choosing principles to regulate *these* sorts of institutions results in the elimination of a disadvantaged class altogether: the highest lowest is equality for all persons.

Note the special importance of the assumption of the contractors' ignorance (of their particular desires, nature, and circumstances) in their agreeing to this principle. Thus, it is because of their ignorance that they find it rational to agree to equalities in institutions which allow each person the greatest equal liberty and opportunity to advance his interests, whatever his particular interests happen to be. And in the case of their agreement to freedom of religion, this is made possible by the contractors' ignorance of their religion, which excludes the use of appeals to religious duties to their Catholic or Muslim or Jewish God to override the equal liberty of religious belief. Not knowing which religion, if any, they are, the contractors will not know whether they have access to any source of religious faith; rather, their reasoning in the original position will be based on ordinary principles of empirical inference and induction and the knowledge which such principles yield, not on the special kinds of principles and knowledge which religious faith may involve. Otherwise, the rational choice problem of the original position would be quite insoluble, for the contractors would entertain such irreconcilable kinds of beliefs (based on different religious sources and perceptions) that the unanimity of decision required in the original position would be quite improbable. Even though the contractors know that they may, in fact, entertain religious beliefs which are incompatible with an equal liberty of religious belief, from the point of view of the original position they will rationally refuse to allow the possibility of their entertaining such beliefs to affect their readiness to agree to a principle of equal liberty in religious belief; for they will know that it is also possible that they may be victims of people holding such beliefs, a fact which will lead the maximining contractors to agree to a principle ensuring against persecution by such people. In general, by depriving the contractors of knowledge of their specific beliefs in religious duties, this contractual view gives expression to the Kantian, and common Christian, conception that the concept of morality is independent of the concept of God's will; and indeed defines the notion of His goodness.[37]

The second principle of justice introduces the notion of typical persons in standard classes, an abstraction developed from economic theory's concept of the average man.[38] The idea is that the contractors find it more rational to consider the question of inequalities of wealth and status in terms of the effects of such inequalities on the typical person in standard classes, since this provides, in *this* case, a more workable and effective standard of conduct, than if the question were considered in terms of all particular persons. Thus, the contractors know that some persons (e.g. of the Rousseau type) never have the standard rational expectations of desire satisfaction from institutions that others typically have, because such institutions are in some way deeply repugnant to their psychologies; and that it would be preposterous to think that, in some *a priori* way, institutions did advance their particular interests, in line with the standard interests of their class. The contractors will find it more rational to accommodate such persons' interests by not requiring them to obey institutions which do not advance their interests (see chapter 9), than by so formulating the second principle of justice in terms of their particular interests that the principle would be nugatory (since such anarchistic spirits are, by definition, frustrated by institutional life).

Since I just discussed the relation of the original position to a principle of equal liberty and opportunity, a natural corollary might seem to be a principle of equal wealth and status.[39] In fact, it can be easily seen that this is not the case, and that the contractors would abandon their egalitarianism in matters of wealth and status because of certain social facts of which they are aware: viz. that the distribution of differential money, property, and status to persons of superior capacity is a necessary incentive to the exercise of that capacity; and that the consequences of the exercise of superior capacities is often a greater level of desire satisfaction for all than without such inequalities (e.g. superior managerial talent, better teachers, more inventions, etc.).

The general appropriateness of something like the second principle in justifying inequalities of wealth and status has been a common feature of the utilitarian tradition, from Hume to Sidgwick.[40] However, it is important to see that the rational contractors would put rather strong constraints on the application of this principle. Thus, not only must the first principle of justice be satisfied, securing basic equal liberties and opportunities for all; but the differences in wealth and status must be a *necessary* means to elicit the exercise of superior capacity, which results in a higher level of rational expectation of desire satisfaction over their lifeplan for typical persons in all standard positions (defined, say, by income) in the institution, as compared to their expectations without such inequalities; and which also results in the level of rational expectation of desire satisfaction of the least advantaged class being as high as possible. This principle, recently formulated by John Rawls as 'the difference principle',[41] would be accepted by the rational contractors of the original position because it satisfies the maximin strategy that the contractors are employing, given their general desire to take advantage of the superior way of life that differences in wealth and status make possible for all. However, it should not be supposed that the egalitarianism implicit in the original position will receive no expression as applied to this area of problems, for I shall propose in the next section that, over time, there will be a requirement to encourage the development of a population of equal and greatest talent.

Unlike the equal liberty requirements of the first principle of justice, which seems to be the main standard which ought to regulate the deliberations of a constitutional convention setting up a constitutional order,[42] the second principle of justice, like the equal opportunity requirements of the first, seems to apply to complex legislative decision-making; thus, the application of the principle to institutions involves well-informed and dispassionate analysis by policy makers of the actual workings of whole systems of economic and social institutions (market structure and relations, e.g. monopolies in restraint of trade; laws of wills and testaments which perpetuate great unearned wealth to the disadvantage of equality of opportunity; class structure, etc.) in order to see whether resulting differences in wealth and status do lead to a higher rational expectation of well-being for all, or whether enlarging or lessening those differences would increase or decrease the life prospect of desire satisfaction of all, and, especially, further increase or decrease the life prospects of the least well advantaged class—all always within the constraints of the first principle of justice.[43] The issue of just taxation, for example, depends on such an assessment. If existing distributive shares are just, then a tax structure should leave undisturbed the existing distribution of relative advantages, i.e. taxing those above subsistence at the same proportional rate on the basis of personal consumption. If distributive shares are unjust, progressive rates not only on personal consumption but on capital wealth (at high levels) may be necessary to mitigate the unjustified inequalities. Also, more vigorous gift and inheritance taxation should limit each person's allowable donative receipts to a moderate amount over life, thus more widely dispersing money and capital wealth.

Three points seem important to note about the application of this principle. First, it always requires that basic institutions ensure at least a minimal level of well-being for all persons in the society. Thus, if the second principle does not apply, because differences of wealth and status will not work out in the way prescribed, then the first principle will require equal wealth and status for all, and thus at least a minimal level of well-being for all, assuming cooperative institutions only exist when they can provide at least such levels. And, if the second principle does apply (the life prospects of the lowest class being maximized), then at least a minimal level of well-being will be required for all persons in the society.[44] Secondly, while the first principle of justice requires roughly the political institutions associated with constitutional democracies, the second principle provides no similar normative selection between different sorts of economic institutions—especially, between capitalist free enterprise and socialism. The Pareto optimality properties of a free enterprise economy under perfect competition have been celebrated from Adam Smith to Koopmans;[45] but, since no modern capitalist economy satisfies the assumptions of perfect competition, and since Lange and Lerner seem to have shown that socialistic institutions are not *theoretically* incompatible with reaping the optimality properties,[46] there seems no clear decision between economic systems on the basis of efficiency alone. And as regards the principles of justice, I do not myself see any necessary theoretical connection between these principles and either of these economic systems, since both principles may equally well satisfy these principles, given the appropriate government intervention. Perhaps, historical circumstance is all that ultimately decides one's preferences here. Thirdly, given that a set of institutions satisfies the first and second principles of justice, then whatever distribution of wealth and status results from the operation of such institutions is what persons deserve. On this account, the concept of fair distribution is explicated by the applicability of the principles of justice; and there is no way of deciding on a fair distribution by appeal to the concept of desert, say, prior to the working out of institutions which satisfy the principles of justice. In Rawls's terminology, the distributive problem as applied to the economic system is an instance of 'pure procedural justice'.[47]

After agreeing on these principles of justice, the rational contractors would further agree that coercion would be justified, in the last resort, in getting people to act on them. This would be so, since these principles are of such fundamental importance in securing a highest lowest life prospect of desire satisfaction: without persons acting on these principles, persons could be justifiably and without complaint enslaved, deprived of income below the subsistence level, etc., if they did end up in the most disadvantaged class of society. To ensure better against this result, and thus secure a higher lowest, the contractors will view coercion as justified in forcing the principles on the recalcitrant. Thus, on my account of chapter 7, these are principles of duty.

That the principles of justice are principles of duty implies that the persons who benefit from them have the right to claim and receive from others the performance of their duty in the relevant respect. Thus, these principles account for the notions of natural rights found in the classical liberals and the similar appeals to human rights that the moral depravities of Hitler's genocide and South Africa's and the American South's racism have revived in this century.[48] Further, the requirement on equality of educational, cultural, and family opportunity of the first principle of justice in part explains the moral relationship of adults to children, and gives content to the notion of children having moral rights to certain things, even if the typical background of the *use* of the concept of a right, implying the actual capacity to claim it, is not found here.[49]

The general question of the use of coercion in enforcing the principles they agree on will naturally lead the rational contractors to consider the appropriate principles which are to regulate the justifiable use of such coercion. The question subdivides into two parts: the use of coercion to force institutional change, and the use of coercion within institutions to support moral requiremens. I wish here to consider only the latter question, focusing on the use of the legal system to enforce moral duties; when I discuss reform and revolution later on, the former question will be considered. Generally, it seems to me that the rational contractors would agree that four sub-principles (derived from the principles of justice) are to regulate the use of legal coercion in enforcing moral principles.

First, the contractors would agree that the equal liberty principle requires that sanctions be applied only to persons who broke the law, who had the full capacity and opportunity to obey the law, and who could reasonably have been supposed to have known such a law existed. In this way, each person is secured a greatest liberty and opportunity of controlling and predicting results of his own actions, compatible with a like liberty and opportunity for all.[50] Such a result is required by the contractors because, from the point of view of the original position, it is a rational way to secure general obedience to moral principles at a tolerable cost. Since legal coercion is a form of desire frustration, the maximiners of the original position are concerned that the amount of such desire frustration required by their principles be a higher lowest than that required by alternative principles. The contractors conclude that a highest lowest is secured by requiring the presence of the above conditions before sanctions are applied, since these conditions provide the fullest possible opportunity for people to avoid these sanctions if they so choose, or, at least, the fullest possible opportunity within the constraint that some system of coercive deterrence is necessary to enforce moral principles. This approach would exclude the application of sanctions to an innocent who had not broken the law at all or to persons lacking the capacity (the insane and infants) or full opportunity (the severely coerced) to regulate conduct by principles, even where the application of sanctions might have some deterrent effect in better enforcing moral principles; it would also tend to make immune from sanctions those unintentional actions which result from quite unforeseeable and unavoidable accident, which there was no real opportunity to avoid. The approach would also tend to justify a different gradation of sanctions for cases of intentional and unintentionally negligent actions, since the latter often do not involve as easy or full an opportunity to regulate conduct by principles as do the former. However, such considerations are outweighed by countervailing considerations in certain cases—e.g. cases of unintentionally negligent wrongdoing where the cost of observing a standard of care is so slight and the benefit so substantial that the contractors may view sanctions equal to those of intentional wrongdoing as justifiable, and even cases of strict liability where making firms responsible for the safety of their employees, or for defects in their manufactured goods, may produce a more fair result if made a requirement of strict liability than otherwise (in the sense that the firm may be in the best possible position to take prophylactic action to avoid dangers and defects and to bear the costs of failure to do so). Further, this principle also applies to the distribution of benefits by the second principle of justice, so that people will have a greater equal liberty of planning the consequences of actions involving the exercise of their special capacities. Note that an important substantive requirement of this principle is reasonable notice that a law exists. In so far as people better understand what the law requires when they understand what the reasons for the law are, a corollary requirement of elementary justice is that public authorities, if possible, explain what the reasons for the law are, whether at the legislative stage of law-making or the judicial or executive stages of law-applying.

Secondly, given that the first principle of justice is satisfied, the application of sanctions is viewed as justified by the contractors only when it acts as a general deterrent to other people's not observing principles of duty, or when it enforces compulsory compensation by which a particular wrongdoer compensates the person wronged, where this is itself a requirement of certain moral principles; and sanctions are to be so arranged in gradations as to discourage persons from the more serious and damaging offences. The rational contractors will give such priority to deterrence and compulsory compensation because they view the application of sanctions as justified only to the extent necessary to secure general and particular obedience to moral principles, within the constraints of equal liberty; thus, they have *no* interest in, or understanding of, intuitionistic notions of the intrinsic goodness of evil plus pain, or Kant's concept of the obligation to punish evil *per se*.[51]

Thirdly, the contractors understand that the first and second principles of justice put quite strong moral constraints on the general system of institutions within which institutions of legal punishment are justified. T. H. Green briefly raised this general issue in the following passage, which he unfortunately failed to elaborate:

This, however, does not alter the moral duty, on the part of the society authorising the punishment, to make its punishment just by making the system of rights which it maintains just. The justice of the punishment depends on the justice of the general system of rights; not merely on the propriety with reference to social well-being of maintaining this or that particular right which the crime punished violates, but on the question whether the social organisation in which a criminal has lived and acted is one that has given him a fair chance of not being a criminal.[52]

But the principles of justice formulated above, especially the equal opportunity requirement, of the first, and the maximization of the life prospects of desire satisfaction of the least advantaged class, of the second, give, I think, Green's idea a more formal expression. These principles apply to the generalized effects of institutions, in so far as they may incline and tempt persons to violate the law. Obviously, it contravenes the first principle of justice if basic institutions do not allow disadvantaged classes an equal opportunity of developing their conception of their rational good and the capacity to achieve it, without the temptations and frustrations of lower-class life leading to a life of crime. And the second principle of justice *a fortiori* requires that institutions be so arranged that they will not have these generalized effects on the worst-off classes.

Fourthly, on the assumption that a generally just legal system exists, the rational contractors will agree that the use of coercion in enforcing moral principles of duty and obligation must be restricted to the legal system, except for certain special cases. The reason for this has been a prominent point made by the contractarian tradition, especially Locke and Kant:[53] viz., when each individual person, in an institutional state of nature, himself acts as an enforcer of moral duties, he is judge, jury, and executioner in each case, including his own, and thus his judgement will often be distorted by personal interest and bias, selfish envy and vindictiveness. The great virtue of a fully just legal system, where the final appeal in the exercise of coercive power is to a group of impartial interpreters and executors of the law, is that the distortions of judgement and execution, found with an individual in the state of nature, are minimized. This is simply to say that such legal institutions tend to be more just in their distribution of punishment: the persons who violate moral duties and obligations, which the law enforces, are more likely to be punished than in the state of nature, where distortions of judgement lead to applying coercion to the innocent, or applying coercion to the guilty to a degree which is out of all relation to the requirements of deterrence. For this reason, when a just legal system exists, coercion is justified in enforcing moral duties and obligations only when these requirements can be effectively enforced by law; those duties and obligations which cannot be effectively enforced by law are not to be enforced by individuals at all; the possible injustices would be too great, and the spirit of self-help would undermine the ethos of the legal system. Of course, there will be exceptions, e.g. coercively stopping a man who threatens to kill or rob you or another, and so on.

There is one interesting implication of these four principles regulating the use of coercion to enforce moral principles: they do not decide on the merits of *particular* sanctions from the point of view of the original position. Thus, it does not seem to me that the members of the original position would decide on the appropriateness or inappropriateness of the death penalty. The matter depends on circumstances—whether it is required for deterrence, whether it contravenes the second principle of justice, lowering the life prospects of the least advantaged class, etc. This result is to be contrasted with the opposing views of the implications of the contract conception in Beccaria and Kant. Beccaria, of course, supposed that the contractors would generally exclude the death penalty as a sanction, whereas Kant argued, on the contrary, that the death penalty would be imposed by the noumenal selves as the just and obligatory sanction in certain cases.[54] It may be supposed, however, that the maximiners of the original position would adopt the Beccaria position, since institutions without the death penalty permit a higher lowest than one without them. This view represents a misinterpretation of the point of view of the original position. The contractors are concerned with the highest lowest position in an institution and the rational expectations of desire satisfaction over life of the person in that position. But there is nothing in this conception which renders it incompatible with the death penalty's raising the expectations of such a person, perhaps by better securing the obedience to moral principles which makes him better off.

Finally, I have, in this section, discussed only principles of justice as regulating legal systems, economic and social institutions, etc. However, the rational contractors will also agree that the principles of justice apply to other institutions, though the specific nature of those institutions results in a different sort of applicability for the relevant principles. For example, the second principle does not apply to the institution of promising, though the first principle does, requiring that a promise only be given and accepted from a position of equal liberty, thus excluding promises given in a state of slavery or under coercion or duress.

(d) The Principles of Justice between Generations and Institutions

So far, I have considered the ultimate standards which would be accepted by the rational contractors in regulating an actual institution at a given time, However, they will also agree to principles which regulate (i) the distributive effects of institutions between different generations which share that institution, and (ii) the distributive relations among institutions.

(i) Institutions, of course, exist over time, e.g. the present legal system of the United States has existed roughly since the latter part of the eighteenth century. That is to say, the ultimate rules of legal validity which determine what counts as law in the United States have been accepted at least by the class of ruling officials, and, of course, many others, over several centuries, though the class of acceptors has changed through births and deaths.[55] Such trans-temporal institutions have important distributive effects on the changing class of persons which live within them, and bear the burdens and incur the benefits of institutional life. I should like to consider here what principles, regulating the trans-temporal effects of institutions, the rational contractors will agree to as regards (a) the rate of economic growth, (b) the size of population, and (c) the capacities of that population.

(a) As regards the rate of economic growth, the contractors know that a certain rate of savings, which is invested in capital accumulation and research and development, is necessary if goods and services are to increase and be improved on for the use of later generations; and that such a rate of savings is a sacrifice for the present generation, since it could be used for their own consumption. Since the contractors do not know what historical generation they are in, they will be concerned that some sort of principle of 'just savings' be accepted,[56] which will require a certain rate of savings over time, in order to ensure that they get the highest lowest result, something which they would not get if they lived in a later generation inheriting institutions which had been exhausted by the indulgence of a previous generation (factories and machines have run down, goods are not increased in amount though there is a larger population, etc.). But conversely, the rational contractors would not accept, as a just savings principle, any standard (like the classical or modified utilitarian principle, or the Pareto optimality principle adjusted to apply over time)[57] which would require too high a rate of savings, impoverishing present generations in order to aggrandize future generations (because this might maximize the total or average of desire satisfaction over time, or yield a result where some in the present generation could only be made better off by making those in the future generations worse off).[58] The form of just savings principle that the maximining contractors would adopt (since it secures a higher lowest than alternative principles) seems to be an adaptation and extension of the second principle of justice, requiring a rate of savings which leads to the highest long-term expectation of desire satisfaction of a typical person in the lowest standard position in the economy over several generations, assuming that the rate of savings raises the level of expectation of desire satisfaction of all classes over time, as compared to no such rate of savings. Such a typical person could be understood as an average member of the lowest class who hypothetically survives for several generations, giving equal weight to his interests in each generation, or, more realistically, as such an average man with Hume's 'confin'd generosity',[59] desiring his own good and the good of his family for the next few generations, all of whom are likely, let us suppose, to be in the same class position. Generally, the application of the just savings principle assumes that the principle of equal liberty and opportunity is satisfied, and that there is a distribution of talent which makes the second principle of justice applicable. The scope of the second principle is limited by the just savings principle which requires that the life prospects of all classes should be raised over *several* generations and the life prospects of the lowest class over *several* generations should be maximized (by setting the required rate of savings), before the life prospects of the *present* lowest class are maximized and the life prospects of all *present* classes are raised (by setting inequalities of wealth and status). If the second principle of justice does not apply, so that there is an equal distribution of wealth and status, then the just savings principle requires maximizing the long-term prospect of desire satisfaction of any typical person in the society over several generations. Note, however, that one important factor telling against very large savings for the benefit of future generations is the unpredictability of the future; there may, for example, be some destructive war in the future which will make present savings quite pointless; or, new inventions may make such savings quite unnecessary. However, to the extent the principle of just savings imposes some requirement for present savings, it would ensure basic life prospects of desire satisfaction; and thus, coercion would be viewed as justified in enforcing it, e.g. younger generations could force legislators to create a higher rate of savings by regulating capital accumulation and creating other savings by taxing incomes.

(*b*) The most important general fact that the maximining contractors will keep in mind in their consideration of the problem of population size is that the *number* of people in an institution, at least beyond a certain point, strains economic and other institutions and reduces the rational expectations of desire satisfaction of persons quite substantially. Being concerned in securing a higher lowest, the contractors will thus not agree to principles of population size (like the classical utilitarian principle, as applied by Sidgwick to population size,[60] or its variant average utility and Pareto optimality forms) which require an almost unlimited population size (since there would be more desires to be satisfied), even at the expense of quite severe privation for some, as long as the utilitarian calculus thereby computes a higher total or average of utility, or a Pareto-optimal point. Rather, the contractors would agree that a certain institution is to have roughly that size of population which raises the life prospects of all classes over several generations and raises the life prospects of desire satisfaction of the worst-off class as high as possible (by allowing people to indulge their natural desire for some children within the constraint of limiting the pressure on scarce resources which, unlimited, can lower everyone's life prospects, including children's); for, this principle will secure a higher lowest than alternative principles. The principle will apply not only to prospective parents, who are to regulate their having children by it, but also to legislators who regulate the size of population by either encouraging persons having children through allowances and tax relief, or by discouraging them through heavy taxes, making birth control knowledge available, and even making birth control legally compulsory, after a certain number of children. And the contractors will also agree that coercion is justified in enforcing this principle. However, it is not to be supposed that this principle of duty implies anything like a duty on persons to have children. Indeed, since the contractors do not know the nature of their sexual aims (e.g. their hetero- or homosexuality), they will not agree upon a principle which regulates them in a certain direction. Rather, the principle applies where people (as they generally do) have the desire and capacity to have children. Further, the egoistic desire to exist of the contractors does not influence their consideration of this problem, for *ex hypothesi* the contractors know they exist at some point of time, and are thus only concerned to ensure that their existence be as satisfying as possible.

(*c*) Assuming the contractors know the genetic facts about hereditary inheritance of superior capacities, especially intelligence, an important fact relevant to the contractors' consideration of the distribution of native capacities over time is that having superior capacities, especially intelligence, contributes to one's greater prospect of desire satisfaction over life. This is so not only because the second principle of justice typically justifies greater wealth and status, but, more importantly, because the possession of greater capacities increases the level and sophistication of satisfaction derived from competence desires; indeed, a native capacity like intelligence seems to be a general good, in the sense that it enables one better to formulate rational plans to advance one's ends, whatever one's ends are. As a consequence of this, the maximining contractors will be concerned to realize the higher lowest which a wider distribution of these capacities involves; however, the forms of regulation they will be prepared to accept will not include those which lower the life prospects of desire satisfaction of the lowest standard class through coercively limiting their desire at least for some offspring (except for cases of mental deficients) or which violate the equal liberty principle through genocidal programmes whose ostensible purpose is eugenic; the maximining contractors will obviously reject *such* forms of regulation *ab initio*. Rather, the principle which the contractors would agree to, as regulating the eugenic effects of institutions over time, would be a principle requiring the development, over time, of a population of equal and greatest talent, since such a distribution of capacity would yield the highest lowest.[61] The contractors' reasons for accepting this principle (i.e. that they can exercise choice over the sort of distribution of capacity over time that they find most acceptable from the point of view of the original position) may be usefully contrasted with their reasoning in accepting the second principle of justice (i.e. that differences in the distribution of capacity within a given institution at some time are given by the natural lottery, as it were, which they can take advantage of for the good of all). Thus, the requirements of the principle of equal and greatest talent may be achieved only over a long time; meanwhile, the existence of differential capacities at some particular time will result in the applicability of the second principle of justice. The principle of equal and greatest talent requires institutions to encourage persons of greater capacity to have children, then persons of greater and less, and least, persons of less native talent, where such encouragement, by forms of tax relief, for example,[62] will over many generations work out to a population of equal and greatest talent. It also requires that persons who are mentally deficient should not be permitted to have children at all (e.g. requiring sterilization), since their offspring are highly likely to lack the minimal equipment for a rational life; the life prospect of desire satisfaction of such offspring is so meagre that the contractors will want a principle which works against perpetuating such a low position in terms of life prospects. Similarly, this principle justifies incest taboos, *if* it is a genetic fact that such sexual unions are likely to be mentally abnormal. Of course, coercion will be viewed as justified in enforcing this principle, whether considered as applying to legislators or to potential parents of mental deficients. Finally, note that when a society of equal and greatest talent has been achieved, the conditions of applicability of the second principle of justice will be removed; and the egalitarian society will be complete. Indeed, it seems to me that an assumption of actually *existent* equal talent is behind many completely egalitarian political theories, e.g. Marx's. Here, the supposition seems to be that once capitalist institutions fall away, then the full potentiality of repressed human talent will emerge; and this talent will be so prodigious that the division of labour will be irrelevant, and men will be equal and sufficient to themselves.[63]

(ii) The principles which the rational contractors will agree to as regulating the relations of institutions, especially nation-states, represent, I think, a simple extension of the principles of justice which they agree upon, as applying within institutions. I shall very briefly illustrate this by reference to two sorts of cases— (a) war (where my account is basically Kant's)[64] and (b) economic aid.

(a) The contractors will consider war an imperfect form of coercion which is justifiably used only when nations are in an institutional state of nature, and only justified then when the coercion is used to enforce there quirements of the principle of equal liberty. Thus, the contractors know that conflicts of economic and political interest will arise between nations; and that war is a way of resolving such conflicts, often resulting in the political or economic subordination of nation x by nation y, or even the absorption of x into y, where this substantially prejudices the interests of the people of x. From the point of view of the original position, where no one knows which nation or tribe he is a member of, and where the contractors are trying to agree upon principles which will ensure a highest lowest life prospect of desire satisfaction, these forms of war will not be acceptable, since they permit too low a life prospect, if a contractor should end up in such a subordinate country or colony.[65] Another way of making the same point is this: since the rational contractors have already agreed to a principle of equal liberty by which the citizens of a given nation are to be guaranteed various political and civil rights, liberties of expression and religion, etc., it would be a contravention of this principle for one nation to deny such rights to another by a *de facto* or *de jure* subordination or absorption. And, it also follows from the principle of equal liberty that a nation x is justified in using force to stop another nation y, which is itself about to use force on x to secure its own aims.

It is natural to suppose that the principle of equal liberty involved here is something of the form: each nation is to be allowed a greatest equal liberty, compatible with a like liberty for all. This is not, however, the case, since the contractors are basically concerned that the institutional structure of a nation itself satisfies the first principle of justice. And thus, where there is a grave violation of equal liberty within institutions, the contractors will view war, in the appropriate context (see next section), and even some form of absorption,[66] a justified means in stopping this. In short, mutual non-interference between states is not, *per se*, justified; however, once there is equal liberty within institutions, then there is to be an equal liberty between them. Importantly, the contractors are concerned not with the well-being of institutions (e.g. continued existence), but with the well-being of persons; and thus, it is perfectly natural that the contractors may approve the destruction of a certain nation, if it severely frustrates the interests of its populace.

These remarks about the justifiability of war are assumed to hold only in an institutional state of nature between nations. Such forms of coercion are highly imperfect, and subject to the same objections as those made above against the individual use of coercion in enforcing moral principles in the state of nature. That is, because an individual nation will be judge, jury, and executioner, often in its own case, the application of such coercion is subject to the distortions of self-interest and nationalistic prejudice; and thus, nations innocent of aggressive intent may be attacked. Indeed, it seems that the contractors would agree that some form of supreme supra-national authority, having the final power over the exercise of coercive power, should be created in order to make wars morally unnecessary, and to ensure that coercion is more justly executed in forcing obedience to moral principles. And such a principle requiring the existence of a supra-national authority would be of such importance that coercion would be justified in enforcing it. This principle of duty would apply to national leaders who are to try to create institutions to realize it. Thus, the ideal contract view gives expression to Kant's notion of a categorical imperative requiring perpetual peace.[67]

(*b*) As regards the economic relations between nations, the contractors know that nations vary widely in their economic development, and thus in the real income *per capita* of their populations, and thus in the life prospects of desire satisfaction of their standard classes. But since the contractors do not know which nation, at which stage of economic development, they are actually in, they will be concerned to agree to ultimate standards regulating the economic relations between nations which will secure the highest lowest life prospect of desire satisfaction, assuming that the relations between nations satisfy the first principle of justice. At first sight, one might suppose that the contractors would simply agree to a principle requiring equality of wealth between all nations, thus requiring the appropriate transfers from rich to poor that would result in such equality. This would not, I think, be so, for reasons similar to those relevant to the contractors' acceptance of the second principle of justice: creating immediate equality of wealth by such transfers may have such adverse effects on the wealthy economy (on the exercise of superior managerial and scientific talent which the wealthy economy makes possible, and thus on productive efficiency, rates of investment, research, and development) as to lower the rates of economic growth of all nations, through reduced trade, investment, and invention, and even reduce the life prospects of desire satisfaction of the least advantaged class over several generations in an underdeveloped country, as compared with a situation of inequality of wealth. While such transfers from rich to poor nations might raise the life prospects of desire satisfaction of all the *present* standard classes of underdeveloped countries, the contractors will not give weight to this consideration as long as it also involves lowering the life prospects of desire satisfaction of future generations in the standard classes of underdeveloped countries. Because of this, the contractors will accept a principle regulating inequalities of *per capita* income between nations analogous to the second principle of justice, with the important difference that the superior talents here are not constitutional endowments, but the specialized capacities fostered by and given expression in developed economies (thus, such capacities may exist in underdeveloped countries, but they lack the institutions to tap them). Thus, inequalities of *per capita* income between nations are only justified if those inequalities are necessary in eliciting the exercise of capacities which raise the life prospects of desire satisfaction of all standard classes, as compared with equality, and raise the life prospects of the lowest standard class (in the underdeveloped country) over several generations as high as possible. Once the interests of future generations are thus promoted, then the interests of the present people in standard classes in underdeveloped countries are similarly to be taken into account. Since trade and economic aid are typically required to facilitate the economic growth of underdeveloped countries and raise the life prospects of the lowest class as high as possible, such trade and economic aid will be requirements of this principle. This principle will be viewed by the contractors as limiting the applicability of the second principle of justice within a developed nation, and the just savings principle as between generations living within such a nation. This is so because the life prospects of desire satisfaction of present and future generations in the standard classes of underdeveloped countries are often lower than all or most of the standard classes of developed countries, and their lowests are usually much lower than the developed country's lowest. Thus, in order to ensure that *these* lows are as high as possible, the contractors will require that developed nations first raise the life prospects over several generations of the lowest class of the underdeveloped country as high as possible; then raise the life prospects of the present lowest class of the underdeveloped country; then, raise the life prospects of one's own (developed country's) lowest class over several generations by setting the requisite savings rate; and then raise the life prospect of one's present lowest class as high as possible by setting the appropriate levels of wealth and status, assuming that inequalities of capacity exist. Each principle only applies within the range of points which satisfy the previous principle.

However, this principle justifying inequalities of wealth between nations, like the similar second principle of justice within nations, will only apply as long as nations have differential capacities, which can be exercised for the good of all nations through increased trade, investment, and research and development. However, as economically underdeveloped countries advance, in part through the assistance of developed countries, their populations will develop the specialized managerial and scientific talents which were previously the monopoly of developed countries. When such equal talents have been realized, consistent egalitarianism will be possible.

Finally, having agreed upon the principle of economic aid, the contractors will find further reasons for accepting the principle requiring a supra-national authority. That is, they will recognize that the principle of mutual aid is of such importance as to justify coercion in enforcing it, but they will also know that making individual nations the sole judge, jury, and executioner, often in their own case, will be subject to the injustices I already mentioned. This will be *a fortiori* so with this principle, since strong motives of national self-interest will prevent developed nations from fully, or even perhaps in part, acknowledging and acting on the principle of mutual aid. Thus, a supra-national authority, which itself regulated the applicability of this principle, would be required by the contractors in so far as it would better secure obedience to this principle, and thus ensure a highest lowest.

(e) *Justice: the Ideal and the Actual*

As I sketched the general outlines of the principles of justice which the contractors would accept, the reader will perhaps have been aware of the extreme artificiality of the assumptions on which the applicability of those principles depended. Thus, I always claimed that the second principle of justice, or the just savings principle, or the principle of economic aid, only applied, given that the institutions in question satisfied the equal liberty requirements of the first principle of justice. Yet this is often not the case; and what does the account say then? This raises the difficult question of the relation between the ideally just institutions, whose principles I have sketched, and actual institutions, and the problem of reform and revolution. Philosophers, since Plato and Aristotle, have typically distinguished these problems, and have often created quite different theories to deal with them (thus, the *Republic* and the *Laws*), often through despair at human nature's capacity to sustain the ideal. Some, like Kant, resorted, ultimately, to providential historical process to bridge the gap, and completely forbade revolution as a means of bridging it. Others, like Sidgwick, distinguish the different requirements of their principles in an imperfect and perfect society.[68] I do not myself have any general or easy solution to this problem, in part because so many matters of fact, relevant to the contractors' consideration of this question, seem obscure and undecided. But, I should like partially to clarify the problem by considering the kind of view the contractors would take concerning two sorts of institutions: (i) nations which do not satisfy equal liberty, but which do realize the equal opportunity requirements of this principle and satisfy the requirements of the second principle of justice and (ii) a nation which seriously contravenes the equal liberty principle. In the next chapter, I shall consider institutions which satisfy certain parts of the equal liberty requirements, but not all—the problem of civil disobedience.

(i) As regards nations which do not satisfy the equal liberty requirements, but do approximate satisfying equal opportunity and the second principle of justice, one thinks here of totalitarian regimes, like the Soviet Union and People's China, which have substantially raised the life prospects of desire satisfaction of their most disadvantaged classes, especially over several generations, through their massive support of economic growth, attaining higher rates of such growth in much shorter periods of time than comparable periods of economic growth in Britain and the United States.[69] It may be supposed that the contractors would unambiguously condemn such institutions in so far as equal liberties of speech, press, political rights, etc., are not *effectively* guaranteed to persons (whatever the formal constitution, as in the Soviet Union, which *reads* so well), and especially since equal liberties were often savagely violated to facilitate economic growth (e.g. the kulak massacres in the Soviet Union). In fact, this would not be so, at least not without qualification. I say this because the general facts which are relevant to the contractors' consideration of this problem are themselves unclear and undecided. For example, if one compares the rates of economic growth in two underdeveloped countries with a similar sort of initial impoverishment[70] and cultural situation, and with quite different political systems, e.g. People's China and India,[71] there is *some* reason to believe that a totalitarian regime is much better able to create equality of opportunity for its people and substantially raise their life prospects, where nations have no experience in democratic institutions and methods and have largely illiterate and uneducated populations living on the edge of subsistence. From the point of view of the original position, the contractors would tend to approve a totalitarian regime, *if* the choice were between democratic institutions which allowed large sectors of the population to fall below the subsistence level, and a totalitarian regime, which effectively secured against such a phenomenon, assuming that once the problems of economic growth were surmounted, there would be a change to democratic institutions. This would be so, because such a regime would more effectively secure a higher lowest. And if the kulak massacres, and the like, are adduced, then if the rational contractors *had* to choose *only* between a regime which permitted the killing of millions to secure effective economic growth, and a democratic regime which allowed the deaths of millions through starvation, it is by no means clear how they would decide. Where is the highest lowest? Of course, the picture drawn here is only a caricature of the actual facts, and one would have thought that there *must* be some sort of intermediate choice which man's ingenuity could devise. However, the facts are by no means clear, and the contractors may well decide that institutions may be justified in certain special contexts of underdevelopment and economic growth which they would not agree to in a different situation.

In general, this question raises a problem for the ideal contract view.[72] The rational contractors are assumed to have knowledge of general laws and are thus in a position to predict future events. However, we often lack this kind of knowledge and, therefore, are unable to predict the future. Only one example of this lack of knowledge and consequent unpredictability was my own hesitation regarding the facts of economic growth and development in the decision problem just considered. To accommodate such situations, the rational contractors would decide that future real individuals, who lacked the contractors' access to the facts, should act as best they know how in the light of the reasoned knowledge available to them.[73] In the terminology of chapter 12, people may justifiably act on the basis of good moral reasons for action, which are not conclusive reasons for action.

(ii) As regards nations which seriously contravene the principle of equal liberty, I have in mind here the policies of racial genocide practised on a massive scale by Nazi Germany, where there is no plausibility in relating such violations of equal liberty to massive problems of economic underdevelopment. As suggested above, the contractors would view the most extreme measures of revolution (on the part of the population of the legal system) and war (on the part of other nations) as justified in forcing a stop in such policies, subject to the following provisions. First, the force exerted should, so far as possible, fall on the persons within the system who created and fostered such policies. This is itself a requirement of equal liberty, whereby persons are allowed a greatest equal liberty in planning their lives and predicting the consequences of their plans, including punishment. The applicability of the equal liberty principle to the use of force through war and revolution in forcing obedience to moral principles is analogous to the similar application of this principle to coercion within a legal system, mentioned previously. Secondly, the force must only be the minimum amount required to accomplish its end; and if the force cannot reasonably be expected to accomplish this, or will accomplish it only with greater injustice (harming and killing the innocent) than the situation to be remedied, it is not to be used. Thirdly, once force has accomplished its objective in ending such policies, the persons who created and fostered such policies are only to be punished further if it can be plausibly supposed that this will act as a deterrent to other leaders of nations in similar circumstances.[74] However, the possibility of injustice in the application of such forms of coercion, even in clear cases, will feed into the contractors' reasoning in accepting a principle requiring a supranational authority to dispense such coercion. Indeed, Kant believed that revolution would involve such profound injustice in the breakdown of the legal system that the noumenal selves would *always* view it as unjustified.[75] However, as long as an institutional state of nature between nations exists, the contractors would, I think, view revolution as justified, subject to the above provisions.

Finally, my remarks here about the serious violation of equal liberty in an advanced and developed country should not be regarded as applying in all possible cases, or even in all historically actual ones. This will already have been indicated by the previous section; but many other examples are possible of early historical institutions like slavery which, strictly speaking, violate equal liberty, but which may, in the circumstances, be a great advance over previous institutions; and thus may be justified as a stopgap in the development to other institutions. For example, consider Rawls's example of two city states which previously killed one another's citizens when captured in battle, but which subsequently freely agree upon a treaty to make the captured citizens into slaves.[76] If, in the circumstances, these are the only available alternatives, then the contractors will approve such a move, though they will also require a change to institutions without slavery, whenever feasible.

11. *The Principle of Efficiency*

In discussing the circumstances of justice at the beginning of the previous section, I claimed that questions of justice arise, in part, because men find it to their advantage to join into co-operative institutions, i.e. because co-operative institutions and practices do, in fact, make all the members of the institution better off than they are without the institution. This represents the situation for which the contractors are trying to agree on ultimate standards, when they come to consider principles of justice. It is in this sense that one may say that considerations of utility are prior to considerations of justice, since the contractors will only regard their principles as having applicability when everyone is made better off by institutions than they are without them[77] (which is not, of course, to say that the principles of justice themselves only require that institutions make everyone better off than they are in the state of nature—the Humean or Lockean mistake of confusing the circumstances of justice with the principles which are to regulate distributive questions arising from such circumstances).

However, once the principles of justice do apply to institutions, the contractors will regard them as having an absolute priority over other considerations, which may be relevant to distributive questions within institutions. This is so because the principles of justice secure the highest lowest life prospect of desire satisfaction within institutions; and the maximining contractors will wish to ensure that such a highest lowest is achieved before other aims are considered. This view of the lexicographical priority of principles of justice to other institutional principles follows Kant's conception that justice always overrides utility, and that justice can only be overridden by a greater balance of justice.[78]

However, given that the principles of justice are satisfied, the rational contractors will then be concerned that institutions be as efficient as possible, so that practices are so arranged as to produce the maximum possible life prospects of desire satisfaction. Having fully realized the rational usefulness of the maximin strategy of choice in an institutional context by agreeing to the principles of justice, the contractors may now rationally abandon that strategy and indulge their propensity for gambling in deciding on other institutional principles which apply if the requirements of the prior principles of justice are satisfied. This, of course, does not mean that the maximin strategy does not still fully apply when the contractors come to decide on non-institutional principles. In the present context, the contractors find it to be a rational gamble to agree on the principle of efficiency since each contractor stands as good a chance as any other to benefit from the principle by being made better off and has no chance of being made worse off. Since there is no chance of real loss (at the worst, a person remaining at the same position in terms of life prospects), the gamble is eminently rational. The formulation of this principle, the Pareto optimality criterion adapted to institutions,[79] would run as follows:

3. Given that principles 1 and 2 are satisfied, or not relevant, then the rules which define and establish an institution are to be so arranged that there is no possible change in those rules which would raise the life prospects of desire satisfaction of a typical person in one standard group (defined, say, by income) without lowering the life prospects of desire satisfaction of a typical person in any other standard group.

I use the Pareto optimality criterion to formulate this principle because I do not wish to get involved in the fine-grained inter-personal comparisons of desire satisfaction that a more traditional form of the utilitarian principle might involve. Note that the principles of justice also do not require such comparisons. With the second principle of justice, one is only to raise the life prospects of all standard classes, and maximize those of the lowest, but no interpersonal comparisons are required here; similarly, the principle of efficiency requires that the life prospects of one class only be raised if the prospects of others are not lowered, but no comparisons between life prospects are called for. Thus, the view is neutral as regards disputes over cardinal utility functions.[80] The notion of standard classes is adopted for the same reasons of practicality as its adoption in the case of the second principle of justice.

The normative relation of the principle of efficiency to the principles of justice may be regarded as that of the indeterminate to the determinate.[81] Thus, as my earlier discussion of the Pareto optimality criterion indicated, it defines an infinite number of possible efficient points, and this holds whether the principle is applied to goods or to institutions. However, the two principles of justice yield a determinate conception of just institutions: they must satisfy the equal liberty and opportunity requirements, and inequalities must raise the life prospects of all classes, and maximize those of the least advantaged. Thus, the proper use of the principles of justice remedies the indeterminateness of the principle of efficiency—picking out that one of the infinite number of efficient institutions which satisfies the principles of justice, viz. that efficient institution which, *ceteris paribus*, maximizes the life prospects of the least advantaged class.

Finally, the principle of efficiency will be of sufficient importance to the contractors in securing the most efficient highest lowest that they will view forms of coercion as justified in enforcing it. But the forms of pressure viewed as justified will be rather different from those appropriate in the case of the principles of justice, especially the equal liberty requirements. For one thing, devising efficient institutions is very much a matter for detailed policy investigation by legislators, of the type that operations research and systems analysis has only begun to formalize.[82] Consider, in this connection, the complexities in developing an effective system of providing public goods, or of advancing competition through antitrust policy, where the principle of efficiency is importantly relevant. Thus, it is not possible simply to establish the requirements of efficiency in the basic constitution; rather, like the equal opportunity requirements and the second principle of justice, it is very much a principle which is to govern legislative decision in the light of particular circumstances. But further, unlike the second principle of justice and the equal opportunity requirements of the first, which may, in certain circumstances, override the equal liberty requirements, the principle of efficiency can never do this; nor is it plausible to suppose that the contractors would ever view war or revolution as justified in enforcing it. Always, the principle of efficiency is to be enforced by the exercise of pressure within the political system. This is so because the principle of efficiency is only accepted because it raises expectations from the original position, given that the maximin criterion is already satisfied through acceptance of the principles of justice; and the contractors would not agree to coercion which would endanger just institutions to attain efficiency.

9

THE PRINCIPLE OF FAIRNESS

HAVING agreed upon the ultimate standards which are to regulate their institutions, the rational contractors must then consider when it is that participants in such institutions are to obey their requirements. I shall first consider the general nature of the ultimate standard they will agree to, and then indicate how this principle can explain political obligation, and the obligations of fidelity, veracity, and certain cases of gratitude.

1. *The Principle of Fairness*

In considering what ultimate standards to agree to in regulating obedience to co-operative, mutually beneficial institutions, the rational contractors will be aware of certain relevant facts about the functioning of those institutions. Thus, the general benefits that these institutions supply are often of the sort that economists call public or collective goods, a notion recently defined by Mancur Olson in this way:

A common, collective, or public good is here defined as any good such that, if any person x_1 in a group $x_1 \ldots x_n$ consumes it, it cannot feasibly be withheld from the others in the group.[1]

The general consequence of this fact is that, in large co-operative schemes, it is often possible for persons to enjoy the benefits of consuming collective goods without sharing in any of the burdens involved in maintaining the institution in question. Hume has this fact in mind when he contrasts two persons agreeing to drain a meadow which they possess in common, and a thousand persons agreeing to participate in such a drainage operation, in so far as with the latter: 'each seeks a pretext to free himself of the trouble and expence and wou'd lay the whole burden on others.'[2] Hume's argument is that with such large co-operative schemes, people are prone not to bear any burdens, since they can get the benefits anyway; and this leads to a basic instability in such institutions, which must be remedied by a centralized government, which uses coercion to make people bear the burdens. The same view has been more recently suggested by W. J. Baumol, an economist who has extended the economic theory of public goods to political institutions by suggesting that government intervention with the threat of sanctions is justified in order to stabilize co-operative institutions which secure such public goods as investment in the future, the education of the population, military forces, the non-inflationary stability of prices, free trade between nations, and so on.[3] And Olson's book is concerned to extend this conception to the theory of groups, arguing, for example, that the explanation and justification for making membership of labour unions compulsory is that in this way unions are a stable form of association, since those who benefit from the organization's policies must bear the burdens of supporting it.[4]

The sort of institutional instability to which the phenomenon of collective goods leads was first noticed and discussed by Hobbes, a philosopher whose work has many analogies with the approach of the economists Baumol and Olson, since his theory works on the basis of egoistic assumptions alone. Thus, Hobbes's discussion of the state of nature, the 'time of war',[5] attempts to clarify the sort of situation that would arise where men, having only the desire for their own good, try to enter into co-operative schemes in order to reap the benefits of such co-operation. Such schemes are subject to two related sorts of instability. First, if they are sufficiently large, they will produce benefits to all persons irrespective of whether or not they have contributed to the support of the scheme. And thus, the Hobbesian rational egoist will not contribute to the scheme, or will only pretend to do so, since it is more in his interest if he can reap the benefits of such institutions without bearing any associated burdens. And second, if each beneficiary of the scheme knows that the other beneficiaries are strongly tempted not to contribute, or only pretend to, then he will wish to be the first, or among the first, who does not contribute, since he will gain more, and lose less, by being among the first.[6] Co-operative schemes will, for Hobbes, always break down, since people will have no security concerning others' obedience, if they obey, and no certainty that others will disobey, if they disobey. The only remedy to such situations, for Hobbes, is the creation of a person with absolute coercive power, whose power is publicly known and acknowledged, who commands obedience to such co-operative schemes. Thus, the stability of co-operative institutions is ensured, since persons will both have the security that others will obey, if they obey, and an overriding prudential reason always to obey, since the certain threat of the sovereign's coercion outweighs any probable benefits from disobedience. Thus, both sources of institutional instability are removed.

The relevance of these remarks about public goods and Hobbesian situations to the choice situation of the rational contractors is, I think, this: knowing that institutions often provide public goods and are subject to both the instabilities of the Hobbesian situation, given the pervasiveness and persistence of egoistic motives, one of the chief concerns of the contractors will be to agree to an ultimate standard which, when accepted and acted on, will best stabilize such institutions. Thus, the contractors may be regarded as applying the economic theory of public goods to the choice of a principle of institutional obedience.

The contractors will, however, only be concerned with the stability of certain sorts of co-operative institutions, namely, those which satisfy at least the principle of equal liberty mentioned in the previous chapter, since such institutions secure a highest lowest. At least in the circumstances of a developed nation, the contractors will not make the equal opportunity requirement and the second principle of justice also conditions of obedience, let alone the efficiency principle, because the issues which these principles involve are so complicated, allowing so much room for disagreement over questions of interpretation and fact, that making them conditions of obedience would lead to too much instability in co-operative institutions, and would result in institutions which, in fact, less fully satisfied the principles of justice than otherwise. Rather, given that the equal opportunity requirement and the second principle of justice are the publicly known and generally acted on standards regulating matters of social and economic justice, the contractors will view them as best realized where they are appealed to as justifying policy and statutory changes, including pressure on legislators through the vote, within a legal system which allows persons the equal liberties of thought, speech, association, political and civic rights, and the like.

It may be supposed that the contractors would simply agree that the principle of equal liberty should be the sole condition which an institution must satisfy if its requirements are to be obeyed. But this would not be so, for the contractors will wish to allow persons the liberty of not obeying institutions whose benefits have not been voluntarily accepted. One good reason for this is that the contractors know that the requirements of institutions may be extremely onerous, including the requirement to expose oneself to the likelihood of death in defending one's institutions from aggressors. The contractors will, therefore, wish to make sure that people have in some way voluntarily accepted the risk of being subjected to such requirements before they are *bound* to obey such requirements; for, in this way, they will ensure the higher lowest of people's being bound to perform onerous duties only when they have also voluntarily accepted corresponding benefits. Also, since the contractors do not know their own particular desires, nature, and circumstances, they will further be concerned to guard against the possibility that they may have an anarchistic temperament (e.g. Thoreau's), which just happens to be born into or find itself in a certain institution, from which benefits are not voluntarily accepted. And thus, while the contractors wish to ensure that just institutions are stable, they will not wish to do so at the cost of forcing people to obey institutions from which they never voluntarily accepted any benefits. Rather, the higher lowest will be achieved by making both the principle of equal liberty a condition of institutional obedience, and also some proviso about voluntarily accepting the benefits of the institution in question.

Given these considerations, the rational contractors would accept the following principle of fairness regulating the institutional obedience of individuals:

4. Given that an existent institution makes its beneficiaries better off than they would be with no such institution, and also satisfies the equal liberty requirements of principle 1, then persons who voluntarily accept the benefits of such co-operative institutions, and depend on others to do their part when it comes their turn to bear the burdens involved in sustaining the institution, are themselves to bear such burdens, when it comes their turn.

I call this the principle of fairness after C. D. Broad, who clearly saw the relevance of the theory of public goods to the question of institutional obedience, and went beyond the usual philosophical and economic treatments of the problem (which relate it to the appropriateness of coercion) by considering the relevance of some 'argument from fairness' here.[7] The only distinguishing feature of my formulation of the principle is that I explicitly incorporate conditions of justice into it, and also do not explain the principle by an intuition of intrinsic value: 'when the group of producers, and that of enjoyers is as nearly identical as possible'.[8] But even these features are not really distinctive, since Hart's similar principle of 'mutuality of restrictions' is not intuitionistic, and Rawls's similar 'duty of fair play' also explicitly incorporates the conditions of justice.[9]

11. *Political Obligation*

The discussion of the moral obligation to obey the law, or what I shall call political obligation, will be divided into the following parts: a development of my conception of the principle involved here through a discussion of Locke's account of political obligation, a view as old as the *Crito*, and which remains, I think, substantially correct;[10] the formulation of a principle of natural justice to supplement the force of the principle of fairness; an elaboration of the form the conditions of justice take when the principle of fairness is applied to legal institutions, and some interesting consequences of this; and a discussion of the special class of laws to which the principle of fairness applies, and of the sense in which the principle of fairness is one of obligation.

(a) *Locke on Political Obligation*

Locke's social contract view, more especially his tacit consent notion, has not, I think, received a sympathetic or careful reading at the hands of recent commentators. C. B. MacPherson, for example, has claimed to find in it 'a moral foundation of bourgeois appropriation' whereby only capitalists with fixed goods are citizens with the right to revolt.[11] John Plamenatz, on the other hand, takes the more philosophical line that one can explain the right to revolt without the concept of consent, and thus the latter notion is 'Logically, an unnecessary addition, but, at the time it was made, a persuasive one; and all the more persuasive for being sincere.'[12] And Alan Gewirth has pictured all such social contract views as caught between 'the anarchic and unrealistic consequences',[13] i.e. the notion that government would be unstable if obligation ceased when consent ceased, and that such a view is hopelessly unrealistic, since such consent is not and has not been true, in any sense, of any actual society. Such critiques, it seems to me, have considerably less force if the text, more explicitly Locke's notion of tacit consent, is sympathetically interpreted.

What such views uniformly fail to take into account of in Locke are passages which imply a concept of *hypothetical* consent as *one* of the conditions for moral obligations to arise, e.g.

For though Men when they enter Society, give up the Equality, Liberty, and Executive Power they had in the State of Nature . . . yet it being only with an intention in every one the better to preserve himself his Liberty and Property; (For no rational Creature can be supposed to change his condition with intention to the worse) the power of the society, or Legislative constituted by them, can never be suppos'd to extend further than the common good.[14]

Similarly in section 135, he speaks of the basic moral limits on the power of the government to be 'Arbitrary over the Lives and Fortunes of the People'.[15] What such passages imply is that it is a necessary condition for a moral obligation of obeying the law to arise that the institutions of the society be just, where the criterion of justice is the hypothetical test that rational men from a position of equal liberty (each is equally uncoerced and equal in the sense of his capacity to understand and act on the law of nature)[16] *could* contract into that society, each being made better off and none worse off than in the state of nature, and without the law of nature (requiring each man to preserve himself, as God's 'Property') being transgressed.[17] While Locke accepts and argues for a historical contract,[18] in an established state the notion of the contract is preserved as a hypothetical notion *intended* (whatever its inadequacies) to be a criterion of the justice of those institutions. Moreover, it is quite clear that when Locke refers to men's equality in rationality he is not speaking, *pace* MacPherson, of a class-dependent attribute, but of 'A capacity of knowing that (the moral) Law' which he supposes only 'Lunaticks and Ideots' and 'Children' to lack.[19] In short, for Locke, 'The state exists not for a class but for all who are willing and able to use it on equitable terms.'[20]

However, such a criterion is not, for Locke, sufficient for a moral obligation to exist. In addition, one must have had some 'Possession, or Enjoyment, of any Government', such that one takes advantage of the benefits of its laws, highways, or what have you, whereby a man gives 'his tacit Consent' to the government.[21] Thus, one may delineate Locke's view of political obligation, at least in his tacit consent notion, as consisting in two conditions, together sufficient and both necessary, for political obligation to arise: (1) the legal system and institutions it supports must be just by the criterion of hypothetical consent and (2) one must have, in some sense, tacitly consented to the legal system.

Locke's account is, it seems to me, basically correct in the sense that the intuitive notion behind the view is an application of the principle of fairness to legal institutions. However, as stated above, it is subject to several objections, and would have to be accordingly revised. Thus, one may point out the incompleteness of Locke's criterion of justice, analogous to the similar defects in Hume's conception. For if one takes the original position of equal liberty and rationality as being some primitive state of a cultural and economic minimum, as Locke seems to, then people could conceivably contract into economic and social arrangements, and thus make themselves better off, and not transgress the natural law of self-preservation without those institutions being just in any strong substantive sense. Thus, if Locke points out:

The Americans . . ., who are rich in Land and poor in all the Comforts in Life; whom Nature having furnished as liberally as any other people, with the materials of Plenty, i.e., fruitful Soil . . .; yet for want of improving it by labour, have not one hundredth part of the Conveniences we enjoy; And a King of a large and fruitful Territory there feeds, lodges, and is clad worse than a day Labourer in England.[22]

one may respond that such a fact is irrelevant to the justice of English institutions in defining the rights and liberties of the 'day Labourer'. For the latter may be better off relative to his expectations in the state of nature and well preserved, yet he may be the victim of economic exploitation, lack the opportunities for social and economic mobility, indeed, lack even the political rights of voting for and participating in government (for no one has supposed that Locke accepted universal adult suffrage).[23] What is required to remedy the deficiencies in Locke's concept of justice is not a rejection of the hypothetical contractual criterion, but a strengthening of the criterion by introducing much stronger constraints on the nature of the contractual choice. Indeed, it is plausible to view Rousseau as generalizing Locke's concept, as *a* condition for political obligation, into a strong general criterion of political right and Kant as deepening Rousseau's notion into a criterion for the principles of moral right generally.[24] In any event, the ideal contract view delineated in the previous chapters has already, I think, indicated the proper way to revise Locke's account of justice.

But further, there are classic difficulties, pointed out by Gewirth and Hume, in Locke's notion of tacit (as opposed to express) consent.[25] To judge by the way Locke speaks of tacit consent, one would be tacitly consenting to a legal system by 'the very being of any one within the Territories of that Government',[26] which seems absurd. In order to make this notion more plausible, one must, I think, use the concept of *voluntary* acceptance of the benefits of a legal system, where there is some mature option of choice exercised—the acceptance occurring with the intention and expectation of encouraging others to rely on you to do your part in bearing the burdens, so that they will be encouraged to do their part.

As against even this reformulation, it may be urged, with Hume, that being the subject of a legal system is, often, no more voluntary than remaining in a vessel in mid-sea;[27] what is, then, the exact sense of voluntary acceptance of benefits that the principle of fairness here involves? For one thing, it means that no young child or even young adult who is not financially independent, and thus capable of choosing his own life, is bound to his native country by the principle of fairness, for he has no real mature option of choice between accepting and not accepting the benefits of the legal system. Such a person is *morally* at liberty to choose whatever country he pleases. However, it seems natural to question whether a person ever has a real option of choosing his country, given, for example, the expenses of travel abroad and the restrictions nations may place on new citizens. However, to the extent that there is increasing rapidity of travel and communications between nations, growing availability of travel to more income classes, and the reduction of immigrant restrictions between nations, Hume's stranded vessel begins to seem less plausible as an analogy to a citizen's relation to his legal system. The possibility of real choice widens, and with it the applicability of the principle of fairness. Indeed, from the moral point of view, one can postulate the desirability of setting up a national institution, whereby each person, at twenty-one, say, could choose whether to stay or go, after a full assessment of the relevant facts, and be assured enough money to cover his choice, if he chose to go. This would imply the unambiguous applicability of the principle of fairness to legal institutions.

But even apart from these considerations, and assuming Hume was correct in claiming that the voluntary choice of one's legal system was an absurd conception, there would still be room for the applicability of the principle of fairness to legal systems. Thus, adult mature persons, who live in a legal system, though they may not have any real choice to accept or reject the system, do have an option to accept more or less of the benefits of the system, or wholly to accept or reject them (e.g. the use of public schools for one's children—at least public schools, U.S. style; or the use of government-financed health services). Thus, the principle of fairness will be taken to apply if such persons have voluntarily accepted benefits, where they could have accepted none at all, or where they accept more, rather than less, of the benefits, given there is no real choice of accepting or rejecting the less (e.g. the use of public roads and bridges).

We see, then, that this view of political obligation is not open to common critiques levelled against it. In so far as its criterion of justice is a hypothetical notion, 'an idea of reason', in Kant's phrase,[28] it is not rebutted by historical arguments. In so far as the notion of tacit consent may be revised to suggest more clearly aspects of voluntary human action, it is not open to the critiques of artificiality and unrealism. In so far as the view has a philosophical plausibility as a principle of morality, given its acceptance in the original position as outlined in the previous section, Plamenatz's notion of its historical persuasiveness, but conceptual inadequacy, is unjustified. The one critique that may seem to have some force is the notion that this view may have anarchic implications; for on this view, if we make the assumption of the justice of the legal system, people have a moral obligation to obey the law to the degree that it makes sense to say of them that they accepted the benefits of the system voluntarily (with some option of choice), so that it is reasonable to suppose that they expect others to do their part, etc. The natural objection to this condition is that, as interpreted here, it makes the moral basis of obeying the law more fragile than we suppose it, in fact, to be. However, from the point of view of the original position, the requirement of voluntary acceptance will be regarded as a necessary condition of political

obligation, since it represents the most rational way for the contractors to reconcile their desire for the stability of just institutions
and for the liberty of people from the often onerous requirements
of such just institutions, when people do not rationally wish such
a system and consistently avoid accepting its benefits, if possible.

(b) The Principle of Natural Justice

I grant, however, that the formulation of the principle of fairness
does not fully express our considered common sense judgements
regarding the strength of our moral requirement to obey the law
of a just legal system. However, the way to answer this valid
objection is not, I think, to revise the formulation of the principle
of fairness. Instead, an adequate answer is given when it is noted
that the rational contractors of the original position will not regard
the principle of fairness as the only principle which is to regulate
obedience to institutions. Rather, the contractors will agree to a
supplementary principle, formulated in this way:

4a. Persons are to advance and promote the existence of institutions
which satisfy the principles of justice (principles 1 and 2), given
that this involves little cost to such persons.

The contractors obviously will agree to this principle because, if
publicly known and generally acted on, the principle will produce a
higher lowest by securing the existence of institutions satisfying
principles which themselves secure a higher lowest. The requirement of 'little cost' is necessary to ensure that action on the principle
will not require such sacrifices that the maximining contractors
would not agree to it. A consequence of this requirement is that
people are not required, on grounds of natural justice, to make
those sacrifices of their interests which they might be required
to make on the ground of the principle of fairness, if it applied.
Since the principle of natural justice is so important to securing
basic life prospects of desire satisfaction, the contractors would
view coercion as justified in enforcing it. Note, however, that the
principle would not be a principle of institutional obligation, but
rather a principle of non-institutional natural duty. For, by its own
terms, the principle applies not only to a participant in an institution (requiring him to advance the justice of its rules and policies,
including obedience to just rules and policies), but also to people

in an institutional state of nature who are to advance the existence of just institutions. Thus, this principle of natural justice gives expression to Kant's idea of a duty to enter into civil society from a state of nature.[29]

(c) Justice as a Condition of Political Obligation

The form that the conditions of justice take, in the application of the principle of fairness to legal institutions, was already indicated in section I; here I shall expand that discussion, and then show two quite interesting consequences of this view: (i) indicating why Wollheim's 'paradox of Democracy'[30] is no paradox, but a consequence of the particular form that the conditions of justice take in the application of the principle of fairness here, and (ii) showing how the phenomenon of civil disobedience to a legal system can be viewed as morally justified by the application of the principle of fairness.

In section I, I argued that the rational contractors would make a distinction between the principles which they wish their actual institutions to satisfy and the principle of institutional obedience which they think most likely to secure such institutions.[31] For reasons presented there, the contractors will only make the equal liberty requirements of the first principle of justice a condition of institutional obedience, though, of course, they wish their institutions to satisfy all aspects of both principles of justice. At this point, in the context of a discussion of legal institutions, it seems important to clarify a point left unclear in the previous discussion, viz. whether the equal liberty requirements between nations are a condition of political obligation. A plausible argument might be made that the contractors would never make the requirements of equal liberty between nations into part of the conditions of justice for political obligation, since this would bring the certain instability of internally just institutions with an uncertain result of securing justice between institutions—a situation not likely to produce justice on balance (e.g. the collapse of internally just institutions through widespread failure to pay taxes, because of the widespread view of the injustice of certain foreign military adventures). It seems to me that this view is correct, *except* in the case of a citizen of a nation who is himself required to kill in pursuance of a foreign policy that he conscientiously, and for good reason, believes to be unjust. In such a case, where the prospect of actual killing is involved, it seems to me that the contractors would make equal liberty between nations a condition of such a person's obligation to obey the legal requirement to kill. This will be so because the contractors will secure a higher lowest by *some* kind of balancing between their desire for the stability of internally just institutions and for the realization of justice between institutions; and a rational way to do this is to allow military service when it is part of the necessary defence of one's nation's equal liberties, but to proscribe killing, as part of that military service, when it is required as part of an unjust war policy. In this way, when a foreign war policy is unjust, the internally just institutions will remain stable (since the injustice of a foreign war does not absolve citizens from their political obligations to pay taxes, etc.), while the specifically unjust war policy will be unstable (since those who are the instruments of the policy are not required to obey). With the exception of this case, however, equal liberty between nations will not be a condition of political obligation, but rather part of the principles of public political morality which citizens are to press on the government through the political process, and which other nations may press on the government, through various forms of coercion, including, if necessary, war between nations.

The fact that the conditions of justice, incorporated into the principle of fairness applied to legal institutions, will generally be limited to the equal liberty requirements applying within the institution has two interesting, and illuminating, consequences.

(i) First, this view explains why Wollheim's so-called paradox of democracy is no paradox at all, but a direct consequence of the application of the principle of fairness to a constitutional democracy. Wollheim claims that a citizen of a constitutional democracy who conscientiously votes for a measure 'q' (which leads to state Q), knowing it to be the morally right measure, and yet who also conscientiously accepts measure 'p' (which leads to state P), which he knows to be wrong but which the majority have approved over measure 'q', is committed to a paradoxical view. This citizen holds, very roughly, that situation Q ought to obtain, and yet also, that situation P ought to obtain, whose existence he knows to be incompatible with the existence of state Q. And how can this be? The answer to this must be seen in the light of the two-fold sense in which justice is relevant to a constitutional democracy. First, there is the justice of the basic constitution which effectively secures the various equal liberties to all adult mature persons in the system. When this is the case, and a person in the system has voluntarily accepted the benefits of it, then the principle of fairness applies, and a person is to do what the legal requirements stipulate, i.e. his legal duties and obligations are now also morally required. But secondly, though this is the case, it is still possible, and perhaps likely, that certain laws enacted, and policies pursued, by the democratically elected legislators and executives are unjust, in terms, e.g. of contravening the equal opportunity principle or the second principle of justice, or the equal liberty requirement between nations. There is nothing in the conception or functioning of a just constitution which can eliminate this possibility. And thus, it is possible for a person to be under a moral obligation to obey the requirements of a certain law, or set of policies, which he knows to be unjust; but which he also conscientiously accepts as binding on himself and others (including the executants of the law or policy) because the principle of fairness applies. In such a case, there is no contradiction in a person's believing both that law or policy 'p' should be put into effect to bring about P (because this is the just law or policy) and that law or policy 'q' should be executed to bring about Q (because the principle of fairness requires this), where states P and Q are known to be incompatible. Thus, Wollheim's paradox is dissolved by seeing the different ways in which justice is relevant to a constitutional democracy.[32]

(ii) The second consequence of this view (concerning conditions of justice on political obligation) is an explanation of and justification for the morality of civil disobedience in a democratic society, when that disobedience is a desperate conscientious appeal to the sense of justice of the community to bring into effect the full requirements of the equal liberty principle. Thus, the equal liberty principle requires that various equal liberties be secured to adult mature persons in the system, among which are the political rights to vote and to participate in the political process and the civic rights to equal protection of life and property by appeal to and redress from the legal system. When these rights are not effectively enforced in the case of a certain class of persons, though the general constitution may require all adult persons to have them, then the very foundation of the obligation to obey the law is undermined. In such circumstances the rational contractors would agree that, were all available appeals to the political process exhausted, the principle of fairness would itself justify certain sorts of disobedience to law, were these public, non-violent, conscientious acts directed at arousing the sense of justice of the community, and were the consequences of the delict (legal fines and imprisonment) voluntarily accepted. Such forms of disobedience would be accepted because they represent an attempt to make the system fully satisfy the basic conditions of justice, on which political obligation depends, and because they are compatible with the stability of the at least partially just institutions that exist, since the acts are non-violent, and voluntary acceptance of punishment evidences general respect for the legal system and the other equal liberties that it does effectively secure. The fact that forms of civil disobedience will be justified within such partially just constitutional democracies, where full revolution would not be, may be contrasted with a system where institutions systematically violate the principle of equal liberty, and no question of adequate enforcement of the equal rights enters in, e.g. institutions with policies of systematic racial genocide and segregation. Here, the principle of fairness would not apply at all, and thus persons would be under no moral obligation to fulfil legal duties like paying taxes and serving in the military. Whether revolution would be justified would depend, as indicated previously, on many other factors— whether it would accomplish its end without pointless suffering, whether in the process it would not harm innocent parties, etc., the sorts of considerations, in fact, that Locke introduces as justifying revolution when persons are freed from their political obligations.[33]

Finally, the emphasis here on the equal liberty requirements as a condition of political obligation should not be construed as applying to the sort of underdeveloped country discussed briefly in the previous chapter. If it were the case that certain deprivations of political rights were necessary to enable a government to keep great masses of its people from starvation, the contractors would not agree that these equal liberties were necessary for political obligation in such cases, since a higher lowest would be secured by a government concerned with matters of economic and social, rather than political, justice. However, once such extraordinary circumstances were surmounted, the requirements of equal liberty would be a necessary condition of political obligation.

(d) Does the Principle of Fairness Apply to the Whole Legal System?

In my consideration, so far, of the applicability of the principle of fairness to a legal system, my view suggested that, once a person's relation to this legal system satisfies the principle of fairness, this person is morally required to perform all his legal duties without distinction. But this has been, at best, a convenient way of speaking; and it is, I think, now necessary to make certain sorts of distinctions between various types of laws to which different moral principles are especially relevant. Thus, if one recalls the exact formulation of the principle of fairness, note that the burdens to which the principle refers are those related to supporting and sustaining the institutions; and in the case of a legal system, while, in a sense, this may be taken to apply to general obedience to most legal duties (since, without such obedience, the legal system will, at a certain point, break down), it most clearly applies to legal duties like paying one's taxes or serving in the military, since the execution of such duties is most clearly related to sustaining the ongoing operation and stability of the legal system. Indeed, the moral propriety of obedience to many sorts of laws is not most profitably understood in terms of political obligation; for, many sorts of laws, e.g. against murder, wilfully causing pain or injury, engaging in fraud in selling products, not keeping contracts, etc., represent acts which we have moral duties and obligations not to do, quite apart from our moral obligation to obey the law (on this, see the rest of this chapter, and the next); whereas in the case of the legal duties to pay taxes or serve in the military, the moral requirements do seem explicable solely in terms of our moral obligation to obey the law, as defined by the principle of fairness.

This qualification to the sense in which the principle of fairness applies to the whole legal system may be further developed by considering the case of legal duties which are not related to the support of the legal system, but which are also not required by *any* of the moral principles agreed to by the rational contractors. Consider, for example, the laws found in several American states which forbid all premarital sexual relations, or the recently repealed English law against homosexual relations between consenting adults. Is one to say that such legal duties are morally binding because of the principle of fairness? Here I wish to say, No. The principle of fairness applies most clearly to legal duties like paying taxes which support the functioning of the legal system, and also further requires the *general* obedience to most other laws, which ensures the stability of the system; but, in most advanced nations, such legal duties can be construed to include those clearly related to the principle of fairness as well as those forbidden by other moral principles. Obedience to such laws as the above, not being required for the support of the system, and not being morally required for any other reason, will not be morally required at all. Indeed, it is interesting that some of those who have supported such laws, e.g. Lord Devlin,[34] have appealed to the importance of such laws for the stability of the whole civilized legal system. While such arguments seem at best misguided,[35] they do illustrate the *kind of* argument that would have to be given to show that disobeying such laws was contrary to our moral obligation to obey the law.

(e) The Principle of Fairness as a Principle of Obligation

The sense in which the principle of fairness is here a principle of obligation can be explained by reference to the conception outlined in chapter 7. First, since this principle is one of great importance to the rational contractors in securing the stability of just institutions, it will be viewed by the contractors as justifiably enforced by coercion, here by the legal system itself; thus, it is a moral principle of obligation and duty. More specifically, it is one of obligation, since it defines what is owed to specific other people in virtue of having voluntarily taken up a position of accepting the benefits of a social practice, where one expects others to do their part, and they have reason to expect you to do your part. Thus, the specific vice of breaking the law (given the assumption of a just legal system), for example, failing to pay one's taxes or avoiding the draft for selfish reasons, is that of freeloading on the sense of fairness of those who accept the burdens as well as the benefits of the legal system, and in whom one's actions have created certain expectations which are now violated. It is *they* who may be justifiably indignant at the tax or draft dodger (not all men, *qua* men).

III. The Obligation to Keep Promises: Fidelity

The plausibility of viewing the principle of fairness as explaining the moral obligation to keep promises necessarily depends on the plausibility with which promising can be viewed as an institutional practice. Thus, my discussion of the moral obligation to keep promises, or what I shall call fidelity, will first delineate promising as an institutional practice; then, the applicability of the principle of fairness to it will be discussed; and finally, the special sense in which the principle, as here applied, is one of obligation.

(a) Promising as an Institutional Practice

The view of promising as a conventional practice is at least as old as Hume, and has more recently been discussed in some detail by Rawls and Searle.[36] Searle, for example, tried to show how, from suitable factual descriptions of the practice of promising itself, one could, without introducing moral premises, arrive at a moral 'ought'.[37] Clearly, the philosophical rediscovery and re-awakened interest in promising, as a practice, has been importantly influenced by J. L. Austin's theory of the conventional nature of illocutionary acts, a view previously briefly sketched by Prichard.[38] However, this general view of promising has been criticized by some, e.g. David Lyons,[39] because it supposedly fails to note that the enabling and requiring rules that promising involves are so different from the sorts of rules involved in other social practices, like a legal system, that a conceptual assimilation is unjustified. What is true and false in all this?

To say that promising is a social institution, as suggested in chapter 2, is to say that its existence depends on the existence of certain generally accepted critical attitudes concerning the use, in certain contexts, of expressions like 'I promise', 'I will', etc., and their equivalents in other languages, as is shown by certain ways of acting, viewing demands and criticisms of oneself and others as justified, etc. A formulation of the content of these critical attitudes, at least in the Anglo-American community, might be briefly and inadequately expressed as follows:

If two persons (A and B) are *roughly* in a position of equal liberty and undeceived knowledge, which is preserved throughout their trans-action (such that one is not a slave of the other, or becoming a slave of the other; or one is not coercing the other, or intentionally leading the other to believing certain falsities on the basis of which the promise is given), then if person A (the promisor) seriously uses 'I promise to do *x*' or its known equivalent in the language, addressing it to B (the promisee), who hears and understands the words in their known use, and the seriousness with which they are said, then A is to do x, and coercion and pressure are justified in forcing him to do x, unless:

1. B releases A from doing x.
2. A *knows* B would release him from doing x, but B is not available to do this (thus, typically when it turns out that keeping the promise would be disastrous to the promisee).
3. Doing x is itself immoral (killing, stealing, etc.), violating prior moral principles.
4. The situation has so materially changed that the *understood* circumstances in which the promise was to be kept are no longer present.
5. Keeping the promise is disastrous to the promisor, resulting, say, in death or serious bodily harm.
6. etc.

This formulation, in large part suggested by Sidgwick's account,[40] gives some idea of the complexity that the institution of promising involves. But it seems, *contra* Lyons, no objection to promising's being a social institution that it have such complexity and that its conditions of defeasibility be so general and open-ended. To think otherwise is to suppose that the concept of a social rule or institution must imply the clarity of application of a legal rule, e.g. against murder; but what is the reason for supposing this to be true?

However, one should not be unfair to Lyons, for what, really, he is criticizing in his attack on the practice conception of promising is not, I think, the practice conception itself, but the misuse of that conception in suggesting that it will yield, or is equivalent to, the concept of morality. And no one has *more* misused this conception, I think, than Searle. Searle's view seems mistaken in two different, but related, ways. First, he seems to have misdescribed the institution of promising, if he supposes that no moral, or morally related, notions enter into the factual description of the institution; consider, for example, the equal liberty requirements on the promisor and promisee. But further, Searle's general view of the relation of such institutions to morality seems basically misconceived. What Searle's construction will at best yield, as long as it works on the basis of social institutions alone, are *social* obligations, social rules of a type that at least the authorities in the institution generally view coercion justified in enforcing. However, what such authorities may view as justified hardly concludes the question of what is morally justified; for quite morally evil institutions may exist which its authorities view as so justified that coercion may be used in enforcing obedience; and yet, there may be no moral obligation at all to obey the rules and policies of such an institution. The question is: what is required in order for social obligations to be moral obligations?

(b) *The Principle of Fairness and Fidelity*

Prichard, in his remarkable paper, 'The Obligation to Keep a Promise', raises the following difficulty about this topic—in making a promise, in the appropriate circumstances, we seem to create the moral obligation to keep a promise, yet a moral obligation is not something that it is (logically) possible directly to create. And Prichard therefore concludes that in making a promise we create something else which directly gives rise to the moral obligation. But after rejecting several possible candidates for this something else, he is left with the unsatisfying and paradoxical result that it is something 'which looks very much like an agreement, and yet, strictly speaking, cannot be an agreement', and says, almost desperately, 'we must admit the reality of any thought which we must have, if we are to have, as we do have, this thought'.[41] Prichard's view here is pitched at a level of philosophical honesty that is, it seems to me, quite uncommon—the willingness to admit that the careful examination of a certain conceptual phenomenon compels one to delineate an idea which one cannot wholly explain, and which one is content to leave as a topic for further investigation without claiming final insight. And I should like to develop here Prichard's insight by relating it to the ideal contract view delineated above, and by showing how the sense of paradox can be removed by a clear understanding of the relation of that view to the practice of promising through the principle of fairness.

In section I, I argued that the contractors would agree to the principle of fairness as the principle of institutional obedience. The ideal contract conception does not strictly imply a promise or contract in the usual sense, for there is no conceptual necessity for the contractors to employ the concepts or language associated with the institutions of promising, and contract (a sub-case of promising). Rather, it suffices that the contractors unanimously approve a certain principle, as an ultimate standard from the position of equal liberty. Thus, one can give a sense to Prichard's notion of something which is not strictly a promise, or agreement to do something, and which gives rise to the moral obligation to keep promises: the contractors' acceptance of the principle of fairness, applying to promising.

The general idea here is quite simple. The institutional practice of promising, cursorily delineated above, is one which satisfies the principle of fairness. It is an institution which fulfils the circumstances of justice in making everyone better off than they would be without the institution, and it also satisfies the principle of equal liberty, since it is a requirement of the practice that the promisor and promisee be in a relation of equal liberty which the promise itself must not violate. The general advantages of having an institution like promising have been well known from Hume to Prichard:[42] it enables us to give others a security of expectation about our future actions, and thus a more rational basis of planning, which we could not give by using only expressions of intention or resolve, or predictions of future behaviour, for we may change our minds or be incorrect about our future behaviour in ways which the practice of promising does not allow.[43] Indeed, much of economic life, where co-operative interdependence secures such great advantages, depends on the security of expectations that the institution of contract, based on the institution of promising, brings to economic units in their planning; and, of course, there is the marriage contract, the observance of which brings security in the area of personal intimacy. In addition, the practice of promising allows for the voluntary acceptance of its benefits. Thus, persons voluntarily accept those benefits, when they are promisees who benefit from promisors' keeping their promises to them, where such acceptance of the benefits is typically taken as evidence of readiness to bear the burdens themselves when their turn comes. And a person could abstain from the institution altogether by not accepting promises when they are offered to him, or immediately releasing the promisor from them, and never making promises to others. Thus, the principle of fairness clearly applies to the institution of promising, requiring that, given the existence of such a mutually beneficial and just institution, persons who accept the benefits of the practice (being promisees to whom promises are kept) are themselves to bear the burdens involved in sustaining the institution (keeping their promises) when their turn comes.

(c) Fidelity as an Obligation

Finally, the sense in which the principle of fairness here is a principle of obligation, in my technical sense, should be clear. Because of the importance of the principle in securing the stability of a mutually beneficial, just institution like promising, the contractors will view coercion as justified in enforcing it, whenever feasible. And the principle will apply within the special institutional relations into which men enter by virtue of accepting the benefits of the practice of promising, not in virtue of their being men, apart from any institutional relation.

To say that the rational contractors will view coercion as justified in enforcing the obligation to keep promises is, of course, only true if such coercion will be effective; and, as I indicated in the previous chapter, the appropriateness of such coercion will be changed once a centralized legal system exists which can further stabilize the practice of promising by its coercive mechanism. Thus, a legal system will clearly not be able effectively to enforce all informally given promises, since the difficulties of proof will be considerable and the immensity of possible cases may undermine the effective functioning of the legal system. Rather, the best that might be possible is that the law enforce certain forms of promise which involve both formal documents (the forms of which are defined by law) and substantial exchange bargains, with some special provision for informal exchange bargains where one of the parties has substantially relied on the bargain so that it would be a gross injustice not to enforce it. Here, of course, I have specially in mind that part of the civil law known as the law of contract, as well as that part of family law known as marriage contracts. Two sorts of coercion seem especially apt in enforcing such contracts— those which force the promisor to do what he promises or else pay compulsory damages to the promisee, and those which impose general sanctions, e.g. imprisonment, on such wrongdoing or the failure to compensate therefor. What specific measure of damages, or what specific kind of imprisonment, or what combination of these sanctions, might here be appropriate would not be decided from the original position; such a question is rather to be decided by legislators in terms of specific facts concerning ease and economy of administration, and how most effectively to enforce promises.

However, given that a legal system exists and supports and

stabilizes at least the most socially important class of promises, the contractors will not view individual persons as justified at all in using coercion to enforce informal promises. Individual coercive enforcement of informal promises, not enforceable by law (because of effectiveness problems), would result in too much injustice, because of the distortions of self-interest when judging and enforcing in one's own case. However, informal demands and pressures may be justifiably exercised in enforcing informal promises.

IV. *The Obligation to Tell the Truth: Veracity*

Moral philosophers, even of the stature of Price and Kant, commonly assimilated promising to a sub-case of truth-telling, thus supposing that promising is simply telling the truth about one's intention to do what one is promising to do.[44] Hume, of course, struggled to an alternative view, as did Sidgwick;[45] but a clear recognition of the non-propositional character of promising, as opposed to truth-telling, had to wait for Prichard and Austin.[46] On this now conventional view in analytic philosophy, promising is correctly analysed not as an assertion about anything, but as a kind of 'function'[47]—an act, performed by speech, which typically has the known intention of placing oneself under an obligation to another person to do what one has promised to do. And the possibility of this depends on the existence of the social institution of promising, which provides that the use of certain words, in the appropriate context, is to be followed by doing what one said one would do. Telling the truth, on the other hand, while it also is an act of doing something (saying what one believes to be true), none the less requires, as part of its analysis, some mention of the proposition which a person is asserting, and which he intends, and is known to intend, to communicate to another. One of the ways in which the difference between such acts may be brought out is by noting that, whereas there is a conventional form of words by which the act of promising may unequivocally be done (the explicit performative, 'I promise'), there is no similar form of words with truth-telling (except in special cases—e.g. on income tax forms, 'I hereby declare that . . .'); and thus, the need for philosophers to formalize the act of truth-telling with the technical terminology of assertion signs. While these differences between promising and truth-telling are important, it seems to me that the traditional philosophical failure clearly to distinguish them was perhaps built on an important truth, namely, that the moral obligation, which both involve, arises from basically the same situation and principle.[48]

The sense in which truth-telling is an institution is clearly not closely analogous, say, to legal or social institutions; for one thing, the activities regulated in these cases are quite different (saying what one believes to be true as opposed to acts of not killing, stealing, breaking contracts, etc.). However, there is an important sense in which it is typically held that a person says what he believes; and philosophers have correctly recognized that the relation between assertion and belief is not a logical one, but something having to do with the presuppositions of ordinary language and thought, or with 'conventions of truthfulness'.[49] Another way of making the same point, I think, is to characterize the typical relation between what we say and what we believe as regulated by a social practice or institution—in the sense that it is a matter of people's typically actually saying what they believe to be true, and regarding this as justified, and criticizing themselves and others if they fail to do so, the sort of critical attitude toward the use of language which is outraged, but not logically, by 'the cat is on the mat; but I don't believe it'.

Such an institution or practice of truth-telling clearly satisfies the conditions of applicability of the principle of fairness. First, it is a social practice which is of immense benefit to men, the general existence of which makes all men better off than they would be without it. It enables each man to take advantage of the knowledge and insight of other men in order to make his own beliefs and plans of action more rational, as well as to correct and render impartial his views in the light of the criticisms of others. A society where truth-telling was not the general practice would be bereft of the benefits of collective knowledge and wisdom, not the least example of which is empirical science. It would be, pragmatically speaking, a society of solipsists, and one in which communication would become impossible, because pointless. It would be more plausibly called 'a collection of people', rather than 'a society', for the fundamental basis for social interdependence and economic co-operation would be absent; men could not, for example, have any assurance that goods purchased or companies invested in had the properties they were alleged to have; and the reliability of people's words would be so dubious as to make difficult the authentic disclosure of self that underlies the growth of friendship and love, let alone the sense of social community. Secondly, the practice of truth-telling satisfies the principle of equal liberty, since the practice does not seem to require truth-telling in a situation that would contravene equal liberty (e.g. the Gestapo asking whether you saw some Jews run by, which you did). Finally, there is a sense in which persons voluntarily accept the benefits of the practice of truth-telling, when others tell the truth to them, where such acceptance of benefits is typically taken to evidence readiness to bear the burdens (telling the truth when it conflicts with self-interest) when it comes their turn; and a person *could* abstain from the institution altogether by making clear to others that he did not expect the truth to be told to him, and would not tell the truth himself.

Of course, it is a consequence of this view, following Sidgwick's,[50] that where one is to tell the truth is determined by the social practice in question, apart from those cases to which prior moral principles have relevance (e.g. equal liberty). This will make the practice of truth-telling heir to all the open-texture that we found earlier in the practice of promising, in so far as the social practice may, for many cases, not be determinate, and thus require the exercise of judgement. But there are many cases to which the practice clearly applies, and others to which it does not. As regards the latter category, consider highly conventional expressions like 'it is a great pleasure to meet you', 'I enjoyed your party so much; thank you so much for inviting me', etc.—terms of courtesy where no one has the normatively based expectation that people are telling the truth;[51] and it seems absurd, and even morally improper, to challenge people as 'liars', because of their desire for politeness and consideration in such cases. The social practice does not obtain here, and similarly, perhaps, for many cases of the social 'white lie', as well as obvious cases of joking, irony, thinking out loud, spinning out hypotheses, and the like.

The sense in which the principle of fairness is a principle of obligation, in the case of veracity, seems clear: since the application of that standard to the practice of truth-telling is of such importance in securing the stability of such a mutually beneficial, just practice, the rational contractors will agree that coercion is justified in enforcing it. However, once a legal system exists, the forms of coercion that individual persons may use in forcing people to tell the truth will be strictly limited, and for reasons identical with those raised above in the case of fidelity. Indeed, those reasons will apply even more strongly here in so far as the coercive support of general truth-telling would involve an impossible task of effective enforcement, because of the difficulties of defining the delict operationally and of dealing with all the cases. However, a certain class of cases will be of such importance to the general well-being of society that they will be enforced by law—e.g. laws against malicious slander and defamation of character, laws requiring that the public be not deceived, either by advertising or otherwise, about the nature of saleable goods and property, companies to be invested in, and the like. Such laws would be likely not only to involve coercive sanctions for failure to tell the truth or to disclose adequately, but also to include prophylactic licensing provisions in the case of saleable items involving fundamental social interests. Thus, such licensing provisions would require prospective sellers periodically to file samples of saleable food and drugs with government agencies (who would check the samples in accord with proper nutrition and health standards) in order to obtain or retain their licence to sell; or, companies about to offer stock for public investment may be required to file the proposed advertising solicitations with a government agency, who will check the solicitations for adequacy of disclosure. Failure to conform with such provisions would also justify the application of coercive sanctions. In other cases, however, such forms of coercion will be inappropriate, and the rational contractors will view only informal criticism as justified.

Finally, in calling veracity an obligation, in my technical sense, I am supposing that it arises because of the special relations between men as co-operating members sustaining the practice of truth-telling. A way of seeing what this involves is contrasting this view of veracity with the fascinating utilitarian justification offered by Sidgwick. Sidgwick, almost a century before David Lyons's consideration of the importance of the social context in the application of the utilitarian principle,[52] clearly acknowledges the fact that, as an act-utilitarian, he must believe that a rational utilitarian will view his prevarication as justified, if he knows, or has overwhelming reason to believe, that others will not follow his example.[53] And he accepts this conclusion as *morally* proper, but simply claims that such circumstances rarely exist. What is wholly missing from Sidgwick's account is *any* sense of the fact that such lying *uses* other people unfairly, for the very possibility of gaining one's ends by telling untruths depends on the general practice of truth-telling (i.e. it is because of this practice that people take one's lies as truths).[54] My view, on the other hand, makes fairness the fundamental moral question here, since veracity involves precisely being fair to others in sharing the benefits and burdens of our common practices.

v. *The Obligation to Return Good: Gratitude*

In claiming that the principle of fairness can explain certain cases of the obligation to return good, or gratitude, I do not mean to imply that this principle can explain all cases of gratitude; indeed, in the next two chapters, I shall relate many cases of gratitude to sub-principles under the principle of mutual aid and the principle of beneficence. However, certain institutionally related cases of gratitude do seem to me to be partially explicable by the principle of fairness. It is interesting to note, in this connection, W. D. Ross's claim that one of the prima-facie duties involved in one's moral duty to obey his country's laws is that of gratitude, and Sidgwick's related claim that justice may be viewed as gratitude universalized.[55] Such views, fastening on the notion of benefits received, extend gratitude by analogy into a general concept central to our normative relation to many social and political institutions; but the cases of gratitude I have in mind are much more circumscribed than these, and fit more closely the ordinary language notion of gratitude, e.g. (1) the relation of gratitude between a person who has been invited to a party, or to dinner, or been given a gift, and the person who has done the benefaction, and (2) the relation of gratitude on the part of adult children to their parents, now perhaps aged.

(1) When we invite people to parties or to dinner or give them presents, these social benefactions often form part of existing social practices of mutual hospitality. The practices require those who voluntarily accept such benefactions to do a similar good in return. Such a social institution satisfies the principle of fairness, other things being equal. That is, there exists a beneficial social institution, whose existence makes everyone better off than they would be without it, and which, let us suppose, is just. The institution's stability depends on persons both accepting its benefits (attending parties or dinners, etc.), and also bearing its burdens (giving parties or dinners, etc.), when it comes to their turn;

clearly, the principle of fairness requires that they do this. Note that the stringency of the principle of fairness, as applied to such cases, will depend on the importance of the particular system of institutions in question. Thus, for example, when a primitive people like the Kwakiutl have a system of mutual gift-giving which is the foundation of their entire social and economic life as a community, then the principle of fairness has a special stringency, which it does not have in less significant gift-giving institutions; this would be shown by the fact that the contractors will view coercion as justified in enforcing the principle of fairness in Kwakiutl-type cases, whereas only informal criticism, rebuke, blame, and the like would be viewed as justified in others.[56]

(2) As regards the relation of gratitude of adult children to their parents, now aged, the general idea here is that conventions regulating the relations of parents to children exist in a society, and these institutions hold between young children and parents, and adult children and parents, and distribute various benefits and burdens, so that if a person accepts benefits from the family system when he is younger, he is, when older, to bear the burdens of support, care, and concern for his parents. However, it seems that the principle of fairness will not unambiguously apply to such an institution, and for a morally important reason—young children and infants do not *voluntarily* accept the benefits of being born or being fed, clothed, nurtured, loved, etc. Birth and early care are simply given to a child; there is no possibility of his exercising choice. For this reason, the principle of fairness can not justify gratitude for benefits received when a child is young and lacks the real capacity for choice, but only when the child is older, has developed the capacities of rationality and control, and is therefore able to choose not to accept the benefits. The benefits at this stage include not only financial aid and support, but, perhaps more important, sympathy, understanding, concern, affection, and even friendship. Assuming that the child does voluntarily accept such benefits, and the institutions in question are just (not requiring obedience to parental orders that contravene equal liberty, e.g. killing Negroes) as well as mutually beneficial to all, then the child is to bear the burdens when his turn comes, i.e. caring for his parents as the institution requires. Here it is understood that the burden involved is necessary for the stability and persistence of the institution, since *one* of the conscious or unconscious points of

having and raising children is to have supports in one's old age; and the general institution of child rearing might be unstable unless prospective parents were assured of this. And the rational contractors would agree to coercion in supporting such institutions, where appropriate and possible; and, as in the previous cases, gratitude would here be an obligation in the sense of a special relation with other persons, voluntarily entered into.

10

THE PRINCIPLES OF INDIVIDUAL DUTY

AFTER the rational contractors have agreed on the ultimate standards which are to regulate their common institutions, and their obedience to them, they will still wish to agree to other ultimate standards, which are to regulate their relations apart from such institutions. Since the contractors do not know whether or not their relations to other persons are completely within or without common institutions, they are concerned that, if there are no common institutions shared, people accept ultimate standards which will ensure a highest lowest life prospect from the point of view of the original position. And a subclass of these ultimate standards will be of such importance in securing basic higher lowests that the contractors will think some forms of coercion justified in enforcing them; these standards are principles of individual duty. In this chapter I propose to discuss a set of four such principles which, I believe, the contractors would accept: the principles of non-maleficence, mutual aid, consideration, and paternalistic guidance, as well as subsidiary and supplementary principles to them, which would also be accepted. In the previous chapter, a fifth such principle was formulated and discussed, the principle establishing a natural duty of justice. That principle, however, importantly relates to facilitating the existence of just institutions. Thus, for analytic convenience, it was presented in the context of a discussion of principles regulating obedience to such institutions. However, nothing said there will, I hope, obscure the fact that the principle is one among the principles of individual duty, in that it applies to people even in an institutional state of nature. A sixth such principle (that of moral development) will be presented in chapter 13.

1. *The Principle of Non-maleficence*
(a) *Its Formulation and Relation to the Original Position*

In considering what ultimate standards to agree to as principles of individual duty, the contractors will be aware of circumstances which bear on the general satisfaction of human interests, no matter what one's particular interests are. One set of facts, of obvious relevance to the contractors' decision, is that forms of injury, cruelty, and killing by persons, whose pursuit of their substantial interests does not indispensably require such acts, typically frustrates the fundamental human interests of others (note that injury and cruelty do this analytically, killing only contingently). Thus, the prescription of such forms of injury, cruelty, and killing, at least in a wide range of typical circumstances, will result in a higher lowest life prospect of desire satisfaction than would be attained without such a proscription. Such reasoning will lead the maximining contractors to their acceptance of the principle of non-maleficence, which would be formulated thus:

5. Given that principles 1 and 4, as applied to and between basic legal institutions, and the economic and social institutions they define and support, are satisfied or not relevant, then persons are not, intentionally or knowingly, to be cruel or to injure persons, or animals, or kill persons, except for cases of necessary self-defence, or kill animals except where this is necessary to the support of persons; and are to take precautions to ensure that they do not accidentally, by mistake, or inadvertently cause such pain, injury, or death to persons, except where the person hurt or killed *rationally* and *voluntarily* requests such pain or death by the intentional act of the other, whom he has asked to cause such pain or death, or except where the victim will *considerably* better achieve his rational ends only through the infliction of pain (whether he voluntarily wishes it or not).

This formulation of the principle of non-maleficence, though it may seem in some respects controversial, follows quite precisely, I believe, from the ideal contract view of morality I have been proposing. This can be easily seen in the case of the most controversial feature of this formulation of the principle, i.e. the limitation of the applicability of the principle to cases where the person hurt or killed does not rationally and voluntarily wish pain or death. Since the rational contractors are maximining, they will not extend the principle of non-maleficence to cases where persons' life prospects of desire satisfaction would be lowered, not raised, by the applicability of this principle. Examples of such circumstances include the following: persons dying of some intolerably painful disease (e.g. terminal cancer), who rationally and voluntarily ask to be killed by another; a case illustrated by Ibsen's *Ghosts*, where Mrs. Alving is asked by her son to kill him when his incurable idiocy comes on him again, because Oswald rationally and voluntarily prefers his death to the (for him) contemptible prospect of life spent in dependent idiocy and childishness; and cases where persons masochistically enjoy being hurt by other persons, where this does not result in bodily or psychic harm of such a sort as to cripple a person for life. In all such cases the rational contractors will not regard the principle of non-maleficence as proscribing killing or the infliction of pain, since a higher lowest is secured by permitting rather than by proscribing them, given that the death or pain rationally advances the person's desired ends. The sense of rationality here depends on the principles of rational choice I formulated and discussed in Part I. Thus, the reason why it is rational for a person painfully dying of terminal cancer to prefer his being intentionally killed by another to his being left to die slowly is that the course of action leading to his death through killing will secure less frustration of his desires than the course of action which allows him to die slowly (the ending of terrible pain through present death as opposed to the continuance of such pain until practically inevitable death, where the probability of recovery is so negligible as not even to approach outweighing the near certainty of death). In the Ibsen case, the sense in which Oswald rationally wishes his death must be understood in the light of his individual desire for personal competence and autonomy which is, for him, the *sine qua non* of satisfying all other desires he may have, so that it will better secure his ends to be killed intentionally by another, and thus end all desire, rather than continue in life with the frustration of his basic ideal of excellence. And similarly, the infliction of pain on a masochist, where no permanent harm is involved, is rational in the sense of being required by the principle of effective means (given that overriding dominance considerations are ruled out by lack of any injury or harm), in that one thus satisfies the person's desire to be hurt, something often related to frustrated sexuality. Further, the sense in which such actions are *voluntarily* desired can be partially understood in terms of the existence of equal liberty between the two parties in question, so that the party killed or pained is not coerced or forced by the other into consenting to such death or pain. However, the general requirement of voluntariness here implies that the person wishing such death or pain has the normal developed capacities of understanding and control associated with formulating and executing rational plans of action,[1] and that these capacities are brought to bear in asking the other person to inflict pain on or kill him. The rational contractors will require both the voluntariness and rationality of a person's requesting pain or death at the hands of another, before the principle of non-maleficence is suspended, as opposed to requiring just either one or the other, because they will thus secure the higher lowest. If only voluntariness were required, the contractors will see that this by itself lets in irrational decisions resulting in pain or death, which they wish to guard against. And if only rationality were required, without a person's voluntary consent to death or pain, the contractors will find that this requirement in itself tends to allow too many mistakes by persons in deciding when it is rational that another be killed or hurt, when such rationality is more likely to exist if the person's voluntary consent is also required (except in special circumstances, to be discussed shortly).

Again, we see the crucial importance of the assumption of the contractors' ignorance concerning their particular desires, nature, and circumstances; for it is because the contractors do not know what their particular theological or religious views are, that they are prepared to agree to the above limitations on the applicability of non-maleficence. If, on the other hand, one introduces Lockean assumptions about men as God's 'Property',[2] by virtue of which men are not entitled, under any condition, to consent to the deprivation of their life by another, then one will, quite naturally, arrive at a very different sort of result. Thus, the ideal contract view enables one to separate out those aspects of moral judgement which are part of the natural concept of morality alone, and those which are introduced by various theological assumptions. Similarly, the common view that there is something degrading in agreeing to having pain inflicted on oneself by another, may similarly depend on certain, perhaps quite unconsciously assumed, theological and quasi-theological beliefs about the proper and ordained exercise of human capacities and propensities.[3] From the point of view of the original position, however, the view is: if moral principles are not relevant, then all desires may and *ought* to be pursued, the only constraint being that the desires be rationally satisfied. In this view, the *fact* that a person may have certain deviant desires (e.g. masochism or homosexuality), in so far as their satisfaction is regulated by the principles of rationality and by the requirements of morality in respect to other persons, seems a quite inculpable fact of his psychology; and there is no plausibility at all in supposing such a person to be somehow responsible for having these desires, something perhaps resulting from circumstances of childhood life quite beyond his control, and now quite irremediable.

The other related provision for the non-applicability of non-maleficence, i.e. that the pain be such as to promote considerably the rational interests of the person hurt, quite apart from voluntariness, is also a natural consequence of the maximining of the rational contractors. The contractors will recognize that inflicting pain, especially psychological pain, on a person is often a necessary and indispensable concomitant of securing a *great* rational good to that person,[4] in the way of changing his whole personality orientation in a more rational direction (so that he can better assess and pursue his actual desires in terms of the real circumstances of life). Consider, for example, the great pain of self-knowledge which tragic dramatists have celebrated since Aeschylus, and on which Freud built a method of psychological therapy; and the need for at least some educational punishment in child development. The contractors would view such pains, even if not voluntarily accepted, as not proscribed by non-maleficence, because, in such cases, the conditions of voluntarily consenting to such pain are rarely satisfied (either because the person is young, or under a deep delusion or neurosis); so that, if such voluntariness were required, persons would remain in a *much* lower life prospect of desire satisfaction than would be achieved if voluntariness were not required. In this case, the contractors will accept the risk of persons' possible mistakes concerning the rationality of inflicting such pain, because of the *great* goods that will, consequently, most likely be secured.

As regards the principle's requirement that principles 1 and 4 are assumed to be satisfied, this also strictly follows from the nature of the contractors' decision problem. Thus, while the contractors wish, generally, to proscribe persons' intentionally killing or hurting other persons, in order to ensure a higher lowest, these considerations do not obtain in cases where such intentional killing or hurting is part of *necessary* efforts to defend the substantial interests of the person killing or hurting from those who threaten him for no good reason—for example, in a just war between nations, revolutions within unjust nations, and the application of the coercive sanctions of a just legal system, including even the use of the death penalty where the sanction is *necessary* for deterrence, especially in cases which undermine the just legal system (e.g. treason).[5] In all these cases, given that intentional killing and infliction of pain is the only available recourse, and is likely to accomplish its end without an overbalance of injustice (e.g. killing and hurting the innocent) in the process, such killing and hurting will secure a higher lowest—persons being allowed a greatest equal liberty compatible with a like liberty for all—than would be the case, if they were not permitted.

A parallel form of argument is also implied in the contractors' acceptance of self-defence as an exception to the proscription on intentional killing and hurting. In the absence of any realistic recourse to public authority to stop attacks on one's life and personal safety, a higher lowest (i.e. one's personal safety and security) will be ensured by permitting, rather than by proscribing, such defences, where they involve only the minimal necessary force to stop such attacks.

These justifications for the above exceptions to the applicability of non-maleficence will also indicate why other institutionally related duties and obligations will not typically override non-maleficence, but rather a condition of their moral acceptability will be that non-maleficence is either satisfied or not relevant. Thus, in a case where a person x may promise person y to kill another person z (who, say, lives in a savage land where no common practices exist, so that institutional equal liberties are not relevant), such a promise, made under otherwise bona fide conditions, will have no moral force at all because it contravenes the prior principle of non-maleficence.[6] This is so, of course, because the rational contractors will thus ensure a higher lowest than if they permitted the moral bindingness of such promises, for they will wish to hedge against the possibility that they may end up as the person z in an institutional state of nature, who is to be killed as a result of the agreement of some other persons x and y. Similarly, the claims of non-maleficence will override the conflicting requirements of truth-telling and institutional cases of gratitude—e.g.

telling a prospective murderer where his victim is, or performing your benefactor's request that you kill some person. But obviously, there will be limits to this priority, especially as regards the proscription on cruelty; for example, consider the minor rebukes which seem indispensable to the general utility of the practice of truth-telling, especially where the cruelty in question tends to correct and educate.

The requirements of non-maleficence as regards animals cannot, on the ideal contract view, be explained by those animals being members of the original position,[7] since they lack the capacities of choice and control required to entitle them to such membership, or rather, they lack the causal possibility of having the capacities of choice and control of members of the original position. Thus, the original position includes mental deficients and the insane because it is quite possible that a contractor may be so embodied. However, animals cannot be included in the original position because it is not in the same way possible that a contractor might be one of them. The notion of moral fortuitousness, mentioned in chapter 6, can be pressed only so far and no further: that a person is American or British, Negro or Caucasian, atheist or Anglican, etc., is fortuitous from the point of view of the original position, but that a creature is an animal or a human is not fortuitous in the same way. However, the contractors will still be concerned to put some restrictions on persons' cruelty and injury to, and killing of, animals; this concern follows from the contractors' knowledge that persons generally have certain basic sympathies with animals and animal life. And while they will agree to the use of animals as food, transportation, clothing, etc., i.e. where they can serve and promote basic human interests, they will desire to guard against the possibility that they may themselves have a basic sense of affection for, and sympathy with, animals, especially in view of the analogies of animal behaviour to that of human persons. Further, in view of these analogies, the contractors will understand cruelty to animals as an extension of a personality orientation which is prone to cruelty to persons; and, as part of their desire to proscribe the latter, they will wish to set limitations on the former. The importance of the assumption of the contractors' ignorance of their particular desires, etc., appears again here—since the contractors will only be able to agree to a provision limiting cruelty to animals, but allowing killing of them if this advances basic human interests, in so far as they do not, for example, know that they entertain specific theological beliefs about their own reincarnation in animals.

Finally, the provision that non-maleficence apply not only to intentional acts (where the maleficence is part of one's plan to reach some end) or knowing acts (where it is part of the known consequences of executing one's plan), but also to negligent acts which, by accident or by mistake or inadvertently, result in maleficence, clearly follows from the decision problem of the original position. The maximining contractors will secure a higher lowest life prospect of desire satisfaction in non-institutional contexts if people publicly know and generally act on a standard of care and attention (when they are in circumstances with a known and relatively high probability of resulting in pain, injury, and death to other persons), which will minimize the likelihood of pain, injury, and death to others.

(b) The Subsidiary Principle of Compensation

Having accepted the above principle of non-maleficence, the contractors will then agree to the following principle of compensation, which is to govern persons' conduct when they violate non-maleficence:

5a.   If a person's actions should be such as to violate principle 5, he is to do whatever is required to compensate either the person hurt or injured for his pain or injury, or the dependants of the person killed for his loss, if there are such dependants

Given that a violation of non-maleficence typically frustrates human interests, the contractors will find that a higher lowest is secured if people violating non-maleficence generally act on a principle requiring them to remedy such frustrations as they have culpably caused; the amount of compensation is to be roughly proportional to the harm done, since this secures the highest lowest. Indeed, though I do not wish to elaborate this in detail, the contractors will obviously agree to a general principle of compensation as subsidiary to any moral principle accepted on the maximining criterion (i.e. moral principles of obligation and duty, and the supererogatory principles of blame), since the transgression of such principles harms the interests of persons, and thus lowers the lowest; and agreement to a compensatory principle secures a higher lowest. The forms of compensation will vary from the great amounts required in the case of injury or death or great injustice, to mere forms of apology which are appropriate in the case of unjustified incivilities, unkindnesses, and the like.

(c) Non-maleficence as a Principle of Duty

There is, I think, nothing controversial in the claim that the principle of non-maleficence is a principle of duty, in the sense of chapter 7. Such a principle (as well as its subsidiary compensatory principle) is to govern conduct quite apart from men's institutional relationships, and is of such importance to fundamental human interests that the contractors will view coercion as justified in enforcing it.

However, though this is a principle of individual duty, the principle of non-maleficence will be an appropriate object of legal enforcement, when legal institutions do exist. Indeed, pursuant to a mode of argument now familiar in this work, once just legal institutions do exist, enforcement of non-maleficence (with the exception of self-defence) is to be left to the legal authorities alone, since such authorities will tend to enforce non-maleficence more justly than individual persons. Such legal enforcement of non-maleficence often (but not always—consider the civil law of torts) falls under the criminal law; this is importantly related to the special nature of the moral duties that non-maleficence involves, where persons with moral rights to personal safety do not have unconditional liberty to enforce or extinguish the associated duties.

However, in considering the relation of moral duties to legal enforcement, there may well again be a gap between the forms of coercion that moral principles strictly seem to justify and those which it is practically feasible for the legal system to enforce. This problem occurs with some acuteness in the case of non-maleficence with respect to the conditions of voluntariness and rationality which, it was claimed, suspended the applicability of non-maleficence in certain cases. Though, from the point of view of the original position, intentional killing and hurting are not proscribed in such cases, it may be difficult for the law to capture such fine distinctions, especially given that the main body of typical cases involving non-maleficence does not satisfy these special conditions: the difficulties of proof, and problems of interpretation, which introducing such conditions into the law may involve, to the detriment of the adequate enforcement of the typical cases of non-maleficence, may be such that they cannot be incorporated into the legal system. It may therefore be necessary in such cases for the law to make illegal what is, strictly speaking, not immoral, because, as a public policy, this yields more moral results on the whole than the alternative policies. If this is so, the contractors will presumably view the use of judicial or executive discretion, in dismissing or only nominally punishing clear cases which fall within the above conditions, as justified. In any event, it is important to see that separable questions are involved, in discussing the moral justifiability of an individual person practising mercy killing, and the justifiability of making euthanasia legally permissible; one cannot naïvely move from one such question to the other, as though they are identical.

11. *The Principle of Mutual Aid*

(a) *Its Formulation and Relation to the Original Position*

Another set of facts, relevant to the contractors' decision concerning principles of individual duty, has to do with forms of assistance and aid which, at only slight cost to himself, one person may render to another in saving the other from grave pain, injury, and even death, when the persons are not in any institutional relationship which requires such aid to be given. The contractors will agree to a principle requiring such aid to be given, because, in this way, they will guard against the possibility that they may themselves end up in such a position of requiring assistance from other persons, where they would wish such assistance to be given —thus ensuring a higher lowest consistent with their maximining strategy.

It is of note that the rational contractors are agreeing on a principle of aid which is to apply in a certain circumscribed set of circumstances, not in all possible circumstances of aid, i.e. they are concerned only with aid, given at slight personal cost, which secures a great good to the person aided. The contractors' making of this distinction between different sorts of circumstances where persons may do good to other persons may be usefully contrasted with the traditional philosophical failure to do so. Consider, for example, Kant's argument, in the *Foundations of the Metaphysics of Morals*, which he repeats elsewhere, as to why it is a moral *duty* to give aid to others in great distress—the argument involving basically the sort of reasoning in the original position that I just sketched.[8] However, when, in the *Metaphysical Principles of Virtue*, Kant comes to discuss explicitly duties of this sort, we learn that they are part of the general category of duties of beneficence, which include taking the morally permissible ends of others as one's own. And thus Kant wishes, on the one hand, to insist that these requirements are *duties*, and, on the other, to indicate that they are forms of imperfect duty which, unlike the imperfect duties of respect, are meritorious, not owed to other persons.[9] Similarly, consider Price's account of the duty of beneficence which covers both a person's doing 'all the good he can to his fellow-creatures' generally and doing good to 'distressed persons he ought to relieve'.[10] Sidgwick, of course, clearly describes both non-maleficence and mutual aid as a 'somewhat indefinite limit of Duty' beyond which 'extends the Virtue of Benevolence without limit'; but he sees these as only relative distinctions within the wider principle of beneficence in reference to which he grants that the 'distinction between Excellence and Strict Duty does not seem properly admissible in Utilitarianism'.[11] What is common to these, and other, traditional philosophers is the assimilation of the circumstances of mutual aid to those of general beneficence, and the consequent failure clearly to distinguish and explain the different sorts of moral principles which are relevant to these different sorts of circumstances. And this, in turn, has resulted in the extension by philosophers of the concept of duty from mutual aid to beneficence generally, with the concomitant introduction of various arbitrary devices which attempt to explain how we naturally, but mistakenly, suppose that duty is an inappropriate category in the analysis of beneficence. In over-reaction against this sort of unnatural extension of the concept of duty, recent philosophers like Hart and Baier have claimed that duty is not only inappropriate in the case of beneficence, but also in the case of non-maleficence and mutual aid, since they wish to restrict 'duty' to contexts of social roles.[12] And this view has, in turn, been justly denied by D'Arcy, Findlay, and G. R. Grice, who maintain, for example, that 'duty' has no more natural use, in moral contexts, than in regard to mutual aid.[13] The feature of the view of moral principles here outlined is that it further explains and defends D'Arcy's, Findlay's, and Grice's view by relating it to a general theory of morality and the concepts of duty and obligation.

The principle of mutual aid would, I believe, be formulated as follows:

6. Given that principles 1 and 4, as applied to basic legal institutions, and principle 5 are satisfied or not relevant, then if a person x encounters another person y, where x may, at only slight cost to himself, relieve y's great pain or injury, or aid y in averting such pain, injury, or even death, then x is to give such relief and aid, assuming that y does not voluntarily and rationally refuse it.

The formulation of this principle follows strictly from the nature of the decision problem of the original position. Thus, the qualification that the person aided must not rationally and voluntarily refuse such aid will be accepted by the contractors for reasons identical to their acceptance of the similar qualification on the applicability of the principle of non-maleficence.

The requirement that the aid in question should be only of slight cost to the person who does the aiding is of fundamental importance to the contractors' acceptance of this principle as one of individual duty. From the point of view of the original position, a contractor will only secure a higher lowest by agreeing to a principle which does not require a person to sacrifice his own life and limb to save another. If it were made a justifiably coercive requirement that people did give aid in such circumstances, a higher lowest would not be secured, because persons would be required to endanger their lives in order to *try* to save the lives of others, where they are likely not to be successful and lose their own lives in the process.

The requirement that giving aid be only of slight cost clarifies the sense of 'encounter', which the principle uses. Encountering a person will include any knowledge of another's plight, and capacity at slight cost to relieve that plight. The clearest cases of such encountering are life-saving examples, where a person may save another from drowning by merely putting out his hand, or throwing out a lifebelt; but, obviously, the principle has implications where one is even told (e.g. by Oxfam or the Red Cross) of another's plight, which one can, at slight cost, relieve.[14] Quite clear and quite peripheral cases of the applicability of the principle of mutual aid can be imagined; however, throughout, the principle remains constant—its implications being ambiguous only to the degree that the costs are not slight, and the benefits are not certain or great.

The requirement that principles 1, 4, and 5 be satisfied, or not relevant, before the principle of mutual aid applies, follows from the contractors' use of the maximining strategy. Thus, if mutual aid were generally observed, even in cases where this conflicts with principles 1 and 4, as applied to basic legal institutions, this would imply great injustices and instabilities in basic institutions, yielding a much lower lowest than if a priority order were generally accepted and acted on (e.g. the guards of men imprisoned by a just legal system would be under a duty of mutual aid to release prisoners, if they could without any possible detection let them free; or, in the case of a just war, soldiers might be under a duty of mutual aid to save enemies from possible injuries and mortalities, even where this is completely incompatible with accomplishing their nation's just end). And similarly, in a non-maleficence–mutual aid conflict (e.g. having to kill one person in order to be able to save another), failure to observe the priority of non-maleficence to mutual aid would lead to the certain death of one person in order only probably to save the life of another.

However, obviously such a priority relation will not hold in all cases; for example, in the case of conflicts between promising and truth-telling and mutual aid, if such conflicts did occur, it seems clear that the contractors would give priority to mutual aid, since they thus guard against the evils of grave pain, injury, and even death, where this does not seem significantly to impair the stability of beneficial institutions like promising and truth-telling. Further, it seems clear that the priority of non-maleficence to mutual aid will not hold in all cases; for example, where getting to save the life of some person x involves rudely pushing another person y aside, perhaps hurting him by his consequent fall, it does not seem improper to do so, if necessary, given the great good that may thus be secured.

(b) The Subsidiary Principle of Gratitude

Having agreed to the principle of mutual aid, the contractors will, I think, agree to the following principle of gratitude:

6a.   Given that a person x has regulated his conduct by principle 6 in reference to a person y, then y is to do something by way of satisfying the desires of x.

Because a person who needs assistance cannot typically enforce his claim in the way which a person with a right to non-maleficence can (i.e. through self-defence), the contractors will wish to provide some further incentive to the exercise of mutual aid besides making it a principle of duty,[15] and they will do this by agreeing to the above principle of gratitude; this reasoning will be supplemented by the fact that such a principle will also ensure a higher lowest to the person who has incurred cost in helping. However, the contractors will not make this principle into one of duty, because this will place too great a burden on the person aided, as compared to the slight cost which the helper in question incurred in giving such aid. Instead, the principle will be accepted as a principle of supererogatory blame, so that people may be in various ways criticized and condemned for not expressing such gratitude.

(c) Mutual Aid as a Principle of Duty

The principle of mutual aid is of such importance in securing a higher lowest that the justifiability of coercion, in enforcing it, will outweigh whatever costs the application of sanctions might involve. It will be a principle of individual duty since it applies between men, as men, quite apart from their institutional relationships. However, once legal institutions do exist, the appropriate application of sanctions, in enforcing mutual aid, will be, or ought to be, in the hands of the legal authorities alone, since they will more justly apply coercion. In so far as legal systems, even in advanced nations, do not recognize mutual aid as a legal duty, enforceable in law, such systems are morally incomplete; and, from the point of view of the original position, it is a requirement on legislators, and citizens generally, that the legal system be reformed in such a way as to incorporate such a legal duty.[16]

III. The Principle of Consideration

(a) Its Formulation and Relation to the Original Position

Another set of general facts, which are relevant to the decision of the rational contractors regarding principles of individual duty, concerns various ways in which persons may arbitrarily, and for no good moral (defined by the above principles) and prudential (defined by the principles of rational choice) reason, interfere with the concerns of other persons, not in the way of causing pain, injury, or death, but through annoying and disturbing the others'

peaceful and legitimate pursuit of their own aims. In such circumstances, the contractors will wish to proscribe such forms of interference, because they frustrate the interests of people, and do
not substantially advance the interests of anyone (including the
interferer), a course consistent with the maximining strategy of the
contractors.

The principle of consideration would be formulated thus:

7. Given that principles 1, 2, 3, 4, 5, and 6 are satisfied, or not relevant,
and given that the principles of rational choice do not require a
certain action n as a matter of substantially advancing the agent's
interests, then if such an agent x is in a position substantially to
annoy and disturb some other person y, in the pursuit of his concerns
and purposes, by doing action n, then x is not to do n, assuming that
such interference will not advance the rational interests of y in some
way, and only enables x to achieve some self-regarding end which
could be equally secured without such annoyance to others.

The requirements that the person not substantially advance his
own interests through such an interference, and that the other person's interests not be advanced by such interference, follow from
the contractors' use of the maximining strategy. If the contractors
did proscribe such interference, when it served the interferer's
interest, they would not ensure a highest lowest, since such a principle requires the frustration of the interests of the interferer at the
expense of securing the interests of the person interfered with.
Similarly, the contractors would not proscribe such interference, if
this, in fact, promotes the interests of the person interfered with,
e.g. a process of education and argument which, while it may
undermine basic beliefs and shibboleths and thus cause great
inner disturbance and turmoil, none the less leads to a person's
more rationally advancing his own interests.

The priority relation of principles 1, 2, 3, 4, 5, and 6 to the
principle of consideration follows from the fact that a higher lowest
will be secured, from the point of view of the original position, by
persons' observing such a priority relation in their general action
on these principles, since the prior principles secure such fundamental interests. For example, the contractors will not wish the
principle of consideration to apply if the required consideration
largely exists as a class dependent attribute, which only unjustly
disadvantaged economic classes have to observe in order to allow
advantaged classes to enjoy the amenities of their more abundant

lives, for to require consideration in such a case would only lower an already too low life prospect of desire satisfaction for the worst-off classes. Further, unlike the above two principles, it seems that even the requirements of promising and truth-telling will typically have priority to those of consideration, if there is a conflict, since institutions like promising and truth-telling would be unstable if persons were permitted to be free of such obligations when this was just a matter of consideration to another. Thus, the kinds of case that satisfy this principle are ones where, assuming complete social and economic justice, etc., people arbitrarily annoy and frustrate the interests and concerns of other persons—e.g. the loud party next door which continues well past the hour when the giver of the party knows that others in the neighbourhood have retired; the loud talkers during a play or concert who disturb all those about them; the loud, brawling couple in a restaurant who disturb the meals of all those about them; the drunk who approaches and bothers persons because of a whim; and the like. In cases of this sort, persons disturb others not because of the indispensable pursuit of their substantial interests, or for some good moral reason, but as part of the pursuit of some isolated self-regarding end, which could equally well be realized without disturbance to others.

(b) Consideration as a Principle of Duty

The rational contractors will agree that coercion is justified in enforcing the principle of consideration, since they will ensure a higher lowest by agreeing to such coercion than by not doing so; and it is a principle of individual duty, since it applies quite apart from persons' being in any institutional relationship to one another. However, again and pursuant to reasoning now familiar, once a legal system does exist, the contractors will agree that the application of coercion in enforcing the principle of consideration must be in the hands of the legal authorities alone. However, it will not be possible for the legal system to enforce consideration in all cases, since the forms of annoyance are often too minor to warrant the application of sanctions, and because the task of such general enforcement seems hardly feasible. Rather, the legal system is to enforce the clear and grave cases of such annoyance (e.g. so-called breaches of the peace), and leave the other cases of consideration to the informal criticisms of individual persons.

IV. *The Principle of Paternalistic Guidance and its Supplementary Principle of Rational Self-harm*

Kurt Baier has claimed that the very concept of moral duties which relate to an agent's pursuit of his interests is incompatible with the concept of morality; for 'to use moral pressure to make people promote their own interest is not morality, but paternalism'.[17] Such a view seems to me mistaken, if it supposes that there is no defensible sense in which the concept of morality can be related to a paternalistic principle. This can be seen by considering the relevance of facts about certain extreme types of human irrationality and non-rationality to the decision problem of the rational contractors of the original position. Thus, the contractors know that, as children, they lack the developed capacity of rational thought and control, and require guidance and control by others (including being forcibly sent to school) if they are to develop such capacities, and if their interests are not to be harmed severely by actions taken when lacking such capacities of rationality. And further, they know that certain persons, even as adults, lack these capacities, or their developed exercise, even as to endanger their own life and limb. From the point of view of the original position, the contractors will wish to hedge against both these possibilities, so that if they should be children, their lack of rationality should be guided and developed; and if they should suffer from such psychological abnormality, their irrationality will be stopped and guided by others. Thus, the contractors will agree to a principle requiring paternalism, since such a standard, if publicly known and generally acted on, will substantially advance human interests, including stopping bodily harm and death, where these are not designed to promote the rational ends or aspirations of the person in question.

The principle of paternalistic guidance would be formulated as follows:

8. If person x either lacks the developed capacity of rational choice and deliberation or the full opportunity to exercise such capacities, which lack of either or both is likely substantially to frustrate the person's interests, where such frustration is extremely irrational, given the persons' desires, competences, and circumstances, then another person y, who is available and can stop x, at no great cost to himself, is to do so, and, if also at little cost to himself, to help

him develop his capacities of rationality, if possible, and aid him in securing the full opportunity to exercise these capacities, if feasible.

It is crucial to the acceptance of this principle by the contractors that the incapacity or inopportunity in question must be likely to have substantially irrational results in terms of frustrating a person's interests. This is so because the contractors would not agree that every sort of irrationality, or even most sorts of irrationality, are such that they run counter to moral principles of duty. On the contrary, the contractors will explicitly refuse to agree to the principles of rational choice as ultimate standards which are to be enforced *by others* by moral coercion, blame, or praise. Rather, given that moral principles are satisfied, the contractors will agree to leave the pursuit of individual rationality up to the agent *alone*, in the light of his own perception and knowledge of his wants, needs, and circumstances, both because people's interests are in fact usually better advanced in this way and because mature people better develop their capacity of rational choice when they are allowed autonomously to make and profit from their own mistakes (if and when they are irrational). However, where a person so lacks the capacities of rationality that this will tend to result in a severe frustration of his interests, the contractors will make an exception to their general strategy in respect to the principles of rational choice and agree upon the principle of paternalistic guidance, because in the circumstances of *its* application, a higher lowest will be secured by its being publicly accepted and acted on.

Further, this principle does not apply to circumstances where rational persons may rationally cause their own deaths, i.e. cases of rational suicide. As I implied in my consideration of the related issue of killing where the person to be killed voluntarily and rationally wishes his death, the contractors will place no proscription on persons' killing themselves, when this is rationally justified by the prospect of a life of pain, bitterness, loneliness, and neglect, or a life which would violate ideals which are valued more highly than life itself. This is a simple consequence of the maximining of the contractors—they secure a higher lowest by permitting rather than by proscribing such rational suicide. And thus, the contractors would agree to the following principle of rational self-harm, supplementary to that of paternalistic guidance:

8*a*.   Given that principles 1, 2, 4, 5, and 6 are satisfied, or not relevant, and that a rational person x is about to cause physical pain, injury, or death to himself, where these are rational ends given his desires and circumstances, then another person y, who is available to stop the person x, at no great cost to himself, is not to do so, though he is to do so if any of these conditions do not obtain.

The priority relation of the other moral principles, to the application of this principle, with the exception of efficiency and consideration, follows from the fact that observing such a priority will secure a higher lowest than otherwise. Thus, the moral permissibility of the suicide of a person, which eliminates him from voluntarily undertaken obligations to others, may result in a much lower life prospect (for those dependent on such obligations) than would be the case if this were proscribed in such circumstances; in such cases, because of the voluntary character of undertaking the obligations in question, the contractors will not give any weight to the unhappiness or self-contempt of the prospective suicide as against the likely frustrations of his dependants (e.g. his children) should he commit suicide, because his interests have already been adequately secured by allowing him freedom from such obligations, if he did not voluntarily choose to undertake them. And in the case of non-maleficence and mutual aid, the contractors will proscribe such suicide if undertaken in such circumstances that it causes the death of others, or forecloses giving mutual aid to a person presently appealing for it. The principles of efficiency and consideration will not be prior to the principle of rational suicide because it will not secure a higher lowest to require a prospective suicide first to secure the institutional requirements of efficiency, if he is in an institutional position to do so, or always to be considerate to others, at the expense of a life of bitter unhappiness and self-contempt. But of course, it is of note that the moral principles, which are incorporated into the conditions of non-applicability of the principle, are typically irrelevant when a person rationally contemplates suicide, where the absence of affection, intimacy, and general social commitment, and the sense of loss of personal competence seem especially important.

In so far as traditional philosophers have thought suicide always immoral, it is largely a consequence of their introducing theological conceptions into their views of morality, a point already suggested in my discussion of non-maleficence.[18]

The requirement of both the above principles, that person y only interfere if at little cost to himself, follows from the fact that requiring a person to interfere at considerable cost may involve personal danger with only a probability of saving the other, and thus will not secure a highest lowest.

Both principles are ones of individual duty, since the contractors will secure a highest lowest by viewing coercion as justified in enforcing them in non-institutional contexts. However, once common institutions exist, the sole enforcement of paternalistic guidance is to be by the legal system, except for special life-saving cases. Obviously, such institutional enforcement will include the maintenance by the state of institutions for the mentally abnormal and the abandoned young, and will involve laws and institutions requiring and facilitating child care, guidance, and education, including laws proscribing harmful early child employment. Further, note that the requirement of the principle of paternalistic guidance, that people be given 'the full opportunity to exercise' their capacities of rationality, imposes, once common institutions exist, a duty on the state of ensuring that people in general (including rational adults) have the full opportunity to exercise their rationality. For example, the state is to ensure that people's opportunity to exercise their rationality is not undermined by false or misleading advertising, or by advertising which fails to note the possible harmful properties of a saleable product, and the like. Here, there is some convergence between the state's enforcement of the moral obligation of veracity and the moral duty of paternalistic guidance. The convergence is not, however, exact; for even if the social institution of truth-telling were not well developed (as was, for example, the case during the days of the low commercial morality expressed by the doctrine of caveat emptor), the principle of paternalistic guidance would still require the state to enforce a higher standard of truth-telling than the commercial practice requires.

As regards the enforcement of the principle of rational self-harm, it may be unfeasible to enforce its strict requirements, since it may be beyond the crude coercive instruments of the law to separate out the different sorts of justifiable and unjustifiable suicide, especially given the preponderance of irrational and immoral suicide, which the law primarily wants to prevent. Whether, however, it is justifiable for the legal system to proscribe suicide *simpliciter* is quite another matter, for how are *its* sanctions to have coercive bite on a person who desires death?

11

THE PRINCIPLES OF
SUPEREROGATION

HAVING agreed upon a set of principles of individual duty, certain facts about the relationships of people will lead the contractors to find rational the agreement to a certain class of ultimate standards, which are to govern the relationships between men as men, since public knowledge of and general action on these standards can only raise, and not lower, the satisfaction of human interests from the point of view of the original position, *assuming* that coercion is not viewed as justified in enforcing the requirements of these standards. The explanation for this derives from the fact that making the requirements of these standards matters of duty would place too great a burden on persons, (i) since the justifiability of coercion in such cases would lower the interests of the wrongdoer out of all proportion to the good secured to others, or (ii) because the required actions frustrate people's pursuit of their basic interests for the sake of advancing the interests of others, contrary to maximining. These two reasons explain two different sorts of principles of supererogation. (i) lies behind the rational contractors' agreement to the principles of civility, mutual respect, and mutual love (what I shall call supererogatory principles of blame); and (ii) explains their acceptance of the principle of beneficence (a supererogatory principle of praise).

Before discussing the specific nature of the principles of supererogation, it seems useful to note that I am interpreting supererogation here in a rather broad, and perhaps technical, sense, related to my technical notion of obligation and duty. By contrast, Urmson, in his now classic article, 'Saints and Heroes', emphasized acts of extraordinary courage and goodness as the clear examples of supererogatory acts, which go well beyond the sphere of duty. And Feinberg, though he acknowledges that the ordinary notion of doing a favour is often supererogatory, and rightly emphasizes, against Urmson, that supererogatory acts often occur as things we ought to do where no duties at all exist, generally holds that supererogation involves '*a meritorious, abnormally risky non-duty*', which emphasizes extraordinariness as the crucial mark of the supererogatory.[1] In these views, as long as the omission of an act may be justifiably reproved or blamed, the act is not supererogatory. In contrast to these conceptions, my theory follows Chisholm in marking off as supererogatory many perfectly ordinary and typical acts, e.g. 'ordinary politeness', defining the supererogatory as what it is good to do, but not obligatory to do.[2] Thus, note that the first two principles of supererogation, civility and mutual respect, define wholly unheroic, unsaintly, and unextraordinary actions and activities, where blame is appropriate if people omit to do what is required. My view only differs from Chisholm's in relating the concept of supererogation to a systematic theory of the concepts of morality, obligation, and duty, whereas he prefers to attempt a reductive analysis of the central normative concepts in terms of good.[3] This may also be usefully contrasted with Grice's view, since he finds it necessary to define supererogation separately from his contract ground, as requiring a wholly different mode of analysis from basic obligations.[4] In my view, this is not so, for the rational contractors will explicitly agree to a set of supererogatory principles which are to apply to individuals apart from any institutional relationships they may have to one another.

1. *The Principle of Civility—a Supererogatory Principle of Blame*

In considering what ultimate standards to agree to as principles of supererogation, one set of facts relevant to the contractors' decision problem is the important bearing on promoting human interests of observing certain minimal forms of politeness in one's interaction with other persons, given that observing such forms of politeness typically involves little cost to the person who does so, and yet brings to other persons security from various forms of arbitrary insult, crudity, annoyance, and the like, and generally facilitates the ease of social interaction. These forms of activity may be characterized as those required by civility, which defines the corresponding attitude which Beatrice shrewdly described Claudio as being in when she said: 'The count is neither sad, nor sick, nor merry, nor well; but civil count, civil as an orange, and something of that jealous complexion.'[5] The rational contractors will agree to a principle which requires the forms of behaviour associated with civility, because the acceptance and action on such a standard will ensure a higher lowest, since the principle will require persons to contain their own trivial moodiness, ill will, or aggravation within their own persons, and not allow its arbitrary expression to others, causing ill feeling in them.

However, the contractors will not agree to the justifiability of coercion in enforcing this ultimate standard; this is a consequence of the relatively minor benefits that observance of civility secures, as compared with the principles of non-maleficence, mutual aid, consideration, and paternalistic guidance, so that making coercion justifiable in enforcing it would lower the prospects of desire satisfaction of the breaker of the principle out of all proportion to the benefits that his observing it brings. Rather, the contractors would agree that forms of informal criticism, rebuke, and blame are justifiable in enforcing the principle's requirements, since such informal blame would aid in securing a higher lowest, while not involving the disproportionate costs that the justifiability of coercion would involve.

This principle of supererogatory blame would be formulated as follows:

9. Given that principles 1, 2, 3, 4, 5, 6, 7, and 8 are satisfied, or not relevant, persons in their *ordinary* social interactions with other persons, apart from special friendship relations, are to observe a minimum level of politeness to other persons, even where this may mean containing their own idiosyncratic moodiness, aggravation, aggression, or ill will, given that observing such civility involves only a minor cost.

The justification for the priority of principles 1–8 to this principle is that the requirements of the principles of obligation and duty are of such importance in securing higher lowests, fundamental to basic human well-being, that if the requirements of these principles should conflict with civility, then the requirements of civility are not to apply. It is a consequence of this priority relation that the principle is formulated to require persons to contain 'idiosyncratic' moodiness, aggravation, etc., it being assumed that these are not related to the requirements of prior moral principles (as with, for example, resentment, indignation, etc.), but rather to personal and, often, self-concerned moods and frustrations.[6]

The requirement that the principle obtain only in 'ordinary' social interactions with persons generally, quite apart from special friendship relations, follows from the fact that the contractors will wish to allow persons some vent and expression for their personal frustrations and aggressions, though they will not wish these generally expressed in all ordinary social interactions which are part of daily life. They will provide for such human needs for self-expression by the applicability of the principle of beneficence, and its subsidiary principle of gratitude, within friendship and love relations, a part of which is the willingness to enter sympathetically into the frustrations and sadnesses of the friend, or of the beloved. It is a consequence of the contractors' allowing for this that typically the observance of civility in general social interaction is of little or no cost to the person who observes it, since he typically has access to friendship and love relations to alleviate his frustration. However, in those cases where people lack such recourse, the principle of civility, at least as a principle of supererogatory blame, does not apply. Here, the contractors would regard persons who observe civility, though at great cost to their personal happiness because of having no vent for their frustrations, as going well beyond the requirements of civility as a supererogatory principle of blame; and they would regard the principle of beneficence as applying to such cases, if any principle does.

11. The Principle of Mutual Respect and the Principle of Mutual Love—Supererogatory Principles of Blame

(a) The Principle of Mutual Respect

Another set of general facts, relevant to the rational contractors' decision problem concerning ultimate standards of supererogation, concerns the importance of the exercise and distribution of respect between persons. This derives from the fundamental importance of the desire for personal competence, among typical human desires; and since respect is the logically appropriate response to an exercise of competence, where one values that competence and would desire to imitate it, if possible, the ways in which such respect is distributed, in terms of the sorts of competence that are valued most highly, importantly affect the promotion or frustration of the basic human desire for competence.[7] In considering the institutional principles of justice in chapter 8, the contractors already acknowledged the importance of such respect when, in formulating the second principle of justice, they required that inequalities of status, which include, of course, various attitudes of respect, are justified only when they are related to facilitating the exercise of greater talent which works out in the interests of all standard classes, and raises the life prospects of the least advantaged class as high as possible. However, when they come to consider principles regulating the relations of men, as men, apart from any common institutions, the contractors will be concerned to regulate the distribution of such respect in a rather different way: i.e. requiring persons to *show* an equal respect for all other persons, as beings with the developed capacities and competence to use and act on the principles of morality. From the point of view of the original position, where the contractors are completely ignorant of their particular desires, nature, and circumstances, the contractors will secure a higher lowest by agreeing to such a principle, since they will thus hedge against the possibility that they may be deficient in various competences, and ensure that, even if they are so deficient, they will still receive an equal respect in virtue of the basic competences central to the exercise of morality. In deciding upon such a *non*-institutional principle, the arguments crucial to the acceptance of the second principle of justice, and its inequalities of status and respect, are *not* relevant, since respect here is *ex hypothesi* not leading to greater benefits from common institutions.

However, the contractors will not agree to the justifiability of coercion in enforcing the requirements of this principle, because this would put too great a burden on persons who omitted to do what the principle required, as compared with the benefits that greater conformity to the principle would bring. Rather, the contractors would agree that various forms of informal criticism and rebuke would be justified in getting people to act on it, since the burdens this would place on omissions would be relatively slight as compared with the benefits (a higher lowest) secured by greater conformity. And thus, the principle of mutual respect would be accepted as one of supererogatory blame, which would be formulated thus:

10. Given that principles 1, 2, 3, 4, 5, 6, 7, 8, and 9 are satisfied, or not relevant, then persons, in their ordinary social interactions with other persons, are to guide their behaviour in regard to other persons in accord with an equal respect for their mature competence to exercise and apply the principles of morality, regulating and, if

necessary, suppressing expressions of their own competence in some other respect, if this conflicts with an equal respect for all persons.

The priority of the principles of obligation and duty to the principle of mutual respect seems obvious; and it is perhaps only illuminating to remark here on the special limits on the sense in which the second principle of justice is prior to the principle of mutual respect. That is, while it is the case that the contractors would agree to the priority of principle 2 over principle 10, where both may seem to apply, since inequalities of respect may be indispensable to securing greater advantages for all, it should *not* be supposed that the existence of co-operative institutions, to which the second principle of justice applies, renders the principle of mutual respect wholly inapplicable. On the contrary, the requirements on justifiable inequalities of respect, set by principle 2, are extremely stringent ones; and it is not to be, without argument, assumed that these stringent requirements are satisfied in any particular case. In so far as any such inequality in respect is not clearly justified by principle 2, it will be proscribed by principle 10; and this may be so in many, if not most, cases.

Setting the principle of civility in a priority relation to that of mutual respect is a wholly arbitrary move, on my part, in so far as it is a convenient way of expressing the fact that the principle of civility typically does not seem relevant, in any conflicting way, when the principle of mutual respect applies. However, if they did conflict, I cannot apprehend any clear decision by the contractors as to which is to apply; perhaps, the best one can do in such a case is to allow persons to choose to follow either the one or the other, but not to choose not to follow either one, at least if their action is to be a right and moral one, though not their moral duty or obligation.[8]

The requirement of this principle that persons suppress their own self-respect for their native superiority or competence, where it conflicts with the requirements of mutual respect, is one of its most important features, and gives some idea of the sort of requirement that this principle involves in particular cases. For example, it proscribes pride and conceit, where these belittle and diminish the personal worth of others; and requires an equal concern in other persons' accomplishments, in so far as this expresses men's basic equal competence as moral agents, and thus proscribes forms of action expressing envy and jealousy; and forbids forms of servility in speech and action which are incompatible with this basic equality. One especially notable feature of the constraints that this principle puts on the expression of pride is a requirement that people, whose conduct for legitimate moral or prudential reasons substantially affects the interests of other people, express, if feasible at little cost, to those affected by their conduct the reasons for their conduct. We have already seen in chapter 8 that the explanation of the reasons for having certain laws by the officials who make or apply the laws is a minimal requirement of the duties of justice of such officials, as a matter of elementary fair notice. Here, the contractors agree to similar requirements applying to such officials and also to many others, not, however, as a principle applying only within institutions, but as principle defining what is owed men, as men; not as a way of giving fair notice, but as a way of acknowledging the nature of others as reasonable and moral men; and not as a principle of duty, but as principle of supererogatory blame. On this principle, it is not enough that one have legitimate prudential or moral reasons for acting in ways that affect (often detrimentally) the interests of others; one must also not act in such a style of unreasoned arrogance that other persons are not put in a position to give weight to one's reasons for action. Note, however, that all these constraints on the expression of pride do not apply to a well-regulated self-respect, which is exercised within the constraints of moral propriety. Indeed, such self-respect is rightly praised as a virtue in so far as it is an ingredient in the moral and good life.

Generally, the principle of mutual respect gives expression to Kant's concept of a principle 'not to exalt oneself above others', a view from which my own account is almost completely derivative.[9] This view, which sees restrictions on pride and conceit as *moral* requirements, may be interestingly contrasted with Hume's rather different view. Thus, Hume puts restrictions on pride for the prudential reason that unregulated pride engenders hate, and urges 'a well-regulated pride, which secretly animates our conduct, without breaking out into such indecent expressions of vanity, as may offend the vanity of others'.[10] This sort of view, which makes humility into a clever strategem of the proud man to ensure that he is really respected, has a certain plausibility and appeal; but it wholly misses the basically moral dimension of such humility, which is a way of expressing respect for the competences central to the moral point of view.[11]

(b) The Principle of Mutual Love

Having agreed to the principle of mutual respect, similar reasoning would lead the contractors to agree to a principle of mutual love, which is analogous to the principle of mutual respect. Thus, as in the case of respect and its relation to the desire for personal competence, the contractors will be aware that the ways in which love and affection are distributed, in terms of the sorts of personal characteristics which are valued most highly, will importantly affect the promotion or frustration of the deep and basic human desire for love; and, as consistent maximiners, they will try to find a principle which will, as regards this set of facts, secure the highest lowest. However, in the case of love, as opposed to respect, the contractors will not consider apt a principle requiring equal love for all, because this would trivialize and render nugatory the very value of personal, intimate, unique affection, a point as old as Aristotle's criticism of communistic systems in the *Politics*, and reaffirmed by McTaggart and Scheler.[12] Rather, the contractors would agree that people, when they *show* affection, show it to others in virtue of their morally dutiful or supererogatory actions, and related personality and character traits, rather than because of arbitrary physical characteristics, e.g. physical beauty. This will be so, because, from the point of view of the original position, the rational contractors will wish to guard against the possibility that they may have such physical attributes (e.g. ugliness, obesity, etc.) that people might, absent acceptance of such a principle, show no affection for them. Such a principle would tend to minimize the incidence of such a lowest, with little sacrifice of the natural desire for beauty, since this could still be pursued, as long as the requirements of mutual love are also satisfied. Further, agreeing to such a principle, the contractors will encourage the development of moral character and benevolent personality, since people are to show affection to persons with such characters; and thus, they will further ensure that the higher lowest, attained by persons' publicly accepting and acting on moral principles, will be attained.

However, the contractors will not agree to coercion in enforcing such a standard, because this will put far too great a burden on individual persons, as compared with the benefits it would secure.

Such burdens would include absurd coercive regulations of loves and friendships (leading to intolerable gaps between persons' feeling and showing affection), the disproportionately heavy penalization of the quite natural desire for beauty, and a perhaps counter-productive distortion of the natural process of the growth and development of natural human affection and love. As McTaggart remarked about this process:

. . . love is not necessarily proportioned to the dignity or adequacy of the determining motive . . .[13]

. . . a trivial cause may determine the direction of very deep emotion. To be born in the same family, or to be brought up in the same house, may determine it. It may be determined by physical beauty, or by purely sensual desire. Or we may be, as we often are, unable to assign any determining cause at all.[14]

Being aware of such facts, the contractors would instead agree to the justifiability of quite mild criticism and blame, if persons omitted to do what the principle of mutual love requires, because the cost of such informal criticism would be slight as compared with the benefits (a higher lowest) secured.

Such a supererogatory principle of blame would, I believe, be formulated as follows:

11. Given that principles 1, 2, 3, 4, 5, 6, 7, 8, 9, and 10 are satisfied, or not relevant, then when persons choose to *show* affection for other persons, they are to do so in virtue of the other persons' characters and personalities, and actions in accord with moral duty and supererogation associated with these dispositions, rather than in virtue of physical characteristics alone—regulating and, if necessary, suppressing the desire to show affection when it would contravene mutual love.

The priority relation of the principles of obligation and duty to this principle follows from the fact that the interests secured by the acceptance of those ultimate standards, as guides to conduct, are extremely fundamental ones, which the contractors will wish to have secured before other principles, securing less fundamental interests, are to apply.

The priority of supererogatory principles 9 and 10 over this principle is a more controversial matter. But, the contractors would, I believe, agree to this priority because it will typically be possible for a person to choose to express affection, in ways in which civility and mutual respect to others will also be satisfied; and the contractors will wish persons to realize this possibility, wherever possible, since a higher lowest is secured.

Finally, the formulation of this principle will make clear that I am not supposing there to be a principle requiring one to *feel* affection or love for another, a supposition which Kant rightly considered absurd.[15] Rather, this principle, as with all the principles I have been discussing, applies to *actions*, in this case, actions of showing affection and love for others, and derivatively, to actions of developing the morally preferable ways of feeling affection (in the same way that one takes action to cultivate one's taste in music, or good wine, viz. by experiencing and directing one's attention to the delicate discriminations in the goodness of things). Obviously, the principle has special point in circumstances where persons can choose to show differential affection between several persons, and where they may have an inclination to do so on the basis of physical characteristics alone. This may be interestingly contrasted with the principle of mutual respect, which also does not require a person to feel such respect, but rather to regulate his conduct in accord with the requirements that such respect would involve. The difference, of course, is that mutual love often obtains where persons do feel affection, but are to show it only when this is not based on physical characteristics alone, whereas mutual respect simply requires various sorts of actions towards other persons generally, no matter what one's actual respect for them.

III. *The Principle of Beneficence*

(*a*) *Its Formulation and Relation to the Original Position*

One final set of facts, relevant to the contractors' decision concerning principles of supererogation, concerns circumstances where persons desire to advance the self-regarding desires of others, where this often does not promote their own interests, and indeed, sometimes substantially frustrates them, resulting in their own pain, privation, injury, or death. Such sympathy for and benevolence toward others take many different forms, ranging from relatively minor kindnesses to others, as part of daily life, to the substantial benevolences of friendship and love relations, to the extraordinary actions of saints and heroes, when their actions are directed towards advancing the interests of others. The contractors would not agree to a principle requiring such forms of beneficence, either as a matter of justifiable coercion or blame if disobeyed. This is because public knowledge and general action on such a standard would not, in any sense, secure a higher lowest than if it were not accepted, since it would lead to a lower lowest than would be the case if it were not accepted (i.e. requiring a substantial sacrifice of self-interest in order to promote the interests of another). Contrast this with the principle of mutual aid, which the contractors accept as a principle of individual duty, precisely because it requires a minimal cost to the helper in securing a great good to the person helped. However, the contractors will not be indifferent to the effects of public knowledge and general action on such a standard, *if* this does not violate prior moral principles, and *if* persons only acted on it when they had the capacity and desire for sympathetic benevolence, which they value more highly than their own interests. If persons acted on this standard in such circumstances, it will secure the promotion of the interests of other persons, and yet the person so acting will voluntarily be performing actions which are a necessary part of his own personal fulfilment and ideals. And thus, the contractors can only gain, and not lose, by agreeing to the principle of beneficence as a principle of supererogatory praise, since they will not make this principle incumbent on themselves if they lack such sympathetic benevolence; and will only make it incumbent on themselves if they do have such capacities, in a way which justifies praise, if they do so act, and no blame, if they do not, and which leaves them at liberty to do as they wish, in any event (there being no justifiable coercion to do or not to do the beneficent act). Thus, the contractors, as in the case of their agreement to the principle of efficiency, will abandon their maximining strategy and rationally accept the gamble that agreement to the principle of beneficence implies, since it is a gamble from which they can only gain. Note, however, that here the contractors' abandonment of the maximining strategy is more extreme than in the case of their agreement to the principle of efficiency; for in the latter case, the contractors continue to maximin to the extent that action on the principle of efficiency does not substantially frustrate an agent's interests, whereas such frustration of an agent's fundamental interests is precisely required by the principle of beneficence. This difference crucially underlies the fact that the contractors agree to the principle of efficiency as a principle of duty and to the principle of beneficence as a principle of supererogatory praise.

The supererogatory principle of praise would, I believe, be formulated as follows:

12. Given that principles 1, 2, 3, 4, 5, 6, 7, 8, 9, 10, and 11 are satisfied, or not relevant, then if a person has the desire and capacity to advance the interests of one or more other people, a desire which he values more highly than the pursuit of his interests, then he is to advance the other's interests, even if this should require the frustration of his own interests.

The priority relation of principles 1–11 to the principle of beneficence is a consequence of the fact that all these principles are accepted by the contractors in order to secure at least a highest lowest, from the point of view of the original position; and the contractors, as consistent maximiners, will wish these principles to be satisfied, before the principle of beneficence is to apply. One interesting feature of this priority relation is that the principle of paternalistic guidance will not apply where rational persons pursue the principle of beneficence, even where it may lead to their privation, injury, or death. The principle of paternalistic guidance only applies to cases of extreme irrationality; but, in the case of the desire to do good to others, where a person values this end above the satisfaction of his own interests and personal advantage (including wealth, health, and even life itself), then it is a perfectly rational course of action for such a person to pursue such an end, at the expense of frustrating his own interests.

Finally, it may be briefly noted that the ideal contract view I have been delineating gives a quite different interpretation of the moral significance of the principle of beneficence than is found in many traditional ethical theories, especially utilitarianism. Utilitarians view the principle of beneficence as fundamental to the moral point of view; as I indicated in my reference to Hume in chapter 6, he supposes that it is the exercise of the perfect sympathies of an ideal observer which is fundamental to the moral point of view; it is this which explains the fact that the utilitarian principle implies the duty that persons sacrifice their own interests, if this maximizes desire satisfaction summed over all sentient beings. This will be a consequence of any view which takes sympathetic benevolence, or, perhaps, love (or, Love), as morally fundamental. In the ideal contract view, however, such benevolence may comprise part of one's justifiable personal ideals, which he is at liberty to pursue, and which it is right that he pursue, and wrong that he not pursue, but it is not part of his moral duty or obligation that he do so. In the Christian West, no doubt such an ideal of love and sacrifice is central to Christian ethics; indeed, for a Christian, the failure of such love may define damnation. Such religious and other traditions of thought and training, which facilitate the emergence and effectiveness of such an ideal in human conduct (assuming the tradition also requires prior moral principles to be acted on, before the principle of beneficence applies), would be preferred from the point of view of the original position over those traditions which did not foster similar ideals. However, it is also important to see that, at least in the ideal contract conception of morality, such a substantive and valuable religious ideal *is* an ideal; for sympathetic benevolence, and the actions associated with it, fall outside the bailiwick of those actions which one may legitimately demand from others, and at least blame them for omitting. It represents, as it were, the area of moral grace—where persons may give what others cannot demand.

(b) The Supplementary Principle of Mutual Kindness: a Supererogatory Principle of Blame

Supplementary to the principle of beneficence, the contractors will accept a principle of mutual kindness which regulates those circumstances where persons may do some small good to others, at negligible cost to themselves, where neither the supererogatory principle of beneficence or the dutiful principle of mutual aid are involved: for example, where a person may do some small favour for another (e.g. give him a match, when asked), or perform some minor kindness or charity. Since they will secure a higher lowest by doing so, they will view slight forms of blame as justified in enforcing this principle, which would be formulated thus:

12a.   Given that principles 1, 2, 3, 4, 5, 6, 7, 8, 9, 10, and 11 are satisfied, or not relevant, then if a person, at negligible cost to himself, is in a position to do some small good for another, he is to do so.

This principle interestingly differs from beneficence in not requiring that the person actually desire the good of the other, a consequence of the fact that the contractors secure a higher lowest by agreeing to the applicability of the principle of kindness quite apart from a person's having the desire to be kind, since persons generally incur such negligible costs in being kind, even if they do not desire the good of others. Further, as a consequence of maximining, this principle is prior to principle 12, and thus principle 12 should be amended to allow for this priority.

(c) The Subsidiary Principle of Gratitude: a Supererogatory Principle of Blame

Having accepted the principle of beneficence, the contractors will be so aware of the goods secured to other persons by a person's acting on this principle that they will wish to encourage such actions further, beyond the mere provision of viewing praise as justified when persons act on it. As in the similar case of mutual aid, the contractors will agree that persons who have voluntarily profited from the goodness of others, are to do something by way of gratitude in advancing the interests of their benefactors. The requirement of voluntary acceptance follows from the maximining contractors' desire that people have a greatest equal liberty in planning the consequences of their actions, whether the consequences are rewards, punishments, or obligations. Though the principle of beneficence is a supererogatory principle of praise, the contractors will agree to the justifiability of quite severe blame in enforcing its subsidiary principle of gratitude, because the justifiability of such blame will substantially increase the likelihood of persons' acting on beneficence without putting a disproportionate burden on the person benefited (since he had the choice of accepting or rejecting the benefaction) and because such a principle will secure a higher lowest through requiring that the benefactor's frustrated interests be remedied by something done in gratitude. However, coercion would not be thought justified in enforcing this principle since such a burden of coercion seems disproportionate to its resulting benefits of greater adherence to beneficence, and especially since the higher lowest which the principle of gratitude secures may be of no relevance to the benefactor's personal ideals and aspirations. Note that this view that the morality of gratitude is importantly related to the morality of beneficence gives expression to Kant's idea that 'Gratitude, moreover, must be regarded especially as a sacred duty, i.e. as a duty whose violation (serving as a scandalous example) can destroy the moral incentive for beneficence in its very principle.'[16] The principle of gratitude would be formulated as follows:

12b.   If a person x has satisfied the requirements of principle 12, given the priority of principles 1–11 and 12a, and has advanced the interests of person y, at the expense of his own interests, by doing some action n, and person y has voluntarily accepted the benefits of n, then person y is to advance the interests of x in return.

The general importance of the principle of gratitude should not be underestimated, for it underlies and explains many of the moral aspects of the relations of friendship and love between mature persons. Thus, since one of the crucial marks of friendship and love relations is the desire to advance the interests of the friend or the beloved, even when so doing contravenes one's own interests, the principle of beneficence applies to such cases, and, by implication, the principle of gratitude, when good is done by one person to another. It is this, I believe, that accounts for the special moral claims of friends and loved ones on our attention and concern, our interest and active sympathy, a consequence of the many goods done for one another by friends and lovers, the sort of continual and systematic human reciprocity that leads to quite deep moral relationships.

The limitation of this principle to mature persons follows from the fact that the principle of gratitude applies only where persons have voluntarily accepted benefits from other persons, which is not the case with infants and young children, who lack the capacity to choose to accept or reject benefactions. Thus, like chapter 9's principle of institutional gratitude, this principle of gratitude regulates the relations of children to parents only where children have grown into mature persons, and then voluntarily accepted parental benefits. This result also follows from the fact that parents' love for young children is not, strictly, the sort of benevolence to which the principle of beneficence applies, since such seemingly beneficent actions are, in fact, part of the moral duties of parents, defined by the principles of justice and paternalistic guidance. In short, parents are not morally at liberty to be or not to be beneficent, since prior moral principles apply. However, when children have grown up, and parents are released from moral duties, then the principles of beneficence and gratitude do apply.

The priority relation specified in 12b seems obvious; for example, it seems clear that the contractors will not wish y to express gratitude to x, when x's benefaction derived from money stolen from z. However, in the light of the above discussion, it is interesting to elaborate some of the consequences of the priority relation of the principles of mutual respect and love to that of beneficence. The priority of the principle of mutual respect, for example, implies that even in the most intimate friendship and love relations, persons are not to use, or misuse, love and friendship as an extension of their own ego (the narcissistic 'projecting one's diffused ego image on another', as Erikson put it),[17] or as a parasitic way of supporting their ego (the desperate imitation, as Scheler noted, 'of the spiritual *vampire*, the hollowness of whose existence coupled with a passionate quest for experience, drives him to the limitless *active* penetration into the inmost reaches of the other's self',[18] a character classically portrayed in Strindberg's *Dance of Death*); but rather, one is to subordinate one's own pride, or lack of it, within the bounds of mutual respect. As Kant put it: '. . . love can be regarded as attracting and respect as repelling; and if the principle of the first bids an approach, that of the second demands that friends halt at a suitable distance from one another.'[19] And the priority of the principle of mutual love to beneficence implies that persons are not to do good to others on the basis of physical appearance alone, since, from the point of view of the original position, a higher lowest is secured by persons not being beneficent on the basis of physical qualities alone.

Finally, if the contractors will agree to a principle of gratitude which is subsidiary to beneficence, they will also agree to one as subsidiary to the principle of kindness, of this type:

12*b*. *cont.*: and if a person x has satisfied principle 12*a*, given that principles 1–11 are satisfied, and a person y has voluntarily accepted the kindness, then y is to do something to advance x's interests in return.

The form that y's gratitude should take should roughly depend on the cost that x incurred in being kind or beneficent, since the contractors only wish gratitude to occur to the point where a higher lowest is secured; thus, a person who incurred great personal cost in being beneficent requires greater gratitude than one who was kind at little or no personal cost. Comparisons such as this are to govern gradations of gratitude, just as related comparisons are relevant to the amount of compensation required by the principle of compensation subsidiary to non-maleficence.

12

NORMATIVE PROPOSITIONS, REASONS FOR ACTION, SPEECH ACTS: THE MORAL CASE

I N the previous six chapters, I tried to develop an ideal contract view of morality, and to relate this view, in a very schematic way, to an account of substantive moral principles, and their priority relations. This account is, in many ways, incomplete. Many contexts in which these principles apply have not been considered at all, e.g. the application of principles 1–4 to various roles voluntarily undertaken (member of a corporation; parent; husband or wife; government officials; professional role; etc.), and the extremely interesting moral questions that this topic would involve, especially the moral force of so-called codes of professional ethics; and even where the application of the principles to a set of circumstances has been considered, the account has been highly general, without the detailed casuistry that complete theoretical adequacy seems to require. And the question of priority relations was treated throughout in a constructive and exploratory way. While, at the start, I bravely pressed the notion of lexicographical priority between the principles, it soon became clear, I think, that this was at best a crude approximation to a much more complex truth; at no point have I even begun to articulate in any satisfying detail what that truth is.[1] And, of course, nothing has been done towards working out a set of moral principles, which would hold in all times and all places, since the set of moral principles formulated above has been derived relative to a set of facts about human life and circumstances that may be of only limited applicability. Generally, the whole question of constructively formulating and justifying substantive moral principles is one of the greatest difficulty, and one which cries out for extended philosophical discussion and exchange in a spirit of theoretical cooperation. Personally, I have no doubt that my own account can be, and will be, superseded by a more illuminating and economical

account, and thus entertain no illusions about its finality and completeness. Indeed, such other accounts are welcome, for moral
philosophy in this century has suffered, I believe, from its for-
malistic emphasis, however much more theoretically sophisticated
we may be because of our education in meta-ethical discussions,
as opposed to 'mere' casuistry; and thus, if my account will lead
others to explore further the relation of the concept of morality
to substantive moral principles, it will have served an important,
perhaps its most important, theoretical purpose.

The general theoretical aim of the extended discussion of moral
principles, above, has been to use that account as part of a general
theory of reasons for action, already briefly sketched in Part I.
What I should like to do in this, and the following two chapters,
is to show precisely how this is so, in a way that satisfies the three
criteria of theoretical adequacy that I set myself as theoretical
benchmarks in chapter 1. The discussion of this chapter will proceed thus: first, I shall relate the above set of moral principles to
various normative propositions whose truth value depends on them;
then, this view will in turn be used to account for expressions
about moral reasons for action, both in their justificatory and
explanatory uses; next, I shall discuss the relation between this
class of reasons for action and that class defined by the principles
of rational choice of Part I; and finally, an account will be offered
for the important uses of various expressions in speech acts,
phenomena for which some have supposed propositional theories
unable to provide an account.

However, before undertaking the task of indicating the kind of
propositional theory of reasons for action that the ideal contract
theory makes possible, I must note one caveat. While I myself
undertook the development of the ideal contract construction in
order to provide a propositional theory of reasons for action, it must
in all candour be granted that the construction itself does not necessarily require a propositional conclusion on the meta-ethical question. Indeed, it seems to me quite likely that a non-propositional
theorist, who remains unconvinced by my arguments for pro-
positionalism, could none the less find the ideal contract theory
useful for the analysis of substantive moral questions. One good
example of such a non-propositional theorist is Hare, whose theory,
as I indicated in chapter 6, could easily incorporate the ideal contract conception, as Hare himself would admit.[2] However, I do

not propose to indicate further specifically how non-propositional theories can make use of the ideal contract view. My view is propositional; and it is this view which it is incumbent on me now to explain and defend.

1. *Moral Principles and Normative Propositions*

(a) *The Language of 'Ought'*

The language of 'ought' is perhaps the most general normative term which can be used in indicating the requirements of standards of widely different kinds, including standards which do not seem to apply, in any direct way, to actions at all, but rather to events or things, or beliefs about such events or things. Consider, for example, the following:

1. The sun ought to be up in twenty minutes.
2. The weather ought to turn rainy tomorrow, from the sky's look.
3. Judging from its colour, it ought to be silicon.
4. If plants are to flourish, they ought to receive sunlight.
5. If the room is to be aired, the door ought to be open.
6. A good car ought to have comfortable seats, surely.

Such not unnatural locutions seem, in various ways, to depend on standards of evidence and induction (1–3), on various causal connections which are assumed to exist (4–5, as variants of von Wright's 'anankastic' statements),[3] or on standards of value defined by normative concepts (6). Obviously, they have important logical relations to reasons for believing x, as opposed to not-x, to be the case. If one were to construct a general theory of reasons, *simpliciter*, such locutions would be important examples with which to show analogies between reasons for action and reasons for belief; however, I point out these 'ought'-expressions only to illustrate the generality and diversity of 'ought' language.

Within the class of standards that apply directly to human actions, 'ought' language, as well as the related 'should', seems to be a quite general term used to indicate the requirements of various sorts of standards. Having already elaborated this in Part I with reference to social rules and the principles of rational choice, it only remains to indicate how this is so as regards the principles of morality. Thus, given that people have the capacity to understand and to act on moral principles, then moral principles exist and apply; so that derivations of the following sort are made possible and true:

1. Men ought not intentionally to kill other men, *ceteris paribus*.
2. *x* is a man; *y* is a man; other things are equal.
3. *x* ought not intentionally to kill *y*.
3*a*. *y* ought not intentionally to kill *x* (hereafter to be referred to as 'vice versa').

Analogous to the similar distinctions in Part I, 'ought'-expressions, depending on moral principles, are analysed as expressing propositions either about the general requirements of a moral principle (primary normative propositions expressed by sentences of type 1), or as expressing propositions about the requirements of those principles in specific cases to which they apply (derivative normative propositions, expressed by sentences of type 3).

Four important aspects of this analysis must be noted. (1) It is, of course, not claimed that, as a psychological fact, persons go through the above process of derivation whenever they use 'ought'; one is delineating, rather, a logical structure of *belief*, which underlies the use of this language; but persons may use such language and have such beliefs, without being able fully to express them, let alone being logically compelled to have engaged in some psychological process of deliberation that philosophical dogmas may require. (2) Importantly, on this account, the *ceteris paribus* conditions (the form and complexity of which the previous four chapters indicated) must be satisfied, or believed to be satisfied, before the 'ought' terminology is either true or appropriate; thus, the basic analytic claim here is that the serious use of 'ought', without any qualification or any understood special context of use, expresses *beliefs* about on balance justification;[4] but, such beliefs may be quite unfounded (e.g. the belief expressed by 'you ought to kill him', where the primacy of moral retribution is assumed; or the belief expressed by criminals saying 'we ought to rob that bank', where the criminals assume that society has been so unjust to them as to warrant such actions). The qualification about special contexts of use covers those cases where the 'ought' terminology is quite sensibly used to indicate the relevance of different sorts of principles to a final decision concerning what is, on balance, justified; and, those other usages of 'ought', where the speaker is explicitly abstracting from moral considerations, and where the tags 'from the prudential point of view' or 'from this technical point of view' are either explicitly stated, or implicitly assumed (e.g. hired killers considering the most efficient way to accomplish their aims; or a nation's policy-maker who, imbued with the theory of *Realpolitik* so common in international affairs, may say '*x* is, of course, the morally wrong thing to do, but we ought to do *x*, if we wish to promote national interests'). However, where 'ought' is used without these qualifications, it implies that *ceteris paribus* conditions are satisfied, so that, though a politician may sensibly assert that the nation ought to do *x*, if it wishes to promote its aims, it will still be true to say, without any such qualification, that the nation ought not. (3) In this view, the language of 'ought' is quite generally used to indicate the requirements of principles of action *simpliciter*, cutting across their distinction into moral principles of obligation or duty and supererogation, or into the principles of morality and those of rational choice. As long as the priority relations embodied in the *ceteris paribus* conditions are believed to be satisfied, the language of 'ought' is appropriate; and true, if the principles in question, with their priority relations, do, in fact, apply. And (4), this view of the language of 'ought' also provides an account for Hare's concept of the universalizability which he supposes to be at least a necessary logical feature of this language.[5] Given that the truth or falsity of normative 'ought' propositions depends, in this case, on the applicability of moral and rational principles of action, *ceteris paribus*, then if two cases are exactly similar as regards the requirements of these principles, the 'ought' terminology is equally true or appropriate. This consideration indicates how little universalizability is a sufficient criterion of moral principles or issues, since it equally obtains in the case of the principles of rational choice, where it seems quite implausible to suppose them to be moral principles (whatever may have been the view of Epicurus or Hobbes); and more extremely, since it holds in the case of literally any standard that a person consistently and sincerely holds to as an ultimate standard, thus making possible his use of the 'ought' terminology. Thus, though universalizability may do as a criterion of the consistency and sincerity of one's principles, it will not do as a sufficient criterion of their morality.

(b) The Language of 'Duty' and 'Obligation': a Reductive Analysis in Terms of 'Ought'

While 'ought' seems to have a sort of generalized ubiquity in indicating the requirements of standards of widely different kinds, the language of 'duty' and 'obligation' has a much more restricted application. Thus, note that there do not seem to be natural uses of 'duty' and 'obligation' where they can be sensibly substituted for 'ought' in expressions of the sort 'plants ought to have sunlight to flourish', though clearly the deontic 'must' is, in some cases, substitutable. Even as regards standards of action alone, 'duty' and 'obligation' seem to cover a much narrower area than the more general 'ought'.

My account of the distinguishing nature of moral obligation and duty is clear, I think, from chapter 7. But, in the context of the present discussion, it is necessary to formalize the view of 'obligation' and 'duty' sentences, as expressing a certain kind of normative proposition, that was given only an intuitive formulation in that chapter. Thus, I should like to suggest that the language of 'duty' and 'obligation', and the related 'must', in a moral context, is susceptible to a reductive analysis in terms of the language of 'ought'. That is, given the existence and applicability of certain moral principles, the following sort of derivation is made possible and true:

1. Men ought not intentionally to kill other men, *ceteris paribus*, and men ought to be forced not to do so, if necessary, by coercion and threat of coercion, *ceteris paribus*.
2. X is a man; y is a man; in both senses, other things are equal.
3. X ought not intentionally to kill y, and ought to be forced not to do so, if necessary, by coercion and threat of coercion; and vice versa.

I should like to claim that this derivation expresses the same propositions as those expressed by:

1a. Men have a duty (or obligation) not to kill other men, *ceteris paribus*.
2a. X is a man; y is a man; other things are equal.
3a. X has a duty (or obligation) not to kill y; and vice versa.

In this view, what is distinctive of the language of 'obligation' and 'duty', as opposed to the language of 'ought', is that standards imposing obligations and duties make possible and true not only 'ought' propositions concerning doing the thing required, but also 'ought' propositions concerning others' forcing one to do the thing in question, *ceteris paribus*.[6] These *ceteris paribus* conditions refer to the considerations of the justice and effectiveness of such coercion on which I have dwelt sufficiently, I hope, in previous chapters.

A consequence of this view is that the language of 'duty' and 'obligation' is not appropriate for all moral principles, let alone for both the principles of morality and rationality, for the formulation of these principles does not always include provisions about the appropriateness of coercion, *ceteris paribus*—e.g. this is not the case for the moral principles of supererogation, or the principles of rational choice. And thus, while the 'ought' terminology is appropriate in indicating the requirements of these principles, *ceteris paribus*, 'obligation' and 'duty' are not. It is this fact which accounts for the sense in which the 'ought' terminology, where used to indicate requirements of the principles of supererogation or the principles of rational choice, *ceteris paribus*, importantly leaves human choice at liberty as regards choosing to do what these principles require: one is at liberty in the sense that one cannot be justifiably forced to do or not to do the thing in question, by coercion or the threat of coercion, even where this may be an indispensable means of securing obedience to the principles, in a particular case. And it is this fact which further accounts for the special normative burden placed on human choice by principles of obligation and duty: one is not at liberty to choose to do or not to do the action required, for one can be justifiably forced to do what is required, by coercion or the threat of coercion, *ceteris paribus*.

A further consequence of this view is that, where 'obligation' and 'duty' are used to indicate the requirements of different moral principles to the consideration of what course of action is, on balance, justified, it will not logically follow from one's being under an obligation to do x that one ought to do x, in the *ceteris paribus* sense, for one's obligation to do x may not obtain in certain circumstances because of the priority relation of other principles in these circumstances. However, when 'obligation' and 'duty', as with 'ought', are used without qualification, they carry with them a claim about *ceteris paribus* conditions being satisfied, and the logical relation to the *ceteris paribus* 'ought' will hold, or be assumed to hold.

Finally, this general propositional account of the concepts of obligation and duty is compatible with the introduction of further differentia for distinguishing obligation and duty in certain contexts, a matter already canvassed in chapter 7.

11. *Moral Principles, Normative Propositions, and Reasons for Action*
(*a*) *Reasons for Action in the Justificatory Sense*

The justificatory use of moral reasons for action is that use whereby such reasons may be proposed to a person, as justifying a certain course of conduct, quite apart from any question of his desire and capacity to accept and act on such reasons for action. Examples of this usage are:

1. There is no reason for killing this innocent man.
2. But, what about your child?; surely, any good reason there may be for suicide is overridden because of the effects it would have on him.
3. There is no reason for such arrogance.
4. You had no reason to be so cruel to a child.
5. National self-interest can give no good reason for such injustice.
6. I don't doubt but you may have some reason for such incivility, but no good reason, in these circumstances.
7. One always has a reason to do good to others, no matter what the cost—at least, this is my view as a Christian.
8. The distress of a friend is always a good reason for assistance.

Coherent with the general view of reasons for action suggested in Part I, I should like to claim that sentences of the type 1–8 express propositions which indicate the requirements of various moral principles. The view may be divided into three parts, covering respectively (i) conclusive reasons for action, (ii) good or generally sufficient reasons for action, and (iii) some or a reason for action.

(i) Concerning sentences which make claims about conclusive reasons for action (e.g. 'there is no reason at all for killing this innocent man'), such sentences express propositions about the requirements of moral principles on balance, with the *ceteris paribus* conditions satisfied; thus, sentences of this type express the same proposition as that expressed by the *ceteris paribus* use of 'ought' sentences, where these indicate the requirements of moral principles (e.g. 'it is not the case that one ought to kill this innocent man'). The claim of conceptual equivalence between the use of certain 'there are reasons for' and 'one ought' utterances does not seem to me an eccentric view, but rather gives an account for what seems an important logical relation between the use of these utterances in the language.[7] Note that in this analysis if there is truly conclusive moral reason to do *x*, then *x* is the morally right thing to do; and if *x* is the morally right thing to do, then there is conclusive moral reason to *x*. And, in this view, also, if a person believes there to be conclusive moral reason to x, when there is not such conclusive moral reason, then the person by definition does not have conclusive reason to x. At best, he has a good reason to x.

(ii) Concerning sentences which make claims about good, or generally sufficient, moral reasons for action (e.g. 'the distress of a friend always provides good reason for assistance', 'there is good reason to give aid', etc.), these sentences express propositions about the requirements of moral principles which generally or typically hold on balance, and which one has good reason to believe hold in a particular case, but which may be overridden by prior principles in a special context; or, such sentences express propositions about the requirements of moral principles which one only reasonably believes the contractors would agree to, since one lacks certain knowledge of the general facts on which the contractors by hypothesis base their decision (e.g. as in the case, mentioned in chapter 8, of principles regulating economically and socially underdeveloped nations). Sentences of these types do not express the same propositions as those expressed by 'ought'-expressions *simpliciter*, but do express the same propositions as sentences like 'generally, one ought to help a friend in distress' and 'there is good reason to believe that one ought'; however, these sentences may be used as evidence for the truth of the propositions expressed by sentences using 'ought' *simpliciter*.

(iii) Concerning sentences which make claims about there being some or a reason for action (e.g. 'one always has a reason to do good to others'), such sentences express propositions about the requirements of one principle, or class of principles, in abstraction from the *ceteris paribus* provisions which other principles place on their applicability; this can occur, for example, where one principle of rational choice is employed in abstraction from a prior rationality principle (as noted in chapter 4); or where the principles of rationality are used in abstraction from the prior principles of morality; or where a principle of morality is used in abstraction from a prior moral principle (e.g. the principle of efficiency is pursued irrespective of the requirements of the principles of justice). Thus, the 'ought' terminology only expresses the same concept as the 'some reason' terminology in those special contexts where 'ought' is used to indicate the different sorts of principles which are relevant to a judgement of justification on balance, or in those contexts where 'ought' is used to indicate the requirements of a certain class of principles, e.g. the principles of rational choice as applied to a special prudential or purely technical problem, in explicit abstraction from the requirements of other principles.

Analogous to the special contexts of the use of 'ought', there seem to be similar special contexts of the use of 'good reasons' terminology. Thus, if it is understood that one is talking from a purely technical or prudential point of view, abstracting from other considerations, then there does seem to be a usage of 'good reasons for doing x', and even 'conclusive reasons for doing x', where both would be naturally followed by 'from this special technical or prudential point of view'. However, without such qualifications, the above account of reasons for action will, I believe, hold, so that it may be that, though one ought to do x, or has good, and even conclusive, reason for doing x, from a certain technical point of view, it still is correct and true to say that one ought not, and has conclusive reason not, to do so. And if, as I believe, the notion of bad or insufficient reasons for action is to be, at least in part, understood in terms of using a principle of action in abstraction from its priority relations (it also may involve the misuse of a single principle, even where prior principles are satisfied), then it will still be true to say that a good, or conclusive, reason, from a certain technical point of view, may be a bad reason *simpliciter*.

Within the framework of this general propositional view of reasons for action, further distinctions may be made analogous to the similar distinctions made in discussing the 'ought' terminology above. Thus, it is possible to set out analogous derivations to those mentioned previously, of the following sort:

1. There are conclusive reasons for persons not intentionally to kill other persons, if prior principles are satisfied or not relevant (i.e. *ceteris paribus*).
2. x is a person; y is a person; other things are equal.
3. There are conclusive reasons for x (you) not intentionally to kill y; and vice versa.

Or, similarly:

1a. Persons have a conclusive reason not intentionally to kill other persons, *ceteris paribus*.
2a. x is a person; y is a person; other things are equal.
3a. x has (you have) a conclusive reason not intentionally to kill y; and vice versa.

Sentences of type 1 and 1a express primary normative propositions, and sentences of type 3 and 3a express derivative normative
propositions, both of which are roughly identical to the propositions
expressed by the related 'ought' terminology, and the truth-value
of which depends on the existence of moral principles, and their
priority relations.

One interesting question arises in this context, which it is worth
considering: do 1 and 3 and 1a and 3a express precisely the same
propositions, or are they in some important way different? Thus,
G. R. Grice suggests that the propositions expressed by sentences
of the type 1 and 3 are true on the basis of the principles alone,
whereas the propositions expressed by sentences of the type 1a
and 3a importantly assume that the agent must have had a good
reason for judging the relevant moral principles to apply.[8] What
Grice is trying to introduce by this distinction is some notion of the
objective requirements on human action of moral principles as
contrasted with the requirements of those principles as subjectively
perceived by agents within their reasoned judgement of matters
of fact, roughly covering the area of problems known in twentieth-
century philosophy as objective versus subjective obligation.[9]
Such a distinction may have little importance at the moment of an
agent's choice of the course of action he believes on balance
justified, since this situation provides little use for the distinction,
a point made by Sidgwick and, more recently, by Baier;[10] but,
it clearly has relevance where another person criticizes the agent's
decision or prospective decision,[11] or where the agent himself
criticizes his decision when past. For example, in the latter case,
the person may say 'I did what I sincerely and for good reason
believed to be right, but I see now it was wrong'; and there are
many different sorts of explanation for this, some of which are
blameworthy and some not. However, it does not seem to me that
this distinction is logically drawn through the 'have' and 'is'
terminology, even when expressed in the past tense. Compare, for
example:

1. In those circumstances, there was good reason for my doing what
    I did, but I see now it was not a conclusive reason, given other
    circumstances which I cannot have known.
1a. In those circumstances, I had good reason for my doing what I
    did, but I see now I did not have conclusive reasons, given other
    circumstances which I cannot have known.

where the language of 'is' and 'have' seems to cover roughly the same logical territory. Such examples seem to me to indicate that we must look elsewhere to find the concepts which will clarify the distinction that Grice is after.

The way in which Grice's distinction can be more profitably drawn, and in which to clarify the real issues involved in the older, and often confused, tradition of objective versus subjective obligation, seems to me to be through an understanding of the different implications of conclusive reasons, and good reasons, for action in their relation to the different, though related, questions of the rightness of acts and the moral worth of agents.[12] As a matter of objective normativity, those actions are right and moral, or rational, which, in fact, conform to the requirements of the principles of morality and rationality, given their priority relations; or, putting the point equivalently, which there is conclusive reason to do in the circumstances, where a conclusive reason for action is to the area of practice what a conclusive reason for belief is to knowledge of empirical fact. However, people often have only good, or generally sufficient, reasons for doing some action x, either because they have only good, but not conclusive, reasons for believing certain relevant matters of fact, or because they cannot be certain that all relevant moral features of the situation have been taken into account because of distortions of self-interest, lack of moral sensitivity and imagination, inconsistency, and the like. As a matter of moral worth, such people are not morally blameworthy if, in the circumstances, they had good moral reasons for doing x (being extremely careful in considering what were the requirements of moral principles), though it later turned out that those reasons were not conclusive reasons and that they did something wrong and immoral. The ideal contract view has, I think, already indicated the explanation for this phenomenon, for the entire view of the justifiability of coercion, blame, and praise (in terms of the criteria of equal liberty and more effectively securing obedience to the relevant principles of action) basically addressed itself to this question of moral worth. In this view, coercion and blame are justified only when the mature agent has intentionally, knowingly, or negligently omitted to do what the relevant moral principles require,[13] and praise is justified only when the agent has intentionally or knowingly done what the relevant principles require, because these requirements both secure to agents the greatest equal liberty in planning their lives, through knowing or having the full opportunity of knowing the consequences of their plans of action, and ensure that a level of exercise of the capacities of understanding and control is observed which most effectively leads to following the requirements of moral principles. And thus, the criteria for the moral worth of an agent, who did wrongful action x, are naturally associated with the question of the existence of good moral reasons for doing x, since such reasons naturally relate to the state of the agent's knowledge and deliberative care. Indeed, the contractors would, I think, explicitly agree that persons should not always act on conclusive reasons for action, because this stringent requirement would not make any allowance for the moral requirement of giving people a fair opportunity to understand and act on moral principles (instead, holding people blameworthy or punishable for all failures to do what is morally right, no matter how unavoidable and reasonable the failure), and would lead to such hesitations in moral action, even where there are good reasons to act, that it would not as effectively secure conformance to moral principles as a less stringent requirement (i.e. requiring good reasons for action). And this will be so even though, in a particular case, this has the consequence of an unavoidable gap between good and conclusive reasons for action (i.e. a person non-culpably doing a wrongful act).

Several final points are relevant to an assessment of the adequacy of this theory of moral reasons for action. First, since this account relates the concept of moral reasons for action to a complex set of principles related to a certain sort of original position, the adequacy of the account must be judged relative to the completeness of these principles in mirroring our considered judgements about moral reasons for action. Is it possible, for example, to map some of my admittedly technical definitions on to ordinary language, and to preserve truth values and logical relations? For example, even if, as Hart claimed, 'duty' is not ordinarily used in indicating reasons not to torture children (and I personally do not find any unnaturalness in so using it),[14] is it the case that the terminology we do use (e.g. 'it's wrong to', 'you mustn't', 'you oughtn't') indicates the existence of a moral requirement, which is not dependent on an institutional relation to the child, and is something we could be justifiably forced to do, if necessary? Even if my formulation of the principles of morality should be, as I suspect,

in various ways inadequate, it will still be possible to offer a constructive reformulation of these principles, which better supports
the claim that there is an analytic relation between reasons for
action and principles of action. Secondly, in making such a claim,
it is not proposed that where persons believe moral reasons for
action exist, or where they sincerely and seriously use a form of the
'there are reasons for' or 'I have reason' terminology, this implies
that there are, in fact, such reasons. The claim, rather, is that their
beliefs about such reasons can be shown to relate, *in some way*, to
the requirements of principles of action, no matter how logically
tenuous or irrational such beliefs may be. A suggestion of the sort of
thing I have in mind was indicated in my discussion of the principle
of non-maleficence, where the introduction into the original position
of certain quasi-theological beliefs about the proper human functions yields a rather different set of principles governing non-
maleficence. And presumably, such beliefs, in fact, explain the
difference in moral beliefs about non-maleficence between persons
who have such assumptions and those who do not. Similarly, the
extravagant racial and genetic theories that often underlie views
of the moral inferiority of certain racial groups may be so related
to the concept of morality as to explain how it is that persons
arrive at such *moral beliefs*. And thirdly, the adequacy of the theory
of reasons for action is not only to be tested by its explanatory
power in accounting for ordinary usage and conviction, for no
moral philosopher of any stature has viewed his enterprise as
merely a lexicographical one of accurately registering ordinary
use, though a general test of adequacy has been that the theory
give expression to the most important and central features of
ordinary use.[15] Moral philosophy, rather, seeks to provide a
theoretical framework and systematic justification for moral belief
and conviction; and where the theory and the beliefs will not jibe,
it is not always the theory that is at fault and that requires cor-
rection, for the systematic clarification and general moral persuasiveness of the theory may indicate the desirability of changes
in ordinary use and conviction. For example, my own views on the
moral justifiability of sexual masochism and related questions were
altered in the process of working out moral principles. While, of
course, it is not always, or even often, correct to alter moral convictions to serve the purposes of a moral theory, part of the substantive importance of moral philosophy to practical living is that

this will sometimes, and justifiably, be so. Indeed, one of the most important marks of an intellectually satisfying moral theory is that it enables us to see, in a perspicuous representation, what is justifiably part of our moral beliefs, and what is introduced by other assumptions which may be the residue of shibboleth and arbitrary convention. And thus, theory becomes a filter which we may use in cleansing our moral beliefs of the extraneous particles which have become patched together with the pure element in the process of moral education and development. Whether this is so in the case of the ideal contract view, I leave it to the reader to decide.

(b) Reasons for Action in the Explanatory Sense

In addition to the employment of the concept of reasons for action in the justification of human action, it is also used in explaining human actions, where persons have, in fact, acted *for* certain reasons. In this sense, truly to claim that a person helped another because it was the right thing to do implies that the person did have certain desires and capacities to regulate his life by the principles of morality, and that these desires and capacities explain the action of helping a certain man. In this use of the concept of reasons for action, there is an analytic relation between such reasons and the agent's desires and motives, a claim which is false as a general view about reasons for action in their justificatory employment. My general view of reasons for action, in the explanatory sense, was set out in chapter 4; since that account applies, *mutatis mutandis*, to the case of moral reasons for action, I shall only very generally indicate how it applies to moral reasons for action. For details, the reader is referred to chapter 4.

Again, then, what seems essential to the general notion of explanation is applying a generalization about the causal relation of two events or circumstances to a particular instance of the generalization. In the case of explanation by good or conclusive moral reasons for action, this view would imply that an explanatory answer to the question—'why did A do x?'—must take a form, of which the following would be a schematic representation:

(i) A was in situation B.
(ii) A was a moral agent in that situation.
(iii) In a situation of type B, any moral agent will do x.
(iv) Therefore A did x.

From this abstract scheme, one can see that the notion of explanatory reasons is conceptually parasitic on the notion of justificatory reasons, for to speak of being a moral agent in (ii) is to speak of a complex set of attitudes, which crucially involves the understanding of the principles of morality, and the desire and capacity to execute moral requirements in situations of type B (e.g. a context of mutual aid). Further, in the causal generalization or law which (iii) involves, the principles of morality are also implied, for they indicate what a moral agent, given the situation, would do. And of course, similar explanatory schemata could be set out to clarify the explanation of human actions in terms of bad or insufficient moral reasons for action, where these would involve causal generalizations about types of immoral actions and agents.

As was noted in chapter 4, the crucial mark of explanations in terms of the agent's reasons for action, as opposed, for example, to explanations in terms of chemical blood levels, neurological brain events, and the like (though not Anscombe's mental causes),[16] is that the agent is aware, or has knowledge of, these reasons, in a way in which he is not necessarily aware of other sorts of explanations and *the* reasons for the agent's behaviour that they may specify. And while this awareness does not imply that the action in question must (logically) have been preceded by a process of conscious deliberation, it does imply that the agent acts from certain desires, capacities, and beliefs, the latter of which could be, in some perhaps quite indirect way, elicited by questioning. For the details of this, the reader is again referred to chapter 4, where this issue has already, I think, been adequately covered; and the repetition of which here seems quite superfluous.

III. *The Relation of Reasons Moral and Rational*

In Part I, when discussing the requirements of the principles of rational choice, it was claimed that these principles only applied when the principles of morality were satisfied, or not relevant; and, in discussing the principles of morality, from the opposite direction, I indicated that the principles of morality were in an absolute priority relation to the principles of rationality. Having now set out a general account of these principles, it is time to consider more explicitly their relation to one another, in order that one may see in its broad outlines the general theory of reasons for action that I am proposing. But first, by way of counterbalancing the claim of a priority relation between the principles of morality and rationality, note that there is an important sense in which, in my view, the concept of morality conceptually depends on the concept of rationality; that is, the ideal contract analysis of the concept of morality incorporates the principles of rational choice since it depends on the concept of those ultimate standards that rational men would unanimously agree to from a certain sort of initial position of equal liberty. The introduction of the rationality concept into the analysis of morality does not, of course, in any way imply that the principles agreed to in the original position are either extensionally or intensionally equivalent to the requirements of the principles of rational choice as used by an individual person to regulate the pursuit of his aims, a point easily seen by considering the principles of morality formulated in the previous four chapters. One simply must distinguish here the use of the concept of rationality in the abstract original position of equal liberty and the application of the rationality concept to the choices of an individual in pursuing his particular aims and desires; in short, following Kant, one must distinguish rationality as autonomy from rationality as heteronomy.

Generally, the following propositional account is offered of sentences employing the concepts of morality and rationality: sentences of the type 'act x is right (or moral)' are analysed as expressing the same proposition as 'act x is required, or not forbidden to be done by principles which would be accepted by rational contractors in an original position of equal liberty and in the absence of any particular knowledge of their own desires, nature, or circumstances, as ultimate standards governing their conduct towards other persons within their common institutions and apart from them, provided that these principles were to be publicly known and generally acted on'; sentences of the type 'act x is wrong (or immoral)' are analysed as expressing the same propositions as 'act x is required not to be done, by principles which would be accepted by rational contractors, etc., as ultimate standards, etc.'; sentences of the type 'act x is rational' are analysed as expressing the same proposition as 'act x is required by the principles of rational choice, given the relevant agent's desires'; and 'act x is irrational' expresses the same proposition as 'act x contravenes the requirements of the principles of rational choice, given the relevant agent's desires'. As regards the analysis of

rationality, note that this account is more general than the view
suggested in Part I, as I indicated in chapter 6; in this view, the
concept of rationality strictly involves the more satisfying ways in
which an agent can achieve his ends, whatever those are, whether
self- or other-regarding; and thus, if an agent *in fact* has the desire
to be moral which he values absolutely higher than the pursuit of
his self-regarding ends, then being moral is the rational course of
conduct, quite apart from the relation of being moral to advancing
the agent's interests. Thus, theoretical completeness, in the formulation of the principles of rationality, would seem to indicate
the formulation of a sixth principle of rational choice, in addition
to the five formulated in chapter 3, precisely to this effect, i.e.

6. Given a class of the agent's desired ends, which, from a dispassionate
   and informed point of view, he values absolutely higher than his
   other ends, plans of action which satisfy the former ends are to be
   adopted, and plans to satisfy the agent's other ends are to be
   adopted only in so far as they are compatible with the satisfaction
   of the former ends

—a principle, which, obviously, will be in a priority relation to the
other principles of rational choice, though the principles of morality
will be prior to it. The point of introducing the phrase, 'from a
dispassionate and informed point of view', into this principle is
to exclude cases of alcoholism and addiction from the principle's
domain of application: the alcoholic's craving for alcohol, or the
addict's for drugs, are not forms of desire which the agent values
absolutely higher than his other ends from a dispassionate and
informed point of view, but are precisely forms of craving which
undermine the agent's very capacity for rational assessment and
planning, let alone control, to the frustration of his substantial
interests. In short, one here has the conviction that, *if* the alcoholic
or narcotics addict were in a position dispassionately to assess and
plan for the satisfaction of his craving, as opposed to his other
desires, he would give no special weight to this craving, but would
try, in some way, to eliminate it, in accord with the dominance
principle. However, with this sketchy explanation aside, the important thing to see is that, in my view, questions of rationality
depend completely on what the agent's desires are. Thus, in this
view, acts may be right and moral, though irrational (e.g. an
amoralist's keeping his promise where he could substantially
advance his interests through breaking it, and no one would

know), and rational, though immoral (e.g. white South Africans' creation of apartheid, which may advance their aims quite well, but which is none the less immoral). The concepts of rationality and morality simply have these different intensions and consequent different possible extensions, for the principles of rationality depend on the notion of best, or satisfactorily, realizing the agent's aims, whatever they are, whereas the principles of morality put certain sorts of substantive constraint on the kinds of ends an agent may legitimately pursue.

Importantly, the claims of synonymy, as regards the propositions expressed by the above sentences, are not to be construed as obvious statements of concept identity, to which a person will immediately assent, as with 'bachelor' and 'unmarried man'. Indeed, I dare say that the philosophically uninitiated ordinary man might well take the proposed definition of morality as a kind of joke, were it offhandedly mentioned. Instead, the above claims of synonymy seem more plausibly understood in Brandt's sense of covert, as opposed to overt, synonymy,[17] i.e. as involving analyses of extremely complex concepts (not unlike 'I know x' or 'that is true'), where the proposed, quite complicated analysis of a certain concept may be accepted as expressing the sense of that concept only after extended reflection on the systematic power and plausibility of the theory, as opposed to other theories, shown to be in various ways inadequate.

This general view of the concepts of rationality and morality can be usefully given detail through an elaboration of the fivefold typology of acts briefly sketched at the end of chapter 7, it being understood that this typology only applies to human actions where principles of action apply, i.e. where persons have the developed capacities of understanding and control associated with regulating one's life in accord with the principles (thus, the principles will not apply to the actions, or behaviour, of infants, or mental deficients, or animals, though, of course, certain of the principles regulate the actions of other persons in regard to these persons or creatures).

(i) The first category of acts are those which are moral, in the sense of being required by principles of obligation and duty 1–8. Right acts of this kind are not only things one is under a moral obligation or duty to do, but things one has no moral right not to do. This follows from the general account of moral rights proposed in chapter 7, i.e. that the concept of Y's having a moral right to some action x (whether it is some action of his own or some action of some other person or persons) is equivalent to the concept of moral principles of obligation and duty either not requiring that Y either do or not do x, or as requiring that other persons do some action x, which the principle relates to Y, e.g. not killing him, keeping promises, etc.); thus, if the derivative normative proposition expressed by 'you have a moral duty to x' is true, the derivative normative proposition expressed by 'you have no moral right not to x' is also true, and if there is another person to whom the duty is owed, then the derivative normative proposition expressed by 'he has a right to your doing x' is also true. The consequence of this is that, though principles do not apply to young children, mental deficients, and animals, it is still, strictly speaking, true to say that these persons or creatures have moral rights, since principles of duty regulate mature persons' conduct toward them. If one distinguishes the normal pragmatic context of use of 'have a right' terminology (where the person with the right normally has the mature capacity to claim his rights) from its strict meaning, I see no difficulty or paradox here.

(ii) The second category of acts are those which are wrong and immoral, in the sense of transgressing the requirements of principles of obligation and duty 1–8. The remarks made in (i) concerning sentences employing the concept of moral rights apply here, since persons who omit to do their moral duty have done what they have no right to do.

(iii) The third category of acts are those which are right and moral, in the sense of not being required to be done or not done by any moral principles at all. A sub-class of these acts are those which are required by the principles of rational choice, acts which it is rational to do, and irrational not to do, but which it is *right* for the agent to do or not to do, as he wishes. In so far as acts of this sort are not required to be done or not done by the principles of obligation or duty, a person has the moral right and liberty to do as he pleases, whether he be rational or irrational (within the limits set by paternalistic guidance). In so far as such acts are required by no moral principles at all, but are required by rationality principles, people have conclusive reason so to act, though there are no *moral* reasons for their so acting; and it will be true to say that people ought so to act, though it is not a moral requirement that they do so. And thus, the forms of coercion, blame, and praise, that are appropriate in the case of the applicability of various of the principles of morality, are not here apt. In such cases (which comprise much of ordinary life), it is, importantly, the individual's concern and business whether and in what ways he pursues his self-regarding desires, and indeed his other-regarding desires (e.g. love and hate). And here, the class of acts which it is rational for people to do is as diverse and variegated as people's diverse and various systems of desires and associated psychological histories; so that the notion of some requirement of uniformity of conduct, so typically (though not always)[18] appropriate in the context of applicable moral principles, is improperly dogmatic and stupidly illiberal. But, throughout, if moral principles are relevant, and the agent's rational pursuit of his interests, aspirations, loves, hates, jealousies, envies, and the like, involves his omitting to do what moral principles require, then the reasons associated with rational choice are to have no weight.

(iv) The fourth category of acts are those which are right and moral, since they are required by moral principles of supererogation 9–12 and associated principles, where the prior principles of duty are satisfied or not relevant. Acts of this sort are like those of (iii) since people have a moral right or liberty to do them, as they wish, since coercion and the threat of coercion are not justified in enforcing them; related to this, the 'ought' terminology is appropriate, and the expressed propositions true, where the principles of supererogation in fact apply, though the 'under a duty' terminology is not. However, these acts obviously differ from acts (iii) in that they are required by moral principles, so that omitting to do them is wrong and immoral, and various forms of blame and praise are justified in others enforcing or encouraging persons to observe their requirements.

(v) The fifth category of acts are those which are wrong and immoral, because they omit to do what moral principles of supererogation on balance require. The remarks made in (iv) apply, with appropriate qualifications, to this class of acts. It need only be noted here that there is a systematic distinction between those principles of supererogation which justify blame, if their requirements are omitted, and no special praise, if they are observed, and the supererogatory principle of beneficence which justifies praise, if it is observed, and no blame, if it is not.

IV. *Moral Propositions and Speech Acts*

Having offered the above propositional account of various 'ought', 'under a moral obligation', 'you have conclusive reason', etc., expressions, a view which can be similarly extended, I think, to cover certain 'must' (= 'obligation or duty') and 'should' (= 'ought') expressions, it is now theoretically incumbent on the theory to show how this account is compatible with, and explanatory of, certain speech acts associated with these utterances, speech acts which some have adduced as phenomena for which no propositional theory can account. I do not propose to offer here a detailed account of such speech acts,[19] but rather, like the argument of chapter 4, to show generally how a propositional view can be plausibly related to certain speech acts—especially, commanding (or prescribing), demanding, advising, exhorting, praising, and blaming, in so far as these acts are often performed in speech through the use of certain of the sentences I have claimed to express certain propositions.

First, of course, it is necessary to know, quite generally, what are the distinctive forces of the acts of commanding, demanding, advising, exhorting, praising, and blaming; I shall draw liberally here on the results of my similar inquiry in chapter 4. Generally, these speech acts seem to fall into two types—prospective acts which are intended to affect others' judgement or actions in some direction through the others' understanding of the speech act in question (commanding, demanding, advising, exhorting) and retrospective acts which seem to bear directly on some action already done (praising, blaming). I shall discuss these two types of speech acts separately.

(a) *Commanding, Demanding, Advising, and Exhorting and their Relation to Moral Propositions*

Commanding, demanding, exhorting, and advising are actions, performed by the use of language, of special kinds, i.e. each action has a distinctive, typical, and known (in the language) intention or aim. Thus, commanding and the related speech act of ordering have the aim of getting another to do what one intends him to do, where there is some known context of authoritative and/or coercive superiority, which will typically tend to give the speaker's intentions effect. Often, authoritative and coercive superiority go together, in the sense that part of a person's perception of the authority of many figures includes the belief that the figure has the right to use coercion to enforce his authority; where this is so, commands and orders occur more or less interchangeably. However, where these kinds of superiority fall apart (a man having coercive, but not authoritative, superiority), an order, not a command, is appropriate; thus, a gangster with a gun may order me to put up my hands, but not command me. Demanding, like commanding and ordering, has the aim of securing one's will from the other, with the one difference that here the known context of authoritative or coercive superiority (which typically gives the speaker's intentions effect) includes some notion of the intended action's being specifically *due* to the speaker, who is entitled to claim it, often because of some relevant rule or principle (e.g. requiring keeping promises, returning loaned books, etc.), though not always (e.g. a thief may demand to know the location of your money, where the associated notion of the dueness of telling him derives from his credible threat to use his gun, if you refuse to tell). Exhorting or urging (like persuading) has the aim of influencing the other to do some action through communicating ideas and views, with the distinctive mark that the action is insistently desired by the speaker: so that exhortation may be successful as much because of the great urgency with which the speaker presents his views, as because of the intrinsic persuasiveness of the views themselves. Advising has the aim of communicating to another one's beliefs about which course of action is prudentially or morally justifiable, where the person spoken to typically wants to be prudent or moral, and thus draws on the judgement of others as to what is rational or right in a particular case. As mentioned in chapter 4, two sorts of advice may be distinguished: advising about or upon some course of conduct (where the speaker does not, unlike all the speech acts so far mentioned, intend that his interlocutor do something) and advising someone to do something (going beyond a mere discussion of pros and cons, perhaps implying the speaker's intention that the other do what he is advised to do). While the former sort of advice does not seem as common in the moral as it is in the prudential case, it can be found—for example, an amoralist employs the concept of morality to advise another upon the course of conduct that would be moral, if the other is really morally consistent, where the speaker does not really want or intend the other to do anything, but just to be clear about the implications of morality: thus, Machiavelli advising upon the course of action that true Christianity requires, and noting how little this accords with political experience in the Italian city-states of the Renaissance.

Clearly, such verbal forms of action are of great importance to a society where the natural attitude of morality is widespread, since the principles of morality will often enter into the authoritative context which commanding and demanding assume, and since persons will wish to urge moral principles on others to whom they apply, whether they wish to obey them or not, and advise them as to the precise requirements of these principles, when they wish to obey such principles. Indeed, given the obvious importance of such speech acts, one might expect the existence of forms of language reserved (and understood to be reserved) for signalling the performance of these acts. Of course, such expectations are fulfilled, for there are explicit forms of words which are understood, in the English language, to perform, *ceteris paribus*, these acts, e.g. 'I order', 'I demand', 'I urge', 'I advise', as well as, generally, the use of the imperative mood, especially in expressing commands. However, there are other linguistic expressions which are used to perform such acts, i.e. sentences which express propositions which are so related to the aim of such acts that, in the appropriate circumstances, they can be used to do the act. For example, as mentioned in chapter 4, consider the use of sentences of the kind, 'there is a bull in the field behind you', which express propositions, and yet are used to *warn*, in the appropriate circumstances. Let us consider how this would be so in the case of each of the above speech acts.

In the case of commands and orders, two sorts of case must be separately considered—(i) the usual, ordinary language notion of a command or order, and (ii) the use of the concept of command as a term of philosophical art, e.g. by Hare, in accounting for the prescriptive force of moral utterances. As regards (i), certain sorts of sentences, of the type given a propositional analysis above, can be so related to the typical purpose and context associated with ordinary commands and orders as to be used to command or order. Consider, for example, a judge's use of 'you must pay Jones damages in the amount of harm caused, in this case, 100 pounds', in the appropriate context where this is used to express a derivative normative proposition concerning the requirements of the moral principle of compensation, where these are embodied in the legal system. Here, a publicly known and accepted context of rules exists which empowers the judge's will, as regards certain sorts of cases, to be obeyed by those to whom the rules apply, so that a propositional form of words can be used by the judge to command in a court order, because the requirements in question are those the judge is authoritatively empowered to enforce. Similarly, consider a superior in the armed forces using 'you must shoot him; that's an order', where this is used to express a derivative normative proposition concerning the requirements of the principle of fairness as this relates to a particular regulation which applies in the case in question. As regards (ii), for purposes of simplicity of exposition, let us assume that the use of command as a term of philosophical art is meant to identify three features of the *use* of moral language, in many typical contexts: (i) such language is used to express the speaker's critical attitude of acceptance of moral principles, (ii) it expresses his will that others act on them, where the critical attitude of morality generally exists, so that an expression of will is typically effective in getting others to act on moral principles, and (iii) such expressions of will occur in the context of principles which give persons the authority to insist that others obey the principles, and which require that other persons do so. If this is a plausible rendering of the sense of prescriptive force in using moral language, it is, I think, wholly unmysterious how a propositional theory of moral expressions can account for such *uses* of moral language; for given that a person has the critical attitude of morality (which is widespread) and that the concept of moral principles implies that acts required by them are not the agent's business alone, but are acts in which others may legitimately interfere in getting a person to act on them (forms of interference differing from coercion to blame to praise), then propositional expressions, which precisely indicate the requirements of such moral principles, are ideally suited to giving expression to a moral person's will that others obey moral principles which apply to them, i.e. are ideally suited to commanding, in the technical philosophical use of this notion (e.g. the use of 'you ought to keep your promise to him' to command, in this sense, where the sentence expresses a derivative normative proposition concerning the requirements of the principle of fairness as applied to a particular social institution). Generally, it seems true that a typical presupposition of persons *using* moral language, of the type given a propositional analysis above, is that the persons have the critical attitude of morality, and wish to express their will that others act on it, where the principles in question justify persons in urging moral requirements on others, and where the critical attitude is so widespread that the expression of will is typically effective, or tends to be effective. It is, simply, necessary to distinguish between the propositions expressed by sentences of this sort and the typical speech acts and contexts within which these expressions have their linguistic life and point.

In the case of demands (the aim or purpose being to express one's intention that another do *x*, where typically some context of rules entitles the speaker to the other's doing *x*), there seem to be forms of moral expression, given a propositional analysis above, which are suited to accomplishing this aim in particular circumstances. For example, 'you must return that book; you have no right to keep it any longer, since I loaned it to you for only a week'; 'you must not kill me, since you have no rights to take my, or anyone's, life'; 'you must give me my civil rights', etc., are all sentences, which express derivative normative propositions, in various ways dependent on moral principles, which can be used in making demands. This is so because the propositions expressed by such sentences indicate actions of others to which one is *entitled* under moral principles of obligation and duty (to which the 'have no right' terminology has reference), so that they can be used in making demands on the basis of the entitlement indicated. Generally, the speech act of demanding seems aptly performed by the use of propositions that depend both on moral principles of obligation and duty and the supererogatory principles of blame, since all these principles are such that persons may legitimately expect that others act on them and, at least, blame them if they do not; and thus, these supererogatory principles also underlie, and provide the truth grounds for, propositions which may be used in performing the speech act of demanding, e.g. those expressed by 'you ought to cease this arrogant behaviour', 'you ought to do me this small favour', 'you oughtn't to be so uncivil', etc.

Given the aim of advice delineated above (i.e. communicating to a person one's views about which course of conduct, in a specific situation, is most justifiable, whether by moral principles or principles of rational choice), it seems obvious that, as regards the moral case, there are forms of expression which are ideally suited to this aim, i.e. 'ought'-expressions used in the 'on balance' sense. Since such sentences express true or false propositions, i.e. that a certain act is justified by the principles of morality, they are exactly the form of information which it is the aim of advising to communicate. Thus, these propositions are, in the appropriate context, used to advise. However, one qualification must be added to this view as applied to moral, as opposed to prudential, advice, which is a consequence of the special nature of moral principles as related to speech acts; while both moral and prudential advice are typically only given to a person x where x sincerely wants to do what is right or rational (so that x wishes to draw upon the judgement of others in arriving at his own decision), in the moral case when x does not desire to do what is right, and the speaker in question knows this, the 'ought' terminology is not used to advise, but rather to command (in the technical sense),[20] demand, exhort, plead, etc. In the prudential case, on the other hand, where x does not desire to be rational, the use of 'ought' does not yield to the analogous range of speech acts as in the moral case: e.g. commanding and demanding are not appropriate here, though pleas may be (assuming, of course, that no moral principles are relevant to the prudential advice). This dissimilarity is a consequence of the distinctive nature of the principles which underlie these speech acts: where moral principles apply to a particular case, a person may justifiably interfere to insist that others obey them (indicating they will be blameworthy if they do not, or praiseworthy if they do); but, where the principles of rational choice alone apply, the principles of morality being satisfied or not relevant, a person may do as he wishes, with no form of such insistence (e.g. command, in the technical sense) being justified in getting him to be rational. Thus, the propositional analysis importantly clarifies the grounds for using certain expressions to make some speech act, as opposed to another; for, in this case, as Kant put it, 'The maxim of self-love (prudence) merely advises; the laws of morality command.'[21]

As regards exhortation, where the typical aim is to get another to do something, by presenting various ideas and views with seriousness and urgency, it is not difficult to see how forms of moral expression, given a propositional analysis above, can, in the appropriate context, be used to exhort. This occurs, for example, when an agent refuses to weigh the moral considerations relevant to his action, and another says 'I know you don't care; but you ought to care' (or, 'you ought to think of her for a change' 'you mustn't be so selfish', 'you mustn't break your promise, just because it's inconvenient'), trying to put the agent's prospective action in such a light that the recalcitrant will acknowledge and act on the moral principles relevant to his action, where the speaker himself has a strong conviction about the importance of the relevant moral principles. Many sorts of case can, of course, be distinguished here as regards the degree of immorality and amorality of the agent in question, e.g. he may be a generally moral man in the midst of a moral lapse, or a generally immoral man who suffers guilt feelings but suppresses them, or a thoroughly amoral man, who has no desire to be moral at all. However, in all these cases, the persons exhorted have the concept of morality and moral principles, and understand the sense in which these principles apply to their actions, however little they may desire to regulate their lives by them. With such persons, we are at the limits of effective argument (if not justification), and forms of exhortation and plea often are the last, and futile, recourse, given that forms of coercion are not justified in a particular case.

(b) *Praising and Blaming and their Relation to Moral Principles*

Praising and blaming are, of course, quite general speech acts, which occur in many non-moral contexts—e.g. praising a football player for his performance, or Mozart for writing *The Marriage of Figaro*, or Shakespeare for writing *Lear*, etc.; and blaming a football player for his ineptitude, Beethoven for writing *Wellington's Victory*, Shakespeare for *Titus*, etc. The characteristic intention or aim of praising involves an expression of approval or admiration for the actions of another as achieving a high level of merit, as defined by standards of value appropriate to acts of a certain kind; and in the case of blame, the aim is an expression of one's disapproval of the actions of another, for reaching so low a level of demerit, as defined by standards of value appropriate to acts of a certain kind. As regards moral praising and blaming, it is, I hope, by now rather obvious how moral expressions, of the sort given a propositional analysis above, may be used in praising and blaming; the propositions expressed by such sentences often bear on the aims of praising and blaming: in the case of praising, where the principle of beneficence has relevance; and in the case of blaming, where the other moral principles have not been obeyed. Thus, for example, 'your actions on the battlefield were beyond the call of duty', 'you did what you ought, but what no man could expect', etc., are sentences, expressing normative propositions about the relevance of the principle of beneficence, which so indicate a high level of merit that they can be used in praising, in the appropriate circumstances. Similarly, as regards blaming, persons may use 'you oughn't to have broken your promise', 'you had no right to be so cruel', etc. (so indicating a low level of demerit) to blame, in the appropriate context. This is so because the propositions expressed by these sentences directly bear on the typical aims of praising and blaming, since they indicate the requirements of principles which themselves justify such praising and blaming, when conditions of voluntariness are satisfied. And, of course, the principles underlying the propositions used in such speech acts clarify the grounds for such speech acts; for example, it is a consequence of the status of the principle of beneficence as a supererogatory principle of praise that it is not an appropriate ground for a proposition used in demanding; thus, one has an explanation for the fact that 'ought' terminology is not used in demanding that persons act on the principle of beneficence, but is more appropriately used by the agent himself in deciding what to do, as a matter of what others cannot demand, but what he may, in good conscience, regard himself as required to do, as a matter of moral right.

(c) General Remarks

In Part II, as part of a general theory of reasons for action, I set myself against the view that a propositional theory of certain 'ought', 'under a moral obligation', etc., expressions, was incompatible with any account of the use of such expressions in various speech acts. I have argued here that, so far from their being incompatible, the adequate analysis of the sense in which such sentences are used to command, demand, advise, exhort, praise, or blame, depends on the propositions they express, which provide the grounds for such speech acts. The second criterion of theoretical adequacy presented in chapter 1 is then satisfied. But the account will not be complete, in accounting for moral reasons for action, until some account of the moving appeal of such utterances to human action is offered. Some attention must next be given to this.

13

THE NATURAL ATTITUDE OF
MORALITY

THE third, and final, criterion of theoretical adequacy, which
I set myself in chapter 1, was to offer some account, or
explanation, for the relation of utterances, here given a
propositional account, to their moving appeal to human action.
As in chapter 5, my solution to this problem, as applied to moral
reasons for action, is, in a way, a quite trivial one. That is, in the
case of the propositional theory of moral reasons for action offered
here, it seems clear that the answer must be: as a brute fact of
human psychology, there is a widespread desire to be moral, and
thus the information conveyed by certain expressions containing
'ought', 'under a moral obligation', 'it is the morally right thing to
do', etc., has an intelligible relation to human desire, and thus to
the human actions that those desires, in part, motivate. This is so
because the propositional theory offered here claims no analytic or
logical relation between moral propositions and the desires of
agents (unlike, e.g. forms of first-person moral approbationism,
which analyse moral statements as equivalent to propositions
about the speaker's desires); and, *qua* propositional theory, my
account cannot solve the moving appeal problem by claiming an
analytic relation between prescriptions expressing desires and
moral judgements, which are thus interpreted, in part, non-
propositionally (e.g. Hare's prescriptivism). In my view, what is
meant in saying '*x* is the morally right thing for you to do' is not
dependent even on the speaker's being disposed impartially to
desire, let alone prescribe, that you do *x*, but rather on what the
principles of morality require (i.e. those ultimate standards which
would be accepted by rational contractors, etc.) which holds quite
apart from the speaker's, or his interlocutor's, desire to do, or to
prescribe, what these principles justify. In short, following the
terminology of chapter 5, mine is an externalist account of moral
expressions; the proposition expressed, e.g. by 'you ought (morally)

to do *x*' does not logically imply the desire to do *x*: the desire to be moral is external to the concept of morality

Given, then, the particular form of propositional account which I am offering, it seems that, in fact, I must be committed to some form of brute fact thesis. However, as I pointed out in chapter 5, such accounts differ, importantly, in terms of their explanatory informativeness in accounting for the relation of concepts and desires. Thus, intuitionist accounts in ethics, like those of Price, Prichard, and W. D. Ross,[1] suffer from the fact that having identified rightness, say, with some intuitable property, they are compelled to explain moral motivations in terms of an inexplicable desire for that intuitable property. Such an explanation leaves one with the same sort of intellectual dissatisfaction that would be felt in a theory of human motivation which accepted the desire to see yellowness as an ultimate fact of human psychology, without requiring further explanation, for such a motivation seems to be precisely what *requires* explanation. What one would like from a moral theory is some more illuminating and explanatory account of the relation of moral concepts and desires. This further explanation will fall into two parts: first, a characterization of the relation of the concept of morality to the natural attitude of morality, which also clarifies the logical nature of various moral feelings and dispositions; and second, some characterization of the relation of the concept of morality to genetic theories of the development of the natural attitude of morality, so that one can have some idea of how it is that persons come to have the desire to regulate their lives by the principles of morality. A paradigmatic example of the *sort* of theoretical attempt I have in mind here is the theory of morality, as related to a general theory of the capacities and desires that comprise human nature, found in Hume's *Treatise*, Book III. Here, Hume relates an ideal observer theory of the concept of morality to a view of basic human capacities for sympathetic identification with others, so that some account is given of how it is that persons, as they approximate to conditions of full knowledge of matters of fact, impartiality, perfect sympathy, and the like, desire to do what is morally right. It seems to me, in two senses, to be a species of theoretical delusion for philosophers to think that they can create their theories of moral concepts in total abstraction from any attempt to relate their views *explicitly* to psychological theories of human attitudes and desires. First, such a sharp demarcation of philosophy and psychology leads to a failure to examine psychological assumptions which may, in fact, underlie the philosophical theory—thus, for example, the obvious, but little noted, dependence of Stevenson's emotivism on Freudian theories of childhood identification, which explain how words come to have emotive meaning, theories for which the empirical evidence is, in fact, quite meagre.[2] Second, such a demarcation, if part of a non-first-person, propositional theory of moral concepts, fails to give any explanation for the moving appeal of moral utterances to action, which is an obvious fact for which any theory with pretensions to adequacy must account. Surely, much of the plausibility and persuasiveness of emotivism and prescriptivism, against naturalistic theories, have been their emphasis on this latter point. What one would like from a propositional theory is some attempt to relate its account to plausible and well-evidenced theories of moral development, which psychological inquiry has made available. From this point of view, it seems clear that a propositional theory which is naturalistic has obvious advantages over an intuitionistic propositional theory; for example, consider the greater theoretical plausibility, from this point of view, of Perry's analysis of the good in terms of what promotes human interests; as opposed to Moore's analysis of the good in terms of a simple, indefinable property, which we inexplicably desire.[3] This will hold analogously, I think, in the case of my theory of morality, which is naturalistic in the sense of defining the right in terms of principles which rational contractors would agree to as best advancing their interests from the orginal position.

In this chapter I propose to address myself both to the task of characterizing the logical nature of the natural attitude of morality and of relating the above propositional theory of morality to well-evidenced theories of moral development. First, I shall try to characterize the natural attitude of morality, and then, relate this view to an account of the associated distinctions between guilt, remorse, shame, and regret, which will be contrasted with the Freudian view and generally used in criticism of social scientists' claim that shame *must* replace guilt in an enlightened morality; related to this, an account of rational shame and guilt will briefly be sketched. Then, my propositional and naturalistic account of moral concepts will be related to the psychological theory of moral development suggested in the works of Piaget, R. W. White, and

Kohlberg. Finally, the relevance of such well-evidenced psychological theories to the decision problem of the rational contractors will be considered, with the conclusion that the contractors will agree to one final principle of morality, the principle of moral development.

1. *The Natural Attitude of Morality*

In elucidating the natural attitude of rationality in chapter 5, it was claimed that the adequate characterization of a rational man would fall into three parts: (*a*) certain beliefs and thoughts of this man, (*b*) the desires and capacities associated with these beliefs, and (*c*) the disposition to certain sorts of feelings, and intentions to act, if one deviates from rationality. An analogous form of analysis seems to me appropriate in describing the natural attitude of morality; and I propose here to show how this analysis would go.

(*a*) The thoughts and beliefs that an existent attitude of morality implies are the thoughts and beliefs that having the concept of morality implies. That is, the moral man believes that the principles of morality define at least a large class of reasons for action, as is shown by the sorts of sentence which he claims or admits to express true propositions about there being some reason, or good reason, or conclusive reason for some action (e.g. 'you have a moral duty to serve', 'you must keep your promise', etc.). These beliefs about reasons for action fall into two parts, those corresponding to the moral principles of obligation and duty and the supererogatory principles of blame, and those corresponding to the supererogatory principle of praise, beneficence. Though the terminology is, in some ways, misleading, in so far as all these principles define what are reasons for action, I propose to distinguish these sets of beliefs into those of reasonableness and those of sympathetic beneficence respectively. The distinction drawn here derives from the fact that certain moral beliefs (those of reasonableness) depend on moral principles which at least satisfy the maximin criterion of the original position (and which the contractors thus agree to as justifying at least forms of blame in enforcing them), while other moral beliefs (those of beneficence) are based on moral principles which do not similarly satisfy this criterion, since they may require an agent to sacrifice his substantial interests for the good of others (and which the con-tractors thus agree to as justifying praise if persons act on them, and no blame if they do not). But, of course, in having such beliefs, the moral man is no different from other men, who do not have the attitude of morality, but who have the concept. They, too, may admit that propositions of the above type are true, and yet they may not act on them, or have any inclination at all to act on them.

(b) What is further required for a person to have the natural attitude of morality is his having the capacity and desire to be moral. People who have the capacity to be moral have the psycho-logical equipment to do what the principles of morality require, both as regards reasonableness and sympathetic beneficence. They are creatures of a kind who are able to perceive and understand their present and future circumstances and desires and the circumstances and desires of others, to satisfy their desires, and to suppress, adjust, or subordinate the satisfaction of their own self-regarding desires, both present occurrent wants and future perceived wants, because of their other-regarding desires, what-ever they may be. They have the capacities of imagination, ingenuity, inventiveness, a firm grasp of facts and possibilities, the power of relevant and controlled hypothetical thought (in-involving the capacity to manipulate dated and universal pro-positions),⁴ as well as self-control. In short, they have all the capacities associated with formulating and executing plans of action which satisfy the principles of morality.

The claim that persons have the desire to be moral must be distinguished into the separable questions of the nature of the desires associated with (i) reasonableness and (ii) sympathetic beneficence.

(i) On the view of chapter 3, the desire to be reasonable is an other-regarding desire, since its general end, being reasonable in one's relation with other persons, has reference to, and is believed to have reference to, the satisfaction of other persons' desires, as well as one's own. In having an end which logically depends upon a class of principles (i.e. the requirements of moral principles 1–11 and 12a), the desire to be reasonable stands in sharp contrast to other desires (e.g. hunger, thirst, sexuality, competence, love, envy, hate, and the like) whose general ends (eating food, drinking liquids, having sex, exercising or realizing a competence, doing another good and being near him, possessing what another has, harming another) logically exist prior to the use of moral or rationality principles in regulating the pursuit of such ends.

Given the ultimate normative value of the principles in terms of which the desire to be reasonable is defined, it is not difficult to see why Kant supposed that such a desire to be reasonable was the only desire of ultimate and unconditional worth, and why he wished to distinguish it sharply from all other sorts of desires, often denying it was any sort of desire at all.[5] Kant's view here may be shorn of its metaphysical trappings, and reinterpreted as expressing an important logical point about the special relation of the natural desire to be reasonable to a certain class of principles of action, which are such that the pursuit of all other self- and other-regarding desires is to be regulated within the constraints that these principles establish

The special nature of this desire may be understood in terms of its general end, defined by moral principles. Thus, given the concept of moral principles as those ultimate standards which would be accepted by all rational men from an original position of equal liberty, the desire to be reasonable implies wanting to give such weight to the desires of others, as would be required from an original position where all are *equally* persons, a concept expressed by Kant in terms of men's status as noumena and ends in themselves, by Piaget in terms of the basic capacities of moral personality, and by Scheler as an equality of personal worth.[6] If a man wholly lacked the desire to be reasonable, though having the natural attitude of rationality, he would plan for and pursue his aims, with the interests of other persons only having weight when they conduced to advancing his aims; as Kant often put it, the desires and wants of others, at least where no love or friendship relation exists, would appear to the agent as a kind of mechanical movement whose only reality for the agent would be like that of artifacts and creatures, whose use conduces to his aims.[7] He would not, as the phrase goes, treat others as persons.

(ii) The desire to be beneficent, or sympathetic benevolence, importantly differs from the desire to be reasonable. First, like love and friendship (which differ from benevolence only in implying a particular relation between individual persons known to one another and the desire for closeness, whereas benevolence seems to imply a general desire to do good to anyone),[8] benevolence seems clearly to be an other-regarding desire whose end involves doing good to others; and, unlike reasonableness, seems to have no logical dependence on principles of any sort. Secondly, as a consequence of this different relation of reasonableness and sympathetic benevolence to moral principles, the moral relevance of these desires differs; that is, the moral principles 1–11 and 12a apply to persons, no matter whether they desire to be reasonable or not, whereas the moral principle of beneficence only applies when persons have sympathetic benevolence, or ideals with benevolent implications, where these are valued more highly by the person than his own interests, assuming no other moral principles are relevant. Thirdly, the attitude of sympathetic benevolence implies a desire of doing good to others, which goes quite beyond whatever desire for doing good reasonableness may involve. This is, of course, a consequence of the special nature of the principles associated with reasonableness, i.e. they are all accepted by the rational contractors because they ensure at least a higher lowest, whereas sympathetic benevolence may lead to a much lower lowest for the benevolent agent as a result of his promoting the interests of others. And fourthly, sympathetic benevolence implies a much greater capacity for sympathy with, and feeling for, others than is the case with reasonableness. The desire to be reasonable draws only upon that minimal capacity of feeling for others that is required for persons to act on the associated moral principles, the attitude associated with treating others as persons; and as Kant well noted, such reasonableness may often exist in a person who wholly lacks any deep or subtle capacity for sympathy with the concerns and emotions of others.[9]

The general nature of sympathy is a vexed philosophical problem, the difficulties of which led a philosopher of Hume's stature to say some patently absurd things.[10] Following Scheler, it seems necessary to distinguish at least five types of fellow-feeling, in order to be clear about the specific sort of sympathy which enters into sympathetic benevolence.[11] First, there is the community of feeling which two persons sharing a common emotion may have, e.g. two children's grief over the bier of their parent. Secondly, there is the emotional infection, which occurs, e.g. as part of a crowd psychology. Thirdly, there is the emotional identification which can occur between the hypnotized and his hypnotist, a young boy and his father, a mentally disturbed man and his hated and loved mother, or the primitive savage and his totem, or the adept in a Dionysian Mystery and his god, and the like. Fourthly, there is the emotional empathy which occurs between an audience and a moving play, or symphony, or opera, or ballet. And fifthly, there is genuine sympathy by one person for another person's pain, anxiety, aggravation, desperation, depression, etc., or for his joy, happiness, ebullience, well-being, accomplishment, etc. In contrast to the involuntary and unconscious process that emotional infection and identification involve, sympathy implies what Scheler called the 'awareness of distance between selves',[12] i.e. that a person sympathizing is aware that the other person's feelings are uniquely his, and that the act of sympathy is an expression of interest and concern by one separate self for the condition of another self. As H. B. Acton put it, 'Sympathy is not a primitive animal feeling, but is an exercise of the imagination involving self-consciousness and comparison.'[13] Sympathy is distinguishable from a community of feeling in so far as the latter involves the common and primitive emotional response of two or several persons to an external event in reference to which the persons share common emotional ties and experiences, but it does not involve the sort of relation between the persons themselves that characterizes sympathy. And, of course, sympathy differs from the empathetic reaction of an audience to a moving work of art, since it assumes awareness of the real emotion or feeling of another person, apart from the special context of a work of art.

This set of contrasts between sympathy and other sorts of fellow-feeling may be summarized in the claim that sympathy involves two logical elements: understanding of the sort of emotion or state of feeling that the *other* is undergoing, and the desire to relieve that emotion, if one of frustration, by expressions of interest and concern and by assistance, and the desire to celebrate that emotion, if one of joy, by expressions of joy, happiness, and congratulation. Understanding and the above friendly desires are distinguishable features of sympathy, a point that can easily be seen by noting that understanding, in this sense, does not necessarily imply the occurrence of sympathy, and, indeed, is a necessary accompaniment of various forms of sadistic cruelty, hate, envy, and general malevolence.[14] Generally, it seems a necessary psychological and logical condition of understanding, in this sense, that the person who understands has himself to some degree gone through the general *kind* of emotion or state of feeling that the other is undergoing, though this does not imply that the specific details of the other's emotional experience must have been undergone, for, were that the case, there could be no understanding of the different experiences and emotions of others.[15] It is sympathy, combining such understanding and friendly feelings and inclinations, that importantly enters into sympathetic benevolence, where the desire to do good to others often is accompanied by the understanding, sensitivities, and desires that characterize sympathy.

(*c*) The final logical mark of the natural attitude of morality involves the various desires and intentions to act to which persons, who have the natural attitude of morality, are disposed, when their actions culpably violate moral principles. However, this is a difficult subject, deserving an entire section to itself.

11. *Moral Feelings and the Natural Attitude of Morality*

I propose here to present an analysis of moral, and related, feelings; the specific method of analysis is derived from John Rawls, with whose account of guilt I am in agreement;[16] but the general approach has been well known since the later work of Wittgenstein, and has been used in the analysis of various feelings by Mrs. Foot, Miss Anscombe, Kenny, Hampshire, J. N. Findlay, and many others.[17] The feature of the view presented here is to extend this general approach and specific method to the comparative analysis of a wide range of moral, and related, feelings. When this account is completed, I shall try to show how the analysis of shame and guilt can be used in answering the widespread view that shame *must* replace guilt in an enlightened morality. Related to this, an account of rational shame and rational guilt will be sketched.

(*a*) *The Nature of the Moral Feelings*

An approach to the analysis of the moral feelings may be characterized by the kinds of questions it asks and considers important. My account is marked by raising each of the following questions separately: (i) what are the characteristic behavioural manifestations, or intentions to behave, of a particular moral feeling, and what are the ways in which a person characteristically betrays how he feels? Does one blush, or one's voice tighten with anger, or what? (ii) What are the characteristic sensations and kinesthetic feelings which go with a moral feeling? Is there some tightening of the stomach or pain in the chest? (iii) What is the definitive type of explanation required for having a given moral feeling, and how do these explanations differ from one feeling to another? (iv) What are the characteristic temptations to actions, the doing of which results in these feelings? And of special importance in the logical characterization of guilt versus shame, what sorts of things does one feel inclined to do by way of relieving or resolving the feeling? (v) Finally, what is the natural attitude with which the moral feeling is connected? The thought here is that natural attitudes and moral feelings are so *logically* related that the absence of certain moral feelings, in the appropriate circumstances, implies the absence of certain natural attitudes, and the presence of certain natural attitudes implies the liability to certain moral feelings.[18] As an example of the kind of logical relation I mean, consider the relation between a natural attitude like love and certain feelings: e.g. if I *love* someone, I would, failing some kind of special explanation, be *afraid* when that person is threatened, and be *angry* at a person who threatened the beloved; I would tend to feel *joy* when the latter was joyful, and *sadness* when grieved. All of these dispositions to experience, I *must*, logically, feel, unless there are special circumstances of conflicting attitudes and feelings, or the like; for if I feel, without special explanation, none of them, it *could* not be love I was feeling; and if I feel such joy and fear, etc., in the appropriate context, it *must* be love I am feeling.

(i) The idea of distinguishing various types of moral feelings by virtue of non-linguistic behavioural manifestation or intentions to behave seems to me generally futile. For example, Erikson and Kenny quite rightly note the disposition to hide, as a distinctive mark of shame;[19] but such a disposition to act is equally characteristic of embarrassment; yet surely, these feelings are distinct. Similarly, as Scheler noted, the redness of my cheek may be a sign of shame, or may 'equally well betray overheating, anger or debauchery, or be due to the light from a red lamp'.[20] What, in short, distinguishes the *flush* of anger from the *blush* of shame or embarrassment cannot be the redness alone. Similarly, the shaking of the voice may accompany anger on one occasion, and indignation on another, yet these seem to be distinguishable notions.

(ii) Further, it does not seem that any special sensation or kinesthetic feeling is either necessary or sufficient for the existence of any class of feelings, as distinct from any other. No doubt the Freudian view of guilt suggests that what is peculiar to guilt versus shame is some experience of internalized versus externalized punishment.[21] But in fact, one may tremble internally and feel a tightening of the stomach when one experiences guilt or shame, or, for that matter, anger, fear, or embarrassment. And further, it seems neither necessary nor sufficient that any internal sensation occur in a particular case, for one appropriately or truly to express one's feeling guilty or ashamed for something, though some such sensations may be necessary if one is overwhelmed with feelings of guilt, or is intensely ashamed.[22]

(iii) If the above behavioural and sensational criteria seem inadequate to distinguish different feelings from one another, one may appeal to the deeper level of beliefs associated with these feelings, as seen in the linguistic expressions which are used, at least characteristically, to explain our having certain feelings, as opposed to certain others. Thus, when someone says he feels guilty, what kind of explanation, in ordinary language and thought, do we expect to be involved? What seems characteristic and essential is that some principle of reciprocity is believed to have been transgressed, in an intentional or knowing or negligent way, by the person who feels guilty (cf. the use of 'guilty' in the law). I feel guilty, for example, because I took more than my share, and treated others unfairly; or because I broke my promise, and thus did not render the promisee his due. Piers and Singer, in their interesting and, I think, basically correct discussion of guilt and shame, characterized the reciprocity principles underlying guilt in this way: 'The Law of Talion does not obtain in the development of shame, as it generally does in guilt.'[23] The Piers–Singer point can be unexceptionably restated by relating the concept of guilt to the concept of transgressing moral principles. Since, in my view, the concept of moral principles involves those reciprocally observed restrictions on people's conduct toward one another, which all persons would agree to from an original position of equal liberty, the sense in which moral guilt involves a breach of human reciprocity is explicable. The notion that such guilt implies the aptness of forms of punishment, and the requirement of giving return to those harmed, is explicable in terms of the

existence of moral principles of coercion and blame, and of reparation and compensation. The relation of guilt to such moral principles
(justifying blame only where there is culpability) explains why
guilt characteristically occurs when one has voluntarily committed
a moral fault through transgressing a principle regarded as a
moral one, and why one does not normally feel guilty for another
person's action, unless that action (as some kind of moral wrong)
is regarded as done because of something one voluntarily did.
Further, note that even cases of what one may call neurotic guilt
(pathological cases for which the psycho-analytic model of guilt as
arbitrary internal punishment seems most natural)[24] are called
cases of guilt because it is believed that the agent feels anxiety not
just for any reason, but because of suppressed beliefs or, at least,
thoughts which it is the task of psycho-analysis to dig out—e.g.
the belief that all women are your mother, and thus it is morally
wrong to have sex with them. If one did not suppose that such
neurotics in some way suppose themselves to be transgressing
moral norms, these would not be regarded as cases of guilt, I think.

The important logical relation of guilt to moral beliefs is not a
unique feature of guilt alone, and could be easily generalized in
characterizing other moral feelings as well, e.g. indignation and
resentment, a point also made by Rawls and Strawson.[25] Thus, if
guilt is the appropriate reaction to one's having voluntarily transgressed a moral principle which is part of one's critical attitudes,
then indignation is the appropriate response to others' transgressing such moral principles in reference to other persons
(e.g. to South African whites establishing an unjust system of
apartheid against South African Negroes), and resentment is the
appropriate response to other persons' transgressing such moral
principles in reference to oneself (e.g. South African Negroes
against the whites for establishing such an unjust system). Indeed,
the logical distinction between, for example, indignation and
anger, importantly depends upon the former's relation to moral
principles, where this is wholly unnecessary in the case of anger
simpliciter, which only implies some belief of frustration from
another and the desire to strike back.

In the case of shame, the defining explanation of having the
feeling involves the belief of failing to attain one's conception of
the self's competence, some self-ideal of excellence. I am ashamed
because I was cowardly and thus did not realize my concept of the

fully competent self triumphing over egoistic fear. In this view, shame is (*pace* Bedford)[26] subject to the peculiar irrationality, not found with non-neurotic guilt, that one may be ashamed of something which is not one's fault, but which one still believes to violate an ideal of the excellent (e.g. one's uncomeliness or mental slowness, etc.) Further, if, as part of a wider identity, one views actions of others as part of the realization of one's ideals of the excellent, then one can be ashamed of their actions (e.g. Americans of Americans in Europe, etc.), a move not similarly present in the case of guilt.

This appeal to characteristic kinds of explanation provides not only a way to distinguish shame from guilt, but also shame from embarrassment, or regret. Thus, what distinguishes embarrassment from shame is that the latter involves the belief of a fall from the excellent, whereas one may be embarrassed in reference to something which one regards as perfectly justified, but which one feels discomfiture in having made public, because of one's quite idiosyncratic sense of social propriety about matters of privacy (e.g. a couple, kissing good night on a dark corner, who are embarrassed when someone flashes a light on them). In this sense, embarrassment does seem to have the public character that many have mistakenly attributed to shame—perhaps precisely because of an unconscious conflation of shame and embarrassment.[27] And as regards the distinction between shame and regret, regret implies the belief that desires generally have been frustrated because of some irrationality in planning, whereas shame narrowly implies that competence desires of some sort have been frustrated, and does not necessarily imply irrationality in planning (e.g. shame over mental slowness). But of course, both have in common being possible feelings held in reference to larger identities with which one associates one's own rational interests or personal ideals (e.g. an Englishman's regret that his country devalued, or an American's shame over Vietnam).

Finally, in this view, it is, of course, quite possible that one may be disposed to regard the same act from the point of view of shame and, later on, from that of guilt. No doubt it sometimes happens that, from one point of view, one is, or feels, ashamed of being the kind of incompetent who has had to cheat in an examination; and yet, from another point of view, one feels guilty because such cheating was unfair to fellow students. That the same act may elicit, alternatively, one response and the other leaves the conceptual distinction intact. Indeed, in the case of the moral principle of beneficence, where a person is assumed to have ideals of generosity and benevolence, shame, rather than guilt, may be the more appropriate response in most cases of failure to obey the principle. It is, also, quite possible, in this view, that, if one regarded obeying the principles of right as realizing one's self-excellence, then shame would supplant guilt as the main moral feeling (one would explain all moral faults as falls from excellence). One may, in fact, interpret Nietzsche's transvaluation of values as urging just this change of conception, among other things.

(iv) The question of what temptations characteristically lead to certain feelings further confirms, I think, the general direction of the differentia described in (iii). For example, the temptations leading to shame involve failures in the competence of the self—in the capacity to control appetites, lack of mastery in execution, lack of courage and confidence in one's ability to do things. Consider, here, Augustine's classic characterization of the shame of our sexual impulses, given his ideal that sexual impulse is to serve no end but legitimate procreation:

This lust, of which we at present speak, is the more shameful on this account, because the soul is therein neither master of itself, so as not to lust at all, nor of the body to keep the members under the control of the will; for if it were thus ruled, there would be no shame.[28]

Contrast this with the characteristic situations that give rise to guilt—temptations from self-interest to transgress established boundaries of moral right.

But further, and of equal importance with (iii) in providing necessary conditions for the existence of shame distinct from those of guilt, is the question of what are the characteristic dispositions to action by which the feelings are resolved. In the case of guilt feelings, given that they occur with the associated belief that some moral principles (requiring forms of compensation when they are violated) have been transgressed, then the characteristic ways of resolving the feeling involve reparation or restitution to the others who have been wrongly treated by one's action, an inclination to admit what one has done and to apologize, a readiness to acknowledge and accept reproofs and penalties, and, sometimes, an inclination to confess and seek reconciliation.

None of these modes of resolving guilt hold in the case of shame. Since shame does not necessarily imply any reciprocity notion of a relation to other persons, there is no one to make reparation to, except oneself. Thus, the sole way of resolving shame, like regret, is one's subsequent success doing that at which one previously failed. While shame may sometimes result in self-punishment, this must be seen as an attempt to strengthen the self so that on subsequent occasions the self may triumph where it previously failed. This sense of self-punishment is to be distinguished from that which is characteristic of remorse; remorse is, I think, characteristically felt when irreparable harm of some kind has been done to someone who is loved—she may be dead or have lost her sight, for example. Thus, the self-punishments associated with remorse involve a frustrated turning in on oneself of feelings that would normally be resolved by restitution or reparation (here impossible). In a sense, one tries a second-best resolution by sharing in the suffering of the person for whom one feels an affection.

(v) The propensity to the moral feelings of guilt has its natural basis in the existence of certain natural attitudes—among which are love, trust, and the sense of moral right. Thus, the existence of the natural attitude of love implies not only certain liabilities to feel the joys and griefs of the beloved as one's own, but also the disposition to feel guilt if one violates the requirements of the love relationship, given that the love relation implies the applicability of moral principle 12b of chapter 11. In the circumstances of childhood, while the child has no independent capacity of moral judgement, the natural attitude of love shows itself in a desire to do what the beloved parents wants the child to do in terms of certain rules, and the mode of guilt resolution takes the natural form of confession and seeking reconciliation with the beloved.[29] The natural attitude of trust, which comes to exist between friends in the child's peer group, necessarily involves exposing oneself to the liability to guilt when that trust is broken, in the sense of violating the moral principle of keeping trust that obtains in the restricted peer group (principle 4 of chapter 9, and principle 12b of chapter 11). Such guilt manifests itself in the inclination to make reparation, to admit what one has done and to apologize, to acknowledge and accept reproofs and penalties, and in a diminished capacity to be angry with others when they fail to do their part. Finally, the existence of the mature sense of right of the reasonable and moral man, the desire to regulate one's life by principles of right which apply beyond any personal love, respect, or trust relationship, implies the liability to guilt feelings, which are characterized by explaining the having of these feelings in terms of voluntarily transgressing moral principles, as well as by the inclination to resolve them by reparation, restitution, reform of the morally wrong practice (if one exists), etc.

Similarly, the natural basis of shame lies in a positive attitude—here, our capacity for self-esteem or self-respect in reference to certain ideals of the excellent which we regard ourselves as aspiring towards, a capacity which depends on the natural human desire to be competent in some respect.[30] It is a necessary and sufficient condition of our having invested our self-esteem in some attribute or activity (which we associate with some aspect of a competence of the self) that we be liable to feel shame if we fall short of our ideal.

And a similar view of the logical relation of feeling and natural attitude seems appropriate for regret and the natural attitude of rationality, embarrassment and the attitude of social propriety, remorse and love, indignation and resentment and the attitude of morality, etc.

From this point of view, the psycho-analytically suggested notion, already mentioned, that the differentiae of guilt and shame centre on some dimension of internality versus externality is simply wrong. Both feelings are equally internal, in the sense of being feelings which are derived from internalized beliefs and attitudes, and which are experienced quite apart from the actual or fantasied blame of others; where they are differentiated is in the characteristic beliefs and attitudes with which they are associated. This view's denial of externality or publicity as an essential part of the concepts of guilt and shame must not be confused with propositions with which it is compatible. Thus, it may clearly be psychologically true, as Isenberg suggested, that the self-conceptions, on which the capacity for shame in part depends, only arise or are sustained when there is public confirmation of *some* kind of them;[31] yet the above account of shame may still be analytically correct. Indeed, such confirmation *may*, as Erikson has noted in reference to that self-conception he has called identity, involve not present people's confirmation or acceptance, but that of 'a very few who may not be living in the same era';[32] Erikson mentions here

Gandhi's psychological relation to Christ, and elsewhere he has noted G. B. Shaw's similar relation to 'the mighty dead'.[33] But the fact that self-ideals may be thus related, in terms of psychological origin or support, to others is clearly compatible with the view that shame occurs on the basis of a falling from one's self-ideals, not logically requiring the notion of others. Further, as indicated previously, this view is quite consonant with the notion that shame may be felt on the basis of an ideal which includes innumerable others acting in certain ways, in which they fail to act.[34] Helen Lynd has cogently pointed out the revelatory power of shame in revealing ideals that may be parts of a culture-wide identity,[35] yet she has constantly emphasized, and rightly, the internal aspect of shame. Also, the notion that being and feeling ashamed are logically dependent on the concept of falling from a self-ideal is also compatible with the view that certain kinds of behavioural manifestations (e.g. blushing) and kinesthetic sensations will specially occur *when* such shame is public. An immigrant child, for example, may be ashamed (however irrationally) of his foreign accent, yet he may blush, etc. (feeling intensely ashamed) only when exposed to the public pressures and cruelties of his native-born peers. The view of shame (as well as of guilt) is clearly consonant with such further distinctions.

Also, in this account of guilt and shame, the neo-Freudian Erikson, when he tries to account for a sense of positive conscience or the 'genuine sense of guilt', by appealing to the notion of internal ideals,[36] is not accounting for guilt but rather for shame. He has seen, on the one hand, the inadequacies of Freud's negative concept of guilt as the arbitrary stipulator of internalized taboos,[37] and sought to discover the psychological background for what he rightly takes to be the more reasonable sense of guilt which is characteristic of much of the moral life. But in this search, he has succeeded not in developing a more sound psychological concept of guilt, but in putting forth an account of shame, which is not his intention. Now, perhaps, the most important general implication of the view suggested here is that Erikson's intuitive notion of positive conscience is expressed by the logical relation of the natural attitudes to the moral feelings;[38] for, in my view, the positive aspects of being capable of the mutualities of love, trust, and a sense of moral right logically imply a liability to the negative aspects of guilt. The liability to guilt, as well as shame, is simply part of the *necessary* price we pay for our capacity to feel attitudes and engage in activities that may, in large part, give living a point and meaning. Further, this way of looking at the moral feelings orients one, I think, to a quite different psychological conception of moral development from the Freudian one. One does not look for the specific time at which certain frustrated aggressions are internalized, as the root conception of guilt, but rather to the quite different notion of examining the growth of the natural attitudes of love and respect, trust, and a sense of right, the existence of which implies the development of the liability to guilt. However, before delineating such an alternative conception, it seems apt first to clear away the confusion, in understanding the logical relation of guilt and shame to an enlightened morality, that Freudian assumptions have fostered.

(b) Shame, Guilt, and the Concept of an Enlightened Morality

The view that an enlightened morality must do away with the notion of guilt, and replace it with some notion of internal ideals of excellence, is a widespread conception in our Freudian educated culture, and was given its most explicit philosophical statement in the works of Nietzsche. I already mentioned Erikson's notion that what is distinctly ethical are 'ideals to be striven for' as 'a definition of perfection';[39] that is, Erikson urges us, not unlike Strawson,[40] to think of mature ethics in terms of certain excellences to which we strive 'with a high degree of rational assent'.[41] As suggested above, what he is, in effect, saying is that the really important ethical concepts are self-ideals and the related notion of shame. This is a quite common point of view among contemporary social scientists, even among those who are much more clear about the concepts of guilt and shame than is Erikson.

Helen Lynd, for example, in her important book, *On Shame and the Search for Identity*, is, I think, quite clear about the distinction between shame and guilt presented above. Thus, she claims that guilt 'is centrally a transgression, a crime, the violation of a specific taboo boundary, or legal code by a voluntary act', and shame 'a wound to one's self-esteem, a painful feeling or sense of degradation excited by the consciousness of having done something unworthy of one's previous idea of one's own excellence'.[42] However, after making this distinction, she goes on to some remarks about the relative importance of shame and guilt as moral feelings.

Thus, guilt involves 'the sanctions and taboos of one's immediate culture', whereas shame involves the possibility of an appeal to 'more universal human values'.[43] Guilt, in this view, characteristically implies 'disobedience to a particular law', whereas shame includes 'basic human decencies'.[44] Further, guilt is 'primarily external and instrumental' with others regarded as deprivatory agents treating the guilty as a means to their ends, whereas shame involves an experience of failure of more personal response to others as ends in themselves.[45] What Lynd has done has been to make a crucial distinction between shame and guilt, and yet continued to regard guilt as the product of Freud's barbaric stipulator of 'taboos', a locution she often and importantly uses to describe the rules transgressed.[46] Thus, she adopts Freud's basic conception of guilt with no question:

> The superego of Freud is relatively clear. It is a prohibiting, restraining, guilt-producing part of the self compounded from instinctual drives, desire for parental approval, and parental threats and prohibitions which have become internalized through identification with the parents or with the parents' ideals.[47]

Given this background view of guilt, it is not difficult to understand why Lynd believes that it is the concepts of excellence and shame that must provide the basis of an enlightened morality. Like Erikson (but unlike him in clearly recognizing that she is opting for the shame notion), she cannot find in the Freudian threat view of guilt the enlightened moral consciousness which she is trying to delineate.

Also, it seems to me that David Riesman's notion of autonomy represents a similar attempt to use concepts of excellence in the basic characterization of enlightened moral attitudes, which social scientists are to seek to promote. Thus, Riesman defines this concept as follows:

> The 'autonomous' are those who on the whole are capable of conforming to the behavioral norms of their society—a capacity that anomics usually lack—but are free to choose whether to conform or not.[48]

The way in which this notion is thought of, in Riesman's work, is extremely striking: 'the struggle for autonomy', we are told, involves 'the personally productive orientation based on the human need for active participation in a creative task'.[49] The ideal here is the creative man, who, with 'spontaneity and privacy', his 'roots of fantasy' not yet deracinated by deadening conformity or 'concern for sheer technique', is able to respect the practices of his society and yet go beyond them in ways his spontaneous creative power may allow.[50]

Riesman's view here may be likened to that of Nietzsche, whose whole moral philosophy is based on the concept of setting up the excellence of certain sorts of creativity as the sole values to be fostered. And generally, it is striking how much Nietzsche's arguments, for rejecting a guilt view of enlightened morality, resemble those of Lynd, for what Nietzsche quite clearly understands as the guilt view of morality is precisely the view that Freud was later to espouse, and which Lynd, like Erikson, rejects as a basis for an enlightened morality. Thus, when Nietzsche characterizes the attitude of justice, which he takes guilt to involve, he analyses it precisely in the way Freud analyses social justice as arising from envy in the nursery;[51] or as Nietzsche interprets the attitude of the 'tarantulas' who celebrate equality:

'What justice means to us is precisely that the world be filled with the storms of our revenge'—thus they speak to each other. 'We shall wreak vengeance and abuse on all whose equals we are not'—thus do the tarantula-hearts vow. 'And "will to equality" shall henceforth be the name for virtue; and against all that has power we want to raise our clamour.'[52]

Or, as he put this attitude elsewhere: ' "If I am canaille, you ought to be too"—on such logic are revolutions made.'[53]Further, Nietzsche interprets guilt precisely in the Freudian way as arbitrary internal punishment: 'we immoralists are trying with all our strength to take the concept of guilt and the concept of punishment out of the world again, and to cleanse psychology, history, nature, and social institutions and sanctions of them.'[54] As against this view, where 'fear is the mother of morals',[55] Nietzsche believes that an enlightened morality can only be based on an excellence–shame view of morality, where the only values are certain sorts of creative powers which are to be fostered. While, of course, Nietzsche's detailed substantive moral conception cannot be identified with that of either Erikson, Lynd, or Riesman, it is none the less of some interest, I think, that theorists who propose a concept of internal ideals of excellence, as basic to the concept of an enlightened morality, all do so because they conceive any alternative conception of morality in terms of a concept of guilt as some form of unreasoned, internalized aggression, whether derived from envy or hate.

Now, given the view of guilt and shame I have taken above, can one say anything about how they relate to the concept of an enlightened morality, in contrast to the views taken by theorists such as Lynd, Riesman, and Nietzsche? On the view I have suggested, the point to make by way of criticism of Lynd would be that she, like Erikson, retains the Freudian view of guilt in such a way that she misconceives what is precisely involved in the distinction of guilt and shame. Thus, it is clearly not the case, in the view of guilt I have taken, that this moral feeling is only or pre-eminently associated with cultural taboos specific to particular societies. It has been argued to the contrary that it is pre-eminently, in the mature morality of a reasonable man, the principles of morality discussed above that are involved. Such principles are, in a strong sense, transcultural: they apply to *all* persons by virtue of their having certain minimal moral capacities, capacities which, in Locke's phrases, only 'Lunaticks and Ideots' and 'Children' lack.[56] Further, such a view clearly contravenes Lynd's notion that guilt has an externality not found in the case of shame, for it analyses moral guilt precisely as the acknowledgement that one has transgressed principles of treating others as ends, and the disposition to make the appropriate compensation, etc. Lynd can only have been led to her inaccurate view because she assumed that guilt was a wholly punitive, uncreative notion. But, as Bernard Williams noted, one must distinguish here between 'persecutory and reparative guilt. That is to say, he who thinks he has done wrong may not just torment himself, he may seek to put things together again.'[57]

In assessing Riesman's view of autonomy, or Nietzsche's related conception of the excellence of certain forms of creativity, the basic question is whether we regard these notions as ultimate *moral* conceptions. Surely not. One has only to imagine a Napoleon claiming that he is capable of realizing his culture's practices, and yet going beyond them to realize his spontaneous creative gifts as a leader of men in peace and war, to see the vicious distortions to which this notion, as stated, can be put. We do not, in fact, regard spontaneous creativity as an unambiguous moral conception, at least not in abstraction from deeper ethical issues. Only if (which seems doubtful) spontaneous creativity were necessarily correlated with the exercise of greater talent for the good of all would there be a special weight (as far as rewards are concerned) to it, but this would only be within the context of *crucial* factual and moral assumptions which must be satisfied (see chapter 8, above). In setting autonomy and creativity as their goals, Riesman and Nietzsche imply, on the contrary, that those more capable of spontaneous creativity are, *per se*, more morally valuable than others: a conception as morally objectionable to me as a view which takes colour or religion as a criterion of moral equality or inequality. But needless to say, Nietzsche explicitly accepted just such a consequence; indeed, he is quite clear, it seems to me, about the sense in which he is an immoralist.[58] However, clearly, none of this is the case with Riesman, or Lynd, or Erikson, who retain the ordinary concept of morality; and in conclusion, I shall limit myself to criticizing their views.

What Riesman has done, I think, is only to do in more extreme form what Lynd and Erikson have done in less: weight the notion of the excellent in a way incompatible with the constraints principles of morality put on one's pursuit of his good or his ideals of excellence.[59] Thus, the notion of a self-excellence is something regarded as an object of *aspiration*, that which we do not now have or do not have completely and which we are, within certain limits, at liberty to strive for. Similarly, our own good, understood as the rational pursuit of relatively long-range desires and interests, is something we can *choose* to pursue as part of the coherent satisfaction of diverse human desires, and which we are, within certain limits, at liberty to pursue. But the analogy breaks down with the principles of morality; it is not legitimate either to strive or not to strive, or choose or not to choose, to follow *these* principles, for they define the basic boundary conditions of a decent social life; indeed, the moral principles of obligation and duty define what we are morally at liberty in aspiring after, or opting for. Thus, it is to be expected that one who desires to act on such principles typically believes himself to be transgressing basic moral norms, not failing to attain self-ideals, and thus experiences guilt, not shame (though, of course, the latter can be felt, in so far as immorality is regarded as a failure to attain self-ideals, which is quite possible, and not infrequent).

Thus, it seems to me that Riesman, Lynd, and Erikson, all of whom seek to espouse an enlightened morality based on Kantian concepts of all men as equally being persons,[60] fail, in fact, to describe accurately the nature of that enlightened morality, in its relation to the moral feelings of shame and guilt. They fail to see the important sense in which a logically central case of guilt depends on principles which comprise an enlightened morality, because they suppose, following Freud, that guilt must always imply unreasoned, internal punishment. Indeed, it seems to me generally absurd to suppose that our present concept of morality, even when enlightened, can do away with the concept of guilt altogether, for this would imply doing away with the associated concepts of reciprocity, reparation, compensation, etc., which are a crucial part of our non-Nietzschean moral point of view.

(c) Rational Guilt and Rational Shame

A more formal way to make the point of the previous section is by claiming that both guilt and shame can be equally rational emotions, and by proposing some account of wherein their rationality or reasonableness may consist. For present purposes, the notions of rationality and reasonableness seem more or less interchangeable, though for other purposes distinctions between them are useful (see chapter 6).

In the case of guilt, the rationality of this emotion consists in the fact that the beliefs on which this emotion is based can be supported by the principles of morality, which define a wide class of reasons for action. Thus, a feeling of guilt is rational if it is based on a true belief that the principles of morality have been culpably violated and that moral principles of reparation apply; and, a feeling of guilt is irrational if it is based on such beliefs or thoughts, which are not in fact true. Note that, even if moral principles have been culpably violated and moral principles of reparation apply, feelings of guilt can be irrational to the extent that they are based on beliefs which are in excess of moral requirements; thus, guilty self-flagellation (both spiritual and physical) is irrational to the extent that it involves no reparation to the person wrongfully hurt and does not improve the moral character of the wrongdoer.

The rationality of shame may also be based on true beliefs about violating moral principles, at least to the extent that such principles are part of one's self-ideals. However, the rationality of shame may also derive from another quarter, i.e. the principles of rationality of Part I.

It was earlier maintained that the possibility of feeling shame derives in part from the capacity to have and be moved by the desire to be competent in some respect. As I indicated in chapter 3, competence desires are quite natural and ultimate human desires. As such, they constitute one important class of desires, the pursuit of which is to be regulated by the principles of rational choice of Part I; thus, for example, the dominance principle requires that the pursuit of such desires is to be co-ordinated with and adjusted to the pursuit of other ends, at least in so far as the ends are valued roughly equally. It follows from this fact that the principles of rational choice importantly enter into the characterization of certain kinds of shame as rational, and other kinds as irrational. Thus, shame about one's physical unattractiveness or mental slowness is irrational in the sense that such shame is not based on a desire for competence which can rationally be pursued and satisfied, for the competence desired is unattainable. Since such competence desires are doomed to frustration (at least at the present stage of science), the rationality principles would require that no plan be adopted to satisfy them, but that instead plans be adopted which will both eliminate such forms of competence desire (perhaps, by the causal mechanism of habitual non-satisfaction) and substitute other forms of competence desire which can feasibly be satisfied. Similarly, shame is rational if it is based on the frustration of a competence desire which the agent could rationally have pursued. Note, in this connection, that the pursuit of certain kinds of competence desires is so strongly justified by the principles of rationality that shame, based on failure to satisfy these desires, is usually rational. Thus, the objects of certain competence desires (e.g. using language with facility, autonomously and intelligently planning one's life in terms of actual desires, exercising the competences which are the basis of one's occupation and financial remuneration) involve the indispensable means to securing many other ends. Assuming a person has the capacities to achieve the ends of such competence desires, the pursuit of such ends is paramountly rational on the ground of the dominance principle; and shame based on failure to attain such ends is eminently rational. Indeed, to the extent we judge a person to have the capacity to achieve such rational ends in which he has not in fact invested his self-esteem, the rationality principles provide at least one ground for the truth of our saying or thinking that such a man ought to be ashamed, for the rationality principles require a man to develop and invest his self-esteem in the competences central to satisfying desires rationally.[61]

In this general connection, it is worthy of note, as I mentioned in chapter 4, that ultimate natural desires take many different forms; thus, typically, all men share the desire for food, yet that desire takes many different forms, accommodating many different tastes. In the present context of a discussion of self-respect and rational shame, this general point again holds true, for people have widely different capacities, and thus develop widely different competences and the desires to exercise them well. Thus, my remarks in chapter 4 about the sense in which the truth-value of 'ought'-expressions differs from case to case, depending on the particular form of desire, apply *a fortiori* in the case of competence desires, where the diversity of such desires is enormous. Thus, where one man may rationally invest his self-respect in athletics, another will do so in academic research, or in professional expertise, or even in his sexual prowess, etc.;[62] and in each such case, the person may feel rational shame over a certain failure, given he has the capacity for the competence in question which could rationally be exercised.

One context of rational choice deserves special mention in the context of a discussion of competence desires and rationality, i.e. that involving the strategic choices of college, career, marriage status, etc., that occur in late adolescence and early adulthood. In such contexts, the agent often chooses plans not only to satisfy desires involving existent competences, but also chooses plans which involve the development of new competences and desires. Here, if anywhere, one finds appropriate the notion of freely opting for ideals and ends in the light of a rational assessment of one's desires, capacities, and circumstances. It is in such a context that one feels the plausibility and point of Sartre's appeals for authenticity, honesty, and free choice unburdened by shibboleth and irrational practice, and of Hare's appeals for choosing one's way of life in the light of one's own convictions and desires apart from rigid and stupid convention. In such contexts, where people are often morally at liberty to make their lives as they see fit (though their choices may result in different moral situations, e.g. choosing to become a parent and thus undertaking the moral duties of parenthood), people are entitled to create a life as unique as their own special capacities and desires. The demand for uniformity of choice and action, so appropriate in the context of moral principles, is here wholly improper and pointless.

III. *The Development of the Natural Attitude of Morality*

What I should like to do here is to show how one can synthesize, with some emendations, the work of R. W. White, Piaget, and Kohlberg to present a view of moral development quite different from the Freudian one. I am, thus, trying to show that there are well-evidenced and plausible psychological accounts, which can be used to support the view of the natural attitude of morality, and the associated account of guilt, which I have just presented. This is not, then, armchair psychologizing, but an attempt to relate psychological theories to philosophical viewpoints, where there can be intellectually illuminating cross-fertilization; for the philosophical theory will be further supported by the psychological theory, and the psychological theory will importantly employ, in the formulation of its psychological laws, the concept of morality, which the philosophical theory will clarify. From the point of view of the philosophical theory of morality, which is my main concern here, the point of this exercise is not so much to show how, in fact, the gap between my view of moral propositions and human attitudes, and thus actions, is filled, but rather to indicate the *kind* of account which, it seems to me, can fill this gap. It is, ultimately, a matter of empirical evidence as to what precise form of developmental theory best fits the data; and the explanatory theories, which are to be delineated here, are not the final word on the matter, though they are, I believe, the best evidenced general theories of moral development we have today.

In presenting a theory of moral development, I shall, at several points, use the motivational assumptions of R. W. White. What Robert White's revision to Freud's motivational theory amounts to is this: he does not deny the existence of the three drives Freud postulated—love (libido), aggression (mortido), and the desire to avoid pain[63]—but rather claims that the classes of behaviour they explain are narrower than Freud supposed. Citing the fact that certain kinds of behaviour—exploration of the environment, manipulation of items in it, playful activity—occur apart from any of Freud's three drives (both operatively and epigenetically), White postulates another source of motivation, the desire competently to exercise capacities (what he calls ego energies), which can occur apart from any of Freud's three drives.[64] As a consequence of his psychological theory, White is able to restore to intellectual propriety the related notions of respect and esteem (which Freud reduced to forms of love and hate), since he clarifies the logical nature of respect and esteem as feelings that someone is competent in the exercise of his capacities.[65] Interestingly, White's views on competence desires and respect have been accepted even by a neo-Freudian like Erikson, and may be found anticipated in Aristotle, Kant, and Nietzsche.[66] The crucial significance of White's theory of competence desires, to general motivational theory, is in indicating that many forms of activity that Freud ascribed to aggression, e.g. playing football, can be better explained in terms of satisfying competence desires; my point will be that this is also the case as regards moral motivation, which Freud explained as forms of aggression or mortido.

The theory of moral development in the classic study of Piaget, supplemented by Kohlberg's recent work, represents a rather different point of view from that found in Freud, or Erikson.[67] The entire Oedipal situation, central to the emergence of morality in the latter two men's work, is not mentioned in either Piaget's or Kohlberg's accounts; indeed, the general Freudian view of conscience as the punitive superego, stamped into the child's person after certain drive conflicts, is the explicit intellectual opponent of their views.[68] On the contrary, 'internal moral standards are rather the outcome of a set of transformations of primitive attitudes and conceptions'.[69] In order to make this view clear, I shall first sketch Piaget's account, then a constructive interpretation of Kohlberg's work, filling in certain things which other data require, throughout relating their accounts to White's motivational assumptions. A conception of guilt will evolve which is identical with that previously proposed.

Piaget divides moral development into two basic stages, that of an 'ethics of authority' and that of 'autonomous personal conscience'.[70] In the first stage, the child's respect for moral rules is unilateral and absolutistic, involving a kind of blind obedience to the rules prescribed by powerful authority figures.[71] For Piaget, this attitude derives from certain early experiences (among which are regularity in motor functions, fundamental to a child's having the concept of a rule, and such primitive attitudes as 'jealousy' and 'altruistic reactions and a tendency to share', fundamental to a child's understanding the point of parental precepts),[72] combined with the child's continued respect for the omnicompetent parent, which leads to his acceptance of parental precepts. This aspect of Piaget's theory suggests that he implicitly accepts R. W. White's view that identification with the values of another can be most profitably and (contra Freud) unambiguously understood as related to competence and imitation:[73] given that people desire to be competent, when a person encounters another person whom he judges in the requisite sense to be competent, he will take him as his model and try to imitate him. Such a notion of identification clearly seems to be present in moral development, as the high confirmation of John Whiting's status–envy theory indicates.[74] Interpreting the latter in terms of White's theory, the child naturally identifies with the parent who seems more effective in controlling social and material resources, since the parent seems more competent and thus deserving of respect (thus, one may dispense with Whiting's notion of envy). In Piaget's view, assuming such a notion of identification, the 'unilateral respect' in the parent–child relationship is said to encourage a 'heteronomous' attitude toward adult rules as being sacred and unchangeable.[75] This attitude is supported by two related cognitive defects in the child's thought: 'egocentrism', the inability to distinguish one's own point of view from that of others (leading to an incapacity to see moral value as relative to different people's purposes); and 'realism', the inability to distinguish subjective and objective phenomena (leading to a notion of moral rules as fixed, eternal entities, not as the basis of psychosocial expectations).[76] The moral point of view deriving from the mixture of heteronomous respect and cognitive realism is described as 'moral realism'.[77]

Piaget's second stage occurs between the ages of eight and twelve, when a major change in the child's moral consciousness occurs. In terms of moral motivation, there evolves mutual respect between equals: respect based on the feelings that others are equally competent in the exercise of their moral capacities of judging and acting in terms of 'the norms of reciprocity and objective discussion'; this is 'admiration for a personality precisely in so far as this personality subjects itself to rules. Mutual respect would therefore seem to be possible only within what the individuals themselves regard as morality.'[78] The underlying conception, here, can be clarified, once again, by bringing in White's views on competence and respect, and applying them to the psychology of morality; thus, ethical action involves a form of competence since a person's self is able to order and suppress egoistic desires, and non-moral desires generally, as part of its desire to exercise its moral capacity of judging and acting in terms of certain moral principles, where such a capacity is supremely valued. In this view, it seems conscience does not exist as internalized aggressive drives, but as a complicated cognitive and motor capacity of judgement and action, with its own intrinsic desire to be exercised. For Piaget, though the complex development of earlier experiences and primitive attitudes mentioned above is presupposed, what is fundamentally responsible for the development of mutual respect is the development of the capacity for trust through participation in peer group ventures of 'co-operation' with those who are roughly equal (not grossly unequal, as in the parent–child relationship),[79] combined with a growing capacity to distinguish one's own ethical perspective from that of others (decline of egocentrism). Piaget regards the moral attitude of mutual respect as a kind of 'state of equilibrium', to which moral attitudes and concepts naturally tend as differences in age are effaced.[80]

Kohlberg's work, while it confirmed Piaget's finding about certain characteristics of youthful moral attitudes (e.g. judging in terms of consequences, not intention; no concern for the moral perspective of others; badness as dependent on probable punishment etc.),[81] did not validate Piaget's two-stage analysis of moral development. Instead, Kohlberg found it necessary to postulate six stages of moral development, stretching between the ages of ten and sixteen, long after Piaget (and Freud, for that matter) thought moral development ceased.[82] Within these six stages, Kohlberg distinguishes three levels of moral orientation: premorality (punishment and naïve hedonism), conventional role-conformity (good boy and authority-maintaining morality), and self-accepted moral principles (contract and individual principles of conscience). Still, it seems to me important to emphasize the continuities between Piaget's and Kohlberg's accounts. Thus, just as Piaget regarded the mutual respect of mature morality as the end of a developmental schedule from earlier experiences and attitudes, combined with growing cognitive reversibility[83] and the exposure to co-operative ventures, so, too, Kohlberg regards a mature ethics of mutual respect as evolving in a developmental schedule of natural attitudes, each of which is transformed into the next, given a convergence of factors (among which are cognitive growth and social experience). Thus, Kohlberg discusses how, when a child comes to *love* a parent (given a psychological law of the development of the natural attitude of love, as a result of the parent's evident concern for the child's well-being, early nurture, etc.), he naturally accepts his parent's moral precepts. It is part of what love means in such circumstances (the desire to do what the other wants one to do, where there is no capacity to judge critically the rationality or morality of what the other wants of one) that, if the love is breached through the child's transgression of the rules which the parent (the loved one) wants the child to follow, the child experiences certain feelings of guilt and is disposed to reveal his fault characteristically by making a confession, in this way seeking a reconciliation with the loved one. There is considerable empirical confirmation of this relation of parental love and confessional behaviour in children,[84] which is exactly the relation of love and guilt, which was suggested, on a conceptual level, in the previous section. One would, following Piaget, White, and Whiting, only like to supplement Kohlberg by adding the natural attitude of respect, as an important additional feature of the child's liability to guilt at this stage. Such respect would be shown by the tendency to obey the parent's rules, and by the feeling of guilt upon transgressing and the related disposition to confession and reconciliation with the authoritative parent. Kohlberg explicitly distinguishes this notion of guilt from later ones, for he sees that there are important distinctions between a disposition to confession and a disposition to critical self-judgement in terms of moral principles with its related dispositions to restitution and compensation.[85] In order for later kinds of guilt to develop, the child must undergo a cognitive development whereby he becomes capable of having his own standards of moral criticism and of taking account of different moral perspectives, and also begin to participate in more extensive 'social participation and role-taking'.[86] While Kohlberg denies the unique causal role of the peer group (*contra* Piaget), his evidence shows that broad social participation outside the family is a main determinant of moral development.[87] Thus, one may suggest, following Rawls in making explicit what seems implicit in Kohlberg's work,[88] that the kind of childhood confessional guilt feeling, necessarily related to love of and respect for (and the consequent desire for approval from) the parent, develops, when one participates in co-operative schemes with equals, into the attitude of *trust* for the equals in the co-operative scheme. The general psychological principle which is, I would propose, involved in such transformations of desire is the following: *where another shows evident intention of doing things for our own good, as we view it, there is a tendency to develop friendly feelings of some kind for the other.*[89] In the case of the young child, this took the form of the emergence of love for the parent, as a result of the parents' evident intentions of doing good to the child (nurture, care, guidance, etc.). In this second stage, the evident intention of our peers to do things for our own good leads to the development of the natural attitude of trust. One may assume, as part of this second developmental law of human attitudes, that the natural attitude of trust can only fully develop, if the capacity for love has been elicited in the previous stage. Similarly, a new form of guilt feeling would evolve, inhibitions and reactions that follow from the existence of mutual trust, e.g. the inclination to make reparation, to admit what one has done and apologize, to acknowledge and accept reproofs and penalties. Finally, I would claim that, given the previous development of the attitudes of love and trust, there is a third psychological law of attitude development whereby, when other persons generally accept and act on the principles of morality, the desire to act on those principles will develop in a person. The basic idea here is that it is part of the concept of their being moral principles that the principles are such that they work, when publicly accepted and acted on, in the interests of all persons, from the point of view of the original position; and thus, a person, who encounters other persons who accept and act on these principles, will benefit from their acting on them; and coherent with the general psychological principle mentioned above, a person, in so far as he perceives others acting on these principles as indicating an evident intention to advance his own good, will develop a friendly feeling toward the principles on which they act and which underlie this intention, given the previous development of the natural attitudes of love and trust. In short, the natural attitude of morality, the desire to act on the principles of morality, would evolve. Needless to say, the forms of social experience, leading to the development of a sense of morality, will be many and varied, but clearly, the experience of life in a democratic state, based on equal liberty and equal opportunity, will be important facilitating circumstances. Further, associated with the emergence of the attitude of morality, there will be a new form of guilt feeling, developed from the former kinds, one characterized by the appeal, by way of explanation of having the feeling, not to principles or rules holding only within a personal love or trust relation, but to principles applying to *all* moral persons. It is this notion of guilt that Kohlberg calls 'conscience' in his sixth stage:[90] 'self-critical guilt', based on 'socialized concerns about good and bad rather than the deep punitive trends implied in the superego concept'.[91]

The view taken here provides a further explanation for Piaget's suggestion that just social and political institutions will tend to be in stable equilibrium, since they tend to elicit a sense of justice in institutional participants, which shows itself in persons seeking to retain the just institutions.[92] In my view, this is so because just institutions are in the interests of all persons alike, and thus satisfy the psychological principle of attitude development. More generally, this view also provides an analogous explanation for the older traditional view that there is a tendency to a stable equilibrium, once moral principles are publicly and generally accepted, such that a violation of these principles results in an unstable situation until the wrong is remedied, the sort of conception that underlies many great works of art in all ages, e.g. Aeschylus' *Oresteia*, Shakespeare's cycle of history plays starting with *Richard II*, and Wagner's great tetralogy. The explanation is, simply, that public acceptance and general action on *moral* principles tend to elicit a sense of morality in persons that participate in the community where the principles are accepted and acted, and this sense of morality shows itself in the desire that moral principles be maintained, and that wrongs be made right, in accord with principles of reparation and compensation.

What, then, is found in common in Kohlberg's and Piaget's theories of moral development is the concentration on the conditions for the evolution, on a developmental schedule, of certain natural attitudes and conceptions, as a response to certain kinds of social experience. The central factors in moral development, in this view, are the internal capacities of feeling and judgement involved in such attitudes as love, trust, and a sense of right. And the propensity to guilt is seen as a necessary condition of the exercise of our capacity for such natural attitudes; it is, in its mature stage, 'the conscious, developmentally advanced, self-critical (and self-controlling) response' in which one criticizes oneself by appeal to what Kohlberg calls 'moral principles rather than moral rules'.[93] There is no *need* to regard conscience as internalized aggressive drives, a concept, as Kohlberg points out, for which the experimental data is meagre.[94] Rather, conscience is a part of a complicated competence of judgement and action in terms of certain principles, a competence which has an intrinsic desire to be exercised, a desire itself the product of a long attitudinal development. What one has here, then, are well-evidenced and plausible psychological theories, which implicitly and explicitly depend on the concept of guilt presented in the previous section; and thus, one has delineated an alternative to the Freudian view not only on the conceptual but on the psychological level as well. And further, and more important for my present purposes, one has indicated the *general* type of explanatory account which will fill the gap between my theory of moral propositions and their relation to human desires; and in doing this, I have also indicated how it is that the very concept of moral principles may enter into such explanatory accounts, as in the third law of attitudinal development, i.e. the account of moral principles as ultimate standards that are in the interests of all, from an original position of equal liberty, enters into the applicability of psychological principles which depend on others showing an evident intention of doing another good. An important advantage of a naturalistic theory of morality, such as mine, is that it can thus be used in clarifying such psychological laws; this is in sharp contrast to intuitionist propositional theories, where no similar clarification seems possible.

Finally, as regards my general anti-Freudian orientation, it should be noted that Kohlberg often mentions that experimental methods are much more easily able to detect guilt, as we find it in ordinary language and thinking, than the pervasive, unconscious, self-punitive tendencies which psycho-analysis has inferred from fantasy and pathology data.[95] Thus, Freudians may be quite correct in claiming that there is a sense of neurotic guilt, which is not characterized by the consciously available explanations and behavioural dispositions that we have seen to be characteristic of certain kinds of normal guilt (e.g. confession to parents, restitution to friends, reparation in terms of universally applicable moral principles); and about this, the developmental theories of Piaget and Kohlberg have little to say. The little they do have to say may be that one should not easily and without argument assume that the concepts derived from pathology necessarily throw light on the more normal developmental process, let alone that they are *in any sense* fundamental to that process in such a way that the normal data *must* be fitted to the pathological model (as Freudian theories generally seem to assume). As Erikson said in a different context, but of relevance here:

In psychoanalysis we repeat for our own encouragement (and as an argument against others) that human nature can best be studied in a state of partial breakdown or, at any rate, of marked conflict because— so we say—a conflict delineates the borderlines and clarifies the forces which collide on those borderlines. As Freud himself put it, we see a crystal's structure when it cracks. But a crystal, on the one hand, and an organism or a personality, differ in the fact that the one is inanimate and the other an organic whole which cannot be broken up without a withering of the parts.[96]

IV. *The Principle of Moral Development*

All the principles, both of morality and rationality, that I have formulated apply to actions of persons. However, at three points, I noted that certain of these principles require certain kinds of actions which lead to the development of special kinds of desires and sensitivities. Thus, the principles of rationality may require the development of certain kinds of competences and the desire to exercise them well, the development of which is in the agent's interests; the moral principle of mutual love may require the cultivation of certain kinds of sensitivities to personality and character traits; and the moral principle of beneficence may at least justify preferences for certain kinds of traditions of thought and training over other kinds (namely, preferences for those traditions that, *ceteris paribus*, foster the development of benevolent ideals). While none of these principles require a person to feel or have a certain desire, they do require that people put themselves in those circumstances which causally tend to develop certain kinds of feelings and desires, given that such circumstances in fact exist.

If the rational contractors of the original position are concerned that people develop certain kinds of desires in the above kinds of case, it seems *a fortiori* that they will be concerned that people develop the general desire to act on moral principles.[97] Given that some general theory of the development of the attitude of morality (analogous to that just presented) is true, the contractors will agree to a principle requiring people to be exposed to such circumstances as causally tend to facilitate the development of the desire to be moral. For, such a principle, if publicly known and generally acted on, will tend to increase people's readiness to act on moral principles, and will thus further secure a higher lowest, from the point of view of the original position.

The principle of moral development would be formulated thus:

13. People are to expose themselves and be exposed by others to those psychological conditions which will causally facilitate the development of the desire to act on moral principles 1–11 and 12*a*, given that people exposing others or exposing themselves do so at not substantial cost.

The principle will be agreed to as a principle of individual duty, since it is so important in securing a highest lowest that coercion is justified in enforcing it and since it applies in an institutional state of nature. However, where institutions do exist, it obviously applies there as well, imposing duties on those in a position to apply the principle, e.g. parents, educators, legislators, etc.

The principle is specifically formulated so as to facilitate the development of what I called previously the attitude of reasonableness (the effective desire and capacity to act on moral principles 1–11 and 12*a*). A requirement of developing the attitude of sympathetic benevolence is specifically not imposed by *this* principle, since action motivated by sympathetic benevolence may involve substantial sacrifices by the agent of his own interests. The contractors, as maximiners, would thus not wish to require the development of this attitude as a matter of duty. The preference of the contractors for people developing such attitudes will rather be expressed by their agreement to the principle of beneficence, a supererogatory principle of praise.

The requirement, 'that people exposing others or exposing themselves do so at not substantial cost', is, of course, necessary in order for the principle to be agreed to as a principle of duty, for the contractors will not secure a higher lowest if action on a principle (to which they are agreeing) severely frustrates the interests of the agent who is to act on such a principle. Note that the requirement of 'not substantial cost' is not equivalent to a requirement that a person exposing himself to such conditions must find being a moral man a more rational course of conduct than not being one (see, on this, chapter 14), before the principle applies. Choosing to be a moral man may well be less rational than not so choosing; but, as long as such a choice does not involve substantial sacrifices of the agent's interests (death, ill health, penury, and the like), it is still an applicable requirement of the principle of moral development that an agent expose himself to those conditions which causally facilitate the development of the attitude of a moral man. Note, in this connection, that the 'not substantial cost' requirement is easily satisfied in a community where people already acknowledge and generally act on moral principles, for here there are such reciprocal benefits from all acting on moral principles that the costs of so acting are meagre indeed. And conversely, the 'not substantial cost' requirement seems likely not to be satisfied in barbaric states of society where moral principles are not generally acknowledged and acted on, and where a person's acting on such principles may bring personal disaster at the hands of the uncomprehending moral barbarian. It is no logical accident that, in such cases, we look not for the reasonable man to find the moral man, but for the enlightened saint who is prepared for the crucifixions, which are necessary to give his message force but which reasonableness neither requires or demands.

The principle of moral development gives expression to certain fairly deep and quite old moral judgements. Thus, it gives a sense to our judgement that certain moral constraints do apply to people when they choose different ways of life, namely, that those ways of life are morally permissible which are least likely morally to corrupt the person choosing. The principle also provides another ground for the truth of our saying or thinking that a person ought to be ashamed who has failed to develop the capacities and desires central to the moral life, for he has failed to develop the competences which he had conclusive moral reason to develop (on the basis of the principle of moral development).[98] The principle also provides a ground for the truth of our saying to, or thinking of, an amoralist that he ought to feel guilty, for he has failed to develop the moral attitudes which he had moral reason to develop. And from the point of view of moral tradition, the principle gives expression to the old notion, found in Kant and many others, that there are duties to develop the moral virtues.[99]

14

WHY SHOULD I BE MORAL?

IN terms of the three criteria of theoretical adequacy which I set myself in chapter 1 (i.e. providing an account for propositions, their use in speech acts, and their moving appeal to action), my account of reasons for action seems to indicate at least the rough outlines of an adequate account, though complete theoretical adequacy would, of course, require considerably more precision and detail, in the account of principles, normative propositions, and speech acts. However, one traditional problem, perhaps *the* traditional problem, of moral philosophy has not yet been considered in sufficient detail, i.e. the problem expressed through the question—why should I be moral? I propose here to address myself, and the above theory of reasons for action, to this problem, because it seems to me to have been, and to continue to be, the source of so much philosophical puzzlement and confusion, especially as regards the concept of reasons for action.

The question—why should I be moral?—may be interpreted in several ways, most of which are based on various philosophical confusions and mistakes, and one of which raises interesting questions about the relation of being moral to the theory of goods for man. I shall divide these interpretations into the following headings and discuss them separately: (i) the relation of being moral to the concept of reasons for action, (ii) the relation of being moral to the concept of rationality, (iii) the relation of being moral to the concept of human virtues, and (iv) the relation of being moral to the theory of goods for man.

1. *Being Moral and the Concept of Reasons for Action*

The traditional *point* of the question—why should I be moral?—e.g. in Plato and Aristotle, was based on the assumption that a person had *no reason at all* for being moral, until it could be shown that, in some sense, choosing to be moral more promoted the agent's wants and interests than not so choosing. This view is, of course, quite explicit in Plato's *Republic*, the main point of which is to show that just such a relation between morality and interest obtains; thus, in the myth of the last book of the *Republic*, where persons can choose which character type they will have in the world of shadows, it is most rational, in terms of the agent's interests, for him to choose the character type of the moral man. Similarly, the entire point of Aristotle's view that 'what is valuable and pleasant to a morally good man actually is valuable and pleasant'[1] rests on the Platonic assumption that this man has the accurate knowledge of those activities that best advance his own wants and interests, unlike other men who lack the experience of having compared the desirability of the moral life with other sorts of life, and having rationally chosen the former.[2] And lest this be supposed an antique philosophical view of no relevance today, consider Mrs. Foot's recent claim that a man has *no* reason to be moral until being moral is shown to relate to advancing his wants and interests; and thus she insists that moral philosophers will not have given an adequate account of reasons for action until they have addressed themselves to answering the Platonic question.[3]

Now, as I already suggested in chapter 6, the view that there being reason for an agent to do *x*, or having reasons to do *x*, logically depends on the agent's wants, is simply false as a general account of the concept of reasons for action in their justificatory employment, for it is based on the confusion of rationality and reasonableness. The relation between being moral and reasons for action is mediated by the principles of morality, which define a large class of reasons for action, and which apply quite apart from a particular agent's wants and desires (e.g. even to an amoralist who has no desire at all to regulate his life by the principles of morality, and who has other desires whose rational pursuit involves contravening moral principles). Given that persons have certain capacities and are in such circumstances that moral principles apply to them, these persons have reasons, and conclusive reasons, to be moral, to regulate their lives by the principles of morality. The question—why should I be moral?—may be interpretable in some philosophically illuminating sense; but, in so far as it is construed as being a request for reasons for being moral, where persons have no reasons at all, if no true answer in terms of self-interest is given, then it is a logically confused and inappropriate question, whose answer is, importantly, irrelevant to the justifiability of being moral.

11. *Being Moral and the Concept of Rationality*

Another way of interpreting the question—why should I be moral?—would be in terms of a request for the justifiability of being moral, in terms of the principles of rational choice and the advancement of self- and other-regarding desires, with the exception of the desire to be moral (which is assumed to be absent), where it is not supposed that a positive answer to this question in terms of considerations of rationally advancing the agent's interests provides the only good reason for being moral. The question, in short, would be—is it in my interest, or is it rational, to be moral? The answer to this question may be interpreted in a hypothetical way, as being determined by a purely hypothetical decision situation where a rational man, lacking the desire to be moral but having other typical human desires and wants, must decide whether he will submit himself to certain circumstances, which will lead to his having the attitude of morality, not unlike the choice of character in Plato's myth or of Kant's noumena.[4] Being rational, the man will decide on the basis of the principles of rational choice, as applied to his self- and other-regarding desires. Now, two remarks may be made concerning the question—why should I be moral?—interpreted in this sense: (i) as regards the answer to it, and (ii) as regards the appropriateness of the question, given the relation of the concept of moral principles to the principles of rational choice.

(i) Interpreted as a question about the rationality of being moral, it seems rather obvious to me that the answer will not always be positive, and that Plato, Aristotle, and Foot are mistaken in suggesting that it is. No doubt, many persons, in the hypothetical decision situation described above, will find it rational to decide to be moral. And clearly, Mrs. Foot's considerations about the importance to many people of spontaneity in social interaction are relevant here;[5] many persons will not be able, or find it profitable, to endure the costs in duplicity and shrewd concealment of their amorality that a rational decision not to be moral must involve, in that candour about this would be against the agent's interests in so far as other persons would react with hostility and even social ostracism from co-operative institutions. However, this will not be so in all cases, e.g. in the case of a person with the capacities and desires of Grice's 'Master Criminal'.[6] Such a person has the capacity to conceal his amorality from others, and thus himself profit from the morality of other persons, without foregoing that profit through others' hostility at his amorality, since he can successfully conceal this from them, only contravening moral principles where he can keep it secret, and where such contravention is in his interests. For such a person, it will be irrational to be moral, assuming most other persons are moral, since he can successfully profit from their morality without himself undergoing all the costs of being consistently moral in all cases.

(ii) The proposition that it may be irrational to be moral is one which many philosophers have vainly sought to disprove. But, it is, I think, a wholly obvious result; and it can only be through misunderstanding and confusion that such a result has been viewed with such philosophical distaste. In part, of course, the confusion is due to the widespread incorrect assimilation of the concepts of rationality and reasonableness, and related misunderstanding of the concept of reasons for action, mentioned above. But such mistaken distaste is also derived from the failure to assess fully the priority of principles of morality to those of rational choice (see Part II, chapter 12). What it means for there to be such a priority relation, and what it means for the prior moral principles to be principles, is simply that there is no appeal, by way of justification, beyond these principles, when they apply. And thus, in so far as the applicability of moral principles conclusively and decisively answers the question—why should I be moral?—*raising* that question, in such a way that the principles of rational choice can in some important way provide the answer, is based on a confusion, not least of which is to be involved in the logical circularity of justifying moral principles by principles of rational choice, whose applicability assumes the prior applicability of the principles of morality.

Another related, and more accurate, way of posing this criticism would be in the following way. If one embarks on the enterprise of trying to show that being moral is rational, it is normally assumed that the answer to this question will in some important way clarify the grounds or reasons for being moral. But, in fact, since the posing of the question abstracts from the priority relations between principles of action, the answer will, at best, provide *a* or *some* reason for being or not being moral; the idea that it can, in itself, provide good, let alone conclusive, reasons for being or not being moral is based on a mistaken conception of reasons for action as exhausted by the concept of rationality and its principles, a view which it is one of the main points of this book to deny.

Perhaps, the view that raising the above question of rationality is crucially relevant to the justifiability of being moral derives also from the following natural confusion. Most moral principles (i.e. the principles of moral reasonableness) only apply if acting on them is not severely irrational. Even the principle of fairness, which may require a person to expose himself to likely death defending his institutions from aggressors, does not require irrational frustration of interests, since death here is a voluntarily accepted price of having lived in and benefited from institutions which made possible a much more rationally satisfying life-plan. Seen in its full context, accepting such exposure to death is here quite rational. It is quite natural to confuse the broad question of the rationality of being moral with the question of whether acting on moral principles would be severely irrational for a certain agent; and to suppose that what is true of the latter question (namely, that if acting on certain moral principles is severely irrational, such principles would not apply to the agent at all) is also true of the former. However, the connection between these questions is in fact notably tenuous. For, as indicated in the previous chapter, the question of the rationality of being moral is not equivalent to the question of the possible severe irrationality of acting on moral principles. Irrationality is of many degrees. Once the mistaken confusion of different questions is seen, the temptation to related confusions is, I think, removed.

III. *Being Moral and the Concept of Virtue*

Still another way of interpreting the question—why be moral?— has been that of supposing that a positive answer to this question, in terms of being moral advancing the agent's interests, was required in order for the desires and capacities, associated with being moral, to be worthy of pursuit, as human virtues. This view, clearly of Platonic and Aristotelian origin, has been expressed recently by Mrs. Foot, who has claimed that if 'someone were to say that courage was not a virtue he would have to say that it was not a quality by which a man came to act well', where the notion of acting well is interpreted, for example, in terms of injustice being 'more profitable than justice to a man of strength and wit' and thus justice not being a virtue (the claim of Thrasymachus in Book I of the *Republic*).⁷ In this view, the concept of a virtue is such that a particular trait of character is a virtue only if it is such as to be chosen rationally, as a character trait, in the hypothetical decision situation sketched in the previous section; and thus, the question— why should I be moral?, interpreted as, is it rational to be moral?— must be raised before deciding whether or not being moral, or separate dispositions comprising being moral, are virtues, things worthy of being adopted and pursued.

This interpretation of the question seems based on an incorrect conception of human virtues or character-traits. Virtues are valuable not because they promote the agent's self-interest, but because they involve the desires and capacities required to regulate one's life by the ultimate standards of morality and rationality. These principles, as ultimate standards of action, *define* what is worthy of being pursued, or what it is to act *well*. The Platonic– Aristotelian conception of virtue mistakenly assimilates all human virtues to those associated with the rationality principles (even if through a complex hypothetical decision situation), as part of its general mistaken assimilation of all reasons for action to those defined by the latter principles. But, once one clearly sees the distinction between principles of morality and those of rational choice, and understands their priority relations, then it is also clear that the theory of virtue must be appropriately revised to account for the independent force of the principles of morality from those of rational choice.

In my general view of human virtue, what will be considered human virtues depends on the capacities and desires which are psychologically required for persons to regulate their lives by various principles of action. In chapter 5 I indicated how this was so in reference to the virtue of prudence and the principles of rational choice. But, it is, I think, clear how this view can be generalized to cover moral virtues, since what are considered to be such virtues can be shown to involve desires and capacities associated with regulating one's life by some moral principle or some class of moral principles, as the case may be. Thus, for example, the Platonic virtue of temperance (the capacity and desire to forego the pursuit of immediate pleasure because of

overriding considerations) is an important requisite for regulating
one's life both by principles of morality and rationality, since the
temptation to immediate pleasure will, if not resisted, often lead to
contravening these principles; and the Platonic virtue of courage
(the capacity and desire to overcome fear of harm and danger
because of overriding goals which are to be achieved) is important
in fulfilling the requirements of the moral principle of fairness,
where this applies in the case of certain military duties. And
similarly, the Aristotelian virtue of generosity is required, in many
cases, for the moral principle of beneficence to be used in regulating
conduct; and the Aristotelian virtue of justice by definition involves
the desire and capacity to regulate one's conduct to others by
principles of justice, and is psychologically necessary if persons are
to regulate their lives by justice systematically, and not just
occasionally because of some special convergence of justice and
self-interest. A similar sort of relation between virtues and
principles can, I think, be made out between honesty and the
principle of fairness requiring veracity; between faithfulness
and the principle of fairness as applied to promise- and contract-
keeping; considerateness and the principle of consideration;
decency and the moral principles of obligation and duty; niceness
and the principles of supererogation; and (that very un-Greek
virtue) humility and the principle of mutual respect; and the like.
Of course, not all ages or all peoples in the same age value the
same character traits as virtues, or to the same extent, since the
requirements of moral principles differ in different conditions of
life and with different social institutions. Thus, for example, the
characteristic Greek emphasis on courage seems rather excessive
today, and is no doubt related to the special conditions of life in
ancient Greece, where military enterprises, concentrating on the
individual hero, were a continual part of life.[8] And the Aristotelian
virtue of magnificence (the desire and capacity to spend money
lavishly on public projects, or entertainments) seems hardly to be
a contemporary virtue of any significance, in part because we do
not have public institutions in which such private lavishness plays
a crucial role. Further, the Aristotelian virtue of high-mindedness
comes very close to being the vice we consider to be pride; and
this is, no doubt, related to the greater importance to social life of
individualistic, noble heroism in Greece than in our present society,
which can, perhaps, better afford to value more egalitarian virtues.

iv. *Being Moral and the Concept of Goods for Man*

One final way in which one may interpret the question—why should I be moral?—is as a confused way of asking whether being moral is *good* for the man who is moral, and as trying to provide a criterion for answering this question in terms of whether it would be rational for an agent, in the hypothetical situation described above, to decide to have the character of a moral man. Understood in this sense, it seems to me that one has both a legitimate question and a legitimate criterion for answering it. To consider this question, in the full detail it obviously needs, would require an extended investigation of the concept of the good, and its relation to the concept of morality, an investigation I cannot undertake here. However, a general view of the good can be *outlined*, at least to an extent that will make the concept of goods for man somewhat clearer.

Very roughly, it seems to me that the concept of x's being a good is generally equivalent to the concept of x's advancing, or conducing to, in some optimal way, the ends of a living thing, whether these ends are the full functioning and continued life of plant (a good root) or primitive animal life, or the general objects of desire of animals, men among them. The qualification that a good must 'in some optimal way' advance the ends of living things has an important consequence for one's understanding of the meaning of the good as applied to good x's, relative to men's ends: the good, in this sense, is not analytically related to human desires, *per se*, but only to satisfying human desires rationally, where this latter concept is understood in terms of the principles of rational choice as applied to actual human desires. The view that the good, as applied to the human case, is analytically related to promoting the rational satisfaction of human desires is at least as old as Aristotle's distinction between 'the real or the apparent good', and is a subject on which there is a remarkable convergence of opinion among traditional philosophers, who disagree on many other issues, e.g. Kant and Sidgwick.[9] And clearly, a similar view is behind Perry's and Ziff's conception that the good is related to promoting human interests, since human interests are defined as things needed for the pursuit of any desires at all (e.g. money), and thus as things which it is, by the dominance principle, supremely rational to secure, since many ends can be attained by achieving them;[10] and a similar view of the good has been suggested by Findlay, Foot, Geach, Anscombe, Harrod, and many others.[11]

This general view of the good, as being analytically related to the rational satisfaction of human desires, must be considerably elaborated on before it can provide an adequate propositional account for many sentences in which 'good' is used.[12] Thus, for example, one must distinguish between the use of 'good for me' or 'good for him', or 'good for them', and the use of 'good' *simpliciter*, as in 'good pen', 'good book', 'good car', etc. The former usages may be explicated as expressing propositions about some x's tending to the rational satisfaction of the particular desires of a certain person, or group of persons; but the use of 'good', without such qualifications, seems to involve the concept of the x's promoting the rational satisfaction of desires which are typically, given the regularities of human desire and circumstance, associated with things of kind x. Thus, for example, 'a good pen' may be analysed as expressing the same proposition as that expressed by 'a pen which has the properties which persons typically desire pens to have, and which has those properties to a degree that rationally advances those desires', where the properties here include ease in writing, not spurting ink, etc. And thus, it may well be the case, as often is the case, that a good car, for example, may not be a good car for me, given the peculiarities of my desires, the fact, for example, that speed and ease of driving would contravene my desire for slowness and my passion for difficulty. Or, given that the concept of a good book is to be explicated relative to the desires of a relatively educated and sophisticated élite, it may well be that a good book is something which many persons may find not to be a good for them at all, except, perhaps, as an artistic filler of bookcases (as with the woman who buys books to match the colour of her wallpaper). And further, an adequate theory of the good, in the human case, would have to elaborate on the sense of the application of 'good' not only to artifacts (pens, cars, books), but also to events (good weather), natural objects (a good stone formation), men in social roles (a good judge, father), institutions (a good bank, system of government), national policies (the common good), men *simpliciter* (good man), reasons for action (good as opposed to bad reasons), and the like. While it may be correct to claim that 'good', in all these cases, expresses the concept of the *x*'s in some way advancing the rational satisfaction of human desires from some point of view (whether the individual's special interests, or the typical interests of individuals, or even the interests of individuals from a hypothetical position of equal liberty, as with good moral reasons for action), one should like an adequate theory to work this out in detail. But, relative to my present purposes, I propose only to consider the sense of 'a good man', 'a good for man', 'a good for this man', and refer to other usages only in so far as they will assist in the understanding of these.

In analysing the concept of a good man and good for man, along the lines of the general view of the good taken here, it seems clear that something very important, in understanding these different concepts, was indicated by Socrates' answer to Thrasymachus, in Book I of the *Republic*, where Socrates responds to Thrasymachus' attack on the view that a good shepherd takes care of sheep well by pointing out that the use of 'good' here pertains to doing good for sheep, not to the good of the shepherd; and similarly, Socrates notes, with the concept of a good ruler.[13] Socrates' point is, I think, quite correct, and is crucial to the understanding of the different meaning of 'good man' and 'good for man'. The sense of 'good man', like that of 'good father', 'good patient', 'good teacher', etc., is explicable in terms of the person in question having those characteristics which advance the rational satisfaction of the desires of other men associated with the person in the particular context in question, e.g. a good father benefits his children, a good patient does not give the doctor or nurses much trouble but obeys their instructions, a good teacher communicates knowledge and curiosity to students, etc. In cases such as these, the concept of father, patient, teacher, etc., introduces the concept of the relevant group of persons in reference to whom the sense of the person's being good is to be understood; the sense of 'good man', however, at least apart from special contexts which assume a particular group (e.g. 'he's a good man', as used by a boss in a textile factory, where the sense of good is assumed to have reference to the man's skills in raising the production levels that advance the boss's interests), does not seem to incorporate the concept of a *special* group of persons in reference to whom the sense of goodness is to be construed. Rather, by contrast to special roles and relationships, which persons may be in, the sense of 'good man' must be explicated by the concept of a man's somehow advancing the rational desire satisfaction of all persons, apart from special institutional (good worker) or other relationships (e.g. good friend). In this usage, the sense of 'good man' naturally implies that the man systematically regulates his life by moral principles, since, by definition, moral principles, if publicly accepted and generally acted on, rationally advance the desires of *all* men, i.e. are for the good of all men. A good man, in this sense, only acts on the basis of good, or generally sufficient, moral reasons for action, except where he has good reason to believe that such moral reasons are not relevant, so that reasons for action in terms of individual rationality can be pursued. Such a man is good and of moral worth, because he is more likely, in fact, to regulate his life by moral principles than a man who does not have the natural attitude of morality as a settled disposition of action, and than a man who has a moral character which will only act when there are conclusive reasons to do so, thus, perhaps, leading to more immorality through inaction than otherwise. Here, of course, as I had occasion to remark in chapter 12, we have a gap between the good reasons associated with questions of moral worth, and praise and blame, and the conclusive reasons associated with questions of moral rightness. The only advance of the present discussion over the previous one is that we are now able to see how the concept of goodness is related to questions of moral worth: by definition, obedience to moral principles advances the interests of all, and thus those men are good who are most likely, in fact, to realize the requirements of moral principles. Obviously, the use of the concept of goodness has special naturalness as applied to those who, *ceteris paribus*, regulate their conduct by the principle of beneficence, since action on this principle implies doing good to others even where it involves substantially sacrificing one's own interests. But, of course, nothing so far said about the concept of a good man, or, for that matter, a good father, patient, or teacher, implies that being a good person as *x* is necessarily a good for that person as *x*. And this is, I think, a consequence of the fact that something's being a good for someone depends, precisely, on the desires of the person in question, and whether the thing, supposed to be a good, does, in fact, rationally advance the desires of the person. Thus, unlike the concept of a good *x*, where *x* is a person under some description, the concept of a something's being a good for a person *does* depend on the desires of the person, so that it is quite possible for a person's goodness, as related to other persons' desires, not to be a good for the person in question, e.g. a good physician may in fact find nothing at all satisfying in his being a physician, and thus find his being a good physician to be an evil *for him*, if it, in fact, frustrates his desires.[14]

But is being a good man a good for man, or a good for some particular man? Now, to *this* question, it seems to me that the above interpretation of 'why should I be moral?' is relevant, and, indeed, provides a criterion for answering the question. That is, what will, I think, decide whether being moral, or being a good man, is a good for a man is whether or not that man would find it rational to decide to be moral, in the hypothetical decision situation delineated above, i.e. decide to submit himself to circumstances which would result in his having the attitude of morality, where he previously lacked the desire to be moral. This will be so, because such a decision situation will provide the relevant criterion for deciding whether the man's being moral will more rationally advance his desires from the decision situation, as opposed to his not being moral. The answer to this question, as indicated above, is, simply, that it depends on the desires of the person in question, as well as on the particular context of choice, e.g. whether or not it is assumed that other persons do have the critical attitude of morality. Perhaps, the closest one may come to agreeing with the traditional view that morality is always a good for man is in the saying that it may be true that morality is a good for man, in the sense that *most* men, given their desires and limited capacity for duplicity and artful secrecy, will find it profitable to decide to be moral, in the context of choice where it is assumed that other persons have the natural attitude of morality. But, it is simply not the case that being moral, or being a good man, is necessarily a good for every particular man, for one may well imagine men, whose capacities and desires are such that it would be irrational for them to decide to be moral, in the hypothetical decision situation; and, for them, if being moral would involve the substantial frustration of their desires, being a good man would be an evil. The important point to see here is that the fact that being moral would be irrational and thus not be a good for a man provides no good reason at all for not being moral, at least as long as the irrationality is not severe. But, enough has, I think, already been said on this.

Finally, in so far as substantive theories of morality have been traditionally classified in terms of their conception of the relation of the right and the good, one would like to know where, in the traditional typology, the present theory belongs. The answer, simply, is that my account is deontological, which is to say that it does not analyse the concept of the right in terms of some notion of maximizing the good, however the latter term is understood. Rather, the concept of morality and that of goodness are independently defined, though in various ways related; and the principles of morality are analysed as placing normative constraints on each person's justifiable pursuit of his own good. Note how little support the present account gives the general view that deontological theories cannot account for consequences, for it is a crucial mark of the ideal contract view that the consequences of moral principles importantly enter into their acceptance as moral principles from the original position, a matter which chapters 8–11 should have made abundantly clear.

v. *A Final Remark on the General Theory*

In working out a constructive theory of reasons for action, I tried, throughout, systematically to satisfy criteria of theoretical adequacy, which seemed to me of evident philosophical importance. And, though, as I remarked at the beginning of this chapter, the view is by no means complete, it does not seem to me wildly implausible or unreasonable to claim that the account is, in its very general outlines, adequate by the criteria that I set myself. But, of course, adequacy, in the sense I have employed that notion, is ambiguous between the theory's actually stating what is ordinarily meant by certain words and sentences and the theory's providing a reconstruction of our concepts, which it is desirable, in some sense, to adopt. This general ambiguity has plagued my account throughout; and underlying it is the troubling problem of where one draws the line between rejecting a theory because it fails to reflect ordinary use, and altering ordinary use because of the theory's systematic plausibility and appeal. Excesses seem obviously possible on both sides; for example, J. J. C. Smart's cavalier rejection of all counter-examples to act-utilitarianism by telling people to change their considered moral judgements and generally to substitute the rational for the moral,[15] seems to go well beyond the tolerable amount of reconstruction that a philosopher, in good conscience, may urge; and, analogously, the common claim, that the deep social opprobrium attached to homosexuality implies that any theory not condemning it must be incorrect, seems to use the appeal to ordinary use in an inconclusive and illegitimate way. But, where and how is one to draw the line between such excesses and more legitimate theoretical moves? I have no simple, non-circular answer to this question; and for want of one, it seems to me that one must, finally, rest content with offering the entire constructive theory to the critical judgements and deliberations of other men, so that they may reflect upon and decide whether or not the theory does in fact accurately reflect their concepts, or provide a reconstruction of them which is found illuminating and useful, or both to some extent, as I, personally, would hope and expect. Ultimately, the value of this, as with any similar theory, will only be proven to the degree that it provides an analytic tool which will aid men in understanding and working out their considered convictions about reasons for action until they reach some sort of reasonable equilibrium between their theories about such beliefs and the beliefs themselves. For, in working out a theory such as I have presented in this work, a person is, at bottom, constructing a complex system of interlocking concepts which, like a baroque cathedral, reverences and gives expression to a certain vision of the unity of ideas and action, a vision which is certainly in origin highly personal and perhaps in effect quite idiosyncratic. Thus, though I have rejected the concept of having freely chosen principles, in Hare's or in the more traditional Platonic–Aristotelian sense, as being fundamental to a person's having reasons for action, perhaps such views have some appropriateness if applied as a criterion of the adequacy of a theory (i.e. that theory is adequate which, after extensive reflection, a man freely accepts as being most accurate and useful). At the last, one offers one's theory to others as a subjective and personal set of ideas which have been found useful in one's own deliberations; and one grants that the issue of the theory's objectivity and impersonal truth-value hinges on the degree to which it illuminates for others the process of an enlightened choice of normative beliefs.

NOTES

Bibliographical details of all books and articles cited in the notes are to be found in the Bibliography (pp. 342–57)

CHAPTER 1

1. A concise and clear statement of Stevenson's theory may be found in his article, 'The Emotive Meaning of Ethical Terms'; but his classic work remains *Ethics and Language*. Hare's main works are *The Language of Morals* and *Freedom and Reason*.

2. Hare's so-called 'inverted commas' cases (*Language of Morals*, pp. 120, 124, 167); Diggs, 'A Technical Ought', p. 310.

3. Diggs, 'A Technical Ought', p. 311; cf. *Freedom and Reason*, pp. 27–8, where Hare allows that all 'ought'-expressions have a propositional component.

4. I am here rather loosely extending H. P. Grice's analysis of meaning from the information-conveying case to the action-inducing or guiding case; for Grice's own view, see 'Meaning'.

5. Diggs, 'A Technical Ought', p. 315.

6. 'Ascriptivism'; and especially, 'Assertion'.

7. 'Meaning and Speech Acts.'

8. See Geach, 'Ascriptivism', p. 223; Searle, 'Meaning and Speech Acts', p. 429.

9. Urmson, 'On Grading'; Hare, *Language of Morals*, pp. 94–110.

10. See chapter 2, *Freedom and Reason*.

11. 'The Emotive Meaning of Ethical Terms', p. 417

12. 'Value and its Moving Appeal.'

13. e.g. *Language of Morals*, p. 85.

14. *Contemporary Moral Philosophy*, pp. 2–3. Of course, as Austin's theoretical account is refined, the account of the implications of his theory for moral philosophy can also be refined.

15. J. L. Austin, *How To Do Things With Words*, p. 100.

16. Thus, cf. Socrates' method of questioning Euthyphro about 'the essential form of holiness which makes all holy actions holy' (p. 174, *Euthyphro*) by appeal to our considered judgements; Aristotle, 'Therefore, we should start from what is known to us. For that reason, to be a competent student of what is right and just, and of politics generally,

one must first have received a proper upbringing in moral conduct',
Nicomachean Ethics, 1095^6 3–6; Hume, *Treatise of Human Nature*,
p. 546, and especially pp. 547–9, where Hume uses the method of appeal
to considered judgements to refute the theories of social contractarians;
Kant, *Foundations of the Metaphysics of Morals*, p. 20; Ross, *The Right
and the Good*, p. 41; Brandt, *Ethical Theory*, pp. 244 ff.; Rawls, 'Outline
of a Decision Procedure for Ethics'.

17. On the concept of the reasonable, see W. H. Sibley's 'The Rational
vs. the Reasonable'.

18. Sidgwick, *Methods of Ethics*, p. 264.

19. This seems to have been an important philosophical motivation
toward non-cognitivism in ethics; thus, given the belief that Moore's
open-question argument refuted all forms of naturalism or that all forms
of naturalism were philosophically inadequate, then only intuitionism
was left as a form of last ditch cognitivism; but this would be rejected
as incompatible with the empiricist verification theory of meaning. Thus,
non-cognitivism was left. See, for an example of this mode of argument,
chapter VI of A. J. Ayer's *Language, Truth and Logic*.

20. Thus, for example, W. D. Falk, at least in his later work (i.e. in his
paper ' "Ought" and Motivation', as opposed to his earlier works,
'Morals Without Faith', and 'Obligation and Rightness'), does not deny
that we make judgements about obligation that imply an 'externalist
view' (' "Ought" and Motivation', p. 501), but he asks us to reject this
'obscurantist objectivism' in favour of 'an avowed skepticism' (p. 510),
which would rest content with his first-person attitude analysis. Similarly,
Westermarck does not deny that we make moral judgements that seem
to be characterizing the world and not our own experience (dispositional
or occurrent), but he asks us to revise our judgements in line with his
first-person approbationist account with the explanation 'that the subjective experience has been objectivized in the speech as a quality
attributed to the object' (*Ethical Relativity*, pp. 143–4), and that consistent empiricism requires our correcting this delusive appearance of
objectivity.

21. G. E. Moore, *Principia Ethica*.

22. 'The Naturalistic Fallacy'; for another related critique of the naturalistic fallacy, see Morton White's *Toward Reunion in Philosophy*, especially
Part III.

23. Moore, *Principia Ethica*, pp. 15–16.

24. On this, see, for example, Quine's 'Quantifiers and Propositional
Attitudes'.

25. This interpretation was suggested to me by Professor R. M. Hare.

26. Brandt, *Ethical Theory*, pp. 163–6.

27. See *Language of Morals*, pp. 79–93.

CHAPTER 2

1. *Practical Reasoning*, p. 169.

2. For an example of an inquiry into the nature of such principles, see Hart's 'Prolegomenon to the Principles of Punishment', pp. 158–82.

3. Consider, for example, Bentham's venomous attacks on the French natural right theorists, who espoused principles of equal liberty and opportunity in social and political institutions. His classic diatribe is his 'Anarchical Fallacies'. It seems to me that the principles Bentham was attacking were precisely those which best justified Bentham's own moral positions on many issues.

4. See *Freedom and Reason*, chapter 9; in saying that Professor Hare 'too easily' accepts the logical possibility of the actual morality of a sincere Nazi's principles of intolerance, I mean to grant Hare's basic point, viz. that it is possible to describe hypothetical fact situations which, if they existed, would make possible the actual morality of such principles.

5. Among examples of views that morality is logically related to free choice are Hare's view that principles are things 'accepted by a man himself as a guide to his actions', otherwise being 'dead things' (*Freedom and Reason*, p. 46); Nowell-Smith's view that 'a moral principle is a disposition to choose' (*Ethics*, p. 307); Gauthier's emphasis that 'we must decide' (*Practical Reasoning*, p. 122) what shall weigh in our conduct as reasons for action; and Barry's view that political principles have their proper place as intermediate standards between 'ultimate considerations' (*Political Argument*, p. 37) and specific issues, being 'conceived as open to personal adoption and rejection' (p. 38).

6. In Hare's case, there is quite frank acknowledgement that his theories are basically directed not to the question of what is right or good, but rather to how an agent comes to believe that something is right or good; thus, for example, see his account of how his theory relates goodness and choice, 'Descriptivism', pp. 127 ff.

7. Cf. Warnock's related criticism of Hare, *Contemporary Moral Philosophy*, p. 47.

8. On rational choice, see Luce and Raiffa, *Games and Decisions*; on the principles of justice, see Rawls, 'Justice as Fairness'; on Pareto optimality, see I. M. D. Little, *A Critique of Welfare Economics*, especially chapters I–VI; J. Rothenberg, *The Measurement of Social Welfare*, especially chapters 3–4; and Barry, *Political Argument*, pp. 49–52, especially, and pp. 237–85, for a critique of it as a general principle of political right; on the principle of fairness, see Hart, 'Are There Any Natural Rights?', especially pp. 185–6, and Rawls, 'Legal Obligation and the Duty of Fair Play', pp. 3–18; on consideration, cf. Findlay's remark about some principle of 'mutual courtesy and graciousness going

beyond the bounds of need', *Values and Intentions*, p. 343; on non-maleficence, cf. G. J. Warnock's remark, *contra* Hare, that one clear ground of moral judgements, *qua* moral, is that an act is one of wanton cruelty, *Contemporary Moral Philosophy*, p. 47.

9. Cf. H. L. A. Hart, *The Concept of Law*, pp. 54–6.

10. Cf. ibid., chapter 6.

11. In the case of a legal system based entirely on custom the legal case would, of course, collapse into the social custom case (cf. M. Weber, *Law in Economy and Society*, pp. 65–73).

12. And there will, of course, be troublesome middle cases where the criteria we use in clear paradigm cases of existence and non-existence will not allow us to know exactly what to say or think (e.g. suppose the legislative, judicial, and executive branches of government all began accepting different fundamental rules for legal authority; it is difficult to say what rules are legal ones here, for the whole notion of legal system has become problematic).

13. See John Rawls's example, 'Constitutional Liberty and the Concept of Justice', *Justice*, pp. 110 ff.

14. See *Politics*, Book I, especially chapters 5 and 6; on the sociological aspects of the Greek city state, see M. Weber, *The City*, chapter 5. Cf. Weber, *General Economic History*, chapter 6, for an account of the later manorial slave system.

15. For an interesting attempt by a non-cognitivist theory to come to terms with the problem of the moral reformer, see pp. 179–84 of Urmson's 'On Grading'. What Urmson does is simply to deny that the moral reformer's claims have objective status, calling them a 'rhetorical device' (p. 182) used for propaganda purposes; this ploy amounts to rejecting the data of moral philosophy in order to save one's theory, for it is precisely the objectivity of the moral reformer's claims, in the appropriate context, that one wishes to have some account for.

16. Section 5, 'The Nature of Concepts', *Mental Acts*, pp. 11–17.

17. P. Foot and J. Harrison, 'When is a Principle a Moral Principle?'.

18. Kelsen in his *General Theory of Law and State*, where he distinguished 'legal norms' from rules of law 'in a descriptive sense' (p. 45). The view as formulated in that book was obscurely put and unconvincing, and was widely criticized as a result; see, e.g. H. L. A. Hart's 'Kelsen Revisited', especially pp. 710–17; also, Alf Ross's *On Law and Justice*, especially pp. 66–70. However, in his later, considerably revised edition of that work, *Theorie Pure du Droit*, Kelsen clarified the distinction, here formulated as that between 'norme juridique et proposition de droit' (p. 96). Von Wright formulates the distinction as being between 'norm-formulations' and 'normative statements' (*Norm and Action*, p. 101). For an earlier suggestion of this distinction, see Sidgwick, *Methods of Ethics*, p. 101 n.

19. 'Must we Mean what we Say?', p. 87.

20. 'Chess, Checkers, Dominoes, Acey-Ducey', p. 1.

21. *Theorie Pure Du Droit*, p. 101. A remarkable view for Kelsen to adopt, since in his earlier book he had made jurisprudential history by rejecting (for good reasons) a command theory of norms (e.g. *General Theory of Law and State*, p. 33).

22. *Norm and Action*, p. 104.

23. For other examples of sentences possibly used to express normative propositions, consider '*x* is done in *y* way'; 'that isn't done'; etc.

24. *Euthyphro*, pp. 169–85.

25. That is, as the distinction would be applied to the moral sphere; see chapter II, *The Concept of Mind*.

26. *The Moral Judgment of the Child*, p. 119.

27. Thus, for St. Thomas, the natural law comprises only one small set of the larger class of laws, called eternal, by which 'the whole community of the universe is governed by the divine reason', *Summa Theologica*, p. 113; and Patrick Devlin has argued that legalizing homosexuality between consenting adults would undermine the moral foundations on which social cohesion rests in his now famous (or infamous) 'Morals and the Criminal Law', pp. 1–25. For an incisive critique of this reasoning, see Hart's *Law, Liberty, and Morality*.

28. Cicero declares that unjust laws 'no more deserve to be called laws than the rules a band of robbers might pass in their assembly' (*Laws*, p. 385). For Aquinas, an unjust law 'is no longer legal, but rather a corruption of law' (*Summa Theologoca*, p. 129); for Suarez, ' "law" is properly applied, in an absolute sense, to that which pertains to moral conduct' (*On Laws and God the Lawgiver*, p. 24), and thus the concept of an unjust law is logically incoherent. And Victoria argues that the rules set down to regulate the lives of Indians in the New World are not laws, because they are unjust; see *On the Indians*. Grotius takes a similar view in his *De Jure Belli et Pacis*. And Locke implies such a view in his remarks about the 'true Notion' of law (section 57, *Second Treatise of Government*, p. 323), and 'what is absolutely necessary to its being a Law' (section 134, p. 374). While Kant does not maintain that it is analytic in the concept of a rule's being a law that it is morally right, he does hold that the concept of a legal system implies substantive criteria of moral rightness (e.g. p. 26, *The Metaphysical Elements of Justice*; see also ibid., pp. 34, 42, 43, 65, 68, 111). In this century, such a view has been taken by Lon Fuller in his 'Positivism and Fidelity to Law— a Reply to Professor Hart', pp. 630–72, and elaborated in his development of that article, *The Morality of Law*; and has also been taken by McIlwain (in his *Constitutionalism: Ancient and Modern*, and *Growth of*

Political Thought in the West), and Leo Strauss (in his *Natural Right and History*); C. J. Friedrich, like Kant and Lon Fuller, does not hold that it is logically impossible for there to be an unjust law (*Philosophy of Law in Historical Perspective*, p. 191), but rather, he seems to maintain that the concept of a legal system, conferring rights and duties, logically implies that the system is morally justified (e.g. ibid., pp. 173–5).

29. That is, legal positivists are willing to accept that the concept of a legal system may incorporate certain criteria of being prospective, intelligible to persons, etc., as part of laws being intended to act as public guides to conduct, criteria which do not involve substantive moral standards; e.g. see Hart, *Concept of Law*, p. 202. For Hobbes, rules impose obligations because they derive from individuals with the credible power to enforce them; thus, the obligation to obey God does not derive from 'gratitude for his benefits; but from his irresistible power' (*Leviathan*, p. 234); and thus legal obligation is understood as deriving from the feared coercion of the civil sovereign, apart from any moral obligation deriving from the fear of God's punishments, though, of course, there was, for Hobbes, an almost complete coincidence or extensional equivalence between our moral and legal obligations, with the exception of cases of self-preservation. With Bentham, 'An obligation . . . is incumbent on a man . . . in so far as, on the event of his failing to conduct himself in that manner, pain, or loss of pleasure, is considered as about to be experienced by him' (*The Theory of Fictions*, p. 87; see also on this point, *The Limits of Jurisprudence Defined*, p. 317), and thus, a moral obligation to obey the law existed apart from a legal obligation, since the likely sanctions of the civil sovereign are logically separable from those of morality. John Austin follows Bentham almost exactly; for his attack on natural law theory, see *The Province of Jurisprudence Determined*, pp. 184–91. For Kelsen, 'to be legally obligated to a certain behavior means that the contrary behavior is a delict and as such is the condition of a sanction stipulated by a legal norm' (*General Theory of Law and State*, p. 59), apart from any moral obligation. For Alf Ross, legal obligation is not only applicable in situations 'in which a person can be subjected to a penalty or rendered liable to specific performance or damage' (*On Law and Justice*, p. 162), but the reaction to it must be 'experienced as a social disapproval' (p. 162); this attitude is one of 'the legal consciousness' (p. 369), which Ross does not view as identical with the moral consciousness, and thus he accepts the usual positivist view of obligation, as separable into moral and legal, without the latter implying the former. And the separability of legal and moral obligation is, of course, one of the main theses of Hart's *Concept of Law*, chapters VIII–IX; but see also, 'Positivism and the Separation of Law and Morals', pp. 593–629.

30. The notion of a monopoly of coercive power, as central to the concept of law, is originally Weber's: *Law in Economy and Society*, pp. 338–48; the account of the legal system, of course, is substantially Hart's: *Concept of Law*, chapters V–VI.

31. Fuller, 'Positivism and Fidelity to Law', p. 645.

32. This notion of a weak kind of equality as simply involved in the existence and application of general rules has long been recognized by political philosophers; see, for example, Book II, chapter V, section 1, of Sidgwick's *Methods of Ethics*; I. Berlin, 'Equality as an Ideal', Part A, pp. 128–50; C. Perelman, *The Idea of Justice and the Problem of Argument*, pp. 36 ff.

33. Fuller, *Morality of Law*, p. 33.

34. Thus, Fuller, implies (ibid., pp. 159–62) that there is something obscure about immoral aims which makes it difficult to realize them, using as one of his examples certain incoherences in the apartheid laws of South Africa. But is it not clear that the over-all aims of such laws have been unambiguously attained, whatever specific obscurities of definition may be involved? For a still more implausible statement of Fuller's view, see his 'Positivism and Fidelity to Law', p. 636.

35. It is 'ought' construed in this sense that Mabbott seems to have in mind when he distinguishes the question of the moral justifiability of punishment, and of legal systems that involve such institutions of punishment, from the judge's or lawyer's question, 'Ought he to be punished?', which can be sensibly answered by appeal to the legal system, without raising any questions about the system's moral justifiability. See 'Punishment', pp. 39–54.

36. *Lectures on Jurisprudence*, vol. ii, p. 909.

37. Kelsen, *General Theory of Law and State*, pp. 110–24, 131–4, 369–73, 395–6; Hart, *Concept of Law*, chapter VI.

CHAPTER 3

1. Among philosophers, I am especially indebted to Professor John Rawls, who, in various lectures and seminars at Harvard University, first suggested to me the relevance of economic and game theory to the philosophical analysis of the concept of rationality and, indeed, formulated principles of rational choice analogous to those presented here; for Professor Rawls's development of these ideas, as part of a general theory of justice and the good, see his *A Theory of Justice*. Another useful, philosophically oriented, account was I. M. D. Little's *Critique of Welfare Economics*. Among the most useful works by economists and games theorists were Luce and Raiffa's *Games and Decisions*; Schelling's *The Strategy of Conflict*; Rothenberg's *Measurement of Social Welfare*; Arrow's *Social Choice and Individual Values*; T. C. Koopmans's *Three Essays on the State of Economic Science*; and R. Dorfman's *The Price System*.

2. *The Economics of Defense in the Nuclear Age*, p. 198.

3. See, Koopmans, *Three Essays on the State of Economic Science*, e.g. pp. 137, 160, 164.

4. See Hitch and McKean, *Economics of Defense in the Nuclear Age*, pp. 200, 251 ff.

5. See, for example, Dorfman's *Price Theory*, chapter 3.

6. See, here, Rothenberg's excellent exposition and critique of Armstrong's view, chapter 7, *Measurement of Social Welfare*; very briefly, the intransitivity is derived from Armstrong's view that the preference intensity for y over z may not be perceivable, and thus they may be perceived as indifferent; and similarly, for x over y; but the cumulative intensities may reach the threshold of perception so that x is preferred to z, violating transitivity. Such intransitivity would have the consequence that indifference functions, drawn for a particular utility level, would not be continuous, since there would be breaks in them due to cumulative preference intensities becoming perceivable.

7. Ibid., chapter 7 and pp. 229–34.

8. See Luce and Raiffa, *Games and Decisions*, pp. 34–7, 50.

9. Ibid., p. 35.

10. *Intention*, p. 79.

11. Foot, 'Moral Beliefs', p. 101; A. I. Melden, *Free Action*, chapter 12; E. D'Arcy, *Human Acts*, chapter 4; Findlay, *Values and Intentions*, pp. 149, 186, 203, 211, 255.

12. Luce and Raiffa, *Games and Decisions*, p. 48; Arrow, *Social Choice and Individual Values*, p. 18; Schelling, *Strategy of Conflict*, p. 4; A. Downs, *An Economic Theory of Democracy*, p. 37.

13. On the question of objectless desires, see M. Scheler's *The Nature of Sympathy*, especially pp. 172–3, 199–200, 235–7; on the relation between desire and belief, see S. Hampshire, *Freedom of the Individual*, chapter 2; for a rather different, and, I think, mistaken view, see Findlay's *Values and Intentions*, pp. 145 ff.

14. On this, see Ryle, *Concept of Mind*, chapter IV, and Findlay, *Values and Intentions*, pp. 166–78.

15. See C. G. Hempel's 'Rational Action', especially pp. 16 ff.; Hempel emphasizes beliefs and goals as being 'epistemically interdependent' (p. 16).

16. *Mental Acts*, p. 8.

17. *Action, Emotion and Will*, pp. 235–6.

18. Act III, scene iii, *Hamlet*. On the importance of capacities in the explanation of human actions, see Hampshire, *Freedom of the Individual*, chapter 1.

19. Anscombe, *Intention*, pp. 67 ff.; Gauthier, *Practical Reasoning*, chapter 3; Kenny, especially chapter 5, *Action, Emotion and Will*; see also Melden, *Free Action*, chapters X–XII.

20. The notion of achievability must be introduced to account for those uses of 'I want *x*' where, for example, '*x*' = 'a wife', not any particular person, Mary M., who now exists. Here, the belief, required for the proper use of 'I want *x*', is not about the existence of a specific object (Mary M.), but a belief about achieving that kind of object in the future; cf. *Intention* pp. 69–70.

21. See *Intention*, pp. 72, 75; Anscombe makes the plausible exception of certain cases where 'for no particular reason' is an intelligible response, ibid., pp. 26, 69 ff. This general view of Anscombe's is approved by Geach in quoting the medieval phrase (of Socratic origin) 'quidquid appetitur appetitur sub specie boni', 'Good and Evil', p. 38.

22. Cf., for similar views, Hampshire, *Freedom of the Individual*, pp. 48–9; Kenny, *Action, Emotion and Will*, pp. 94–5; and Hare, 'Descriptivism', pp. 122–7.

23. For a useful critique of psychological hedonism, see Brandt, *Ethical Theory*, chapter 12.

24. For a suggestive account of this concept of pleasure, see Kenny, *Action, Emotion and Will*, chapter 6; it is extremely important to see how clearly distinguishable this concept of pleasure is from the general concept of desire satisfaction, which is the aim of pursuing desires *simpliciter*.

25. I am indebted for this point to certain criticisms of Professor R. M. Hare.

26. Similarly, in the case of a mother whose love for her child leads her to sacrifice her own life to save its life, it seems rather inappropriate to say that she thus satisfied one of her wants, unless following Gauthier (*Practical Reasoning*, pp. 133–4), we are literally imagining that, for her, the saving of her child was saving her own life. However, more naturally, I think, we would describe such a case as something which, as a mother, she *had* to do.

27. *Freedom of the Individual*, pp. 15, 40, 50, 68; also, *Thought and Action*, pp. 147, 167–8.

28. e.g. *Foundations of the Metaphysics of Morals*, p. 46.

29. *Political Argument*, pp. 173–86.

30. On the concept of needs, see S. I. Benn and R. S. Peters, *Social Principles and the Democratic State*, pp. 143–8; Kenny, *Action, Emotion and Will*, p. 45; and Peters, *The Concept of Motivation*, pp. 17 ff., 23, 106, 123.

31. Cf. here, Anscombe, 'Modern Moral Philosophy', p. 7.

32. As Little noted, without adequate analysis, in his discussion of the use of 'welfare' in welfare economics, *Critique of Welfare Economics*, chapter 5.

33. On the concept of welfare, see Barry, *Political Argument*, pp. 187–9.

34. And which led to a sort of ethics of flourishing capacities; on the resultant contrast between their and our conception of ethics, see Anscombe, 'Modern Moral Philosophy', and, for a clear expression of the Greek view, see Aristotle, *Nicomachean Ethics*, Book I.

35. On the concept of intention, see Anscombe's *Intention* and Hampshire's *Thought and Action*.

36. In the law, the concept of intention is extended to cover not only an agent's end, and means, in doing *x*, but also those things which happen as a consequence of doing *x*, and which the agent knows will happen as a consequence of doing *x*, though they are unwanted; on this, and related issues, see Hart's 'Intention and Punishment'.

37. Anscombe, *Intention*, pp. 37–47; D'Arcy, *Human Acts*, chapter 1.

38. See Anscombe, *Intention*, pp. 66–7.

39. *A Treatise of Human Nature*, especially Book II, Part III, sections III–X, pp. 413–54.

40. 'Butler's Sermons', p. 226.

41. Mabbott, 'Reason and Desire', pp. 113–23; and 'Prudence', pp. 51–64; for a similarly illuminating account, see Findlay, *Values and Intentions*, pp. 152, 182.

42. Cf. Hare's notion of choosing 'what sort of man to try to become', *Language of Morals*, p. 128.

43. On the game theoretic concept of dominance, see Luce and Raiffa, *Games and Decisions*, pp. 99, 117, 202, 286–7.

44. *Ethical Theory*, pp. 346–52.

45. I am indebted for this analysis to conversations with Diane R. Richards.

46. *Economics of Defense in the Nuclear Age*, p. 160.

47. Ibid., p. 187; see also ibid., pp. 198, 265, 287.

48. *De Anima*, 434^{a}8–9.

49. *Summa Contra Gentiles*, Book III, Part I, p. 100.

50. *Critique of Practical Reason*, p. 22. Cf. Kant's claim that 'the feeling of pleasure, by virtue of which they constitute the determining ground of the will (since it is the agreeableness and enjoyment which one expects from the object which impels the activity toward producing it) is always the same' (ibid., p. 21). It is this view which lies behind Kant's tendency to view principles of rational choice as involving effective means (*Foundations of the Metaphysics of Morals*, p. 33), and postponement (ibid., pp. 32–3) alone, and also to some extent explains Kant's sharp distinction between human desires and moral motivation, since the former necessarily

involve calculation in terms of sensations of pleasure, while the latter clearly do not (e.g. *The Metaphysical Elements of Justice*, pp. 10–14; *Critique of Practical Reason*, pp. 24, 40, 74–5, 77, 82–3, 121, 152).

51. *Methods of Ethics*, p. 406; see also ibid., pp. 106, 479.

52. Ibid., p. 121; see also ibid., pp. 127, 129, 131, 177, 205.

53. *Models of Man*, p. 204.

54. J. G. March and H. A. Simon, *Organizations*, p. 140.

55. Hitch and McKean, *Economics of Defense in the Nuclear Age*, p. 217; see also ibid., pp. 221, 265.

56. 'A Technical Ought', p. 306.

CHAPTER 4

1. e.g. *Practical Reasoning*, chapter XI.

2. *The Moral Point of View*, chapter 6.

3. On the kind of awareness here involved, see Anscombe on knowledge without observation, *Intention*, pp. 6, 8, 13–15, 19–20, 49–53, 57, 87–9.

4. Ibid., pp. 17–18.

5. Benn and Peters, *Social Principles and the Democratic State*, pp. 198–205; Peters, *Concept of Motivation*, especially chapter 1; Findlay, *Values and Intentions*, especially pp. 191–202.

6. This seems the correct description in Findlay's case; see, for example, ibid., p. 200.

7. 'Rational Action', especially p. 12; for a plausible defence of the thesis that reasons for action can be causes, against, for example, Melden's objections (chapters 12–13, *Free Action*), see D. F. Pears, 'Are Reasons for Action Causes?', pp. 204–28.

8. A view suggested by Gauthier, e.g. *Practical Reasoning*, p. 26.

9. P. Alexander, 'Rational Behaviour and Psychoanalytic Explanation', especially, p. 331.

10. See T. Mischel, 'Concerning Rational Behaviour and Psychoanalytic Explanation', especially pp. 76–7; and N. Care, 'On Avowing Reasons', pp. 208–16.

11. Indeed, it seems a conceptual mark of belief that it is not closely related to physical time; see Geach, *Mental Acts*, Part 23; Hampshire, *Thought and Action*, pp. 149–50.

12. *Intention*, p. 80.

13. e.g. *Concept of Mind*, pp. 91, 111–12; Nowell-Smith, *Ethics*, pp. 122–3.

14. See, on this, D'Arcy, *Human Acts*, pp. 132–3.

15. See especially Hart and Honore, *Causation in the Law*, pp. 48–55.

16. See, on this, ibid., p. 51.

17. On performatives, see Austin's *How To Do Things With Words*.

CHAPTER 5

1. Prichard, 'Duty and Interest'. For an illuminating consideration of this topic, see W. K. Frankena's 'Obligation and Motivation in Recent Moral Philosophy'.

2. Westermarck, *Ethical Relativity*, chapter, 5; Falk, 'Morals Without Faith', and 'Obligation and Rightness'; for Westermarck, I take it, '*x* is wrong' is not conceptually equivalent to 'I now am feeling disapproval of *x*', but rather to the more complex and plausible, 'I have a tendency to disapprove *x*, when in full knowledge of the facts, disinterested, etc.'. Falk's is perhaps best viewed not as a form of approbationism, but rather as something like: '*x* is my duty' is conceptually equivalent to 'I have a tendency to feel required or compelled to do *x* when fully informed, disinterested, etc.'.

3. Broad's classic typology of these views can be found in his 'Some Reflections on Moral-Sense Theories in Ethics'.

4. The terminology, of course, was originally Falk's (' "Ought" and Motivation'), but Frankena's elaboration and clarification of that distinction, in 'Obligation and Motivation in Recent Moral Philosophy', has been the seminal work in my own consideration of this topic.

5. See, for example, Prichard, 'Does Moral Philosophy Rest on a Mistake?', and 'Moral Obligation'; Ross, *The Right and the Good*.

6. e.g. *Principles of Morals and Legislation*, p. 313.

7. In using utilitarianism as an example of a naturalistic moral theory, I do not mean to claim that utilitarianism is necessarily a naturalistic theory, for one can be a utilitarian and hold non-naturalist views about the analysis of moral judgements. This, for example, seems to be Urmson's position in his 'The Interpretation of the Moral Philosophy of J. S. Mill'; and there are some passages in J. S. Mill which at least strongly suggest such a view, e.g. *A System of Logic*, Book VI, chapter XII.

8. 'Butler's Sermons', p. 226; Erikson, e.g. in his 'The Problem of Ego Identity'.

9. Erikson, 'The Problem of Ego Identity', p. 118.

10. See, for example, Hampshire, *Thought and Action*, p. 75; P. F. Strawson, *Individuals*, chapters III–IV.

11. Hampshire, *Thought and Action*, p. 69.

12. 'Butler's Sermons', p. 227.

13. The presence of this higher-order capacity seems to be one of the crucial differentia between animals and humans, as Findlay suggested, relating it to our special means of linguistic communications, e.g. *Values and Intentions*, pp. 181–2. Hampshire has claimed that, while animals can have purposes or ends, they cannot have intentions, since the latter depend on thoughts and the capacity to communicate them, e.g. *Freedom of the Individual*, pp. 37–8.

14. *Concept of Mind*, pp. 189–90; cf. Hampshire's remark: 'I identify myself with my will', *Thought and Action*, p. 153; also Sidgwick, *Methods of Ethics*, pp. 65–6.

15. *Childhood and Society*, chapter 5.

16. Cf. Ryle's contrast of intelligent capacities and habits, *Concept of Mind*, pp. 42, 47, 132, 144–6, 160, 312.

17. In his *The Herring Gull's World*; for examples of this instinctive stupidity, see pp. 28–32 (dropping shellfish—to get at the meat through breaking them—continually on water or sand, where the shells never break); pp. 140–1 (clumsiness of egg retrieval, when the gull has equipment for an easier method); pp. 144–5 (brooding on an empty nest when eggs are at a distance from it); p. 153 (inconsistent method of choosing real eggs when fakes are placed among them); and pp. 186–210 (chick responding continually to crude dummy parent, which never supplies it with food). All these stupidities are a consequence of the simple stimulus-response mechanisms which control many of the gulls' responses (pp. 232–3).

18. On the concept of animal intelligence, see J. Bennett, *Rationality*, pp. 35–43; and, on the distinctive marks of human intelligence, as involving reasons for belief, see ibid., pp. 80, 85, 94.

19. Adopting Erikson's word and method, 'The Problem of Ego Identity', p. 122.

20. A virtue to which only Mabbott, in recent philosophy, has given anything approaching adequate attention; see 'Prudence'.

21. A more difficult question, that Mabbott (ibid., pp. 57 ff.) has raised, is why prudence is often regarded as being a moral virtue, when it seems to have reference only to self-regarding ends.

22. Especially 'Moral Beliefs', pp. 98 ff.

23. 'The Rational vs. the Reasonable', p. 559.

24. *Thought and Action*, p. 239.

25. *Action, Emotion and Will*, p. 190.

26. *Nicomachean Ethics*, 1166^{a}29, p. 253.

CHAPTER 6

1. 'The Rational vs. the Reasonable'; see also W. Kneale, 'Objectivity in Morals', especially pp. 692 ff.

2. See Sibley, 'The Rational vs. the Reasonable', p. 558; Sibley may, however, just be distinguishing their being reasons for action from their being accepted reasons for action.

3. Anscombe, *Intention*, p. 79 (but consider ibid., pp. 65–6, where Anscombe seems to be drawing some sort of distinction between reasons for action, as actually used to guide, and thus explain, human actions, and reasons in a justificatory sense); Melden, *Free Action*, chapter 12; Foot, 'Moral Beliefs', p. 101.

4. K. Baier, *The Moral Point of View*, chapter 6. See Gauthier's criticism of Baier's argument here, *Practical Reasoning*, pp. 104–10.

5. G. R. Grice, *The Grounds of Moral Judgement*, chapter 1, pp. 95, 135–40.

6. For such a view, see Price's reference to the moral as 'what is *reasonable* and *fit* as such', p. 144, *A Review of the Principal Questions in Morals*; cf. the more modest claim that morality is a species of reasonableness, e.g. Benn and Peters, *Social Principles and the Democratic State*, p. 56.

7. 'Recent Conceptions of Morality.'

8. 'Cardinal Utility in Welfare Economics and in the Theory of Risk-Taking', pp. 434–5; see also his 'Cardinal Welfare, Individualistic Ethics, and Interpersonal Comparisons of Utility'. On strategies under uncertainty, see Luce and Raiffa, *Games and Decisions*, chapter 13. Elsewhere, Harsanyi confuses the special features which a contract conception implies with an ideal observer account—see his 'Ethics in Terms of Hypothetical Imperatives', pp. 305–16. This is a not uncommon confusion, e.g. Kneale suggests a contract analysis of morality, which he then unthinkingly equates with an ideal observer account—see his 'Objectivity in Morals'. This confusion derives, I think, from the common view that an ideal observer account is the only possible way to account for the objectivity of moral judgements.

9. *The Calculus of Consent*, pp. 78, 96.

10. See, for example, ibid., p. 80.

11. The view was first suggested by Professor Rawls as an account of the concept of justice, e.g. in his 'Justice as Fairness', and 'Constitutional Liberty and the Concept of Justice'. But his recently published book, *A Theory of Justice*, makes clear that the account is also intended as an explication of the concept of morality, though Professor Rawls (as a matter of methodology) is in that book primarily concerned with getting clear the concept of the principles of justice and related institutional principles.

12. Cf. Baier, *Moral Point of View*, p. 197. The notion is, of course, Kantian in origin; indeed, the example I here use was suggested to me

by an example of Kant's, *Foundations of the Metaphysics of Morals*, p. 40.

13. *Grounds of Moral Judgement*, p. 150. Grice maintains that basic moral obligations are explicable in terms of the applicability of his contract ground: 'It is in everyone's interest to make a contract with everyone else to do *x*' (ibid., p. 95), where it is assumed that everyone else will do *x*, and that the contract ground applies only to all mature adults living now.

14. In addition to several formal requirements on moral principles, Baier postulates one substantive one: that the principles must be for the good of everyone alike, *Moral Point of View*, pp. 200–4. Gauthier postulates an analytic relation between moral reasons for action and 'all wants of all persons', *Practical Reasoning*, p. 86. Grice's use of his contract ground (see n. 13 above) is as a criterion for when principles are in the interests of everyone.

15. That is, they all suggest that a central test for moral principles is that the principles must at least make everyone better off and no one worse off; on the economic concept of Pareto optimality, see Little, *Critique of Welfare Economics*, chapters I–VI, and Rothenberg, *Measurement of Social Welfare*, chapters 3–4.

16. *Grounds of Moral Judgement*, chapter 3.

17. See ibid., pp. 102 ff., 144–5.

18. Grice's view here is similar to that of Buchanan and Tullock who assume that their contract notion is only to apply when the contractors' position is governed by certain moral principles of equality and liberty, *Calculus of Consent*, p. 86; and is also similar to Anthony Downs's postulation that his model of democratic institutions only applies when certain moral principles of equal liberty are given as inviolate, *Economic Theory of Democracy*, p. 12. The difference between these theories and Grice's, however, is that they are not *claiming* to offer a general account of morality, but are concerned with much more circumscribed questions having to do with the justification (Buchanan and Tullock) and explanation (Downs) of certain political institutions, given certain moral assumptions.

19. See, especially, *Freedom and Reason*, pp. 92–4.

20. In general, see ibid., chapter 9. Hare has not perhaps made as clear as he might his view that the fanatic he has centrally in mind is one whose moral opinions could survive agreement about the facts. I had myself misunderstood his views until Professor Hare clarified them for me in private correspondence. However, such misunderstanding is not wholly warranted, given certain passages in *Freedom and Reason*, e.g. those on pp. 219–20 and 180–2. For an even clearer statement of Hare's view, see pp. 10 f. of his lecture 'Peace', delivered on 19 July 1966, at the Australian National University, Canberra.

21. I am indebted for this point to certain criticisms by Dr. A. J. P. Kenny.

22. For Locke, the moral law existed prior to the social contract, which occurred solely to realize effectively the moral law in men's social relations; see, for example, *Second Treatise of Government*, sections 6–7, pp. 288–90. For Rousseau, see *The Social Contract*, pp. 34, 134.

23. The most plausible presentation of the ideal observer theory is that found in Firth's now classic paper, 'Ethical Absolutism and the Ideal Observer'. For a similar account, cf. Brandt's qualified attitude theory, *Ethical Theory*, pp. 244 ff. Firth's paper is not subject to the criticisms which I level against Hume's use of the ideal observer conception, since Firth does not use the view in the way Hume does, rather regarding what the ideal observer approves as essentially an empirical, contingent matter. The main difficulty with Firth's rather sophisticated ideal observer theory comes, I think, with the logical circularity which is involved in Firth's use of certain feelings of his ideal observer as defining the concept of morality, a problem which many intuitionist critics of moral-sense theories have often mentioned (see Sidgwick, *Methods of Ethics*, pp. 26–8; W. D. Ross, *Foundations of Ethics*, pp. 25–6). That is, in order for Firth's theory non-circularly to define the concept of morality, it must isolate certain feelings of the ideal observer which do not imply any moral beliefs, as Firth admits ('Ethical Absolutism and the Ideal Observer', pp. 326 ff.). Firth, following Broad ('Some Reflections on Moral-Sense Theories in Ethics', pp. 386–8), tries to distinguish between moral feelings which arise as a consequence of moral beliefs, and other moral feelings which are evidence for such beliefs—e.g. where one feels moral approval of an act, but yet is in doubt about whether it is right or wrong (say, I feel moral approval for a certain act of disobedience against the war in Vietnam, but am in doubt whether it is right or wrong). But Firth's distinction will not do, for the correct description for the latter sort of case seems to be not that certain *sui generis* feelings exist in the presence of certain cognitive doubts, but rather that the person has certain thoughts and beliefs, which underlie his feelings, and which are relevant to the rightness of such actions (e.g. the belief in the injustice of the Vietnam war), but which do not conclude the question of the rightness of such actions. It seems a logical fact about *moral* feelings, even quite irrational ones (e.g. neurotic guilt, or instinctive approval of retribution), that they imply at least certain kinds of moral thoughts, if not beliefs (e.g. the thought of some transgression of moral norms, or the thought of some moral principle like *lex talionis*). Firth's account, thus, rests on an untenable conception of the logical nature of human emotion and feeling, as though human feelings are certain sorts of sensations which bear their nature writ on them, in abstraction from the associated context of thoughts and beliefs, desires, and intentions and dispositions to act. Consider, in this context, Firth's suggestion that moral feelings are to the analysis of 'right' what colour sensations are to the analysis of 'really yellow' (Firth, p. 327), which further reveals this deeply confused way of thinking.

24. Of course, it is possible for there to be legitimate differences in interpretation of Hume's view of morality; for example, in the text of the *Treatise*, within four pages, Hume suggests at least three different views of morality—first-person moral approbationism (p. 469), emotivism (p. 471), and an ideal observer view (p. 472). But impartial reflection on the whole of Hume's theory, especially as presented in Book III of the *Treatise*, reveals, I think, an ideal observer conception as his considered view. But for a different Humean exegesis, see C. D. Broad, *Five Types of Ethical Theory*.

25. Hume understood sympathy as 'the conversion of an idea into an impression' (*Treatise of Human Nature*, p. 595), given certain conditions of conversion, among which were physical contiguity, similarity of language and culture, and the like. That is, he supposed that when someone is in pain, such that you, upon observing him, have the idea of his being in pain in your mind, and given that the conditions of conversion are satisfied (there being no distorting condition, e.g. pride or malice), then your idea of his being in pain will be converted into *your* having the sort of pain associated with the idea. The ideal observer, having perfect sympathy, will thus perfectly catch all the pleasures and pain of others.

26. In *Freedom and Reason*, Hare imagines an individual person who sympathetically extends himself into the interests of all other parties ('or, if there are many, of a representative sample of them', *Freedom and Reason*, p. 123) involved in a certain co-operative system, and then, having made the round of all these persons, and having come back to his own person, decides what moral principle to adopt concerning the distribution of goods between the persons in the system; and Hare thinks it plausible that such a person will arrive at the utilitarian principle, or some variant of it. While Hare does give some weight to the claims of equality in his account, and does not seem to suppose that any un-qualified utilitarianism would be morally acceptable, his account does illustrate that any view which takes the decisions of *one* person as morally fundamental, and relates other persons to this by means of sympathy alone, will have a tendency to the utilitarian principle and fail to allow for the basic moral constraints on its application. Thus, Hume's reasoning is no antique philosophical curio, of no stature today.

27. On this, see Gauthier, *Practical Reasoning*, p. 126; G. R. Grice, *Grounds of Moral Judgement*, pp. 190–7; Rawls, 'Justice as Fairness', pp. 101–6; and Findlay, *Values and Intentions*, pp. 235–6.

28. Price, *Review of the Principal Questions in Morals*, p. 160.

29. *Values and Intentions*, p. 399.

30. On the concept of a person, see Scheler, *Nature of Sympathy*, pp. 58–61, 64–5, 70, 224–5.

31. My own blindness was cured by certain criticisms by Professor R. M. Hare.

32. e.g. *Foundations of the Metaphysics of Morals*, pp. 50 ff.

33. 'The positive concept of freedom' (ibid., p. 65) or 'autonomy' (ibid., p. 71) is regarded by Kant as analytically involved with 'the universal principle of morality' (ibid., p. 71). Autonomy, as opposed to heteronomy, involves the capacity of a member of the phenomenal world to abstract himself from his particular desires, nature, and circumstances, and to consider and follow the requirements that his membership of the noumenal world places on the pursuit of his particular ends in the phenomenal world.

34. See, for example, *Critique of Practical Reason*, pp. 101–3; Kant holds that, as members of the noumenal world, the normal categories of judgement, e.g. space, time, causality, etc., do not apply, or apply only by analogy (see, for example, ibid., pp. 70–4, where Kant considers the use of 'law' as extended from science to morals).

35. Consider Kant's third, implicitly contractual, formulation of the categorical imperative, with its suggestion of 'the idea of the will of every rational being as making universal law' (*Foundations of the Metaphysics of Morals*, p. 49).

36. e.g. *Metaphysical Elements of Justice*, pp. 58, 72, 80, 111–12, 119, 129; 'Concerning the Common Saying: This May be True in Theory, But Does Not Apply in Practice', pp. 164, 166–7, 169.

37. In the *Critique of Judgement*, especially pp. 108–9, 153, but also pp. 97–8 (footnote) and p. 100 (footnote), Kant makes clear his Aristotelian assumption that an end in itself is of intrinsic worth, and that men as noumena are ends in themselves. Kant uses this assumption as follows. The noumenal selves, since they do not act under the category of time, must choose their whole life-character in the phenomenal world. Two things are relevant to this choice—one a matter of justification, the other of explanation. First, given the Aristotelian assumption, the only thing of intrinsic worth is a morally good will which desires to act on and from the moral law, since the moral law best express men's nature as members of the noumenal world, where they are ends in themselves. Thus, since one ought always to maximize intrinsic worth, the noumenal selves ought to choose the character with a good will, since this is the most justifiable choice. But, on the other hand, the noumenal selves have freedom as 'absolute spontaneity' (*Critique of Practical Reason*, p. 50), which Kant claims to underlie our concept of voluntary action (*Foundations of the Metaphysics of Morals*, p. 81) and without which he regards responsibility to be an empty concept (e.g. *Religion Within the Limits of Reason Alone*, p. 20; *Critique of Judgement*, pp. 116–17 n.). This concept of freedom, clearly distinguishable from freedom as autonomy (see n. 31, above), gives the noumenal selves the capacity to choose whatever life-character they wish, though the choice is not justifiable; however, because this concept of freedom is a noumenal notion, we cannot strictly understand it, especially when they choose

contrary to reason (e.g. *Metaphysical Principles of Virtue*, p. 37 n., *Metaphysical Elements of Justice*, p. 87; *Religion Within the Limits of Reason Alone*, p. 17).

38. In his 'Justice and Equality'.

39. As R. M. Blake noted in 'The Ground of Moral Obligation'.

40. e.g. in Frankena's 'Recent Conceptions of Morality', especially chapter V.

41. See *Grounds of Moral Judgement*, pp. 111–15.

42. Hare's fanatic Nazi example is intended to make this point, by suggesting that different systems of desires will lead to different kinds of moral principles. However ill-chosen the example, the point is important and valid.

CHAPTER 7

1. *Treatise of Human Nature*, Book III, Part II.

2. *Methods of Ethics*, Book III, chapters IV–X.

3. The subjects respectively, of, *Metaphysical Elements of Justice* and *Metaphysical Principles of Virtue*.

4. *Review of the Principal Questions in Morals*, chapters VI–VII.

5. For an excellent exposition and critique of Kant's theory of supererogation, see P. D. Eisenberg, 'From the Forbidden to the Supererogatory; the Basic Ethical Categories in Kant's *Tugendlehre*'.

6. Price, *Review of the Principle Questions in Morals*, pp. 119–23.

7. *Methods of Ethics*, p. 492.

8. e.g. *Foundations of Ethics*, p. 43.

9. e.g. *Values and Intentions*, p. 341.

10. See *Methods of Ethics*, pp. 327 ff., where Sidgwick postulates and discusses the 'Duty of Prudence'; but cf. ibid., p. 217, where Sidgwick grants that 'duty' is often a less than apt term to characterize this requirement. Related to this principle, Sidgwick also espouses a duty to preserve life even if the life is miserably unhappy, for example, ibid., pp. 327, 331, 356, a corollary to which being that suicide is forbidden absolutely. See, for Price, *Review of the Principal Questions in Morals*, pp. 148–9, where he claims that prudence is a duty, giving as his reason for this claim the fact that the language of 'ought' is often naturally used to characterize the appropriateness of being prudent; cf. also ibid., p. 105.

11. Kant's distinction of hypothetical and categorical imperatives expresses his understanding of the difference between the 'ought' of prudence and the 'be under duty' of morality, for example, *Foundations of the Metaphysics of Morals*, pp. 30 ff. Kant's concept of moral duties to

increase natural and moral perfection (see *Metaphysical Principles of Virtue*, pp. 108–11) seems clearly meant to characterize requirements which are logically distinct from prudence, since these duties contemplate not advancing the interests of the individual but rather the interests of the species which are to prevail even if at the sacrifice of personal happiness.

12. *Methods of Ethics*, pp. 32–3.

13. For the intuitionist argument, see, for example, Ross, *Foundations of Ethics*, chapter 2; Ewing, *The Definition of Good*, chapter 2. Moore took good as basic (see, for example, *Principia Ethica*, pp. 23–7, 146–8, 152–4, 167–70), and, with the qualification of the appropriateness of 'obligation' where there are counter-desires (ibid., p. 170), defined the obligatory in terms of maximizing it (the notion of conceptual identity was later retracted by Moore; see, for example, *Ethics*, p. 73; see also 'A Reply to my Critics', pp. 597–601); Prichard, on the other hand, took duty as '*sui generis*, i.e. unique and therefore incapable of having its nature expressed in terms of the nature of anything else' ('Moral Obligation', p. 94), and seems to take right as in some sense derivative (however, Prichard does suggest that there is some sort of basic difference between the notions, 'Duty and Ignorance of Fact', pp. 36–7); Ross took right as basic and viewed it as meaning 'very nearly, but not quite the same, as "obligatory" or "what is my duty" ' (*Foundations of Ethics*, p. 43; see, also, *The Right and the Good*, pp. 3–4).

14. Sometimes they claim that, in so far as it has not been done, there is a presumption that it will not be done—see, for example, Ross, *Foundations of Ethics*, p. 43; Carritt, *Ethical and Political Thinking*, p. 111; in other cases, much stronger claims are made, e.g. see Ewing, *Definition of Good*, pp. 43–4.

15. *Practical Reasoning*, p. 179. While Gauthier distinguishes obligation and duty in terms of how they arise or are determined, he none the less holds that the basic normative notion both involve is that of determining 'generally sufficient reasons for action' (ibid., p. 201), which override other reasons.

16. The view was perhaps first suggested by Bentham, when he divided the law into two parts: 'the directive part, which must of itself be a complete expression of will, and an article of a different nature, a prediction' (*Limits of Jurisprudence Defined*, p. 228); it was followed by Austin (e.g. *Province of Jurisprudence Determined*, p. 14); Holmes ('The Path of the Law', p. 169); Gray (especially chapter IV, 'The Law', *The Nature and Sources of the Law*); Llewellyn (see *The Bramble Bush*, pp. 13–14, where the predictive view of law suggests the same account of legal obligation); and Frank (*Law and the Modern Mind*, pp. 133 ff.). Interestingly, Sidgwick, generally so critical of the analysis of obligation in terms of sanctions, accepts the predictive view of legal, though not moral, obligation (*Methods of Ethics*, p. 29; see also ibid., p. 505, for a contrasting view of the moral case).

17. This objection is found, e.g. in Kelsen (*General Theory of Law and State*, pp. 165 ff.) and Hart (*Concept of Law*, p. 82).

18. Ibid.

19. Ibid., p. 84. Mill's formulation is to be found in *Utilitarianism*, pp. 59–60.

20. Bentham, *Limits of Jurisprudence Defined*, pp. 229–30; Austin, *Lectures on Jurisprudence*, vol. ii, p. 790.

21. Hobbes relates obligation to coercion in terms of actual 'fear of some evil consequence upon the rupture', *Leviathan*, p. 86; for criticisms of this theory, see, for example, Kelsen, *General Theory of Law and State*, pp. 71–4, and Hart, *Concept of Law*, p. 81. Interestingly, Kelsen criticizes Austin for holding such a theory. For Ross, see, for example, *On Law and Justice*, pp. 160–2, 369.

22. e.g. Hart, *Concept of Law*, p. 88; 'Legal and Moral Obligation', pp. 90-1; Baier, 'Moral Obligation', pp. 216–17.

23. *Concept of Law*, pp. 85–6.

24. I say that whether sanctions are viewed as justified is typically determined by examining the relations and content of legal rules, because this is not the case in all instances where we are prepared to speak or think of legal obligations. Thus, in the case of the so-called duties of imperfect obligation, e.g. the obligation imposed by the United States Constitution on the President to take care for the due execution of laws, it is not the case that there is any secondary law which stipulates formal sanctions on non-performance of the duty, yet, as Hart admitted, 'we do not hesitate to refer to such cases as cases of official duty or obligation' ('Legal and Moral Obligation', p. 99). But such cases are compatible with the general account, for though there are no formal sanctions present here, it is clear that, within the system as a whole, various forms of sanctions would be viewed as justified in forcing the President to do his duty, e.g. the Congressional threat to withhold funds and refuse to approve his proposed legislative programme, severe public criticism and the threat not to re-elect, and even the threat of impeachment.

25. In his 'Are there any Natural Rights?', and in his lectures on rights and duties delivered during Michaelmas term 1966 at Oxford University.

26. *Fundamental Legal Conceptions*; I differ from Hohfeld in my account of the concept of liberty, which he supposes to involve only the absence of a duty not to do x (e.g. ibid., pp. 38–50).

27. 'Are there any Natural Rights?', p. 179; see also R. Wollheim, 'Equality and Equal Rights', pp. 120–1. For a traditional statement and employment of this concept of freedom, see Sidgwick, *The Elements of Politics*, chapter IV; and, for an illuminating consideration of the proper use of this concept of freedom in a substantive political theory, see W. L. Weinstein, 'The Concept of Liberty in Nineteenth Century English Political Thought'.

28. See *Concept of Law*, pp. 26-48, 78-9, 238-40.

29. On this, see Hart ('Are there any Natural Rights?', p. 179 n.); Lemmon (especially 'Moral Dilemmas', pp. 140-3); Feinberg (e.g. 'Supererogation and Rules', p. 277; and, 'Duties, Rights, and Claims'); and Gauthier (*Practical Reasoning*, chapters XII-XIII).

30. 'The Concepts of Obligation and Duty', pp. 387, 388. Such natural, distinctive usages of 'obligation' and 'duty' are obscured, Brandt claims, by the fact that, today, many positions are voluntarily held and relinquished at will, such that the use of 'obligation' is appropriate (unlike, for example, the feudal case, where positions were largely by status, not contract, such that 'duty' alone was appropriate).

31. Thus, in the Roman law, the concept of obligation seems to have been reserved for the requirement that answered to a right *in personam*, e.g. a contract (see, on this, Austin, *Lectures on Jurisprudence*, pp. 47, 60, 956), whereas requirements which avail against persons generally and indeterminately tended to be distinguished from obligations as being duties (ibid., pp. 380-1). Austin seems to give expression to the distinction through his differentiation between relative duties (obligations, in the Roman sense) and absolute duties (duties, in the Roman sense), the former of which have correlative rights held by determinate persons, the latter of which do not; see, on this, ibid., pp. 412-19).

32. This basic view of the concept of moral obligation is suggested in Baier's article 'Moral Obligation'. The special feature of my account is to free Baier's view of certain confusions, and to indicate how this sort of account is compatible with a logical distinction between moral and legal obligation (which Baier denies). Thus, in my view, to say that there is a legal obligation to do x is to say that there is a law requiring persons to do x of such a sort that coercion is viewed as justified in enforcing it. And to say that a moral obligation to do x exists is to say that a principle to do x would be accepted by the rational contractors of the original position, and they would view coercion as justified in enforcing it. But, of course, legal obligations can occur in quite substantively evil legal systems, where there is no moral obligation to obey the law; and the knowledge of the existence of the one does not bring with it the knowledge of the other. Note, further, that, while I developed my views of moral obligation from Hart's account of legal obligation, my view is quite different from the way in which Hart has suggested that his account of obligation be extended to the moral case: see his 'Moral and Legal Obligation'. What Hart has done is to reduce the concept of moral obligation to the existent social morality of a group, a view closely analogous to T. H. Green's (e.g. *Principles of Political Obligation*, pp. 151 ff.) and open to the same objections as those offered by Prichard (see his 'Green's Principles of Political Obligation').

33. Contrast Kant's view that the noumenal selves require the death penalty for a murderer, even where it serves no deterrent purpose, *Metaphysical Elements of Justice*, p. 102.

34. Kant, *Foundations of the Metaphysics of Morals*, pp. 29–31, 58, 67–8, 73; Sidgwick, *Methods of Ethics*, pp. 35, 217; Marx, *The German Ideology*, p. 78.

35. Hart, 'Legal and Moral Obligation', p. 82; Gauthier, *Practical Reasoning*, p. 194; Baier, *Moral Point of View*, pp. 226–7; for a similar view of non-maleficence, see ibid., p. 221.

36. *Practical Reasoning*, pp. 203 ff.

37. *Human Acts*, pp. 50–7.

38. For a similar view, see Hart, 'Are there any Natural Rights?'; cf. with this Feinberg, 'Duties, Rights, and Claims', and R. Wasserstrom, 'Rights, Human Rights, and Racial Discrimination'; also, Feinberg's critique of the Wasserstrom article, 'Wasserstrom on Rights', ibid., pp. 641–5.

39. Cf. with this Eisenberg's sixfold typology, 'From the Forbidden to the Supererogatory', and R. Chisholm's ninefold typology, 'Supererogation and Offence'.

CHAPTER 8

1. Hart's account of justice importantly draws on Hume; see *Concept of Law*, chapters 8–9.

2. *Treatise of Human Nature*, p. 485.

3. Ibid., p. 495.

4. Ibid.

5. *Enquiry Concerning the Principles of Morals*, p. 190.

6. *Treatise of Human Nature*, p. 490.

7. Ibid., p. 526; cf. Hart, *Concept of Law*, pp. 189–95.

8. See *Treatise of Human Nature*, pp. 502, 532, 534 ff.

9. In *An Economic Theory of Democracy*.

10. *Treatise of Human Nature*, p. 497.

11. For this line of criticism, see, for example, J. Rawls, 'Justice as Fairness'; for Brandt's claim, see *Ethical Theory*, chapter 16; for a further development of Brandt's theory, see his 'Toward a Credible Form of Utilitarianism'.

12. *Treatise of Human Nature*, p. 497; cf. ibid., p. 534. Cf. B. Barry's similar critique of Hume, *Political Argument*, pp. 319–22.

13. On this, see Luce and Raiffa, *Games and Decisions*, chapter 13; J. Milnor's 'Games Against Nature'; and also, Koopmans, *Three Essays on the State of Economic Science*, pp. 155–65.

14. See Milnor, 'Games Against Nature', pp. 121–2.

15. e.g. in his article 'Cardinal Welfare, Individualistic Ethics, and Inter-personal Comparisons of Utility'.

16. In *Calculus of Consent*, e.g. pp. 78, 95–6.

17. See 'Justice as Fairness', p. 87; also 'Distributive Justice', p. 61. For a much more ample and complete justification for the assumption that the contractors would maximin than any presented in this book, see also Rawls, *A Theory of Justice*.

18. Luce and Raiffa, *Games and Decisions*, pp. 279–80. Other objections have been that the maximin criterion will be irrational in all circumstances, except where one knows that one's enemy is reacting to one's choices in such a way as to damage you—see, for example, Brian Barry's 'On Social Injustice', especially pp. 36–8. Barry's objection to the use of the maximin criterion in the original position is obviously quite irrelevant, for he considers the appropriateness of maximining in choosing, e.g. whether to take one's raincoat, by reference to situations where complete uncertainty does not obtain, i.e. there is some knowledge that the probability of rain is below some level. Of course, maximining will be absurd if people have some idea of the probabilities with which it will rain or be sunny; but the point is that it is an appropriate strategy where they lack *all* such probabilities, which is, by definition, exactly the position of the rational contractors in the original position.

19. Sidgwick, *Methods of Ethics*, pp. 411–19; Hume, *An Enquiry Concerning the Principles of Morals*, pp. 272–3; Bentham, *Principles of Morals and Legislation*, pp. 1–7.

20. e.g. Hume, *Enquiry Concerning the Principles of Morals*, pp. 193–4; on this, see Barry, *Political Argument*, pp. 319–22.

21. This is the main point of Rawls's critique in 'Justice as Fairness'.

22. The most convincing way to get to the utilitarian principle from the original position would, I think, be to assume a loss of the sense of individual identity, such that the contractors literally thought of themselves as one person: a common move in Hegelian idealist thought ending in a form of ideal observer theory, where distinctions between persons are eradicated. Cf. also Aristotle's notion that a 'friend really is another self' (*Nicomachean Ethics*, 1166[a]32, p. 253), and the Christian doctrine of love.

23. Cf. Sidgwick's remarks about 'Unconscious Utilitarianism', *Methods of Ethics*, p. 454.

24. e.g. in 'Cardinal Utility in Welfare Economics and in the Theory of Risk-Taking'.

25. The whole of Aristotle's *Nicomachean Ethics* is an attempt to describe the human excellences which morality requires us to maximize; but,

see, especially, Book 10 for a characterization of the special weight Aristotle gave to the human excellence of theoretical wisdom; for perhaps the clearest statement by Nietzsche of this principle, and a clear recognition of its implications, see *Twilight of the Idols*, p. 534.

26. *Politics*, Book I, chapter 4.

27. On slavery, see Aristotle, *Politics*, Book I, chapters 3–7; and Nietzsche, *Beyond Good and Evil*, pp. 189, 196, and *The Antichrist*, p. 639; on caste systems, see Nietzsche, *The Antichrist*, pp. 644 ff.; on aristocracies, see Aristotle, *Politics*, Book III, and Nietzsche's critique of feminist movements from the point of view of 'the military and aristocratic spirit', *Beyond Good and Evil*, p. 188.

28. *The Rise of the Meritocracy*; of course, a meritocratic conception is not only justifiable on perfectionist grounds; a Platonic form of utilitarian could be a quite vigorous meritocrat if he believed that pleasure could only be maximized (throughout society) if the wise and good were selected by competitive examination and made rulers.

29. Pareto, *Manuel d'Economie Politique*, especially chapter III, 'Notion Generale de l'Equilibre Economique'.

30. For an excellent discussion of economists' attempts to make the Pareto optimality criterion operational, and to replace it by a more adequate criterion, see Rothenberg, *The Measurement of Social Welfare*, chapters 3–5. For Buchanan and Tullock, see, especially, *Calculus of Consent*, Part III; for a very persuasive critique of this view, see Barry, *Political Argument*, chapters XIV–XV; for Runciman and Sen, see 'Games, Justice and the General Will'.

31. For a still more sophisticated and plausible statement of the view, see Brandt, 'Toward a Credible Form of Utilitarianism'; it will be noted that David Lyons excepts this form of rule-utilitarianism from his general thesis of extensional equivalence, presented in *Forms and Limits of Utilitarianism*, chapter III, though he still feels there are other objections to it, ibid., pp. 136–43.

32. Brandt, *Ethical Theory*, chapter 16; Benn and Peters, e.g. *Social Principles and the Democratic State*, pp. 183, 191–2.

33. *Political Argument*, chapter I.

34. e.g. J. Rawls, 'Two Concepts of Rules'; J. R. Searle, 'How to Derive "Ought" from "Is"'; G. E. M. Anscombe, 'Brute Facts'.

35. On this, see Hart, *Concept of Law*, chapter III.

36. For the first, see, for example, *Metaphysical Elements of Justice*, p. 35; cf. with this the Kantian principles of equal liberty suggested by Hart, 'Are there any Natural Rights?', and Rawls, 'Justice as Fairness'. For the second, see, for example, *Metaphysical Elements of Justice*, pp. 80, 96; 'Concerning the Common Saying: This May Be True in Theory, But Does Not

Apply in Practice', pp. 162-4. Rawls's theory, involves, in addition to the sketch I give, an elaborate classification of political institutions into different functional sub-institutions and discusses the different ways in which the principles of justice apply to these sub-institutions. See Rawls's article, 'Distributive Justice', and his book, *A Theory of Justice*.

37. For the Kantian conception, see, for example, *Foundations of the Metaphysics of Morals*, pp. 25, 27 n., 58, 62. For a negative example of the Christian conception, note that the nature of Ockham's heresy has to do not with his nominalist or general logical views, but rather with his adoption of a voluntarist theory of ethics; see Francis Oakley, 'Medieval Theories of Natural Law: William of Ockham and the Significance of the Voluntarist Tradition'.

38. e.g. Little, *Critique of Welfare Economics*, pp. 49-50.

39. Cf. Wollheim's illuminating consideration of two different types of principles of equality, and their relevance to the liberal tradition, 'Equality and Equal Rights'; also, Berlin's 'Equality as an Ideal'.

40. Hume, *Enquiry Concerning the Principles of Morals*, section III, Part II; Sidgwick, *Methods of Ethics*, pp. 288-90, 436, 442, 446.

41. 'Distributive Justice', p. 66.

42. On this, see J. Rawls, 'Constitutional Liberty and the Concept of Justice'.

43. Cf. Rawls, 'Distributive Justice', pp. 69 ff. On just taxation in the unjust society', see Meade's *Efficiency, Equality and the Ownership of Property*.

44. A similar concept is expounded in Buchanan and Tullock, *Calculus of Consent*, chapter 13, where they claim that the rational contractors, at the time of constitutional choice, will agree on some sort of insurance plan by which any person whose income falls beneath a certain minimal level will have it supplemented by a redistribution of income from others. Such a principle would be appropriately accepted in the original position had the contractors not already agreed on principles to cover the question.

45. *Three Essays on the State of Economic Science*, essay I.

46. The relevant texts here are O. Lange and F. M. Taylor, *On the Economic Theory of Socialism*, and A. P. Lerner's *The Economics of Control*.

47. In this, my view is diametrically opposed to the principal thesis of Feinberg's fine article, 'Justice and Personal Desert'. See Rawls, 'Distributive Justice', p. 77; cf. Sidgwick's similar view, *Methods of Ethics*, p. 290.

48. A subject interestingly described in R. Wasserstrom, 'Rights, Human Rights, and Racial Discrimination'; and also, in J. Feinberg, 'Duties, Rights, and Claims'.

49. Hart, 'Are there any Natural Rights?', pp. 181, 190; it seems not unlikely that Hart is confusing a point of pragmatic use with the strict meaning of the 'have rights' terminology.

50. For an illuminating elaboration of this sort of view, see Hart's 'Prolegomenon to the Principles of Punishment', and also his 'Legal Responsibility and Excuses'.

51. See, for example, Moore, *Principia Ethica*, pp. 214–16; Ross, *The Right and the Good*, pp. 57–8; Kant, *Metaphysical Elements of Justice*, pp. 99–108.

52. *Lectures on the Principles of Political Obligation*, p. 190; for a rather different moral conception, cf. Sidgwick's remark concerning the inappropriateness of a government's ensuring minimal incomes for the benefit of children, and providing 'sustenance for adults, in order that they may not be driven into criminal courses' (*The Elements of Politics*, p. 141), on the basis that 'if either kind of governmental assistance is once admitted as justifiable in principle, it is not very easy to limit the burden that may be thrown on industrious and provident individuals by the improvidence of others' (ibid.).

53. See, especially, Locke, *Second Treatise of Government*, chapters I–III; Kant supposed there to be a moral obligation for persons to leave the state of nature and enter into civil society, e.g. *Metaphysical Elements of Justice*, pp. 69–72.

54. Beccaria made an exception of cases of treason leading to unjustifiable anarchy, civil war, and revolution, *On Crimes and Punishments*, pp. 45–52; for Kant's arguments, see, for example, *Metaphysical Elements of Justice*, pp. 101–2, 104–7 (where he explicitly argues against Beccaria, who, he claims, has been mistakenly moved by a 'sympathetic sentimentality and an affectation of humanitarianism', p. 105). For an example of an account which seems to me to raise at least some of the central questions relevant to the justifiability of the death penalty, see H. L. A. Hart's 'Murder and the Principles of Punishment: England and the United States'.

55. Cf. Hart's concept of the continuity and persistence of legal systems, for which any adequate legal theory must account, e.g. *Concept of Law*, pp. 50–64.

56. I take the word and concept from Rawls, 'Distributive Justice', p. 74.

57. So that an economy 'behaves in an efficient manner only if at each point of time it would be impossible to make some citizen better off at that point of time without making someone worse off at the same point of time or at some other point of time', J. E. Meade, *Efficiency, Equality, and the Ownership of Property*, p. 19.

58. An independent objection is that the Pareto optimality criterion would be too indeterminate, since it would yield an infinite number of optimal distributions over time; see ibid., pp. 21–6.

59. *Treatise of Human Nature*, p. 495.

60. e.g. *Methods of Ethics*, pp. 415–16, 487.

61. Note that I use the notion, 'equal and greatest talent', not the notion, 'greatest equal talent', in formulating this principle. The difference in formulation is quite intentional. The latter formulation is ambiguous between a requirement that natural talent be distributed as equally as possible (which is not the notion I intend expressing) and a requirement that *both* natural talent be distributed as equally as possible *and* the greatest amount of talent as possible be distributed. The former kind of requirement would involve the counterintuitive result that a conscious programme of discouraging genius be adopted, whereas the latter kind of dual requirement emphasizes the point that, so far from genius being discouraged, programmes are to be adopted to make it more likely that everyone will have genius of some kind.

62. Cf. Barry's *Political Argument*, pp. 165–6, n. 2, and Meade's *Efficiency, Equality and the Ownership of Property*, pp. 63–5.

63. See *The German Ideology*, p. 22, where Marx claims that the self-sufficient, unalienated communist man will 'hunt in the morning, fish in the afternoon, rear cattle in the evening, criticize after dinner'. For Marx's most explicit indictment of capitalist society as repressing the fullness of talent, see *Karl Marx: Early Writings*, especially pp. 120 ff.

64. e.g. *Metaphysical Elements of Justice*, pp. 114–29; and also, *Perpetual Peace*.

65. Cf. Kant's remark: 'the founding of colonies that are linked with a mother country provides an occasion for doing evil and violence to some place on our globe that will be felt everywhere', *Metaphysical Elements of Justice*, p. 26. Kant's remark suggests he had in mind colonies of emigrants from the mother country (e.g. the American colonies, rather than colonies like Fiji or Hongkong), which act as outposts from which to molest neighbouring regions. However, the view would apply to any form of colonial rule where the equal liberties of the citizens of the colony were violated, or where the colony itself (perhaps consisting of emigrés with equal liberties with their stay-at-home former fellow-citizens) was used to violate the equal liberties of neighbours.

66. I am indebted for this point to Professor R. M. Hare.

67. *Metaphysical Elements of Justice*, pp. 123–9; *Perpetual Peace, passim.*

68. Kant, ibid., pp. 106–16; Sidgwick claims that, though to guarantee a minimum wage would not be justified by the utilitarian principle in the imperfect conditions of late nineteenth-century England, it would be justified were it the case that equality of educational opportunity were secured to all classes, and the interest on capital was largely diverted to the remuneration of labour, *Principles of Political Economy*, pp. 531–2.

69. See, on this, R. T. Gill, *Economic Development: Past and Present*.

70. Thus, Russia is not strictly comparable, since the process of economic growth had begun under the Czars; and Japan is not, since economic growth began under the Meiji restoration. For useful accounts of the Soviet Union's approach to economic planning, see A. Bergson, *The Economics of Soviet Planning*, and R. W. Campbell, *Soviet Economic Power*. For a very useful account of the Japanese process of economic development from the Meiji restoration onwards, see W. W. Lockwood, *The Economic Development of Japan: Growth and Structural Change, 1869–1939*.

71. See, on this, Gill, *Economic Development*. For a useful account of the Indian approach to economic planning, see W. B. Reddaway, *The Development of the Indian Economy*.

72. The problem raised by the difference between people's actual knowledge of empirical facts and the ideal knowledge of the rational contractors is a problem for other moral theories as well, e.g. the ideal observer theory. In the theological formulation of the ideal observer theory, the problem was formulated as the difference between the individual's limited attempts to consult his conscience and thus discover what God wills and what God (who is omniscient and omnipercipient) in fact wills: the gap which doctrines of theodicy attempted to fill.

73. Cf. Prichard, 'Duty and Ignorance of Fact'.

74. For a more sociological treatment of the general question of the justifiability of war crimes tribunals, see J. N. Shklar, *Legalism*, especially Part I. My own emphasis on a requirement of plausible deterrence, before such tribunals are justifiable, would, I think, tend to indicate that such tribunals are morally quite dubious, since the notion of deterrence seems here much more threadbare than in the typical case of punishment within a national legal system.

75. It also derives from his concept of sovereignty, which held it contradictory that the people could have the final voice over the sovereign, e.g. *Metaphysical Elements of Justice*, pp. 86–7.

76. 'Constitutional Liberty and the Concept of Justice', pp. 110 ff.

77. Cf. D. Lyons, *Forms and Limits of Utilitarianism*, pp. 165–7.

78. No claim is made about the priority of justice in all contexts; and thus, Barry's sort of counter-example, 'On Social Justice', pp. 40–1, will not do, since it is a non-institutional use of the concept of justice. From Kant's conception of the priority of justice over utility arises his view that a person 'must first be found to be deserving of punishment before any consideration is given to the utility of this punishment for himself and for his fellow citizens', *Metaphysical Elements of Justice*, p. 100; cf. ibid., pp. 127, 132; and from his conception that justice can only be overriden by a greater balance of justice, arises his view that the justice of the death penalty for a murderer with innumerable accomplices may be overriden by the greater injustice of returning one's people

to the state of nature by killing off too many people (ibid., p. 104), or his view that the justice of a revolution will always be outweighed by the greater injustice of returning one's people to the state of nature (ibid., p. 127); for an explicit statement in Kant's works of such a lexicographical priority order, see his remarks on conditional and unconditional duties in his 'On the Saying "Necessity Has No Law" '.

79. First suggested by J. Rawls, 'Distributive Justice', pp. 63–6.

80. On these, see Rothenberg, *Measurement of Social Welfare*, Part III, chapters 6–10.

81. For a suggestion of an exactly similar view, see Koopmans, *Three Essays on the State of Economic Science*, p. 166.

82. See Hitch and McKean, *Economics of Defense in the Nuclear Age*, for an illuminating application of these techniques of analysis to various types of defence institutions and policies.

CHAPTER 9

1. *The Logic of Collective Action*, p. 14.

2. *Treatise of Human Nature*, p. 538

3. Baumol, *Welfare Economics and the Theory of the State*, pp. 37, 131–3, 135–41, 142–7; on price stability, cf. Benn and Peters, *Social Principles and the Democratic State*, p. 275.

4. *The Logic of Collective Action*, Part III.

5. *Leviathan*, p. 82.

6. On this, see Baumol, *Welfare Economics and the Theory of the State*, pp. 146, 176–7.

7. In his remarkable article, 'On the Function of False Hypotheses in Ethics', especially pp. 387–8, 391.

8. Ibid., p. 388.

9. Hart, 'Are there any Natural Rights?', p. 185; Rawls, 'Legal Obligation and the Duty of Fair Play', p. 3. For a much fuller development of Rawls's analysis, see his *A Theory of Justice*.

10. Such a principle seems involved in Socrates' justification for not fleeing Athens, *Crito*, 51ᶜ7 ff., pp. 27–39. To say that any principle could be operative over such a tradition of political thought is perhaps only to confirm Berlin's view of political philosophy's task in investigating 'the most familiar and inalienable kinds of characteristics in terms of which we think and act', 'Does Political Theory Still Exist?', p. 25.

11. *The Political Theory of Possessive Individualism*, p. 221.

12. *Man and Society*, vol. I, p. 232.

13. 'Political Justice', p. 135.

14. *Second Treatise*, p. 371.

15. Ibid., p. 375.

16. The subject of *Second Treatise*, chapter II; the 'Fundamental Law of Nature' (pp. 296–7), for Locke, is comprised in the notion: 'Every one as he is *bound to preserve himself*, and not to quit his Station wilfully, so by like reason when his own Preservation comes not in competition, ought he, as much as he can, *to preserve the rest of* Mankind' (ibid., p. 289). Men are equal in the sense that they are equal in their capacity to know and act on this principle, though, no doubt, only the philosopher will know how to derive it (as Locke supposed he did in *Essays on the Law of Nature*).

17. *Second Treatise*, section 6, p. 289.

18. Ibid., chapter VIII.

19. Ibid., sections 59–60, pp. 325–6.

20. A. Ryan, 'Locke and the Dictatorship of the Bourgeoisie', p. 227.

21. *Second Treatise*, section 119, p. 366.

22. Ibid., section 41, pp. 314–15.

23. See, for example, Ryan, 'Locke and the Dictatorship of the Bourgeoisie', p. 226. Locke also suggests that inequalities in wealth and status are only justified when they make all better off than they are in the state of nature; see *Second Treatise*, section 48, p. 319. This view fails, I think, to reflect our sense of the proper relation between justice and inequalities in wealth and status, for it allows much that we would consider unjust. For a discussion of the conditions when the principle of equality may be justifiably departed from and of how that principle is to be understood, see W. Frankena, 'The Concept of Social Justice'; for a very interesting discussion of the meritocracy issue, see G. Vlastos, 'Justice and Equality'.

24. Runciman and Sen, in 'Games, Justice, and the General Will', suggest interpreting Rousseau's criterion of political right as the Pareto criterion. Such an interpretation seems clearly inadequate. In certain circumstances, it might be that some would be made better off and none worse off by making slavery an institution. Yet clearly, for Rousseau, slavery is excluded as a moral possibility (e.g. *The Social Contract*, Book I, chapter IV). This realization seems to be behind Runciman's change of conception in *Relative Deprivation and Social Justice*, especially chapter XII; for a conception much closer to Rousseau's intention, see Rawls, 'Justice as Fairness'.

25. Gewirth, 'Political Justice', pp. 132 ff.; Hume, 'Of the Original Contract', especially pp. 203 ff. Locke also supposes that one can be 'Subject or Members of that Commonwealth' (*Second Treatise*, section 122, p. 367) only 'by positive engagement and express Promise and

Compact' (*Second Treatise*, p. 367), where he may mean some feature of English law by which persons accept 'the Inheritance of their Ancestors' (ibid., section 73, p. 333). For my analytical purposes, I choose to ignore this quite implausible notion, and emphasize Locke's tacit consent notion.

26. Ibid., section 119, p. 366.

27. 'Of the Original Contract', p. 203.

28. 'Concerning the Common Saying: This May Be True in Theory But Does Not Apply in Practice', p. 166. For an extended critique of historical views of the social contract, see Austin, *Province of Jurisprudence Determined*, lecture VI.

29. e.g. *Metaphysical Elements of Justice*, pp. 76, 116. This way of answering the fragility objection was suggested to me by Professor John Rawls.

30. 'A Paradox in the Theory of Democracy', p. 84.

31. A distinction not unlike Sidgwick's continual claim that men may act most morally if they act on the basis of various maxims and rules, and not on the basis of a benevolent desire to advance the greatest happiness of the greatest number, *Methods of Ethics*, pp. 345, 370, 395, 405 (analogous to self-interest, p. 136), 413, 422, 431.

32. Cf. B. Barry's rather different consideration of Wollheim's paradox, *Political Argument*, pp. 293–4; for some other interesting considerations of this general problem, see R. Wasserstrom, 'The Obligation to Obey the Law', pp. 797 ff., and I. M. D. Little, 'Social Choice and Individual Values', pp. 430–2.

33. Thus, Locke insists that revolution is only justified when all other forms of redress are denied, e.g. *Second Treatise*, pp. 299 (cf. p. 342), 404, 421.

34. 'Morals and the Criminal Law.'

35. See Hart's criticisms of this view, *Law, Liberty, and Morality*, especially lectures II–III.

36. Hume, *Treatise of Human Nature*, pp. 516–25; Rawls, 'Two Concepts of Rules'; Searle, 'How to Derive "Ought" from "Is" '.

37. Searle's view is the subject of a large, and largely critical, literature; for one of the more interesting critiques, see R. M. Hare, 'The Promising Game'.

38. Austin, *How To Do Things With Words*; see Prichard, 'The Obligation to Keep a Promise'. For an illuminating consideration of this topic, see P. F. Strawson's 'Intention and Convention in Speech Acts'.

39. *Forms and Limits of Utilitarianism*, pp. 177–97.

40. *Methods of Ethics*, pp. 295–311.

41. 'The Obligation to Keep a Promise', pp. 178–9.

42. Prichard seems correct further in noting that, on the basis of such advantages alone, we should not think promising a moral obligation but 'should only think doing the action wise and sensible', ibid., p. 176.

43. On this, see J. Rawls, 'Two Concepts of Rules', especially pp. 213–18, 30–1.

44. Price, *Review of the Principal Questions in Morals*, pp. 155–7; Kant, *Metaphysical Principles of Virtue*, pp. 90–3; Kant, 'On a Supposed Right to Tell Lies from Benevolent Motives', pp. 362–3.

45. Hume, *Treatise of Human Nature*, pp. 516–17; Sidgwick, *Methods of Ethics*, p. 304.

46. Prichard, 'The Obligation to Keep a Promise'; Austin, *How To Do Things With Words*; also 'Other Minds', pp. 66 ff.

47. G. R. Grice's term, *The Grounds of Moral Judgement*, p. 45.

48. Cf. Sidgwick's view that both fidelity and veracity have much in common, since they seem to depend on existent social practices, *Methods of Ethics*, Book III, chapters VI–VII.

49. D. Lewis, *Convention: a Philosophical Study*, p. 177. Lewis's distinctions are quite compatible with my own account, including his suggestion that the moral obligation to tell the truth is related to 'an obligation of fair play to reciprocate the benefits he has derived from others' truthfulness', ibid., p. 182.

50. *Methods of Ethics*, pp. 312–19.

51. Cf. Bernard Williams's related claim that highly conventionalized speech acts like greetings do not admit the concepts of the sincere or insincere, 'Morality and the Emotions', p. 11.

52. *Forms and Limits of Utilitarianism*, especially chapter III.

53. *Methods of Ethics*, pp. 318–19, 487–8.

54. Cf. Lyons, *Forms and Limits of Utilitarianism*, pp. 112, 130, 163 ff. See here Gauthier's similar remarks on the sense in which insincere advising is 'parasitical' on the practice of sincere advising, *Practical Reasoning*, pp. 54, 79, 137.

55. Ross, *The Right and the Good*, p. 27; Sidgwick, *Methods of Ethics*, p. 279.

56. On this, see F. Boas, *Kwakiutl Ethnography*, especially chapter IV, 'The Potlatch', pp. 77–104. Of course, to the extent a society actually does view such coercion as justified, the notion of gift (as something freely given) becomes inapplicable.

CHAPTER 10

1. For a similar, and more extended, consideration of the concept of the voluntary, see D'Arcy, *Human Acts*, chapter 3; also, Hart, 'Varieties of Responsibility'.

2. Locke, *Second Treatise*, section 6, p. 289.

3. Thus, for example, Kant's arguments against the moral justifiability of suicide, masturbation, immoderate eating and drinking (*Metaphysical Principles of Virtue*, pp. 82–90) all depend on his conception of the proper functions of human nature, which may implicitly depend on Kant's unquestioning assumption of theological views about the ordained use of human functions; in so far as this seems to be the case, Kant's view here seems appropriately described as quasi-theological.

4. On this, see Findlay, *Values and Intentions*, pp. 233, 248, 261, 266, 358.

5. Thus, Beccaria, who argued against the moral justifiability of the death penalty as a general deterrent in legal systems, still held that the death penalty was justified in those cases where persons tried to undermine the stability of a just society, where this clearly seems to cover both internal revolution and treason to a foreign power, e.g. *On Crimes and Punishments*, p. 46.

6. But, cf. Grice's rather different view, *Grounds of Moral Judgement*, pp. 55, 84–6.

7. Such a conception was suggested by utilitarianism (e.g. *Methods of Ethics*, p. 414); since the point of the utilitarian principle was to maximize desire satisfaction, and since there is no reason to doubt that animals have desires and wants as much as human beings, quite severe constraints would be placed on the use of animals as food, beasts of burden, etc., perhaps proscribing such uses altogether. Clearly, if animals were members of the original position, in my sense, as maximiners, they would never consent to being food, or beasts of burden, etc. A plausible way to defend the utilitarian position is to note that animals may have desires, but not to the extent that humans do, or not of the sorts (exactly) that humans have; and thus, the wants of animals have correspondingly less moral weight; e.g. see Hare, *Freedom and Reason*, pp. 222 ff.

8. Namely, that a requirement of mutual aid is a minimum requirement that one would be willing to agree to obey oneself, since it would secure a great good to oneself, if one were distressed and others obeyed, and that others would also agree to obey, from an original position of equal liberty; *Foundations of the Metaphysics of Morals*, p. 41; see also, for example, *Metaphysical Principles of Virtue*, pp. 52, 115, 117; *Critique of Practical Reason*, pp. 34–5. See Eisenberg's comments on Kant's argument here, especially 'From the Forbidden to the Supererogatory', pp. 263 ff.

9. *Metaphysical Principles of Virtue*, pp. 112 ff.

10. *Review of the Principal Questions in Morals*, pp. 120–1.

11. *Methods of Ethics*, pp. 253, 492.

12. Against there being a duty of non-maleficence, Hart, 'Legal and Moral Obligation', pp. 82–3; against there being a duty of mutual aid, Baier, *Moral Point of View*, pp. 226–7; against there being a duty of non-maleficence, ibid., p. 221; similarly, Gauthier maintains there is no duty of non-maleficence (*Practical Reasoning*, p. 194), yet, surprisingly, holds there is a duty of mutual aid (ibid., p. 203).

13. D'Arcy, *Human Acts*, pp. 50–7; Findlay, *Values and Intentions*, pp. 310, 343, 363; Grice, *Grounds of Moral Judgement*, pp. 124, 155, 159 ff., 173.

14. This point was suggested to me by certain criticisms of Dr. A. J. Kenny.

15. Cf. Kant's claim that the special moral vice in ingratitude is its destruction of the moral impulse to beneficence, *Metaphysical Principles of Virtue*, pp. 119, 124.

16. Sidgwick, *Methods of Ethics*, p. 437.

17. *Moral Point of View*, p. 230.

18. e.g. Kant, *Metaphysical Principles of Virtue*, pp. 82–4 (but note the exceptions under 'Casuistical Questions', ibid., pp. 84–5); Price, *Review of the Principal Questions in Morals*, p. 171; Sidgwick, *Methods of Ethics*, pp. 327, 331, 356. Sidgwick may be an exception to this, since he appeals to the utilitarian principle in justifying the absolute proscription on suicide, ibid.; and does not, unlike the others, seem to assume theological notions. Whether utilitarianism does, in fact, justify such an absolute proscription is quite another matter.

CHAPTER 11

1. 'Supererogation and Rules', pp. 279, 281.

2. Chisholm, 'Supererogation and Offence: a Conceptual Scheme for Ethics', p. 3.

3. See, especially, ibid., pp. 10 ff.

4. *Grounds of Moral Judgement*, chapter 4.

5. *Much Ado About Nothing*, Act II, scene i; cf. also Olivia's similar comment: 'Where is Malvolio? he is sad, and civil, / And suits well for a servant with my fortunes: / Where is Malvolio?', *Twelfth Night*, Act III, scene iv.

6. On guilt, resentment, and indignation, as distinctive types of *moral* feeling, see J. Rawls, 'The Sense of Justice'; and P. F. Strawson, 'Freedom and Resentment'.

7. The relation of respect to the exercise of competence has been one of the central features of the psychological theory of competence desires of R. W. White; White's best statement of his view is *Ego and Reality in Psychoanalytic Theory*, but his short paper, 'Competence and the Psychosexual Stages of Development', interestingly relates his theory to Erikson's development stages.

8. Something like this seems to be what Kant meant by his notion of imperfect duties of broad obligation, as applied to a certain class of acts one has a duty to do, e.g. *Metaphysical Principles of Virtue*, pp. 48–9, and what Price similarly meant in discussing the distinctive nature of duties of beneficence, e.g. *Review of the Principal Questions in Morals*, pp. 120–3; the distinctive feature of my use of this notion is applying it as between conflicting duties, whereas Kant and Price seem to use it mainly as applying within a class of acts one has a duty to do.

9. *Metaphysical Principles of Virtue*, pp. 112 ff.

10. *Treatise of Human Nature*, p. 600.

11. Cf. Sidgwick's utilitarian justification of humility as falling under a principle which prescribes 'the expression of general goodwill and abstinence from anything that may cause pain to others in conversation and social demeanour' (*Methods of Ethics*, p. 253; see also ibid., pp. 336, 429). Also, cf. Piaget's use of the concept of a principle of mutual respect as generally equivalent to moral principles *simpliciter*, e.g. *Moral Judgment of the Child*, pp. 95–6, 97–8, 352–3, 368–9, 383, 397.

12. *Politics*, Book II, chapters 3–4; see also Aristotle's unrivalled discussion of friendship, *Nicomachean Ethics*, Books VIII and IX; McTaggart, *Studies in Hegelian Cosmology*; Scheler, *The Nature of Sympathy*, pp. 67–8, 101–2, 142, 160, 167–8.

13. *Studies in Hegelian Cosmology*, p. 278.

14. Ibid., p. 279.

15. e.g. *Foundations of the Metaphysics of Morals*, pp. 15–16.

16. *Metaphysical Principles of Virtue*, p. 119; cf. ibid., p. 124.

17. *Childhood and Society*, p. 262.

18. *The Nature of Sympathy*, p. 43.

19. *Metaphysical Principles of Virtue*, p. 136.

CHAPTER 12

1. Professor John Rawls has suggested to me that the priority problem may lead the rational contractors to abandon their maximining strategy, and seek to maximize the average of utility, at least in considering the principles of priority which are to govern when substantive principles conflict.

2. Professor Hare has made this quite clear to me in his criticisms of the doctoral dissertation which led to this book and in his subsequent correspondence with me.

3. e.g. *Norm and Action*, p. 101.

4. A fact commonly remarked on in recent discussions of the subject, e.g. J. Feinberg's 'Supererogation and Rules', pp. 278–9; also his 'Justice and Personal Desert', p. 74; R. B. Brandt, 'The Concepts of Obligation and Duty', p. 378; E. J. Lemmon, 'Moral Dilemmas', pp. 142–3.

5. See *Freedom and Reason*, p. 37, where Hare makes clear that universalizability is a necessary, not a sufficient, condition of moral judgements. I am indebted to Professor Hare for pointing this out to me.

6. Cf. Baier's analysis: 'As I construe the claim " 'Do *x*' has moral binding force", it implies that "Do *x*" is a directive in regard to which there *ought to be* a person whose job it is to ensure that all those to whom addressees of the directive applies follow it', 'Moral Obligation', p. 224.

7. For a similar analytic claim, see G. R. Grice, *Grounds of Moral Judgement*, e.g. pp. 24–33, 93–8, 174–6.

8. Ibid., pp. 17 ff.

9. A problem classically raised by Prichard in his 'Duty and Ignorance of Fact'; however, the first philosophical statement of the problem seems to go back to Richard Price's distinction between abstract and practical virtue, e.g. *Review of the Principal Questions in Morals*, pp. 177–8, 208.

10. Sidgwick, *Methods of Ethics*, pp. 207–8, 394–5; Baier, *Moral Point of View*, pp. 143–7.

11. Sidgwick's point, *Methods of Ethics*, pp. 207–8.

12. The distinction between good and conclusive reasons for action was suggested to me by D. Lyons, *Forms and Limits of Utilitarianism*, e.g. pp. 19–22.

13. On the concept of negligence, see D'Arcy, *Human Acts*, pp. 119–24.

14. Hart refers to all examples of non-institutional duties as 'absurd', 'Legal and Moral Obligation', p. 82, on the basis that we do not tend to speak of our duties, for example, not to torture children. Hart's argument, here, seems to rest on a confusion between the pragmatic uses of concepts and what strictly such concepts mean. Even if 'duty' is not typically *used* to refer to certain requirements, it does not follow that using 'duty' to refer to these requirements is an incoherent or contradictory thing to do.

15. Cf., for example, Kant's remark, *Foundations of the Metaphysics of Morals*, p. 20.

16. e.g. *Intention*, pp. 16–18.

17. *Ethical Theory*, pp. 159–66.

18. The exceptional moral principle that I have here in mind is the principle of beneficence, whose applicability does depend on whether or not a person has benevolent desires, something which is very much part of people's psychological histories.

19. For a suggestion of the form such an account would take, see Gauthier, *Practical Reasoning*, chapters IV, V, X. My own account here is extremely crude. However, that all distinctions are not drawn does not imply that the distinctions actually drawn are invalid.

20. It seems to me that there is some doubt as to whether 'ought' is ever used to command, in the ordinary restricted sense. Note that my previous examples of the use of propositional expressions to command centre on 'must', not 'ought'.

21. *Critique of Practical Reason*, p. 32.

CHAPTER 13

1. In his *Review of the Principal Questions of Morals*, Price argues that it is unjustified to infer the logical identity of moral judgements and feelings from their undisputed concomitance (p. 63), but maintains, none the less, that there is a necessary relation between such judgements and motivating feelings (pp. 186–7, 213–14), which we must simply accept as a brute fact of human nature. The thesis of Prichard's 'Duty and Interest' is that we must accept as a brute fact, unrelated to the desire for our own good, 'the existence of a desire to do what is right' (p. 485), where the right is a primitive, indefinable property. W. D. Ross, following Prichard, defends the view that, in matters of moral psychology, we must accept the existence of a desire to do what is right, where the right is a primitive intuition, e.g. *Foundations of Ethics*, chapter IX.

2. See Lawrence Kohlberg, 'Moral Development and Identification', pp. 288 ff.

3. On this, see Perry, 'Value and its Moving Appeal'; Moore's analysis is to be found in *Principia Ethica*, chapter 1.

4. On this see J. Bennett, *Rationality*, pp. 79–86.

5. e.g. *Foundations of the Metaphysics of Morals*, pp. 16–17, 46–7.

6. e.g. ibid., pp. 56–9; Piaget, *Moral Judgment of the Child*, pp. 95, 98, 352, 368, 397; Scheler, *The Nature of Sympathy*, pp. 58–61.

7. e.g. *Foundations of the Metaphysics of Morals*, pp. 46–7; 'What is Enlightenment?', ibid., p. 92.

8. The distinctive relation of the concept of love to the uniqueness of the person loved is a central feature of Scheler's suggestive account, e.g. *The Nature of Sympathy*, pp. 67–8, 101–2, 142, 160, 167–8; on the desire for closeness, see Sidgwick, *Methods of Ethics*, pp. 244–5.

9. *Foundations of the Metaphysics of Morals*, pp. 14–16.

10. For a cogent criticism of the Humean view (described at n. 25, p. 309, *supra*), see Scheler, *The Nature of Sympathy*, pp. 10–12; Scheler not only notes, as a fact of human psychology, that sympathy does not imply a reproduction in the sympathizer of the other's pleasure or pain, but interestingly points out that the cases where such reproduction does occur, for example, the infection by others' emotions, as a fact of crowd psychology (not unlike post-hypnotic suggestion), are the very opposite of genuine understanding and sympathy.

11. *The Nature of Sympathy*, chapter II.

12. Ibid., p. 23.

13. 'The Ethical Importance of Sympathy', p. 66.

14. See Scheler, *The Nature of Sympathy*, pp. 14, 132–3.

15. On this, see Acton, 'The Ethical Importance of Sympathy', pp. 62–4; and Scheler, *The Nature of Sympathy*, pp. 47–50; but, cf. with this, Scheler, pp. 96–8. While Scheler maintains that it is not necessary that a person should have gone through the same precise experience of another in order to be able to sympathize with that experience, he does maintain that a person must have *identified* himself with another going through a certain kind of experience, feeling others' feelings as one's own, without a realization of the separateness of persons, as with 'the little girl playing at "mother" . . . the herd, the horde and crowd . . . the mysteries of antiquity', p. 97.

16. See his 'Sense of Justice'. I also profited by attending Professor Rawls's lectures and seminars at Harvard University where he further developed his theory of moral feelings, especially the theory of shame.

17. On pride and fear, see Foot, 'Moral Beliefs', pp. 86 ff.; on anger, see Anscombe, 'Pretending', especially pp. 281–9; on fear, see Kenny, *Action, Emotion and Will*, especially pp. 60–75, and Hampshire, *Freedom of the Will*, chapter 3, e.g. pp. 76 ff., 85 ff.; see also Findlay, *Values and Intentions*, pp. 166–78.

18. Cf. Rawls's similar statement of this relation, 'Sense of Justice', p. 297.

19. 'Shame supposes that one is completely exposed and conscious of being looked at: in one word, self-conscious.' Erikson, *Childhood and Society*, p. 252; Kenny has claimed that there is a logical relation between shame and 'the desire to conceal whatever it is that makes one ashamed', *Action, Emotion and Will*, p. 100.

20. *The Nature of Sympathy*, p. 263.

21. The notion that shame involves some kind of fear of public exposure and blame is a primary part of Freud's account of this notion, where shame is the moral feeling aimed at inhibiting the child's 'shameless . . . pleasure in displaying its body and especially its sexual organs' (*Three Contributions to the Theory of Sex*, p. 52) as well as inhibiting the child's curiosity about the genitalia of other children (ibid., p. 21). Guilt, by contrast, involves not fear of public exposure, but fear of unleashing the aggressive energies embodied in the superego, when one disobeys the injunctions of the superego; for the clearest statement of Freud's view that guilt is derived from internalized aggression, or *mortido*, see *Civilization and its Discontents*. Freud's distinction of shame and guilt has had wide influence. Thus, Erikson views shame as a form of fear of public exposure (*Childhood and Society*, pp. 252–3), whereas guilt, whether that of 'negative conscience' (e.g. *Young Man Luther*, pp. 193, 214, 219) or 'the good conscience of true indignation' (ibid., p. 242), involves essentially fear of some punishment from some internalized rule or ideal. Freud's view has, of course, been popularized in the anthropological notion of shame and guilt cultures; see, for example, R. Benedict, *Chrysanthemum and the Sword: Patterns of Japanese Culture*, p. 223; and M. Mead, *Cooperation and Competition among Primitive Peoples*, p. 493, and Mead, 'Some Anthropological Considerations Concerning Guilt', p. 203. Cf. also Riesman's suggestion that tradition-directed men would emphasize the moral feeling of shame, while inner-directed men would emphasize guilt, *The Lonely Crowd*, p. 24. Note that, if my way of distinguishing shame and guilt is correct, then it will have important implications for the reinterpretation of anthropological data heretofore analysed on the Mead–Benedict guilt–shame culture model. For example, tribes or peoples interpreted by Mead as manifestly being guilt cultures— the Eskimo's fear of loss of strength (*Cooperation and Competition among Primitive Peoples*, p. 498), the Iroquois' pride (ibid., p. 502), the Samoans' pride in playing social roles well (ibid., p. 502), the Maori's sense of keeping their positions inviolate (ibid., p. 505)—may, in my view, all be interpreted as manifesting an excellence–shame view of morality. Similarly, Benedict seems to me to misdescribe the moral dynamics of Japanese culture when she characterizes failure in 'living up to one's own picture of oneself' (Benedict, p. 223) as a form of guilt. From Benedict's own descriptions it seems to me that shame much more precisely characterizes the value commitments of Japanese culture, its celebration of 'generalized technical self-control and self-governance' (p. 229; cf. pp. 120, 121, 130, 148 ff., 152, 171 ff., 219, 220–1, 290, 293). Further, it seems to me that the shame–guilt distinction I suggest is far more suggestive of possible causal relationships than the Mead–Benedict view. For example, it has always seemed to me that an excellence–shame ethic like Aristotle's, with its emphasis on sacrifice and self-control, is a distinctly heroic conception, which a culture dominated by constant military enterprises emphasizing the individual hero, like ancient Greece (see on this, Weber, *The City*,

Part 5), would find particularly natural. A similar argument could be made in the case of Japan, I think. While I have no idea of the validity of this view, it is a possible causal relationship which my view of shame clearly suggests.

22. Cf. Rawls, 'Sense of Justice', p. 294.

23. *Shame and Guilt: a Psychoanalytic and Cultural Study*, p. 11.

24. On this, see G. A. Paul, 'The Problem of Guilt'.

25. Rawls, 'Sense of Justice', pp. 298–9 ; Strawson, 'Freedom and Resentment', pp. 199–201.

26. Bedford supposed shame logically to imply the notion of voluntary fault, e.g. 'Emotions', pp. 290–1.

27. On the public character of shame, I refer here not only to Freud, Erikson, Benedict, Mead, and Riesman (see note (21, above), but to an older *philosophical* tradition, including Spinoza (see, for example, *Ethics*, *Spinoza: Selections*, Part III, proposition XXX, p. 235); Descartes (see, for example, *Passions of the Soul, Philosophical Works of Descartes*, vol. i, article LXVI, p. 361, and article CCV, p. 422); Hume (who suggests that shame must be based on some process of emulous and invidious comparison, where you seek to find the attributes that others lack and you have, *Treatise of Human Nature*, Book II, p. 291); Sartre (*Being and Nothingness*, pp. 222, 261); and perhaps Kenny (*Action, Emotion and Will*, p. 100). The confusion betweens hame and embarrassment is quite apparent in Erving Goffman's 'On Face-Work'; elsewhere, Goffman truly and importantly notes the relativity of embarrassment to the idiosyncracies of social training, e.g. 'Embarrassment and Social Organization'.

28. *City of God*, Book XIV, chapter 23, p. 471.

29. See Kohlberg, 'Development of Moral Character and Moral Ideology', vol. i, pp. 409 ff., where he indicates this is the prevalent mode of guilt resolution in childhood.

30. It has been not uncommon to view the reciprocal of shame as not self-respect, but pride—see, for example, Hume, *Treatise of Human Nature*, p. 277, and Arnold Isenberg, 'Natural Pride and Natural Shame'. Such views are insufficiently general, for they fail to note the many cases where people are or feel ashamed not because of pride (for they have no inclination to exhibit or compare their achievements), but rather because of a completely personal ideal in which they have invested their self-esteem. Thus, Hume's contention that shame implies emulous comparison (*Treatise*, p. 291) clearly derives from his view that pride is the natural attitude basic to shame, for such emulous comparison seems to be a part of the concept of pride, though not of self-respect.

31. Isenberg, 'Natural Pride and Natural Shame', pp. 2–3.

32. *Childhood and Society*, p. 412.

33. 'The Problem of Ego Identity', p. 112.

34. For example, as an American abroad, I may be ashamed of the actions of fellow Americans abroad. This feature of my account runs directly contrary to Hume's view that shame implies some feature of emulous comparison whereby one notes the things one has and others lack (see notes 27, 30 above).

35. e.g. *On Shame and the Search for Identity*, p. 227.

36. *Young Man Luther*, p. 212.

37. Note Freud's remark about 'the essential similarity between taboo prohibitions and moral prohibitions', *Totem and Taboo*, p. 32.

38. See Rawls, 'Sense of Justice', p. 297.

39. 'The Golden Rule in the Light of New Insight', p. 222.

40. Strawson suggests that the diversity of individual ideals falls within the realm of the ethical, if not the moral; 'Social Morality and Individual Ideal', p. 4.

41. 'The Golden Rule in the Light of New Insight', p. 222.

42. *On Shame and the Search for Identity*, pp. 23–4.

43. Ibid., pp. 257, 227.

44. Ibid., p. 221.

45. Ibid., p. 236.

46. e.g. ibid., pp. 208, 230.

47. Ibid., p. 230.

48. *The Lonely Crowd*, p. 242. Part III of this book is concerned with a discussion of the notion of 'autonomy'.

49. Ibid., p. 263.

50. Ibid., pp. 301, 294. The entire concern with 'false personalization' (ibid., p. 261) and the bizarre suggestion of constructing 'indexes' to weight it (ibid., p. 273) must be seen in the context of Riesman's basic concern with letting the natural and spontaneous impulses of friendship, trust, affection, respect, etc., operate where the agent feels them, not where arbitrary convention prescribes them.

51. *Group Psychology and the Analysis of the Ego*, pp. 65 ff.

52. *Thus Spoke Zarathustra*, pp. 211–12. Thus, one can understand Nietzsche's conception of the Christian God of equality as a spider, *The Antichrist*, p. 585; interestingly, God appears as a spider to the psychotic heroine of Bergman's film, *Through a Glass Darkly*.

53. *Twilight of the Idols*, p. 535.

54. Ibid., p. 500.

55. *Beyond Good and Evil*, p. 124.

56. *Second Treatise of Government*, section 60, p. 326.

57. 'Morality and the Emotions', p. 18.

58. Consider the titles of several of his books, *Beyond Good and Evil*, *The Antichrist*, and his continual remarks about, for example, 'we immoralists', *Twilight of the Idols*, p. 500.

59. Thus, when Riesman uses his concept of autonomy largely to criticize patterns of other-directed conformity, which presumably dominate the areas of dress or eating or entertainment in American life (especially *The Lonely Crowd*, Part III), I wonder what the fuss is all about. If patterns of conformity dominate the area of the *morally* indifferent, then such conformity is morally unexceptionable. At best, in such a situation, one is only entitled to advise, on the basis of the supposed applicability of the principles of rational choice; and it is not *a priori* clear that human desires will be better satisfied one way than another. Indeed, in giving such advice, there is always the danger that one may be foisting his own special capacities and circumstances on others, something that seems quite likely in the case of Riesman's ideal of spontaneous creativity, which seems to me a dubious candidate for a *universally* satisfying end or ideal.

60. Thus, the entire point of Lynd's objection to guilt as 'primarily external and instrumental' (*On Shame and the Search for Identity*, p. 236) is that a substantive moral ideal must involve personal response to others as ends in themselves, which Lynd (wrongly) associates with shame, as opposed to guilt. Similarly, cf. Erikson's statement: 'My base line is the Golden Rule, which advocates that one should do (or not do) to another what one wishes to be (or not to be) done by' ('The Golden Rule in the Light of New Insight', p. 220). And Riesman's concept of autonomy, while, as stated, it has non-egalitarian, élitist implications, is clearly used by him in a way that supposes such a 'human need for active participation in a creative task' (*The Lonely Crowd*, p. 263) to belong equally to men, as persons.

61. Another ground is provided by the principle of moral development, to be presented shortly.

62. Consider White's remark: 'a campus Don Juan reduces his sexual drive while also congratulating himself on the success of his technique of seduction', 'Competence and the Psychosexual Stages of Development', p. 7.

63. On this, see White, *Ego and Reality in Psychoanalytic Theory*, pp. 6–10, 154–6.

64. The common neo-Freudian way in which to fill the gap left in Freud's theory, by its failure adequately to account for competence desires, was to grant that such desires *operated* independently of Freud's three drives, but then to claim that such competence desires *epigenetically* developed from Freud's three drives by mechanisms of 'delibidinization' and 'deaggressification'. This is, of course, Hartmann's influential theory of secondary autonomy (on Hartmann's theory, see Merton Gill, 'The Present State of Psychoanalytic Theory', especially p. 2, and David Rapaport, 'A Historical Survey of Psychoanalytic Ego Psychology', pp. 12–14), which Erikson employs as a theoretical stopgap, *Childhood and Society*, pp. 95–6. However, considerable evidence from studies of children (especially, here, the work of Piaget) and animal behaviour has invalidated such theories, for desires for competent exercise of various capacities were found to exist prior to any possibility of their development from Freud's three drives (on this, see White, *Ego and Reality in Psychoanalytic Theory*, chapter 3).

65. See ibid., pp. 129 ff. And by implication, White has clarified the distinctive nature of shame, in so far as it depends on the existence of self-respect and -esteem. For White's excellent discussion of the latter two attitudes, see ibid., chapter 7.

66. In his more recent work, e.g. 'Human Strength and the Cycle of Generations', Erikson seems to accept White's view; in Book 10 of the *Nicomachean Ethics*, Aristotle seems to me to be discussing White's concept exactly; cf. Kant's notion of 'Respect for the moral law' (*Critique of Practical Reason*, p. 76), which he constantly attempts to distinguish from 'the faculty of desire of rational finite beings' (ibid., p. 114)—an attempt which may be viewed as an exaggerated distortion of White's distinction between Freudian drives and independent competence desires; cf., also, Kant's remark that 'we ultimately take a liking to that the observation of which makes us feel that our powers of knowledge are extended' (ibid., p. 164), where Kant quite explicitly postulates a desire for intellectual competence, 'the store of talents which are elevated above the mere animal level' (ibid.); and Nietzsche's notion of a 'will to mastery' (*Twilight of the Idols*, p. 512) seems to express White's concept exactly.

67. Piaget, *Moral Judgment of the Child*, and Kohlberg, 'The Development of Children's Orientation Towards a Moral Order'; 'Moral Development and Identification'; 'Development of Moral Character and Moral Ideology'. For Freud, morality emerged through resolution of the Oedipus Complex. The male child develops pregenital longings for his mother and hate for his father, since his father sleeps with the mother, thus frustrating the child's libidinal desires. This 'economically difficult situation' (*Civilization and its Discontents*, p. 76) is resolved through repression of the son's aggression against his father and the internalization of that aggression in the child's superego, which now accepts the father's proscription of incest, thus inhibiting the child's libidinal desires. Freud regards this method of drive resolution, on

which 'the beginnings of religion, morals, society, and art converge' (*Totem and Taboo*, p. 156), as inherited by Lamarckian transmission from a primal horde situation where the guilty sons of the original Adam resolve their guilt for killing their father (in order to get sexual access to the women of the tribe, heretofore hoarded by the father) by accepting the incest taboo (see *Totem and Taboo*). Erikson's views on moral development have evolved over time, and receive their most advanced statement in his 'The Golden Rule in the Light of New Insight', where he divides moral development into three stages—moralism, ideology, and ethics. Erikson goes beyond Freud in introducing the latter two stages of moral development; but, his basic conception of guilt derives from his view that the sense of guilt emerges in the third psycho-sexual stage, initiative versus guilt (e.g. pp. 225 ff., *Childhood and Society*, and pp. 74 ff., *Identity and the Life Cycle*), as a psychological resolution of the Oedipus Complex, with the superego emerging as the binder of man's aggressive energies, beginning with the child's primitive rage at the frustration of his pregenital maternal love by the all-powerful father.

68. See, for example, Kohlberg, 'The Development of Children's Orientation Toward a Moral Order', pp. 11 f.; also, see 'Moral Development and Identification', for an extensive critique, by appeal to experimental data, of Freudian theory.

69. 'The Development of Children's Orientation Toward a Moral Order', p. 11.

70. *Moral Judgment of the Child*, pp. 228, 174.

71. Thus, see ibid., pp. 191 f., 287, 294, 324, 336, 366; and Erikson, 'The Golden Rule in the Light of New Insight', pp. 223–4, where Erikson outlines his concept of moralism, which is quite similar to that Piaget is here discussing.

72. e.g. *Moral Judgment of the Child*, pp. 30–4, 51, 52, 87, 88, 196, 318.

73. *Ego and Reality in Psychoanalytic Theory*, chapter 6.

74. See R. Brown, *Social Psychology*, pp. 399–401.

75. *Moral Judgment of the Child*, pp. 138, 110.

76. Ibid., pp. 35–6, 111.

77. Ibid., p. 111. Piaget was later to develop explicit stages of intellectual development. For a lucid discussion, see Brown, *Social Psychology* chapter 5.

78. *Moral Judgment of the Child*, pp. 95–6, 98. The sense of objectivity includes intersubjective validation generally. Thus, he views there as being a necessary psychological relation between the evolution of scientific and moral attitudes in the child; for discussions of the relations between the theoretical and practical judgement, see ibid., pp. 64, 85, 86, 113–14, 116–20, 136–7, 145, 174–5, 176, 184, 274. For a development of the

concept of moral equality, based on Piaget, see J. Rawls, 'The Sense of Justice', pp. 281 ff.; and, for rather different developments of the concept of equality, see B. Williams, 'The Idea of Equality', and Wasserstrom, 'Rights, Human Rights, and Racial Discrimination', p. 637. On the latter, cf. Feinberg's plausible critique, 'Wasserstrom on Rights', p. 644.

79. *Moral Judgment of the Child*, p. 70.

80. Ibid., p. 96.

81. 'The Development of Moral Character and Moral Ideology', pp. 396-8.

82. Kohlberg, 'The Development of Children's Orientation Toward a Moral Order', pp. 13 ff.

83. See Brown, *Social Psychology*, pp. 211-14, for a lucid discussion of this; see also Piaget's early work, comprising more experimental results than theoretical analysis, *Language and Thought of the Child*.

84. See Kohlberg, 'The Development of Moral Character and Moral Ideology', pp. 409 ff.

85. As responses, confession behaviour and appeal to principles for self-judgement seem quite unrelated, ibid., p. 411. For a statement of the distinction between these kinds of guilt, see, especially, 'Moral Development of Identification', pp. 290 ff.

86. 'Development of Moral Character and Moral Ideology', p. 395.

87. Ibid., p. 406.

88. The rest of the construction is inferred from Kohlberg's work, and was suggested to me by Rawls, 'Sense of Justice'. The only part of it that is really implicit in Kohlberg is the interpretation of confessional guilt—see 'Moral Development and Identification', p. 302; also, 'Development of Moral Character and Moral Ideology', p. 414.

89. For similar suggestions of this psychological principle, see Sidgwick, *Methods of Ethics*, pp. 320, 433; Scheler, *The Nature of Sympathy*, pp. 102, 164; there would, in fact, seem to be a sound evolutionary explanation for the existence of such a psychological principle. If, for example, others' evident intentions of doing things for our good resulted in hate and aggression, the species could not long survive, given the importance of co-operation to human survival. Similarly, if such stimuli led to attitudinal indifference, human survival would not be advanced. The evolutionary adaptive response would clearly be some form of friendly feeling, leading to forms of co-operation.

90. 'The Development of Children's Orientation Toward a Moral Order', p. 28.

91. 'Development of Moral Character and Moral Ideology', p. 412; 'Moral Development and Identification', p. 292.

92. Piaget, *Moral Judgment of the Child*, pp. 65, 71, 74, 76, 325, 346, 363; see Rawls, 'Sense of Justice', pp. 291–3.

93. 'Moral Development and Identification', p. 294; 'The Development of Children's Orientation Toward a Moral Order', p. 28.

94. See 'Moral Development and Identification', pp. 288 ff.

95. e.g. 'Development of Moral Character and Moral Ideology', p. 413; 'Moral Development and Identification', p. 294.

96. 'Inner and Outer Space: Reflections on Womanhood', p. 594.

97. Another concern, which it seems plausible to impute to the contractors, is the relevance of psychological laws of attitude development to the question of which principles they will agree to as moral ones. Thus, it may be argued that one reason (among others) for agreeing to the principles of morality (which I have formulated) is that these principles somehow more easily cohere with the facts of human psychology than other principles, which may be more unnatural in the sense of putting more strain on human nature. While I respect the efforts of theorists to develop such a view (especially Rawls, see his *Theory of Justice*), I have not chosen myself to develop it, since it seems to me so easily to lend itself to circularity.

98. The principles of rationality would provide the other ground, in so far as the competences which are required for the moral life seem in large part also required for the prudent life (e.g. the development of intelligence, self-control, and the like).

99. See Kant, *Metaphysical Principles of Virtue, passim*.

CHAPTER 14

1. *Nicomachean Ethics*, 1176^{b}25–6, p. 287.

2. The relevant Platonic text here is *Republic*, Book IX, 580, line 24, to 583, line 12, pp. 354–8; cf. Plato's similar argument, *Philebus*, pp. 237–9, 375–7. The comparison of the arguments of the *Republic* and *Philebus* is a fruitful one, since the works represent earlier and later discussions by Plato of the theory of the good, in its relation to a person's ultimate choice of the good life. Of special interest is Plato's abandonment, in the *Philebus*, of the intuitionistic form-theory of the good found in the *Republic*, identifying the concept of the good, rather, with the self-sufficient object of men's rationally informed desires (e.g. *Philebus*, pp. 233–5, 355, 375, 397), a view later developed by Aristotle.

3. 'Moral Beliefs', pp. 98 ff.

4. Kant believes that the phenomenon of moral responsibility requires there to have been some sort of choice by noumenal selves of their whole character as phenomenal selves (see chapter 6, note 37, p. 310 above). Kant imagines that the noumenal self chooses his phenomenal self as

some *combination* of three characters—animality, humanity, and personality (*Religion Within the Limits of Reason Alone*, pp. 21 ff.). It is to the noumenal self, in making *this* choice, that the Categorical Imperative is addressed. Thus, one may understand the sense in which the Categorical Imperative is synthetic a priori (*Foundations of the Metaphysics of Morals*, pp. 38, 59, 65). Given that the imperative makes possible and true the proposition expressed by 'noumenal selves ought to choose the character with a good moral will', the proposition is not analytically true, since the noumenal selves, having absolute freedom, do not necessarily will the end of being moral. Not being analytic, the proposition is synthetic. And since the truth of the proposition does not seem a matter of contingent empirical fact, it is a priori as well.

5. Foot, 'Moral Beliefs', pp. 103–4.

6. e.g. *Grounds of Moral Judgement*, pp. 101–2, 135–40.

7. Foot, 'Moral Beliefs', pp. 98–9.

8. See on this, Weber, *The City*, Part 5.

9. Aristotle, *De Anima*, 433ᵃ29, p. 598; Kant, 'The sole objects of a practical reason are thus those of the good and the evil. By the former, one understands a necessary object of desire, and by the latter, a necessary object of aversion, both according to a principle of reason', *Critique of Practical Reason*, p. 60; see also, ibid., pp. 61, 63, 114; Sidgwick, 'a man's future good on the whole is what he would now desire and seek on the whole if all the consequences of all the different lines of conduct open to him were accurately foreseen and adequately realised in imagination at the present point of time', *Methods of Ethics*, pp. 111–12.

10. Thus, 'Having thus defined positive and negative interest, we have by implication defined the antithesis of good and evil; *a* being good in so far as interest is taken in it, and evil in so far as interest is taken in not-*a*', Perry, *General Theory of Value*; and, 'The main hypothesis that has been under consideration is this: that "good" has associated with the condition of answering to certain interests.' Ziff, *Semantic Analysis*, p. 247.

11. Findlay, *Values and Intentions*, chapter V, sections III–IV; Foot, 'Goodness and Choice'; Geach, 'Good and Evil'; Anscombe, *Intention*, pp. 72–8; Harrod, 'Utilitarianism Revised', pp. 138–47; and Hampshire, *Freedom of the Individual*, p. 41; Kenny, *Action, Emotion and Will*, pp. 91–7, 123, 144–5; Melden, *Free Action*, pp. 177–9; G. R. Grice, *Grounds of Moral Judgement*, pp. 187–90. Grice does not explicitly relate the good to facilitating ends, but rather to 'the proposition that some characteristic is possessed in a relatively high degree' (ibid., p. 188), but it seems implicit in his view that the relevant characteristic is understood relative to certain ends, as determined by a certain context of speech and thought. The relevance of the theory of rationality to the theory of the good was first suggested to me by Professor John Rawls.

12. Once such a propositional theory was given detail, it is not difficult to see how it could also be used to account for the speech acts in which 'good' is used and the moving appeal to action of use of this expression. Thus, as regards the use of 'good' in commending and praising—given the typical aims or intentions of commending (expressing approval of the high merits of a person, or his work, where there is typically some authoritative relation of superiority of the approver in reference to the person, or his work, which he is approving) and praising (expressing approval of the high merits of a person, or his work or accomplishment, in some respect), then it is not difficult to see how my propositional analysis of the use of 'good' in sentences like 'that was good work', 'you are a good man to have around', etc., can be used in accounting for the use of such sentences in commending or praising. Thus, in my view, the propositions expressed by such sentences, e.g. that the person's work is such as to satisfy rationally the desires of his employers in regard to such work, are of a kind which will indicate the merit in virtue of which the man is being commended or praised, in the appropriate circumstances; and thus, such propositions can be used in accomplishing the speech act, and indeed provide the grounds for making it. Similarly, the concept of the bad or evil, explicated as equivalent to conducing to the frustration of rational desire, can be analogously shown to be appropriately used in the speech act of blaming, in so far as this speech act has the typical aim of expressing disapproval for a person's demerit in some respect, given responsibility for the fault in question. Further, my view will have no difficulty in accounting for the moving appeal to action of such utterances. Thus, when a person knows that x will be for his good, this theory will explain why such knowledge often has a moving appeal to his acting, i.e. x will rationally advance his desires, and people often have the natural attitude of rationality which implies the desire to be rational in pursuing their aims. In this, contrast the concept of the good with the concept of morality and the right: viz. in my view, the relation between the good and the agent's desires, at least in many contexts of the concept's employment, is analytic, so that the meaning analysis will itself elucidate the concept's moving appeal to action; whereas in the case of morality and the right, no similar analytic claim seems plausible; and I have thus had to relate the latter concept to theories of moral psychology, in order to show that the desire to be moral is wholly natural and unmysterious.

13. *Republic*, Book I, 343–5, line 30, pp. 72–4.

14. Cf. Grice's similar view, *Grounds of Moral Judgement*, pp. 183–7.

15. In his 'Extreme and Restricted Utilitarianism', especially pp. 173–4, 176–8, 182.

BIBLIOGRAPHY

(Where dates of original publication were known, works of each author have been listed in chronological order of publication date; otherwise, the order of works is alphabetical)

ACTON, H. B. 'The Ethical Importance of Sympathy', *Philosophy*, vol. xxx, no. 112 (January 1955), pp. 62–6.

ALEXANDER, PETER. 'Rational Behaviour and Psychoanalytic Explanation', *Mind*, vol. lxxi (1962), pp. 326–41.

ANSCOMBE, G. E. M. *Intention*. Cornell University Press: Ithaca, N.Y., 1963 (originally published, 1957).

—— 'Brute Facts', *Analysis* (January 1958), pp. 69–72.

—— 'Modern Moral Philosophy', *Philosophy*, vol. xxxiii, no. 124 (January 1958), pp. 1–19.

—— 'Pretending', *Proceedings of the Aristotelian Society*, supplementary volume xxxii (1958), pp. 279–94.

AQUINAS, ST. THOMAS. *On the Truth of the Catholic Faith: Summa Contra Gentiles*, Book III, 'Providence', Part I, translated, with an introduction and notes, by Vernon J. Bourke. Image Books, Doubleday & Co., Inc.: Garden City, N.Y., 1956.

—— *Selected Political Writings*, edited with an introduction by A. P. D. D'Entreves, and translated by J. G. Dawson. Basil Blackwell: Oxford, 1959.

ARISTOTLE. *De Anima*, translated by J. A. Smith, *The Basic Works of Aristotle*, pp. 534–603, edited and with an introduction by Richard McKeon. Random House: New York, 1941.

—— *Nicomachean Ethics*, translated, with introduction and notes, by Martin Ostwald. The Library of Liberal Arts, Bobbs-Merrill Co., Inc.: New York, 1962.

—— *Politics*, translated with an introduction, notes, and appendices by Ernest Barker. A Galaxy Book: New York, 1962.

ARROW, KENNETH J. *Social Choice and Individual Values*. John Wiley & Sons, Ltd.: New York, 1963 (originally published, 1951).

AUGUSTINE, ST. *City of God*. Two editions used: (i) an abridged version from translation by Walsh, Zema, Monahan, and Honan, Image Books: Garden City, N.Y., 1958; and (ii) complete version, translated by Marcus Dods. The Modern Library: New York, 1950.

AUSTIN, JOHN. *Lectures on Jurisprudence, or the Philosophy of Positive Law*, in two volumes, edited by Robert Campbell. John Murray: London. (Both 1869 and 1873 editions used.)

—— *The Province of Jurisprudence Determined*, with an introduction by H. L. A. Hart. Weidenfeld & Nicolson: London, 1954. (Comprising first six lectures of *Lectures on Jurisprudence*.)

AUSTIN, J. L. 'Other Minds', *Philosophical Papers*, edited by J. O. Urmson and G. J. Warnock, pp. 44–84. Oxford at the Clarendon Press, 1961 (first published, *Proceedings of the Aristotelian Society*, supplementary volume xx, 1946).

—— *How To Do Things With Words*. Harvard University Press: Cambridge, Mass., 1962.

AYER, A. J. *Language, Truth and Logic*. Victor Gollancz, Ltd.: London, 1936.

BAIER, KURT. *The Moral Point of View: a Rational Basis of Ethics*. Cornell University Press: Ithaca, N.Y., 1958.

—— 'Moral Obligation', *American Philosophical Quarterly*, vol. 3, no. 3 (July 1966), pp. 210–26.

BARRY, BRIAN. *Political Argument*. Routledge & Kegan Paul: London, 1965.

—— 'On Social Justice', *Oxford Review* (Trinity 1967), pp. 29–52.

BAUMOL, WILLIAM J. *Welfare Economics and the Theory of the State*. G. Bell & Sons, Ltd.: London, 1965 (originally published, 1952).

BECCARIA, CESARE. *On Crimes and Punishments*, translated, with an introduction, by Henry Paolucci. The Library of Liberal Arts, The Bobbs-Merrill Co., Inc.: New York, 1963 (originally published, 1764).

BEDFORD, ERROL. 'Emotions', *Proceedings of the Aristotelian Society*, vol. lvii (1956–7), pp. 281–304.

BENEDICT, RUTH. *Chrysanthemum and the Sword: Patterns of Japanese Culture*. Houghton Mifflin Co.: Boston, Mass., 1946.

BENN, S. I., and R. S. PETERS. *Social Principles and the Democratic State*, George Allen & Unwin Ltd.: London, 1959.

BENNETT, JONATHAN. *Rationality: an Essay Towards an Analysis*. Routledge & Kegan Paul: London, 1964.

BENTHAM, JEREMY. *Principles of Morals and Legislation*. Hafner Library: New York, 1948 (originally published, 1789).

—— 'Anarchical Fallacies', *The Works of Jeremy Bentham*, Book II, pp. 491–529, published under the superintendence of Bentham's executor, John Bowring, Edinburgh, 1843.

—— *The Theory of Fictions*, edited by C. K. Ogden. Harcourt, Brace & Co.: New York, 1932.

—— *The Limits of Jurisprudence Defined*, edited by Charles Warren Everett. Columbia University Press: New York, 1945.

BERGSON, ABRAM. *The Economics of Soviet Planning*. Yale University Press: New Haven, Conn., and London, 1964.

BERLIN, ISAIAH. 'Equality as an Ideal', *Justice and Social Policy*, pp. 128–50, edited with an introduction by Frederick A. Olafson. Prentice-Hall, Inc.: Englewood Cliffs, N.J., 1961 (originally published, *Proceedings of the Aristotelian Society*, vol. 56, 1955–6).

—— 'Does Political Theory Still Exist?', *Philosophy, Politics and Society*, second series, pp. 1–33, edited by Peter Laslett and W. G. Runciman. Basil Blackwell: Oxford, 1962.

BLAKE, RALPH M. 'The Ground of Moral Obligation', *The International Journal of Ethics*, vol. xxxviii, no. 2 (January 1928), pp. 129–40.

BOAS, FRANZ. *Kwakiutl Ethnography*, edited and abridged, with an introduction by Helen Codere. University of Chicago Press: Chicago and London, 1966.

BRADLEY, MILTON. 'Chess, Checkers, Dominoes, Acey-Ducey', book of rules supplied by Milton Bradley Co. with its combined chess-checkers-dominoes set, 1944.

BRANDT, RICHARD B. 'The Definition of an "Ideal Observer" Theory in Ethics', *Philosophy and Phenomenological Research* (March 1955), pp. 407–13.

—— 'Some Comments on Professor Firth's Reply', *Philosophy and Phenomenological Research* (March 1955), pp. 422–3.

—— *Ethical Theory*. Prentice-Hall, Inc.: Engelwood Cliffs, N.J., 1959.

—— 'Towards a Credible Form of Utilitarianism', *Morality and the Language of Conduct*, pp. 107–43, edited by Hector-Neri Castaneda and George Nakhnikian. Wayne State University Press: Detroit, 1963.

—— 'The Concepts of Obligation and Duty', *Mind*, vol. lxxiii, no. 291 (July 1965), pp. 374–93.

BROAD, C. D. 'On the Function of False Hypotheses in Ethics', *International Journal of Ethics*, xxvi (April 1916), pp. 377–97.

—— *Five Types of Ethical Theory*. Littlefield, Adams, and Co.: Paterson, N.J., 1959 (originally published, 1930).

—— 'Some Reflections on Moral–Sense Theories in Ethics', *Readings in Ethical Theory*, pp. 363–88, edited by Wilfred Sellars and John Hospers. Appleton-Century-Crofts, Inc.: New York, 1952 (originally published, *Proceedings of the Aristotelian Society*, vol. 45, 1944–5).

BROWN, ROGER. *Social Psychology*. The Free Press: New York, 1965.

BUCHANAN, JAMES M., and GORDON TULLOCK. *The Calculus of Consent: Logical Foundations of Constitutional Democracy*. The University of Michigan Press: Ann Arbor, 1962.

BUTLER, BISHOP JOSEPH. *Sermons*, as excerpted in *Ethical Theories*, edited by A. I. Melden. Prentice-Hall, Inc.: Engelwood Cliffs, N.J., 1955 (first published, 1726).

CAMPBELL, ROBERT W. *Soviet Economic Power*. The Houghton Mifflin Company: Cambridge, Mass., 1960.

CARE, NORMAN. 'On Avowing Reasons', *Mind*, vol. lxxvi, no. 302 (April 1967), pp. 208–16.

CARRITT, E. F. *Ethical and Political Thinking*. Oxford at the Clarendon Press, 1947.

CAVELL, STANLEY. 'Must We Mean What We Say?', *Ordinary Language*, pp. 75–112, edited by V. C. Chappell. Prentice-Hall, Inc.: Englewood Cliffs, N.J., 1964 (first published, *Inquiry*, vol. i, 1958).

CHISHOLM, RODERICK M. 'Supererogation and Offence: a Conceptual Scheme for Ethics', *Ratio*, vol. v, no. 1 (June 1963), pp. 1–14.

CICERO, MARCUS TULLIUS. *Laws*, translated by C. W. Keyes. Loeb Classical Library, Harvard University Press: Cambridge, Mass., 1961.

D'ARCY, ERIC. *Human Acts: an Essay in their Moral Evaluation*. Oxford at the Clarendon Press, 1963.

DECARTES, RENÉ. *The Passions of the Soul, Philosophical Works of Descartes*, vol. i, translated by Haldane and Ross. Dover Publications, Inc., 1955 (originally published, 1649).

DEVLIN, PATRICK. 'Morals and the Criminal Law', *The Enforcement of Morals*, pp. 1–25. Oxford University Press: London, 1965.

DIGGS, B. J. 'A Technical Ought', *Mind*, vol. lxix, no. 275 (July 1960), pp. 301–17.

DORFMAN, ROBERT. *The Price System*. Prentice-Hall, Inc.: Engelwood Cliffs, N.J., 1964.

DOWNS, ANTHONY. *An Economic Theory of Democracy*. Harper & Row: New York, 1957.

EISENBERG, PAUL D. 'From the Forbidden to the Supererogatory: the Basic Ethical Categories in Kant's *Tugendlehre*', *American Philosophical Quarterly*, vol. 3, no. 4 (October 1966), pp. 255–69.

ERIKSON, ERIK. *Childhood and Society*, second edition. W. W. Norton & Co., Inc.: New York, 1963 (originally published, 1950).

—— 'The Problem of Ego Identity', *Identity and the Life Cycle*, pp. 101–64, *Psychological Issues*, vol. i, no. 1, monograph 1. International Universities Press, Inc.: New York, 1959.

—— *Young Man Luther*. W. W. Norton & Co., Inc.: New York, 1962.

—— 'The Golden Rule in the Light of New Insight', *Insight and Responsibility: Lectures in the Ethical Implications of Psychoanalytic Thought*, pp. 219–43. W. W. Norton & Co., Inc.: New York, 1964.

—— 'Human Strength and the Cycle of Generations', ibid., pp. 111–57.

—— 'Inner and Outer Space: Reflections on Womanhood', *Daedalus* (Spring 1964).

EWING, A. C. *The Definition of Good*. The Macmillan Co.: New York, 1947.

FALK, W. D. 'Morals without Faith', *Philosophy*, vol. xix, no. 72 (April 1944), pp. 3–18.

—— 'Obligation and Rightness', *Philosophy*, vol. xx, no. 76 (July 1945), pp. 129–47.

—— ' "Ought" and Motivation', *Readings in Ethical Theory*, pp. 492–517, selected and edited by Wilfred Sellars and John Hospers. Appleton-Century-Crofts, Inc.: New York, 1952 (originally published, *Proceedings of the Aristotelian Society*, vol. 48, 1947–8).

FEINBERG, JOEL. 'Supererogation and Rules', *Ethics*, vol. lxxi, no. 4 (July 1961), pp. 276–88.

—— 'Justice and Personal Desert', *Nomos VI: Justice*, edited by Carl J. Friedrich and John W. Chapman. Atherton Press: New York, 1963.

—— 'Wasserstrom on Rights', *Journal of Philosophy*, vol. lxi, no. 20 (October 1964), pp. 641–5.

—— 'Duties, Rights, and Claims', *American Philosophical Quarterly*, vol. 3, no. 2 (April 1966), pp. 137–44.

FINDLAY, J. N. *Values and Intentions*. George Allen & Unwin, Ltd.: London, 1961.

FIRTH, RODERICK. 'Ethical Absolutism and the Ideal Observer', *Philosophy and Phenomenological Research* (March 1952), pp. 317–45.

FIRTH, RODERICK. 'Reply to Professor Brandt', *Philosophy and Pheno-menological Research* (March 1955), pp. 414–21.

FOOT, PHILIPPA. 'When Is a Principle a Moral Principle?', symposium with Jonathan Harrison, *Proceedings of the Aristotelian Society*, supplementary volume xxviii (1954), pp. 95–110.

—— 'Moral Arguments', *Mind*, vol. lxvii, no. 268 (October 1958). pp. 502–13.

—— 'Moral Beliefs', *Proceedings of the Aristotelian Society*, vol. lix (1958–9), pp. 83–104.

—— 'Goodness and Choice', ibid., supplementary volume xxv (1961), pp. 45–60.

FRANK, JEROME. *Law and the Modern Mind.* Anchor Books, Doubleday & Co., Inc.: Garden City, N.Y., 1963 (originally published, 1930).

FRANKENA, WILLIAM K. 'The Naturalistic Fallacy', *Readings in Ethical Theory*, pp. 103–14, selected and edited by Wilfrid Sellars and John Hospers. Appleton-Century-Crofts, Inc.: New York, 1952 (originally published, *Mind*, vol. 48, 1939).

—— 'Obligation and Motivation in Recent Moral Philosophy', *Essays in Moral Philosophy*, pp. 40–81, edited by A. I. Melden. University of Washington Press: Seattle, 1958.

—— 'The Concept of Social Justice', *Social Justice*, pp. 1–29, edited by Richard B. Brandt. Prentice-Hall Inc.: Englewood Cliffs, N.J., 1962.

—— 'Recent Conceptions of Morality', *Morality and the Language of Conduct*, pp. 1–21, edited by Hector-Neri Castaneda and George Nakhnikian. Wayne State University Press: Detroit, 1963.

FREUD, SIGMUND. *Three Contributions to the Theory of Sex*, translated by A. A. Brill. Dutton & Co.: New York, 1962 (first published, 1905).

—— *Totem and Taboo*, translated by James Strachey. W. W. Norton and Co.: New York, 1950 (first published, 1913).

—— *Group Psychology and the Analysis of the Ego*, translated by James Strachey. Bantam Books: New York, 1960 (first published, 1921).

—— *The Ego and the Id*, translated by Joan Riviere, edited by James Strachey. Anchor Books: Garden City, N.Y., 1960 (first published, 1923).

—— *Civilization and its Discontents*, translated and edited by James Strachey. W. W. Norton & Co., Inc.: New York, 1961 (first published, 1930).

—— *New Introductory Lectures on Psychoanalysis*, translated by W. J. H. Sprott. W. W. Norton & Co., Inc.: New York, 1933 (first published, 1932).

FRIEDRICH, CARL JOACHIM. *Philosophy of Law in Historical Perspective.* University of Chicago Press: Chicago, 1958.

FULLER, LON L. 'Positivism and Fidelity to Law—a Reply to Professor Hart', *Harvard Law Review*, vol. 71, no. 4 (February 1958), pp. 630–72.

—— *The Morality of Law.* Yale University Press: New Haven, Conn., and London, 1964.

GAUTHIER, DAVID P. *Practical Reasoning*. Oxford at the Clarendon Press, 1963.
—— 'Morality and Advantage', *Philosophical Review*, vol. lxxvi (October 1967), pp. 460–75.
GEACH, P. T. 'Good and Evil', *Analysis*, vol. 17, no. 2 (December 1956), pp. 33–42.
—— *Mental Acts: their Content and their Objects*. Routledge & Kegan Paul: London, 1957.
—— 'Ascriptivism', *Philosophical Review*, vol. lxix, no. 2 (April 1960), pp. 221–5.
—— 'Assertion', ibid., vol. lxxiv, no. 4 (October 1965), pp. 449–65.
GEWIRTH, ALAN. 'Political Justice', *Social Justice*, pp. 119–69, edited by Richard B. Brandt. Prentice-Hall, Inc.: Englewood Cliffs, N.J., 1962.
GILL, MERTON. 'The Present State of Psychoanalytic Theory', *Journal of Abnormal and Social Psychology*, vol. 58, no. 1 (January 1959).
GILL, RICHARD T. *Economic Development: Past and Present*. Prentice-Hall, Inc.: Englewood Cliffs, N.J., 1964.
GOFFMAN, ERVING. 'On Face-Work', *Psychiatry: Journal for the Study of Interpersonal Processes*, vol. 18, no. 3 (August 1955).
—— 'Embarrassment and Social Organization', *American Journal of Sociology*, vol. 62 (1956–7), pp. 264–71.
GRAY, JOHN CHIPMAN. *The Nature and Sources of the Law*. The Macmillan Co.: New York, 1921.
GREEN, THOMAS HILL. *Lectures on the Principles of Political Obligation*. Longmans, Green & Co.: New York, 1917 (first published, as part of the complete works, 1885–8).
GRICE, GEOFFREY RUSSELL. *The Grounds of Moral Judgement*. Cambridge at the University Press, 1967.
GRICE, H. P. 'Meaning', *Philosophical Review*, vol. lxvii, no. 3 (July 1957), pp. 377–88.
GROTIUS, HUGO. *De Jure Belli et Pacis*, translated by William Whewell. John W. Parker: London, 1853 (first published, 1625).
HAMPSHIRE, STUART. *Thought and Action*. Chatto & Windus: London, 1960 (first published, 1959).
—— *Freedom of the Individual*. Chatto & Windus: London, 1965.
HARE, R. M. *The Language of Morals*. A Galaxy Book, Oxford University Press: New York, 1964 (originally published, 1952).
—— 'Descriptivism', *Proceedings of the British Academy*, vol. xlix, pp. 115–34. Oxford University Press: London, 1963.
—— *Freedom and Reason*. Oxford at the Clarendon Press, 1963.
—— 'The Promising Game', *Theories of Ethics*, pp. 115–27, edited by Philippa Foot. Oxford University Press, Oxford, 1967 (first published, *Revue Internationale de Philosophie*, no. 70, 1964).
—— 'Peace', the Sixth Annual Lecture of the Research Students' Association given at Canberra on 19 July 1966, the Australian National University, Canberra, 1966.

HARRISON, JONATHAN. 'Utilitarianism, Universalization, and Our Duty to Be Just', *Justice and Social Policy*, pp. 55–79, edited with an introduction by Frederick A. Olafson. Prentice-Hall, Inc.: Englewood Cliffs, N.J., 1961 (first published, *Proceedings of the Aristotelian Society*, vol. 52, 1952–3).
—— 'When Is a Principle a Moral Principle?', symposium with Philippa Foot, *Proceedings of the Aristotelian Society*, supplementary volume xxviii (1954), pp. 111–34.
HARROD, R. F. 'Utilitarianism Revised', *Mind*, vol. xlv, no. 178 (April 1936), pp. 137–56.
HARSANYI, JOHN C. 'Cardinal Utility in Welfare Economics and in the Theory of Risk-Taking', *The Journal of Political Economy*, vol. lxi, no. 5 (October 1953), pp. 434–5.
—— 'Cardinal Welfare, Individualistic Ethics, and Interpersonal Comparisons of Utility', *The Journal of Political Economy*, vol. lxiii, no. 4 (August 1955), pp. 309–21.
—— 'Ethics in Terms of Hypothetical Imperatives', *Mind*, vol. lxvii, no. 267 (July 1958), pp. 305–16.
HART, H. L. A. 'Are There Any Natural Rights?', *Philosophical Review*, vol. lxiv, no. 2 (April 1955), pp. 175–91.
—— 'Legal and Moral Obligation', *Essays in Moral Philosophy*, pp. 82–107, edited by A. I. Melden. University of Washington Press: Seattle, 1958.
—— 'Legal Responsibility and Excuses', *Determinism and Freedom in the Age of Science*, pp. 81–104, a philosophical symposium edited by Sidney Hook. New York University Press: Washington Square, 1958.
—— 'Murder and the Principles of Punishment: England and the United States', *Northwestern University Law Review*, vol. 52, no. 4 (1958).
—— 'Positivism and the Separation of Law and Morals', *Harvard Law Review*, vol. 71, no. 4 (February 1958), pp. 593–629.
—— and A. M. HONORÉ. *Causation in the Law*. Oxford at the Clarendon Press, 1959.
—— *The Concept of Law*. Oxford at the Clarendon Press, 1961.
—— 'Prolegomenon to the Principles of Punishment', *Philosophy, Politics and Society*, second series, pp. 158–82, edited by Peter Laslett and W. G. Runciman. Basil Blackwell: Oxford, 1962.
—— 'Kelsen Revisited', *U.C.L.A. Law Review*, vol. 10, no. 4 (May 1963), pp. 709–28.
—— *Law, Liberty and Morality*. Stanford University Press: Stanford, Calif., 1963.
—— 'Intention and Punishment', *The Oxford Review*, no. 4 (Hilary 1967), pp. 5–22.
—— 'Varieties of Responsibility', *The Law Quarterly Review*, vol. 83, (July 1967), pp. 846–64.
HEMPEL, CARL J. 'Rational Action', *Proceedings of the American Philosophical Association* (1961–2), pp. 5–23.

HITCH, CHARLES J., and ROLAND N. McKEAN. *The Economics of Defense in the Nuclear Age*. Harvard University Press: Cambridge, Mass., 1960.

HOBBES, THOMAS. *Leviathan*, edited, with an introduction, by Michael Oakeshott. Basil Blackwell: Oxford, 1960 (originally published, 1651).

HOHFELD, WESLEY NEWCOMB. *Fundamental Legal Conceptions*, edited by Walter Wheeler Cook, with a new foreword by Arthur L. Corbin. Yale University Press: New Haven, Conn., and London, 1946 (first published, 1923).

HOLMES, OLIVER WENDELL. 'The Path of the Law', *Collected Legal Papers*, pp. 167–202. Harcourt, Brace & Co.: New York, 1952 (first published, *Harvard Law Review*, vol. 10, 1897).

HUME, DAVID. *A Treatise of Human Nature*, edited, with an analytical index, by L. A. Selby-Bigge. Oxford at the Clarendon Press, 1964 (originally published, 1739–40).

—— 'Of the Original Contract', *Hume: Theory of Politics*, pp. 193–214, edited by Frederick Watkins. Thomas Nelson & Sons, Ltd.: London, 1951 (originally published, 1741).

—— *An Enquiry Concerning the Principles of Morals*, in *Enquiries*, edited with introduction by L. A. Selby-Bigge. Oxford at the Clarendon Press, 1902 (originally published, 1751).

ISENBERG, ARNOLD. 'Natural Pride and Natural Shame', *Philosophy and Phenomenological Research*, vol. x, no. 1 (September 1949), pp. 1–24.

KANT, IMMANUEL. 'What Is Enlightenment?', *Foundations of the Metaphysics of Morals*, pp. 85–92, translated by Lewis W. Beck. Liberal Arts Press: New York, 1959 (originally published, 1784).

—— *Foundations of the Metaphysics of Morals*, translated by Lewis W. Beck. Liberal Arts Press: New York, 1959 (originally published, 1785).

—— *Critique of Practical Reason*, translated, with an introduction, by Lewis White Beck. Liberal Arts Press, The Bobbs-Merrill Co., Inc.: New York, 1956 (originally published, 1788).

—— *Critique of Judgement*, translated, with analytical indexes, by James Creed Meredith. Oxford at the Clarendon Press, 1952 (originally published, 1790).

—— 'Concerning the Common Saying: This May Be True In Theory, But Does Not Apply In Practice', *Society, Law, and Morality*, pp. 159–72, edited, with introductions, by Frederick A. Olafson. Prentice-Hall, Inc.: Englewood Cliffs, N.J., 1961 (originally published, 1793).

—— *Religion Within the Limits of Reason Alone*, translated, with an introduction and notes, by Theodore M. Greene and Hoyt H. Hudson. Harper Torchbooks, Harper & Row: New York, Evanston, and London, 1960 (originally published, 1793).

—— *Perpetual Peace, On History*, pp. 85–135, edited, with an introduction, by Lewis White Beck, translated by L. W. Beck, R. E. Anchor, and E. L. Fackenheim. Library of Liberal Arts, The Bobbs-Merrill Co., Inc.: New York, 1963 (originally published, 1795).

KANT, IMMANUEL. *The Metaphysical Elements of Justice*, translated, with an introduction, by John Ladd. The Library of Liberal Arts, The Bobbs-Merrill Co., Inc.: New York, 1965 (originally published, 1797).
—— *The Metaphysical Principles of Virtue*, translated by James Ellington. The Library of Liberal Arts, The Bobbs-Merrill Co., Inc.: New York, 1964 (originally published, 1797).
—— 'On a Supposed Right to Tell Lies from Benevolent Motives', *Kant's Critique of Practical Reason and Other Works on the Theory of Ethics*, pp. 361–6, translated by T. K. Abbott. Longmans, Green & Co.: London, 1883 (originally published, 1797).
—— 'On the Saying "Necessity Has No Law"', ibid., pp. 365–6 (originally published, 1797).
KELSEN, HANS. *General Theory of Law and State*, translated by Anders Wedberg. Harvard University Press: Cambridge, Mass., 1945.
—— *Theorie Pure Du Droit*, traduction française par Charles Eisenmann. Dalloz: Paris, 1962.
KENNY, ANTHONY. *Action, Emotion and Will*. Routledge & Kegan Paul: London, 1963.
KNEALE, WILLIAM. 'Objectivity in Morals', *Readings in Ethical Theory*, pp. 681–97, selected and edited by Wilfrid Sellars and John Hospers. Appleton-Century-Crofts, Inc.: New York, 1952 (first published, *Philosophy*, vol. 25, 1950).
KOHLBERG, LAWRENCE, 'The Development of Children's Orientations Toward a Moral Order', *Vita Humana* (1963), pp. 11–33.
—— 'Moral Development and Identification', *Child Psychology*, pp. 277–332, the Sixty-Second Yearbook of the National Society for the Study of Education. University of Chicago Press: Chicago, 1963.
—— 'The Development of Moral Character and Moral Ideology', *Review of Child Development Research*, vol. i, pp. 383–431. Russell Sage Foundation: New York, 1964.
KOOPMANS, TJALLING C. *Three Essays on the State of Economic Science*. McGraw-Hill Book Co.: New York, 1957.
LANGE, O., and F. M. TAYLOR. *On the Economic Theory of Socialism*. University of Minnesota Press: Minneapolis, 1938.
LEMMON, E. J. 'Moral Dilemmas', *Philosophical Review*, vol. lxxi, no. 2 (April 1962), pp. 139–58.
LERNER, A. P. *The Economics of Control*. Macmillan: New York, 1946.
LEWIS, DAVID. *Convention: a Philosophical Study*. Harvard University Press: Cambridge, Mass., 1969.
LITTLE, I. M. D. *A Critique of Welfare Economics*. Oxford Paperbacks, Oxford at the Clarendon Press, 1960 (first published, 1950).
—— 'Social Choice and Individual Values', *Journal of Political Economy*, vol. lx, no. 5 (October 1952), pp. 422–32.
LLEWELLYN, K. N. *The Bramble Bush: On Our Law and Its Study*. Oceana Publications: New York, 1960 (first published, 1930).
LOCKE, JOHN. *Second Treatise of Government*, in *Locke's Two Treatises of Government*, edited by Peter Laslett. Cambridge at the University Press, 1960 (originally published, 1690).

—— *Essays on the Law of Nature*, edited by W. von Leyden. Oxford at the Clarendon Press, 1958.

LOCKWOOD, W. W. *The Economic Development of Japan: Growth and Structural Change, 1869–1938*. Princeton University Press: Princeton, N.J., 1954.

LUCE, R. DUNCAN, and HOWARD RAIFFA. *Games and Decisions: Introduction and Critical Survey*. John Wiley & Sons, Ltd.: New York, 1957.

LYND, HELEN. *On Shame and the Search for Identity*. Science Editions, Inc.: New York, 1956.

LYONS, DAVID. *Forms and Limits of Utilitarianism*. Oxford at the Clarendon Press, 1965.

MABBOTT, J. D. 'Punishment', *Justice and Social Policy*, pp. 39–54, edited, with an introduction, by Frederick A. Olafson. Prentice-Hall, Inc.: Englewood Cliffs, N.J., 1961 (first published, *Mind*, vol. xlix, 1939).

—— 'Reason and Desire', *Philosophy*, vol. xxviii, no. 105 (April 1953), pp. 113–23.

—— 'Prudence', *Proceedings of the Aristotelian Society*, supplementary volume xxxvi (1962), pp. 51–64.

MACPHERSON, C. B. *The Political Theory of Possessive Individualism*. Oxford at the Clarendon Press, 1962.

MARCH, JAMES G., and HERBERT A. SIMON. *Organizations*. John Wiley & Sons, Inc.: New York, 1958.

MARX, KARL. *Karl Marx: Early Writings* (*On the Jewish Question, Contribution to the Critique of Hegel's Philosophy of Right, Economic and Philosophical Manuscripts of 1844*), translated and edited by T. B. Bottomore. C. A. Watts & Co., Ltd.: London, 1963 (works originally published, 1844, 1844, 1932).

—— and FREDERICK ENGELS. *The German Ideology*, Parts I and III, edited, with an introduction, by R. Pascal. International Publishers: New York, 1947 (first published in full, 1932).

MCILWAIN, CHARLES HOWARD. *Growth of Political Thought in the West*. Macmillan: New York, 1932.

—— *Constitutionalism: Ancient and Modern*. Great Seal Books, Cornell University Press: New York, 1947 (first published, 1940).

MCKEAN, ROLAND N., and CHARLES J. HITCH. *The Economics of Defense in the Nuclear Age*. Harvard University Press: Cambridge, Mass., 1960.

MCTAGGART, J. M. E. *Studies in Hegelian Cosmology*. Cambridge at the University Press, 1901.

MEAD, MARGARET. *Cooperation and Competition Among Primitive Peoples*. Beacon Press: Boston, Mass., 1961 (first published, 1937).

—— 'Some Anthropological Considerations Concerning Guilt', *Anthropology: a Human Science*, pp. 198–212. Van Nostrand Co.: Princeton, N.J., 1964 (first published, 1950, in Reynert, *Feelings and Emotions*, pp. 362–73).

MEADE, J. E. *Efficiency, Equality, and the Ownership of Property*. George Allen & Unwin Ltd.: London, 1964.

MELDEN, A. I. *Free Action*. Routledge & Kegan Paul: London, 1961.

MILL, JOHN STUART. *A System of Logic*. Longmans, Green & Co., Ltd.: London, 1961 (originally published, 1843).

—— *Utilitarianism*, in *Utilitarianism, Liberty, and Representative Government*, introduction by A. D. Lindsay. J. M. Dent & Sons, Ltd.: London, 1951 (originally published, 1863).

MILNOR, JAMES. 'Games Against Nature', *Game Theory and Related Approaches to Social Behaviour*, pp. 120–31, edited by Martin Shubik. John Wiley & Sons, Inc.: New York, 1964 (first published, 1954, Thrall, Coombs, and Davis, eds., *Decision Processes*, pp. 49–59).

MISCHEL, THEODORE. 'Concerning Rational Behaviour and Psychoanalytic Explanation', *Mind*, vol. lxxiv, no. 293 (January 1965), pp. 71–8.

MOORE, G. E. *Principia Ethica*. Cambridge at the University Press, 1960 (originally published, 1903).

—— *Ethics*. A Galaxy Book, Oxford University Press: New York, 1965 (originally published, 1912).

—— 'A Reply to my Critics', *The Philosophy of G. E. Moore*, especially pp. 597–601, edited by Paul Arthur Schilpp. Northwestern University Press: Evanston, Ill., and Chicago, 1942.

NIETZSCHE, FRIEDRICH. *Beyond Good and Evil: Prelude to a Philosophy of the Future*, translated by Helen Zimmern. T. N. Foulis: Edinburgh and London, 1907 (first published, 1886).

—— *Twilight of the Idols, The Portable Nietzsche*, pp. 465–563, selected and translated with an introduction, prefaces, and notes, by Walter Kaufmann. The Viking Press: New York, 1954 (first published, 1889).

—— *Thus Spoke Zarathustra*, ibid., pp. 121–439 (first published, 1891).

—— *The Antichrist*, ibid., pp. 568–656 (first published, 1895).

NOWELL-SMITH, P. H. *Ethics*. Penguin Books: Harmondsworth, Middlesex, 1954.

OAKLEY, FRANCIS. 'Medieval Theories of Natural Law: William of Ockham and the Significance of the Voluntarist Tradition', *Natural Law Forum*, vol. vi, pp. 65–83. Notre Dame Law School, 1961.

OLSON, MANCUR. *The Logic of Collective Action: Public Goods and the Theory of Groups*. Harvard University Press: Cambridge, Mass., 1965.

PARETO, VILFREDO. *Manuel d'Economie Politique*, translated into French from Italian by Alfred Bonnet. Marcel Giard: Paris, 1927.

PAUL, G. A. 'The Problem of Guilt', *Proceedings of the Aristotelian Society*, supplementary volume xxi (1947), pp. 209–18.

PEARS, DAVID. 'Are Reasons for Action Causes?', *Epistemology: New Essays in the Theory of Knowledge*, pp. 204–28, edited by Avrum Stroll. Harper & Row: New York, 1967.

PERELMAN, CHAIM. *The Idea of Justice and the Problem of Argument*, with an introduction by H. L. A. Hart. The Humanities Press: New York, 1963 (first published, 1945).

PERRY, RALPH BARTON. *General Theory of Value*. Harvard University Press: Cambridge, Mass., 1954 (first published, 1926).

—— 'Value and Its Moving Appeal', *Philosophical Review*, vol. lxi, no. 4 (July 1932), pp. 337–50.

PETERS, R. S. *The Concept of Motivation*. Routledge & Kegan Paul: London, 1960.

PIAGET, JEAN. *The Language and Thought of the Child*, translated by Marjorie Gabain. Meridian: Cleveland, Ohio, 1963 (published originally, 1924).

—— *The Moral Judgment of the Child*, translated by Marjorie Gabain. Collier: New York, 1962 (published originally, 1932).

PIERS, GERHART, and MILTON B. SINGER. *Shame and Guilt: a Psychoanalytic and a Cultural Study*. Charles C. Thomas, Publisher: Springfield, Ill., 1953.

PLAMENATZ, JOHN. *Man and Society*, vol. i. Longmans, Green & Co.: London, 1963.

PLATO. *Crito*, translated by Hugh Tredennick, *Plato: the Collected Dialogues*, pp. 27–39, edited by Edith Hamilton and Huntington Cairns. Pantheon Books: New York, 1964.

—— *Euthyphro*, translated by Lane Cooper, ibid., pp. 169–85.

—— *Philebus, Plato: Statesman Philebus*, pp. 203–399, translated by Harold N. Fowler. Loeb Classical Library, Harvard University Press: Cambridge, Mass., 1962.

—— *The Republic*, translated with an introduction by H. D. P. Lee. Penguin Books: Harmondsworth, Middlesex, 1955.

PRICE, RICHARD. *A Review of the Principal Questions in Morals*, edited by D. Daiches Raphael. Oxford at the Clarendon Press, 1948 (originally published, 1758).

PRICHARD, H. A. 'Does Moral Philosophy Rest on a Mistake?', *Moral Obligation: Essays and Lectures*, pp. 1–17. Oxford at the Clarendon Press, 1949 (first published, *Mind*, vol. xxi, 1912).

—— 'Duty and Interest', *Readings in Ethical Theory*, pp. 469–86, edited by Wilfrid Sellars and John Hospers. Appleton-Century-Crofts, Inc.: New York, 1952 (originally delivered as Oxford inaugural lecture, 1928).

—— 'Duty and Ignorance of Fact', *Moral Obligation: Essays and Lectures*, pp. 18–39. Oxford at the Clarendon Press, 1949 (originally delivered as British Academy lecture, 1932).

—— 'Green's Principles of Political Obligation', ibid., pp. 54–86.

—— 'Moral Obligation', ibid., pp. 87–163.

—— 'The Obligation to Keep a Promise', ibid., pp. 169–79.

QUINE, W. V. 'Quantifiers and Propositional Attitudes', *The Journal of Philosophy*, vol. liii, no. 5 (March 1956), pp. 177–87.

RAPAPORT, DAVID. 'A Historical Survey of Psychoanalytic Ego Psychology', *Identity and the Life Cycle, Psychological Issues*, vol. i, no. 1, monograph 1, pp. 5–17. International Universities Press, Inc.: New York, 1959.

RAWLS, JOHN. 'Outline of a Decision Procedure for Ethics', *Philosophical Review*, vol. lx, no. 2 (April 1951), pp. 177–97.

RAWLS, JOHN. 'Two Concepts of Rules', *Philosophical Review*, vol. lxiv, no. 1 (January 1955), pp. 3–32.

—— 'Justice as Fairness', *Justice and Social Policy*, pp. 80–107, edited, with an introduction, by Frederick A. Olafson. Prentice-Hall, Inc.: Englewood Cliffs, N.J., 1961 (first published, *Philosophical Review*, vol. lxvii, 1958).

—— 'Constitutional Liberty and the Concept of Justice', *Nomos VI: Justice*, pp. 98–125, edited by Carl J. Friedrich and John W. Chapman. Atherton Press: New York, 1963.

—— 'The Sense of Justice', *Philosophical Review*, vol. lx, no. 2 (April 1963), pp. 281–305.

—— 'Legal Obligation and the Duty of Fair Play', *Law and Philosophy: a Symposium*, pp. 3–18, edited by Sidney Hook. New York University Press: New York, 1964.

—— 'Distributive Justice', *Philosophy, Politics and Society*, third series, pp. 58–82, edited by Peter Laslett and W. G. Runciman. Basil Blackwell: Oxford, 1967.

—— *A Theory of Justice*. Harvard University Press: Cambridge, Mass., 1971.

REDDAWAY, W. B. *The Development of the Indian Economy*. Richard D. Irwin, Inc.: Homewood, Ill., 1962.

RIESMAN, DAVID. *The Lonely Crowd*. Yale University Press: New Haven, Conn., and London, 1961 (first published, 1950).

ROSS, ALF. *On Law and Justice*. University of California Press: Berkeley and Los Angeles, 1959.

ROSS, W. D. *The Right and the Good*. Oxford at the Clarendon Press, 1930.

—— *Foundations of Ethics*. Oxford at the Clarendon Press, 1939.

ROTHENBERG, JEROME. *The Measurement of Social Welfare*. Prentice-Hall: Englewood Cliffs, N.J., 1961.

ROUSSEAU, JEAN-JACQUES. *The Social Contract*, in *The Social Contract and Discourses*, translated with an introduction by G. D. H. Cole. J. M. Dent & Sons, Ltd.: London, 1950 (originally published, 1762).

RUNCIMAN, W. G., and AMARTYA K. SEN. 'Games, Justice and the General Will', *Mind*, vol. lxxiv (1965), pp. 554–62.

—— *Relative Deprivation and Social Justice*. Routledge & Kegan Paul, Ltd.: London, 1966.

RYAN, ALAN. 'Locke and the Dictatorship of the Bourgeoisie', *Political Studies*, vol. xiii, no. 2 (June 1965), pp. 219–30.

RYLE, GILBERT. *The Concept of Mind*. Barnes & Noble: New York, 1949.

SARTE, JEAN-PAUL. *Being and Nothingness*, translated by Hazel E. Barnes. Philosophical Library: New York, 1956 (first published, 1943).

SCHELER, MAX. *The Nature of Sympathy*, translated from the German by Peter Heath, with a general introduction to Max Scheler's work by W. Stark. Routledge & Kegan Paul, Ltd.: London, 1954.

SCHELLING, THOMAS C. *The Strategy of Conflict*. A Galaxy Book, Oxford University Press: New York, 1963 (first published, 1960).

SEARLE, JOHN R. 'Meaning and Speech Acts', *Philosophical Review*, vol. lxxi, no. 4 (October 1962), pp. 423–32.
—— 'How to Derive "Ought" from "Is"', ibid., vol. lxxiii, no. 1 (January 1964), pp. 43–58.
SHKLAR, JUDITH N. *Legalism*. Harvard University Press: Cambridge, Mass., 1964.
SIBLEY, W. H. 'The Rational vs. the Reasonable', *Philosophical Review*, vol. lxii, no. 4 (October 1953), pp. 554–60.
SIDGWICK, HENRY. *The Methods of Ethics*, seventh edition. Macmillan & Co., Ltd.: London, 1963 (originally published, 1874).
—— *The Principles of Political Economy*. Macmillan & Co.: London, 1883.
—— *The Elements of Politics*. Macmillan & Co., Ltd.: London, 1919 (originally published, 1891).
SIMON, HERBERT A. *Models of Man*. John Wiley & Sons, Inc.: New York, 1957.
SMART, J. J. C. 'Extreme and Restricted Utilitarianism', *Theories of Ethics*, pp. 171–83, edited by Philippa Foot. Oxford University Press: Oxford, 1967 (first published, *Philosophical Quarterly*, vol. vi, 1956).
SPINOZA, BENEDICT DE. *Ethics*, translated by W. H. White, in *Spinoza: Selections*, edited by John Wild. Charles Scribner's Sons: New York, 1930 (originally published, 1677).
STEVENSON, CHARLES L. 'The Emotive Meaning of Ethical Terms', *Readings in Ethical Theory*, pp. 415–29, selected and edited by Wilfrid Sellars and John Hospers. Appleton-Century-Crofts, Inc.: New York, 1952 (first published, *Mind*, vol. xlvi, 1937).
—— *Ethics and Language*. Yale University Press: New Haven, Conn., and London, 1944.
STRAUSS, LEO. *Natural Right and History*. University of Chicago Press: Chicago, 1963 (first published, 1953).
STRAWSON, P. F. 'Social Morality and Individual Ideal', *Philosophy*, vol. xxxvi, no. 136 (January 1961), pp. 1–17.
—— 'Freedom and Resentment', *Proceedings of the British Academy* (1962), pp. 187–211 (Philosophical lecture read 9 May 1962).
—— *Individuals: an Essay in Descriptive Metaphysics*. Anchor Books, Doubleday & Co., Inc.: Garden City, N.Y., 1963.
—— 'Intention and Convention in Speech Acts', *Philosophical Review*, vol. lxxiii, no. 4 (October 1964), pp. 439–60.
SUAREZ, FRANCISCO. *Selections from Three Works*, translated by Williams, Brown, Waldron, and Davis, with an introduction by James Brown Scott. Oxford at the Clarendon Press, 1944 (*Tractatus de lege ac Deo legislatore*, originally published, 1612).
SUMNER, W. G. *Folkways*. Ginn & Co.: Boston, Mass., 1934.
TINBERGEN, N. *The Herring Gull's World: a Study of the Social Behaviour of Birds*. Collins: London, 1953.
URMSON, J. O. 'On Grading', *Logic and Language*, second series, pp. 159–86, edited by A. G. N. Flew. Basil Blackwell: Oxford, 1966 (first published, *Mind*, 1950).

A a

URMSON, J. O. 'The Interpretation of the Moral Philosophy of J. S. Mill', *Theories of Ethics*, pp. 128–36, edited by Philippa Foot. Oxford University Press: Oxford, 1967 (originally published, *Philosophical Quarterly*, vol. iii, 1953).

—— 'Saints and Heroes', *Essays in Moral Philosophy*, pp. 198–216, edited by A. I. Melden. University of Washington Press: Seattle, 1958.

VICTORIA, FRANCISCUS. *De Indis et de Jure Belli Relectiones*, edited and translated by Ernest Nys. Carnegie Institute of Washington, 1917.

VLASTOS, GREGORY. 'Justice and Equality', *Social Justice*, pp. 31–72, edited by Richard B. Brandt. Prentice-Hall, Inc.: Englewood Cliffs, N.J., 1962.

VON WRIGHT, GEORG HENRIK. *Norm and Action: a Logical Enquiry*. Routledge & Kegan Paul: London, 1963.

WARNOCK, G. J. *Contemporary Moral Philosophy*. Macmillan & Co.: London, 1967.

WASSERSTROM, RICHARD. 'The Obligation to Obey the Law', *U.C.L.A. Law Review*, vol. 10, no. 4 (May 1963), pp. 780–807.

—— 'Rights, Human Rights, and Racial Discrimination', *Journal of Philosophy*, vol. lxi, no. 20 (29 October 1964), pp. 628–41.

WEBER, MAX. *The City*, translated and edited by Don Martindale and Gertrud Neuwirth. Collier Books: New York, 1962 (first published, 1921).

—— *Law in Economy and Society*, edited and annotated by Max Rheinstein. Harvard University Press: Cambridge, Mass., 1954 (first published, 1922).

—— *General Economic History*, translated by Frank H. Knight. Collier Books: New York, 1961 (first published, 1923).

WEINSTEIN, W. L. 'The Concept of Liberty in Nineteenth Century English Political Thought', *Political Studies*, vol. xiii, pp. 145–67. Oxford at the Clarendon Press, 1965.

WESTERMARCK, EDWARD. *Ethical Relativity*. Harcourt, Brace & Co.: New York, 1932.

WHITE, MORTON. *Toward Reunion in Philosophy*. Atheneum: New York, 1963 (first published, 1956).

WHITE, ROBERT W. 'Competence and the Psychosexual Stages of Development', *Nebraska Symposium on Motivation*. University of Nebraska Press, 1960.

—— *Ego and Reality in Psychoanalytic Theory: a Proposal Regarding Independent Ego Energies*, *Psychological Issues*, vol. iii, no. 3, monograph 11. International Universities Press, Inc.: New York, 1963.

WILLIAMS, BERNARD A. O. 'The Ideal of Equality', *Philosophy, Politics and Society*, second series, pp. 110–31, edited by Peter Laslett and W. G. Runciman. Basil Blackwell: Oxford 1962.

—— 'Morality and the Emotions', an Inaugural Lecture, Bedford College, University of London, 4 May 1965.

WOLLHEIM, RICHARD. 'Equality and Equal Rights', *Justice and Social Policy*, pp. 111–27, edited with an introduction by Frederick A.

Olafson. Prentice-Hall, Inc.: Englewood Cliffs, N.J., 1961 (first published, *Proceedings of the Aristotelian Society*, vol. lvi, 1955–6).

—— 'A Paradox in the Theory of Democracy', *Philosophy, Politics and Society*, second series, pp. 71–87, edited by Peter Laslett and W. G. Runciman. Basil Blackwell: Oxford, 1962.

YOUNG, MICHAEL. *The Rise of the Meritocracy.* Penguin Books: Harmondsworth, Middlesex, 1958.

ZIFF, PAUL. *Semantic Analysis.* Cornell University Press: Ithaca, N.Y., 1960.

INDEX

The Index covers main text and notes but the title of a work is included only when that work is cited by name in the text